Genocide and Democracy

in

Cambodia

Administrative Divisions of
Democratic Kampuchea, 1975-1979

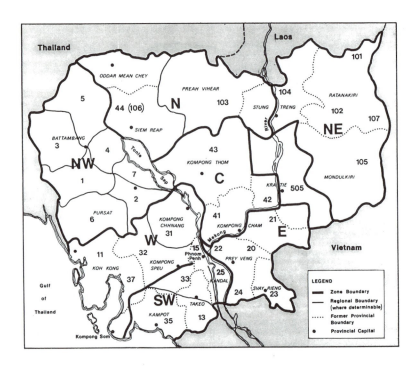

Map drawn by Margaret Pitt.

Genocide and Democracy

in

Cambodia

The Khmer Rouge,
the United Nations
and the
International Community

Edited with an introduction by
Ben Kiernan

Monograph Series 41/Yale University Southeast Asia Studies
Yale Center for International and Area Studies
Orville H. Schell, Jr. Center for International Human Rights
Yale University Law School

Yale University Southeast Asia Studies
James C. Scott: Chairman
Dan Duffy: Guest Managing Editor
Kalí Tal: Production

Consulting Editors
Hans-Dieter Evers, Universität Bielefeld
Huynh Sanh Thông, Yale University
Sartono Kartodirdjo, Gadjah Mada University
Lim Teck Ghee, Institute for Advanced Studies, Kuala Lumpur
Alfred W. McCoy, University of Wisconsin
Anthony Reid, Research School of Pacific Studies, Canberra
Benjamin White, Institute for Social Studies, The Hague
Alexander Woodside, University of British Columbia

Library of Congress Catalog Card Number: 93-060073
International Standard Book Number: 938692-49-6

©1993 by Yale University Southeast Asia Studies
New Haven, CT 06520

Distributor:
Yale University Southeast Asia Studies
Box 13A Yale Station
New Haven, CT 06520

Printed in the U.S.A.

Genocide and Democracy

in

Cambodia

The Khmer Rouge,
the United Nations
and the
International Community

Edited with an introduction by
Ben Kiernan

Monograph Series 41/Yale University Southeast Asia Studies
Yale Center for International and Area Studies
Orville H. Schell, Jr. Center for International Human Rights
Yale University Law School

Yale University Southeast Asia Studies
James C. Scott: Chairman
Dan Duffy: Guest Managing Editor
Kalí Tal: Production

Consulting Editors
Hans-Dieter Evers, Universität Bielefeld
Huynh Sanh Thông, Yale University
Sartono Kartodirdjo, Gadjah Mada University
Lim Teck Ghee, Institute for Advanced Studies, Kuala Lumpur
Alfred W. McCoy, University of Wisconsin
Anthony Reid, Research School of Pacific Studies, Canberra
Benjamin White, Institute for Social Studies, The Hague
Alexander Woodside, University of British Columbia

Library of Congress Catalog Card Number: 93-060073
International Standard Book Number: 938692-49-6

©1993 by Yale University Southeast Asia Studies
New Haven, CT 06520

Distributor:
Yale University Southeast Asia Studies
Box 13A Yale Station
New Haven, CT 06520

Printed in the U.S.A.

Contents

Preface

The Orville H. Schell, Jr. Center for International Human Rights is very pleased to present—in conjunction with the Yale Council on Southeast Asia Studies—the book *Genocide and Democracy in Cambodia*. At a time when the international community's willingness to promote democracy and respect for human rights is being tested in several parts of the world, Cambodia stands out by the enormity of its past suffering and the complexity of the challenges posed by its reconstruction.

Cambodia has been an issue of international concern ever since the Nixon-Kissinger secret bombing of the country during the Vietnam War. But it was the genocidal regime of the Khmer Rouge in the 1970s and the cynical geopolitical use of the very same Khmer Rouge as an anti-Vietnamese instrument, coupled with the denial of international assistance in the 1980s, that transformed Cambodia into what Ben Kiernan calls "an international symbol of disaster."

As Cambodia embarks on a difficult and problematic transition to democracy, a thorough reexamination of the origins, nature and extent of the country's predicament is long overdue. Thus, in this comprehensive study, the record of the Khmer Rouge regime is analyzed and assessed, while at the same time the international community's response is evaluated in the context of both its disturbing indifference in the 1980s, and the controversial UN Cambodian Peace Plan of 1991-1993.

This volume is the result of written papers, informal presentations and a most lively series of exchanges at a two-day conference entitled 'Genocide and Democracy in Cambodia' which was held on 21-22 February 1992 at Yale Law School under the auspices of the Schell Center and as part of the Center's Raphael Lemkin Symposium Series. This volume could not have come into being without the assistance of a number of people. In particular I would like to thank Ben Kiernan, my colleague at the History Department who was instrumental in shaping the themes and structure of the conference as well as those of the resulting volume; Jim Scott, Chairman of the Council on Southeast Asia Studies, for the Council's co-sponsorship of the conference and of this publication; our administrative assistants Joan Paquette-Saas and Marge Camera for their invaluable help throughout this project; Dan Duffy of the Council on Southeast Asia Studies for overseeing the production of this volume; and last, but not least, the contributors to the volume who made the whole thing possible. I sincerely hope that the end result lives up to their endorsement.

George Andreopoulos,
New Haven, June 1993

Introduction

Ben Kiernan

Cambodia is one of the few countries to have sparked separate controversies over its international representation in each of two historical periods.[1] During the early 1970s, and again in the 1980s, the United Nations General Assembly regularly had to decide who represented Cambodia—a *de facto* government, or an insurgent/ exile coalition.

The plight of the Cambodian people had seized the minds of citizens of the world as early as May 1970. Four students at Kent State University, protesting the Nixon Administration's invasion of Cambodia, were shot dead by the US National Guard.[2] Public protest not only filled the streets but also reached surprisingly high levels in Nixon's administration. According to historian Marilyn Young, two of Henry Kissinger's principal aides, Roger Morris and Anthony Lake (who would become National Security Adviser to President Clinton in 1993), "thought the invasion was not only useless but wrong, and resigned." Moreover, "two hundred and fifty employees of the State Department, including fifty Foreign Service officers, signed a letter of protest to Secretary of State William Rogers...Rogers was instructed to hand over the names... (he refused)."[3]

The previous year, the Nixon-Kissinger bombing of Cambodia had secretly begun. A brief report in the *New York Times* provoked Kissinger to order wiretaps on some Administration officials, and thus to begin the process of suppression that led to Watergate.[4] While that scandal grew to eventually rock Washington throughout 1973, the US Air Force dropped over half a million tons of bombs on Cambodia, more in six months of 1973 than had been dropped on Japan during World War Two.[5] Congress imposed a bombing halt in August of that year. But Cambodia became an illustration of the effects of the policies of those Russell Baker calls "the bombing classes."[6]

The Vietnam War ended on 30 April 1975. Cambodia's new rulers had already captured world attention two weeks before, with their unprecedented evacuation of the country's urban centers.[7] Though the Khmer Rouge then closed the country off to the outside world,

Cambodia was not allowed to drift from international consciousness. Refugees who escaped to neighboring countries brought mounting evidence of massive repression, and the regime responsible also launched military attacks against all three of those neighbors: Vietnam, Thailand, and Laos.[8] The Khmer Rouge rejected foreign "interference in Cambodia's internal affairs," but their actions made Cambodia an international issue.

Then in the late 1970s, Cambodia became a worldwide concern. The Vietnamese invasion of 1979 not only provoked international condemnation. It also opened the country to hundreds of international observers who reported first-hand on the legacy of the ousted Pol Pot regime. Jean-Pierre Gallois, the first Western reporter into Cambodia after the fall of the Khmer Rouge, wrote in March 1979:

> The Cambodia that survived Pol Pot is like a dismembered body that is trying to come back to life. Its economy is shattered, its communications severed. Millions of hectares of rice paddies have been temporarily abandoned. A population of refugees is returning home along pitted roads and highways or assembling in the suburbs of empty and dilapidated cities.
>
> Phnom Penh... is in the image of the rest of the country. There is no drinking water, no telephone, no mail service, no transport, no registry office, no money, no markets, hardly any electricity, hardly any schools, hardly any medical dispensaries. The city is so quiet that bird-song has a sinister ring to it. Its residents survive like nomads by eating roots, wild fruit, leaves and fish, and sometimes rice and flour distributed by the authorities... Only faith and hope can save the Cambodian people from extinction.[9]

The Cambodian international relief operation of 1979-1980 was the largest until the campaign against the 1984 Ethiopian famine. It was successful, but the country had become an international symbol of disaster. "Cambodia" was a hit by pop star Kim Wilde, singing of a pilot flying in relief supplies. A rock band called The Dead Kennedys, in a shock album titled *Fresh Fruit for Rotting Vegetables*, included an ironic track, "Holiday in Cambodia." It pictured a place of oppression, "where the people dress in black," the peasant uniform of the Khmer Rouge years.[10] Cambodia joined a litany of disasters in the more sympathetic lyrics of another rock band, Midnight Oil, on the ominously-titled album *10,9,8,7,6,5,4,3,2,1*: "The story of El

Salvador, the silence of Hiroshima, destruction of Cambodia, short memory..." Margaret Drabble's novel, *The Gates of Ivory*, portrays Cambodia as a symbol of disappearance and death.[11] In his creative *Cambodia: A Book for People Who Find Television Too Slow*, Brian Fawcett calls the country "the subtext of the Global Village... its purest apotheosis yet," adding: "Cambodia is a visible manifestation of elements in human polity that appear to seek expression as relentlessly and resourcefully as the more kindly impulses to sing, to paint, to compose different textures of reality, and to articulate new and old ideas lucidly. Genocide, Violence, Cambodia and Art."[12]

Cambodia also became a political cliché. "Pol Potist" became an international insult, thrown at the enemy of the moment. French neo-Marxist philosopher Louis Althusser was blamed for the Khmer Rouge genocide. America's dissident intellectual Noam Chomsky was called a Pol Pot supporter, or worse.[13] "Pol Pot has passed," intoned a hardly prescient conservative in 1979, but "Chomsky, I fear, persisteth."[14] Washington labeled the guerrillas in El Salvador "the Pol Pot left."[15] US Ambassador to the UN, Jeane Kirkpatrick, compared the Salvadoran insurgents—not the murderous regime she supported—to the Khmer Rouge.[16] She nevertheless voted for the ousted Khmer Rouge to represent Cambodia's people in the United Nations.[17] Guerrillas threatening other pro-US governments, from the Philippines to Peru, were likewise called the "new Khmer Rouge."[18] This label was not applied to the US-backed Nicaraguan Contras, even when the acting chief of the Contra high command confessed: "Our strategy is to let blood flow and walk on through it."[19]

Later, more distant anti-communist insurgents like Mozambique's unspeakably brutal Renamo, and the Afghan terrorist Gulbuddin Hekmatyar (now his country's Prime Minister), did evoke their own parallels.[20] Though usually implied, and documented for Shining Path and Renamo, genocidal potential was not a common factor among all these candidates for the Khmer Rouge mantle. A closer link seemed to be insurgency itself, as distinct from *state* brutality; and for leftist insurgents, some degree of Maoist ideology. *Behavior* approaching genocide by established US-backed regimes, for instance in Guatemala and El Salvador, though far closer to the Khmer Rouge record than that of the guerrillas they faced, failed to elicit the analogy.[21] The only comparison made with an established government seemed to prove the rule of the political convenience of the Cambodian case. Samir al-Khalil, author of *Republic of Fear*, wrote after the Gulf

War that "Cambodia is the appropriate metaphor for what is happening inside Iraq."[22]

In 1985 the film *The Killing Fields* coined a new, non-ideological term for mass murder. It was also one of the most successful Hollywood films with an Asian story line. Its star, Dr. Haing S. Ngor, a survivor of the Khmer Rouge period, played the part of Cambodian journalist Dith Pran, friend of *New York Times* reporter Sidney Schanberg. Ngor won an Academy Award.

A minor character was played by Spalding Gray, who published an account of the making of the film (in Thailand) in a collection of his solo stand-up dramas entitled *Swimming to Cambodia*. Gray's description of his experience ends with his return to the United States, with exotic Cambodia under his fingernails:

> And I had had this idea that as soon as I got back I would catch up on everything—I would be a changed man. I'd adopt a Cambodian family, I'd have my teeth taken care of, pay my taxes, clean my loft— try to put it at perfect white, right angles—wash the windows, get out all the old sweaters I never wear and take them to the Cambodian refugees in Far Rockaway. I'd heard that the Cambodians march from Far Rockaway to Chinatown on the Beltway every day to buy rice because they are so confused by the subway system that they prefer walking. I saw myself as their new brother, hiking and chanting along at their sides. They'd be wearing all the old mothball-reeking V-neck sweaters that Gram Gray made for me so many years ago, that now lie at the bottom of that black trunk. At last I would do something for them. At last I'd be of service.[23]

Cambodia was now a lightning rod for afflictions of "modern conscience." In his 1984 book, *The Quality of Mercy: Cambodia, Holocaust and Modern Conscience*, British journalist William Shawcross abstracted the country to a figment of the Western mind. He wrote that US involvement in supplying the Khmer Rouge from 1979 "exhibited at best a loss of *memory* and lack of *imagination*, at worst a cynicism that will have long and disturbing repercussions on international *consciousness*."[24] The repercussions on Cambodia itself are of course quite another matter.

The UN's $2 billion Cambodian peace plan of 1991-1993 is the biggest and most expensive the UN has ever undertaken. It was also one of the largest gambles ever taken by the international community, one that risked the return of genocidists to the scene of their crimes.

The Khmer Rouge

In the 1960s, a group of young, radical, mostly French-educated communists took over the leadership of the more orthodox, pro-Vietnamese Workers' Party of Kampuchea, which had led the struggle against French colonialism in the 1950s. The new leadership changed the party's name to "Communist Party of Kampuchea" (CPK) in 1966, and set out on their path to power the next year by staging an uprising against Prince Norodom Sihanouk's neutralist government. After victory in 1975 over Sihanouk's successor regime, that of the US-backed Marshal Lon Nol, the communist leadership proclaimed the state of Democratic Kampuchea (DK). The DK or "Pol Pot regime" lasted nearly four years and caused the deaths of 1.5 million of Cambodia's eight million people,[25] before being overthrown by the Vietnamese army in 1979.

DK's ruling body comprised the members of the Standing Committee of the Central Committee of the CPK. The leaders with maximum national power and responsibility for what was a legally defined case of genocide, were those based in the capital, Phnom Penh, and not specifically responsible for a limited geographic area of the country. These national leaders were known as the Party "Center."

In 1993, fourteen years after their ouster, nearly all these people remain active as Khmer Rouge leaders, and on the eighteenth anniversary of their accession to power on 17 April 1975, their diplomatic representative still occupied Cambodia's mission at the United Nations in New York. These are the Khmer Rouge, led by Saloth Sar (alias Pol Pot), Secretary-General of the CPK since 1962, who was DK's Prime Minister, and Nuon Chea, Deputy Secretary-General of the CPK since 1960. Their subordinates in the CPK political and military hierarchies are shown in Tables 1 and 2.

Under CPK rule, Democratic Kampuchea was divided into six major Zones, each Zone into a number of Regions the size of former provinces, each Region into districts, and the districts into subdistricts and villages. The military hierarchy, parallel to the CPK administration whose head at each level held concurrent military command, illustrates the depth of the CPK's military organization. Table 2 shows, for instance, the relatively junior positions in the chain of command of the rebels such as Heng Samrin and Hun Sen, who mutinied against the CPK and helped Hanoi overthrow the Pol Pot regime, replacing it with their own government in 1979.

Table 1: The Political Chain of Command
The Standing Committee of the CPK Central Committee, 1975-1979[*]

Rank, Name	Aliases	Positions
1. Saloth Sar b. 1928	**Pol Pot**, "87," Brother No. 1	CPK Secretary-General, 1962- ; Prime Minister of DK, 1976-79.
2. Long Bunruot b. 1927	Long Rith, **Nuon Chea**, Brother No. 2	CPK Deputy Secretary-General, 1960- ; President of the DK People's Representative Assembly, 1976-79.
3. Kim Trang b. 1930	**Ieng Sary**, Van	DK Deputy Prime Minister for Foreign Affairs.
4. So Vanna	Sos Sar Yan, So Phim	CPK Secretary, Eastern Zone (suicided 3 June 1978).
5. Penh Thuok	Sok Thuok, **Vorn Vet**	DK Deputy Prime Minister for the Economy (executed November 1978).
6. Moul Sambath	Ros Nhim, Moul Un	CPK Secretary, Northwest Zone (arrested 11 June 1978, executed).
7. Ek Choeun	**Mok**, "Ta 15," Chhit Choeun	CPK Secretary, Southwest Zone; 1977- , Chief of General Staff, Armed Forces.
8. **Son Sen** b. 1930	Khieu, "B," "89"	DK Deputy Prime Minister for Defense; responsible to the CPK Standing Committee for security matters.
9. **Khieu Samphan** b. 1931	Hem	President of the DK State Presidium; head, Office of the CPK CC, 1978-79.

Candidate Members

Rank, Name	Aliases	Positions
10. Keu		Military Commander, NW Zone (1978)
11. Khieu Thirith (Mme. Ieng Sary)	**Ieng Thirith**, Phea, Hong	DK Minister of Social Action and Education.
12. **Yun Yat**	(Mme. Son Sen)	DK Minister of Culture and Information.
13. Ke Vin b. 1934	**Ke Pauk**	CPK Secretary, Central Zone; 1977- , Dep.Chief, General Staff, Armed Forces.
14. Sua Vasi	Doeun	Head, Office of the CC (1977).
15. Phouk Chhay	Nang, Touc	Minutes secretary, Standing Committee (1977)
16. Men San	Ney Sarann, Ya, Achar Sieng	CPK Secretary, Northeast Zone (1976)
17. Ek Sophon	Phuong, Veung Chhaem	Minister of Rubber Plantations (1978)
18. Seng Hong	Chan	Deputy CPK Secretary, East Zone (1979)
19. Kang Chap	Sae	CPK Secretary, Northern Zone (1978)
20. (?) Chou Chet	Thang Sy	CPK Secretary, Western Zone (1978).

[*] CPK "Center" or specifically national officeholders in bold type. Year of birth is given where known. Year of execution in parentheses.

Table 2.
The Democratic Kampuchea Military Chain of Command

A. Center

1. **Pol Pot**   Commander-in-Chief; Head of the Military Commission of the Standing Committee of the CPK Central Committee
2. **Son Sen**   Deputy Prime Minister, Defence Minister, and CC SC member responsible for Defence and Security
3. **Mok**   Chief of the General Staff, Revolutionary Armed Forces of Democratic Kampuchea, and Commander-in-Chief, Southwest Zone Armed Forces
4. **Ke Pauk**   Deputy Chief of the General Staff, Revolutionary Armed Forces of DK, and Commander-in-Chief, Central Zone Armed Forces
5. **Siet Chhe**   Member of the General Staff (executed April 1977)

Center "Divisions" (or Brigades)		Regiments
164th (ex-3rd Southwest) Division	502nd Division	75th
170th (ex-1st Eastern) Division	703rd Division	152nd
310th (ex-Northern) Division	801st Division	377th
450th (ex-Northern) Division	920th Division	488th

[1977-78 additions: 108th, 280th, 290th Divisions]

plus: "Battallion for Guarding Office 870 [Party Center]"

B. Zone Level (example: Eastern Zone)

1. So Phim   CPK Zone Secretary, Commander Zone Armed Forces (suicided 1978)
2. Seng Hong   CPK Zone Deputy Secretary, Deputy CIC (executed 1979)
3. Kev Samnang   Chief of the Zone Military Staff (executed 1978)
4. Ly Phen   Chief Political Commissar, Zone Armed Forces (executed 1976)
5. Heng Samrin   1st Deputy Chief, Zone Military Staff (rebelled 1978)
6. Pol Saroeun   2nd Deputy Chief, Zone Military Staff (rebelled 1978)

Eastern Zone Divisions

One company of 2 tanks plus:

3rd Division, commander: Poeu Hak (executed 1976),
     replaced by Kry (executed 1978)
4th Division, commander: Heng Samrin (rebelled 1978)
     political commissar: Phan (executed 1976)
     CPK Secretary: Heng Kim (executed 1978)
5th Division (1977-8), CPK Secretary: Paen Cheuan (executed 1978)

C. Region Level (example: Region 21)

By 1978, each of the five Regions of the Eastern Zone had one *kong pul* (Division or brigade—three or more regiments of troops), except Region 20 which had one regiment.

1. Chen Sot   CPK Secretary, Region 21; Commander (executed 1978)
2. Ouch Bun Chhoeun   Deputy CPK Region Secretary; Dep. Commander (rebelled 1978)
3. Kun Deth   Chief of Region 21 Military Staff (executed 1978?)
4. Sok Sat   Pol. Commissar, Special (Memut border) Regiment (killed 1977)
5. Chum Horl   Regimental Commander, Special Regiment. Defected 1977.
6. Chum Sei   Deputy Political Commissar, Special Regiment (killed 1977)
7. Hun Sen   Deputy Regimental Commander, Special Regiment (from 1977); chief of Special Regimental staff from 1975. Defected June 1977.

Genocide and Democracy

This book deals with two aspects of Cambodia's international existence: the record of the Khmer Rouge, and the international community's involvement in the country's affairs. Specialists from seven disciplines examine the policies and practices of the Khmer Rouge period; the responsibility or accountability, if any, of the Khmer Rouge for those policies and practices under international law; and the capacity, responsibility, and performance of the international community under international law.

First, political scientist Kate G. Frieson examines the rise of the Khmer Rouge. Through interviews with peasants who came into contact with the Khmer Rouge before their seizure of power in 1975, she assesses the evidence for a "peasant revolution."[26] She finds the case unpersuasive. She also opens up some further questions: What was the appeal of moderate rural reform, as advanced by the Khmer Rouge leaders while hiding their extremist agenda, to a society that was more egalitarian than polarized rural Vietnam, but still stratified, with a large minority (twenty percent) of landless peasants and a larger percentage of landowning peasants whose plots were too small for subsistence?

Secondly, what was the role of the 1969-1973 United States bombardment in mobilizing enough peasant support for the Khmer Rouge to defeat their enemies, even if without majority popular support (however that may be gauged)? The CIA's Directorate of Operations reported on 2 May 1973 that the Khmer Rouge had launched a new recruiting drive in Kandal province:

> *They are using damage caused by B-52 strikes as the main theme of their propaganda.* The cadre tell the people that the Government of Lon Nol has requested the airstrikes and is responsible for the damage and the "suffering of innocent villagers."... The only way to stop "the massive destruction of the country" is to ... defeat Lon Nol and stop the bombing.
>
> This approach has resulted in the successful recruitment of a number of young men... Residents ... say that *the propaganda campaign has been effective* with refugees and in areas ... which have been subject to B-52 strikes.[27]

Thirdly, what are the possibilities for peasants to organize against a revolutionary movement which appeals to them as its primary base of support, but on achieving power suddenly unveils policies inimical to the features of rural life which peasants hold most dear: land, family, and religion?

Anthropologist May Ebihara shows in Chapter Two that the Cambodian peasantry were caught in a trap. Here was no peasant revolution, but a cruel, distant conqueror who worked, starved and beat to death half of a community in Kandal province which Ebihara had known for thirty years. Her unique study of this Cambodian village makes the chapter gripping reading.

Demographers Judith Banister and E. Paige Johnson assess the long-term growth trends of the Cambodian population since 1970. Using data made available for the first time, they provide powerful statistical evidence of the country-wide death toll during the Khmer Rouge period. They also analyze Cambodia's population growth during the 1980s, and provide projections for the future.

Anthropologist and international lawyer Gregory Stanton analyzes two broader issues, the national record of the Khmer Rouge regime and the question of genocide under international law. In a succeeding chapter, sociologist Serge Thion assesses genocide from a different angle, its use and abuse as a political concept. Different perspectives emerge. While Stanton proceeds from the definition of the term "genocide" set out in the 1948 Convention on the Prevention and Punishment of the Crime of Genocide, a treaty to which Cambodia had long been a party, Thion prefers the informal definition used by "most people," and rejects its applicability to the Khmer Rouge record.

Stanton, for instance, points out that the Muslim Cham minority in Cambodia were suppressed as a community. They were subjected not only to massive killings and destruction of their religious life like other Cambodians, but *also* to enforced dispersal of every single Cham village in the country, prohibition of the Cham language on pain of death, sadistically enforced consumption of pork, and other treatments worse than those meted out to their Khmer peasant neighbors—all on the basis of their different ethnic origin.[28] Thion, on the other hand, interprets this very narrowly as simply an attack on Islam, little different from the Khmer Rouge's destruction of all other religions, including the Buddhism of the Khmer majority, and therefore not a case of racial discrimination or persecution.

Stanton calls for action in the World Court under the Genocide Convention, taken by a state party to the Convention, which could mean any of a large number of Western states. Thion, on the other hand, proposes that the Khmer Rouge be brought to trial for their crimes in Cambodia itself.

My own chapter analyzes the diplomatic responses to the Cambodian question from 1979 to 1993. It identifies three different theaters of conflict and diplomacy: within Cambodia, at the regional Southeast Asian level, and at the level of the great powers, the five permanent members of the United Nations Security Council: the USA, the USSR, China, the UK, and France. It traces the opening during the 1980s of a more viable path to peace, one originating in regional developments and initiatives rather than the interests of the great powers. That alternative route to a Cambodian settlement, obstructed by the "Perm-5" powers, did not require the cooperation of the Khmer Rouge. This assessment highlights the costs of their inclusion in the peace process.

It is sometimes asserted that there was no alternative. In this view, the UN Security Council, including the Chinese patrons of the Khmer Rouge, had to "save" Cambodia because from 1979 to 1991 its government was "utterly incapable of sustaining itself as a member of the international community." Cambodia required rescue as a "failed nation state," which was "incapable of governing itself."[29] There is no truth to this. To a great extent, Cambodia was rebuilt in 1979-1991.[30] UN personnel who began to arrive in 1991 found a very different country from that described by Jean-Pierre Gallois twelve years earlier. A World Bank report published in 1992 praised "the dedication that the authorities mustered to put the country back on its feet," noting that "the progress made during the past decade in recovering from the devastation of the 1970s has been impressive."[31] But this progress was achieved only in the teeth of international resistance, including a crippling economic embargo not acknowledged by the authors of the thesis of "failed state" meeting international generosity.[32]

Economist Chanthou Boua outlines the impact of the world's economic isolation of Cambodia. The Khmer Rouge regime had sealed off the outside world as a matter of policy. But the successor regime requested international assistance. However, apart from the emergency period of 1979-1981, Phnom Penh was consistently rebuffed.[33] Cambodia was excluded from the United Nations, where the Khmer Rouge represented their victims for no fewer than fourteen years after their overthrow. Through the 1980s the United Nations Development Program accumulated funds earmarked for Cambodia, reaching as much as $110 million by 1991, but UNDP spent none of it. For over a decade, other UN agencies sent massive aid to the Khmer Rouge camps in Thailand. China sent them arms. Britain provided military assistance to allies of the Khmer Rouge, including training in the destruction of Cambodian civilian targets.[34]

For its part, the USA applied its Trading with the Enemy Act to both Cambodian regimes in turn. Washington thus embargoed Cambodia all through the 1980s. The embargo was relaxed only after Phnom Penh signed the UN Peace Plan in October 1991. The USA regarded the Paris Agreement as an achievement of its embargo. But Boua shows that it came at a high price, namely a debilitating impact on civilians, particularly Cambodia's women and children. Her chapter highlights the real "failure," that of small countries like Cambodia to withstand concerted international pressure.

The Appendices offer the perspectives of three participants in the Cambodian "peace process." Hédi Annabi, director of the UN's Department of Peacekeeping Operations, who for many years dealt with Cambodian matters for the Secretary-General's Special Representative for Humanitarian Affairs in Southeast Asia, outlines the basics of the UN Plan, and its requirements. The UN's mandate was a "comprehensive settlement," that is, one acceptable to all the parties, including the Khmer Rouge, and resolving all issues to the satisfaction of the great powers. It involved disarming all the Cambodian forces, repatriating 350,000 refugees from Thailand, verifying the withdrawal of any "foreign forces," and establishing a United Nations Transitional Authority in Cambodia (UNTAC) to supervise the country's foreign affairs, finance, defense, interior and information sectors, and to organize free nationwide elections.

In February 1992, as his contribution shows, Annabi warned that "the operation can only succeed if all the parties abide by the commitments that they freely entered into when they signed the agreements." This proved extremely prescient, given the subsequent refusal of the Khmer Rouge to carry out any of their commitments.[35] A more recent claim by a former US official that the United States never expected Khmer Rouge compliance,[36] raises questions about whether Washington anticipated the Plan that it proposed would succeed in its announced aims.

Cambodian journalist Khieu Kanharith, once a student at Phnom Penh's Faculty of Law, was editor of the weekly *Kampuchea* from 1979 until 1990. His contribution to this book was commissioned and written after his dismissal from that post, as a "liberal," by the Chea Sim faction of the State of Cambodia. He then began translating human rights documents into Khmer, and was subsequently appointed a special adviser to Prime Minister Hun Sen. In early 1993, Kanharith regained the editorship of *Kampuchea*, and after the UN-organized general elections, he was appointed Minister of Information in the new government. Cambodia's best-known journalist, he is well qualified to examine the political make-up of the Cambodian scene and its potential for splits and alliances.

In the 1960s, Douc Rasy served as Dean of Phnom Penh's Faculty of Law as well as editor of the newspaper *Phnom Penh Presse*. An elected member of the Cambodian National Assembly for the district of Kompong Tralach from 1962 to 1972, Rasy now leads the fifth and newest human rights advocacy group to be established in Cambodia. A distinguished lawyer, journalist, politician, and diplomat, Rasy's analysis of Cambodia's legal tradition and the democratic process makes an important contribution to understanding the current and future status of democracy in his country.

Some Reflections on the Process

In March 1993, the Khmer Rouge massacred thirty-three civilian Vietnamese men, women and children in a fishing village on Cambodia's Tonle Sap lake.[37] Both Khieu Kanharith and Douc Rasy were among the few courageous Cambodian voices to publicly condemn the Khmer Rouge for the crime.[38]

This outrage was only the latest and bloodiest in a new series of Khmer Rouge racial pogroms to strike Cambodia, along with continued Khmer Rouge military attacks, since the UN Peace Plan commenced operation.[39] UNTAC director Yasushi Akashi declared soon afterwards that his massively-funded and well-armed operation involving 20,000 personnel had failed to achieve either "peace" or "national reconciliation" in Cambodia. Another UNTAC official explained that "in practice, these goals no longer exist."[40]

April brought further escalation of the violence. Twenty-nine Khmers were killed and thirty-one injured by Khmer Rouge forces who machine-gunned a video hall. In the same week, Khmer Rouge forces also murdered six UNTAC soldiers and international personnel.[41] On 13 April, Khmer Rouge representatives abandoned their UN-protected compound in Phnom Penh for the movement's clandestine headquarters in the countryside.

The Khmer Rouge withdrew from the peace process with the gains they had made from it. They had quadrupled the territory and population under their control,[42] increased their regular forces from ten thousand to fifteen thousand in the past year,[43] and doubled their annual income to US$250 million through trade with Thailand.[44] What distinguished the proponents of the UN plan from its critics was the proponents' insistence on including the Khmer Rouge in the peace settlement and elections. That strategy foundered badly—especially if it was an attempt to undermine Khmer Rouge power.

Will the failure of the "comprehensive settlement," in which Washington invested much political capital, provoke reflection on the political dogmas that inspired it?

Two problems seem to have plagued discussion of the Cambodia issue. Firstly, a near monopoly of pundits and opinion shapers accepted the perspective of the great powers who designed the Plan. Politicians like Congressman Stephen Solarz, assuming credit for it, faced little pressure to defend American-inspired displacement of a pro-Vietnamese government in a small country—despite the risks of a denial of justice, or even a return to genocide. One of the few critical assessments published in the US media noted in 1990 that "the UN plan has been a public relations success, requiring lip-service praise from all parties." But the author, Michael J. Horowitz, warned with foresight that the plan was "deeply troublesome," and that "actual progress in Cambodia is likely to be a function of the time it takes for the plan's major features to collapse of their own weight."[45] Cambodia's tragedy is that three years proved a long enough time for the Khmer Rouge to improve their position.[46]

In early 1990, as the peace plan was being drawn up, Khmer Rouge defectors predicted Pol Pot's refusal to disarm his forces in the event of a settlement. "Our troops will remain in the jungle for self-defense," Pol Pot had told his commanders in a secret 1988 briefing. No US newspaper found space for this or other inside information, some of it already available abroad, casting doubt on the Khmer Rouge's commitment to a "comprehensive settlement."[47]

Other views got a better hearing. In the *New Republic*, Stephen J. Morris hastily predicted that the Khmer Rouge were not the major problem: "The real Khmer Rouge military aim... is to force Phnom Penh to accept a comprehensive political settlement such as the UN peace plan... The danger lies in the Vietnamese Communists' determination to subvert such an agreement."[48] In the Boston *Globe*, Morris then labeled critics of the UN plan, and of its inclusion of the Khmer Rouge, as proponents of "an immoral, lost cause" beholden to Hanoi. The UN plan, he asserted, "is morally right and offers real hope of success." It gave the Khmer Rouge, Morris predicted, an "incentive to lay down its arms." Thus, the US should "work toward a comprehensive political settlement involving an interim United Nations takeover of Cambodia, which will end the war and preclude the Khmer Rouge from achieving a military victory."[49]

After the Agreement, media hardheads marshmallowed. The *Economist* pleaded: "To help Cambodia, help the Khmers Rouges," adding "no Khmers Rouges, no peace plan."[50] When a majority of both houses of the US Congress (fifty-five senators and 247 representatives) expressed concern at the capacity of the Khmer Rouge to gain from the Agreement, Washington journalist Elizabeth Becker, author of *When the War Was Over*, invited the most concerned congressman to "go home." She claimed that "the world's powers have come up with a fine compromise to end the Cambodian war."[51]

Two months after the Khmer Rouge had explicitly stated they would not comply with the disarmament or any other clauses of the agreement they had signed, the Heritage Foundation assured the *New York Times* that "word of mouth alone draws Khmer Rouge followers and their families out of the jungle and into the cantonment camps." The world should avoid "a critical error," namely: "To allow the Khmer Rouge to slip back to its jungle strongholds under a veil of secrecy, shielded from the international community's attention."[52] The fantasy of the lifted veil was pervasive. Becker, also in the *New York Times*, again cautioned against excluding the Khmer Rouge. "Sanctions against the Khmer Rouge are not the answer," she asserted. "The Khmer Rouge have been forced to come a long way," so their movement was now merely "a hollow version of its former self." Pol Pot's forces, she claimed, "oversee only 1 percent of the population." Others put the figure very much higher,[53] but Becker saw "problems greater than the Khmer Rouge's intransigence," namely the dangers of "economic and ecological disaster."[54]

In the *International Herald Tribune* in late 1992, Becker claimed that the Cambodian peace mission was "far more secure" than that in El Salvador: "the loss of Khmer Rouge participation is not going to ruin either the plan or the country's prospects for peace."[55] Continuing conflict in Cambodia could not challenge such conviction.

Besides one-sided public debate of the facts, a second problem for Cambodia has been wishful thinking by human rights leaders. Even as Asia Watch, for instance, kept an eye on the Khmer Rouge,[56] the executive director of its parent body Human Rights Watch, Aryeh Neier, underestimated the danger. After visiting Cambodia in April-May 1992, Neier devoted two of his *Nation* magazine columns to it. "Cambodia is the most striking example of the UN's new interventionist role in ending the fighting," Neier asserted, adding "though some fear that war could break out again." He concluded that "much is being done well" and "there is a chance of success" in a "historic opportunity to assist a destroyed nation in reconstituting itself."[57] But the UN had by no means "ended the fighting." It raged during Neier's April-May visit. For instance on 4 May, after moving in four hundred truckloads of weaponry, the Khmer Rouge launched "coordinated attacks," according to an UNTAC official, in "the worst violation yet seen."[58] In mid-June, UNTAC director Akashi denounced the Khmer Rouge's refusal to disarm, and reported that the Khmer Rouge "seems to have returned to the offensive," committed "pretty serious violations," and "gravely compromised the settlement."[59] New attacks in mid-July killed civilians in central, northern and southern Cambodia. Akashi again blamed the Khmer Rouge for violations which "continue to increase in number and seriousness," and for "a deliberate policy of terror against ordinary Cambodians.[60]

In his September column, Neier ignored all this violence. He repeated that the war was "largely concluded." He assured readers of his "optimism that the UN mission in Cambodia will give the country a new lease on life," and described "the UN record in Cambodia" as "on the whole, positive." Neier conceded that "a few longtime observers" were "more skeptical," but only because "the Khmer Rouge is exploiting popular resentment over corruption," which the UN presence fueled, and because "the group's racist campaign to whip up hatred of the Vietnamese minority...could inflate support for the Khmer Rouge."[61] In other words, the Khmer Rouge danger was political, not military. Referring to unattributed "violent attacks on the Vietnamese," Neier did not report UNTAC's conclusion that "Khmer

Rouge guerrillas" had themselves perpetrated the slaughters—which went well beyond "whipping up hatred."[62]

Nor did Neier mention the UN's condoning of the 1975-1979 Khmer Rouge genocide. In the case of Bosnia, by contrast, he called for "a tribunal to bring to trial those who have engaged in war crimes." And what Neier called "the biggest research project we have ever undertaken," Human Rights Watch's genocide case against Iraq, was obviously consuming his attention.[64] What else explains such myopia on the part of professional human rights activists? Certain genocide cases are surely more palatable to great powers-that-be.[65] Just as Iraq, an official enemy, was the only established government to gain intellectual comparison with the Khmer Rouge, so the prosecution of Iraq for genocide distracted human rights officials from that committed by the Khmer Rouge. One might wonder whether Cambodia actually exists outside its political pigeon-hole.

Similar views were propounded by David Hawk, director of the Cambodian Documentation Commission (CDC). The CDC, which had begun with the aim of bringing the Khmer Rouge to justice in the World Court, abandoned that aim in favor of the "comprehensive settlement" including them. In the spring of 1991, Hawk described the "risks—not an inevitability" inherent in the UN peace plan. He saw these risks as limited to "the Khmer Rouge coming to power through an electoral coalition rather than in an armed struggle." Hawk falsely predicted that the UN plan would "produce a ceasefire" as well as "reduce the number of men under arms and create an opportunity to search out and disarm or destroy mines and hidden arms caches." Such wishful thinking was only overshadowed by Hawk's fear that the Khmer Rouge may "gain a significant number of votes enabling it to become part of a winning coalition."[66] The Khmer Rouge knew better. They maintained their army, hid their arsenals, continued to attack, boycotted the election, denied the right to vote to thousands of residents of their newly expanded zones of military control, and then, when they had gained maximum ground, thumbed their nose at the UN by formally abandoning its peace process. Cambodia suffered from the miscalculations of those to whom human rights groups mistakenly left the task of bringing the Khmer Rouge to justice.[67]

The result of the one-sided policy discussion in both the media and in human rights circles is that the war went on, the Khmer Rouge gained control of far more of Cambodia and its people than they had before the Plan's implementation, and they continued to murder innocents with a brutality unequaled since their 1979 ouster.

Have the successful May 1993 elections and the anticipated August constitution resolved the problems facing Cambodia's future? The ongoing relationships between genocide and democracy, between a "peace process" and continuing war,[68] and between Cambodia and the international community, make the themes of this book all the more urgent.

In the elections, the royalist party FUNCINPEC, led by Prince Sihanouk's forty-nine-year-old son Norodom Rannariddh, won fifty-eight out of 120 seats. The People's Party of incumbent Prime Minister Hun Sen won fifty-one seats. The elections were held despite the Khmer Rouge attempt to sabotage them, killing 131 civilians in a string of massacres between 1 March and 31 May.[69] At the last minute, however, they changed tactics, instructing their followers to vote for FUNCINPEC.[70] A FUNCINPEC spokesperson said after the election that if the Khmer Rouge wanted the Defense Ministry, it was "negotiable."[71] According to the *Far Eastern Economic Review*, it now appears the Khmer Rouge "will be included in a new coalition government to be formed in September, as the UN withdraws from the country."[72] As this book went to press, negotiations were continuing.

---

[1] See Douc Rasy, *Khmer Representation at the United Nations: A Question of Law or of Politics?*, London 1974 (French edition, A. Pedone, Paris, 1974); Ramses Amer, *The General Assembly and Kampuchean Issues: Intervention, Regime Recognition and the World Community, 1979 to 1987*, Report No. 31, Department of Peace and Conflict Research, Uppsala University, 1989; Amer, "The United Nations and Kampuchea: The Issue of Representation and Its Implications," *Bulletin of Concerned Asian Scholars*, 22:3, 1990: 52-60; and Craig Etcheson, "The Khmer Way of Exile: Lessons from Three Indochinese Wars," in Yossi Shain, ed., *Governments-in-Exile in Contemporary World Politics*, New York: Routledge, 1990: 92-116.

[2] See *Kent and Jackson State*, 1970-1990, Susie Erenrich, ed., *Vietnam Generation*, 2:2, 1990.

[3] Marilyn Young, *The Vietnam Wars, 1945-1990*, New York: HarperCollins, 1991, ch. 10: 247-8.

[4] William Shawcross says these wiretaps "marked the first of the domestic abuses of power now known as Watergate." Shawcross, *Sideshow: Kissinger, Nixon and the Destruction of Cambodia*, London: Deutsch, 1979: 33-35; Seymour Hersh, *The Price of Power: Henry Kissinger in the Nixon White House*, New York: Summit Books, 1983: 54-65; and Edward S. Herman and

Noam Chomsky, *Manufacturing Consent: The Political Economy of the Mass Media*, New York: Pantheon, 1988: 270-1.

5   See Ben Kiernan, "The American Bombardment of Kampuchea, 1969-1973," *Vietnam Generation*, 1:1, Winter 1989: 4-41; Kiernan, *How Pol Pot Came to Power*, London: Verso, 1985, ch. 8; and Shawcross, *Sideshow*

6   Russell Baker, "Like Lead to the Romans," *New York Times*, 29 May 1993.

7   See François Ponchaud, *Cambodia Year Zero*, London: Allen Lane, 1978.

8   See Ben Kiernan, "New Light on the Origins of the Vietnam-Kampuchea Conflict," *Bulletin of Concerned Asian Scholars*, 12:4, 1980: 61-65.

9   Jean-Pierre Gallois, Agence France-Presse, report from Phnom Penh, 25 March 1979. For a longer quotation, see Ben Kiernan, "Kampuchea 1979-1981: National Rehabilitation in the Eye of an International Storm," in Huynh Kim Khanh, ed., *Southeast Asian Affairs 1982*, Singapore: Institute of Southeast Asian Studies/Heinemann, 1982: 167-195.

10   Other tracks on *Fresh Fruit for Rotting Vegetables* include "Kill the Poor," "Forward to Death," "Let's Lynch the Landlord," "Chemical Warfare," "I Kill Children," "Stealing People's Mail" and yes, "Ill in the Head."

11   New York: Penguin, 1991.

12   Brian Fawcett, *Cambodia: A Book for People Who Find Television Too Slow*, Vancouver: Talonbooks, 1986 (reprinted New York: Grove Press, 1989): 54, 95.

13   See for instance William Shawcross, "Too Many Holocausts Have Made Mankind Numb," *Washington Post*, Outlook, 2 September 1984, and Noam Chomsky's reply, "Skepticism and Pol Pot," Washington Post, 30 September 1984.   An egregious attack on Chomsky and the journalist John Pilger is Richard West, "Who Was to Blame?," *Spectator,* 29 September 1984. See their replies, "Chomsky on Cambodia," and "Inauspicious Pilger," *Spectator,* 13 October and 10 November 1984. For a recantation of my own mistaken initial view of the Khmer Rouge regime, see Ben Kiernan, *Bulletin of Concerned Asian Scholars* 11:14, 1979: 19-25, and 12:2, 1980: 72.

14   Robert Manne, "Pol Pot and the Persistence of Noam Chomsky," *Quadrant* (Sydney), October 1979: 8. See the response by Gavan McCormack, *Quadrant*, Jan.-Feb. 1980: 115-6.

15   For references see Herman and Chomsky, *Manufacturing Consent*: 302, 389.

16   Jeane Kirkpatrick, "US Security and Latin America," *Commentary,* January 1981. Kirkpatrick wrote this as Pentagon officials privately conceded the Salvadoran military's "barbaric conduct." Cynthia Arnson, "Unburying El Salvador's Skeletons," *New York Times*, 13 March 1993: 21, citing a Pentagon document released in January 1993. The United Nations Truth Commission on El Salvador singled out Jeane Kirkpatrick for her cover-up of death squad crimes: see *New York Times*, "UN Report Urges Sweeping Changes in Salvador Army," 16 March 1993: A1, 12. See also the *Times* Editorial, "Exposing the Lies About El Salvador," 26 March 1993, and Aryeh Neier, *Nation*, 12 April 1993: 475.

[17] Like the Carter Administration in 1979 and 1980, the Reagan Administration voted in 1981 for the Khmer Rouge government of "Democratic Kampuchea" to represent Cambodia's people in the United Nations. In 1982 Jeane Kirkpatrick reiterated: "We expect to support the coalition Government of Democratic Kampuchea including... the Khmer Rouge" in the UN (*Australian*, 25-6 September 1982), and again supported the Khmer Rouge in the 1982 UN vote. See also Anthony Barnett, "The Pol Pot Fan Club: Still Open For Business," in John Pilger and A. Barnett, *Aftermath: The Struggle of Cambodia and Vietnam*, New Statesman, London, 1982: 135-141.

[18] See for example the series on the Philippine New People's Army by *Time* reporter Ross H. Munro, "The New Khmer Rouge," *Weekend Australian*, starting 21-22 December 1985: 14-15. On Sendero Luminoso, *Newsweek* reported on 26 August 1991: "Carlos Ivan DeGregori, a leading Senderologist, recently offered an interpretation of Shining Path's aims that sounds ominously similar to the Khmer Rouge's vision...In DeGregori's view, Shining Path's extreme violence arises from the group's obsession with forcing reality to fit ideology — an explanation that could apply equally well to the brutality of the Khmer Rouge (24)." Craig Etcheson and Dario Moreno will address this issue in a forthcoming study, *The Eagle and the Jaguar.*

[19] "Contras Collapse in Boredom Waiting for US Paymaster," by a correspondent of the *Economist*, published in the *Australian*, 5 May 1989. The Contra leader was complaining about Washington's alleged pressure "to be like a crab hiding under its shell to avoid bloodshed."

[20] John Battersby says Renamo "has been compared to Cambodia's notorious Khmer Rouge." *Christian Science Monitor,* 15 January 1993: 13, quoted in Elaine Windrich, "Mozambique: Naming Names," *Lies of Our Times*, April 1993: 19-20. In the same journal, Nabeel Abraham describes extremist Mujahadeen leader Gulbuddin Hekmatyar as "the Afghani Pol Pot." "The Threat of Islam," *Lies of Our Times*, April 1993: 9-10.

[21] *New Republic* magazine, in support of Reagan's policy in El Salvador, called for US military aid "regardless of how many are murdered" (2 April 1984). See the discussion in Noam Chomsky, *Turning the Tide*, Boston: South End, 1985: 167-8, 281 n. 211.

[22] Samir al Khalil, "The Republic of Fear and the Killing Fields," *Institute for the Study of Genocide Newsletter*, No. 7, Spring 1991: 3-4. See also Ben Kiernan, "Cambodia's Saddam: Pol Pot is Still Ignored," *Australian Left Review*, No. 129, June 1991: 7-8.

[23] Spalding Gray, *Swimming to Cambodia*, London: Picador, 1986: 87-88.

[24] See William Shawcross, *The Quality of Mercy: Cambodia, Holocaust and Modern Conscience*, London: Deutsch, 1984: 415, emphases added. For a critical review see Ben Kiernan, "William Shawcross, Declining Cambodia," *Bulletin of Concerned Asian Scholars*, 18, 1, 1986: 56-63.

[25] For statistical evidence of this, see Ben Kiernan, "The Genocide in Cambodia, 1975-1979," *Bulletin of Concerned Asian Scholars*, 20, 2, 1990: 35-

40. I disagree with the authors of Chapter 3 of this volume, whose estimate of 1.05 million is based on a 1975, pre-DK population of 7.3 million. UN and independent statisticians put it at 7.89 million (W.J. Sampson, *Economist,* 26 March 1977), and DK sources in 1975-1976 gave consistent figures, all suggesting a higher toll of around 1.5 million.

[26] Michael Vickery, *Cambodia 1975-1982,* Boston: South End, 1984, presents the most persuasive argument for this theory. For a different view see Kate G. Frieson, *The Impact of Revolution on Cambodian Peasants, 1970-1975,* Ph.D. dissertation, Department of Politics, Monash University, Australia, 1991.

[27] US Central Intelligence Agency, Directorate of Operations, Intelligence Information Cable, 2 May 1973, "Efforts of Khmer Insurgents to Exploit for Propaganda Purposes Damage Done by Airstrikes in Kandal Province," 3-page document declassified to the author by the CIA on 19 February 1987. Emphasis added.

[28] For the evidence for this, see Ben Kiernan, "Orphans of Genocide: The Cham Muslims of Kampuchea under Pol Pot," *Bulletin of Concerned Asian Scholars,* 20:4, 1988: 2-33.

[29] Gerald B. Helman and Steven R. Ratner, "Saving Failed States," *Foreign Policy,* No. 89, Winter 1992-93: 3-20, at: 3, 14.

[30] See for instance Ben Kiernan, "Kampuchea 1979-1981: National Rehabilitation in the Eye of an International Storm," in Khanh, *Southeast Asian Affairs 1982;* Chanthou Boua, "Observations of the Heng Samrin Government, 1980-1982," in David P. Chandler and Ben Kiernan, eds., *Revolution and Its Aftermath in Kampuchea: Eight Essays,* New Haven: Yale University Southeast Asia Council Monograph No. 25, 1983: 259-290; Michael Vickery, *Kampuchea: Politics, Economics and Society,* London: Frances Pinter, 1986; Eva Mysliwiec, *Punishing the Poor: The International Isolation of Kampuchea,* Oxford: Oxfam, 1988; C. Scalabrino et al., *Affaires Cambodgiennes 1979-1989,* Paris: L'Harmattan, 1989.

[31] *Cambodia: Agenda for Rehabilitation and Reconstruction,* World Bank, East Asia and Pacific Region, June 1992, 219 pp., at: i, 35. The report adds: "The situation of public administration in the State of Cambodia is better than might be expected after the hardships that the country endured" (v). As for agriculture: "After having dropped to famine levels at the end of the 1970s, paddy production had by 1990 been restored to the level of the late 1960s," and "its pace of development has been increasing satisfactorily." (i, 11). Moreover: "Since 1979, there has been considerable quantitative progress in providing education... Remarkably, ... unlike the situation in many other countries, the primary school network has received first priority... and is, comparatively, in much better condition than one would expect... In qualitative terms, however, achievements while still impressive are more uneven." (10)

[32] Helman and Ratner, *Foreign Policy,* Winter 1992-1993, cite "twenty years of civil war, outside arms supplies, gross violations of human rights, massive dislocations of its population and destruction of its infrastructure" (14), and

they also note the Khmer Rouge genocide, but they ignore the US and UN embargoes on Cambodia's development and ability to "sustain itself as a member of the international community."

[33] For different views of this, see Barnett and Pilger, *Aftermath: The Struggle of Cambodia and Vietnam*; Shawcross, *The Quality of Mercy;* and Mysliwiec, *Punishing the Poor.*

[34] See *Official Report* (London), 25 June 1991, Vol. 193 c. 454, and the report by Asia Watch and Physicians for Human Rights: "China and the United Kingdom are, or have been, involved in training Cambodian resistance factions in the use of mines and explosives against civilian as well as military targets." *Land Mines in Cambodia: the Coward's War*, New York, September 1991, see pp. 25-27, 59. See also John Pilger, "Culpable in Cambodia," *New Statesman and Society*, 27 September 1991, and the exchange between Pilger and Derek Tonkin, *New Statesman and Society*, 11 December 1992: 10, and 15 January 1993: 26.

[35] For an equally prescient critical view of the UN Plan, see Chet Atkins, "Cambodia's 'Peace:' Genocide, Justice, and Silence," *Washington Post*, 26 January 1992. More recent analyses include William E. Colby and Jeremy J. Stone, "Bypass the Khmer Rouge," *New York Times*, 9 July 1992; Ben Kiernan, "Rouge Awakening," *Australian Left Review*, No. 148, March 1993: 10-11; Nayan Chanda, "The UN's Failure in Cambodia," *Wall Street Journal*, 11 March 1993; and Henry Kamm, "Cambodia Election Snared as Peace Pact Unravels," *New York Times*, 18 March 1993.

[36] Shep Lowman (Director of US State Department's Office of Vietnam, Laos and Cambodia, 1986-87), *Christian Science Monitor*, 28 August 1992. Excerpted in *Indochina Digest*, 4 September 1992.

[37] Henry Kamm, *New York Times*, "33 Vietnamese Are Slain in Cambodia," 12 March 1993: 3, and "Cambodia Village Quiet Again After Massacre," 16 March 1993: 11.

[38] *Phnom Penh Post*, "Massacre Condemned But...," by Kevin Barrington, 26 March 1993: 1, 4, 5. See also Chanthou Boua, "Cotton Wool and Diamonds," *New Internationalist*, April 1993: 20-21.

[39] See Ben Kiernan, "Appeasement in Cambodia," *Indochina Newsletter* (Cambridge, Ma.), No. 78, November-December 1992: 1-6.

[40] Henry Kamm, "Cambodia Election Snared as Peace Pact Unravels," *New York Times*, 18 March 1993. Kamm quoted Akashi as saying that "we have not been able to achieve peace and national reconciliation."

[41] *Indochina Digest*, 2 and 9 April 1993.

[42] On the increase in Khmer Rouge territory, see Craig Etcheson's map, based on UN sources, *New Statesman*, 9 July 1993: 14. For a similar view from a quite different perspective, see Nate Thayer, *FEER*, 27 May 1993: 11. According to Australia's Foreign Minister Gareth Evans, by 1993 the Khmer Rouge administered perhaps "500,000-600,000 Cambodians" (quoted in *Indochina Digest*, 22 January 1993), compared to about 150,000 in 1991.

[43] UNTAC director Yasushi Akashi, quoted in *Indochina Digest*, 21 May 1993, and Cambodia Peace Watch, *Folio* 2, 5:1, May 1993.

[44] William Shawcross, *Weekend Australian*, 15-16 May 1993, gives a figure for Khmer Rouge income of $22 million per month.

[45] Michael J. Horowitz, "The 'China Hand' in the Cambodia Plan," *New York Times*, 12 September 1990. US Congressman Stephen Solarz, an architect of the UN Plan, described Horowitz's prescience as "lunatic scribblings."

[46] In "Cambodian Elections Can't Wait," *Asian Wall Street Journal*, 16 December 1991, Michael Horowitz again warned: "Time is not on the side of an interim government composed of competing factions locked together under an impossible mandate to achieve consensus... Hostile battlefield patterns could emerge, from which the Khmer Rouge will benefit."

[47] See Ben Kiernan, "War and Forgetting: Obstructing Peace in Cambodia," *Lies of Our Times*, June 1991: 14-15.

[48] Stephen J. Morris, "Skeletons in the Closet," *New Republic*, 4 June 1990: 19, 17. See also Morris, "Thailand's Separate Peace in Indochina," *Asian Wall Street Journal*, 4 September 1989, on the newly-elected Thai government's "decision to break ranks with its ASEAN allies" while ASEAN still supported the Khmer-Rouge dominated coalition. Morris also complained that "Thai commanders have provided Phnom Penh's artillery commanders with precise intelligence on the location of Khmer Rouge units." For a different perspective, see Chanthou Boua, "Thailand Bears Guilt for Khmer Rouge," letter to *New York Times*, 24 March 1993. For Morris' reliability on Vietnam, see Nayan Chanda, "Research and Destroy," *Far Eastern Economic Review*, 6 May 1993: 20-1.

[49] Stephen J. Morris, "US Choice in Cambodia," *Boston Globe*, 7 August 1990.

[50] *Economist*, 7 December 1991: 14. Its logic was: "Excluding them [the Khmer Rouge] from the Supreme National Council would only encourage them to unlock their arsenals and take up arms again. They may do this anyway," but "they will have had to give up at least some of their arms." They did not.

[51] Elizabeth Becker, "Up From Hell," *New Republic*, 17 February 1992: 37. For a different view, detailing the options rejected by the world's powers, see Kiernan's chapter in this volume.

[52] William J. Bonde, Heritage Foundation, "Khmer Rouge Only Gains by Exclusion," letter to the *New York Times*, 8 August 1992.

[53] Australia's Foreign Minister Gareth Evans stated that the Khmer Rouge controlled perhaps 500,000 to 600,000 Cambodians — more than triple the number they controlled in 1991. Quoted in *Indochina Digest*, 22 January 1993.

[54] Elizabeth Becker, "Cambodia Comes Back to Life," *New York Times*, 25 August 1992.

[55] Elizabeth Becker, "Cambodia: The Khmer Rouge Can Be Circumvented," *International Herald Tribune*, 10 November 1992. Again, she recommended no sanctions against them for violating the Agreement, though they had

signed "believing it would never get off the ground." (Becker, "Cambodia Comes Back to Life," *New York Times,* 25 August 1992.)

56 See for instance Asia Watch, *Khmer Rouge Abuses Along the Thai-Cambodian Border* (New York: Human Rights Watch, February 1989); Asia Watch, *Violations of the Rules of War by the Khmer Rouge* (New York: Human Rights Watch, April 1990), and Asia Watch, *Political Control, Human Rights, and the UN Mission in Cambodia* (New York: Human Rights Watch, September 1992).

57 Aryeh Neier, *Nation,* 8 June 1992: 775. Ironically, Neier's major criticism of UNTAC, the likelihood "that not all the refugees will be repatriated in time for next year's elections," proved unfounded.

58 *Indochina Digest,* 8 May 1992; "Khmer Rouge Launch Fierce Attacks," Reuters, Phnom Penh, *Bangkok Post,* 6 May 1992. After his 8 June *Nation* column appeared, I sent Neier this information, contained in an article I had just published in Australia and Thailand, detailing the continual Khmer Rouge violations of the ceasefire since October 1991. See Ben Kiernan, "Khmer Rouge Exploiting UN Accord?" *Nation* (Bangkok), 9 June 1992.

59 *Indochina Digest,* 19 June 1992.

60 "Top Peacekeeper Lashes KR over Accord Violations," *Bangkok Nation,* 24 July 1992.

61 Aryeh Neier, *Nation,* 28 September 1992: 317.

62 "UN Investigation Concludes KR Slayed Vietnamese Families," *Phnom Penh Post,* 27 August 1992. See also "Slaying of VN Family Called Racist," Bangkok *Nation,* 20 August 1992. This result of the UNTAC investigation was available weeks before Neier's column went to press.

63 Aryeh Neier, *Nation,* 28 September 1992: 317. In an 8 June 1992 letter to the author, Neier had written: "I did not deal with the Khmer Rouge's participation per se in the peace process in my *Nation* column because I have been unable as yet to resolve my own position on this. My inclination is to separate this question from... Khmer Rouge violations of the Paris accords." Neier undertook to "try to address" both these "very important matters" in future, but did not do so in his September column, nor by the time of writing (July 1993). The *Nation* declined to publish a letter from Kathy Knight pointing out that "the UN Peace Plan, because it incorporates the genocidists, still primarily exemplifies the vulnerability of the UN to manipulation by the world's strongest" (15 October 1992).

64 Aryeh Neier, *Nation,* August 31/September 7, 1992, and quoted in the *New Yorker,* 28 September 1992: 46.

65 For the record on Cambodia of mainstream international human rights groups, see Ben Kiernan, "The Cambodian Genocide and Human Rights Organizations," *Institute for the Study of Genocide Newsletter*, No. 7, Spring 1991: 10-11. The worst offender has probably been Amnesty International, which has almost ignored the Khmer Rouge record for fifteen years.

66 David Hawk, "The CDC View of the UN Peace Plan for Cambodia," *Institute for the Study of Genocide Newsletter,* No. 7, Spring 1991: 11:14. In

"Cambodia: An Action Memorandum," prepared for the International Negotiation Network and dated 15 January 1992, Hawk failed to foresee the Khmer Rouge violations of the Agreement, asserting only that "it is almost inevitable that glitches [*sic*] will occur in a program so massive and complicated." He did wrongly predict that a "massive influx of international aid...will accompany the arrival of the UN" (See Henry Kamm, "Most Cambodians See Nothing of Aid," *New York Times*, 21 February 1993.) The last journalistic prediction of Khmer Rouge "participation in the 1993 elections" on the basis of their "steadily gaining popular legitimacy" was probably Nate Thayer, "KR Blueprint for the Future Includes Electoral Strategy," *Phnom Penh Post*, 27 August 1992.

[67] For instance in 1985 the Lawyers Committee for Human Rights stated: "The bestiality that roamed large throughout Kampuchea in the 1970s remains unpunished. Violations of the nearly unprecedented scale practiced in the Pol Pot years demand a full historical and legal accounting. Under the supervision of David Hawk, the Cambodia Documentation Commission is working toward that objective." [*Kampuchea: After the Worst*, New York: Lawyers Committee for Human Rights, 1985: 7, 8.] By 1988, this was not the case. The CDC abandoned its goal, giving priority to demanding a Vietnamese troop withdrawal from Cambodia even after that withdrawal actually occurred. No mainstream human rights group has ever published a study of the Khmer Rouge genocide.

[68] In the weeks following the election, Khmer Rouge forces increased their attacks. They murdered over a dozen ethnic Vietnamese in Cambodia's southwest, blew up five bridges in the northwest, captured a historic temple on the Thai border from the government garrison (see *Indochina Digest*, 9 and 16 July 1993), shelled and overran a UN base, and machine-gunned a passenger train in southern Cambodia, killing ten people (*New York Times*, 3 and 4 August 1993).

[69] *Far Eastern Economic Review*, 3 June 1993: 10. As well as the 131 killings, UNTAC held the Khmer Rouge responsible for 250 injuries and fifty-three abductions. The People's Party was responsible for fifteen of the total of two hundred politically motivated killings in March, April and May 1993, and nine injuries. The other crimes remain unsolved. Lois B. McHugh, US Congressional Research Service, Issue Brief, *United Nations Operations in Cambodia*, updated June 7, 1993, IB92096: 5.

[70] *New York Times*, May 1993.

[71] "Royalists Say Khmer Rouge Should be Included in Government," by Sutin Wannabovorn, Reuters, Bangkok, 5 June 1993.

[72] "Back in the Fold," *FEER*, 22 July 1993: 12.

Revolution and Rural Response in Cambodia: 1970-1975

Kate G. Frieson

Few revolutionary movements can claim a legacy of radical political change more swift and violent than that of the Khmer Rouge. Between 1970 and 1975, the Red Khmer movement transformed itself from a marginalized group of committed communists forced to work underground into a nation-wide resistance movement that wrested state power.

Popular support is usually considered a necessary and crucial factor in the success of any revolutionary movement. This factor, Lenin stated, was the "fundamental law" guiding revolution to success: "Only when the 'lower classes' do not want the old way, and when the 'upper classes' cannot carry on in the old way-only then can revolution triumph."[1] The Cambodian revolution may represent one case in which popular support was not sufficiently developed, contributing to the fall of the regime in 1978. To understand one of the most bloody revolutionary regimes in this century it is useful to analyze the social and cultural context of the Red Khmer movement as it rose to power.

Cambodia was and is a predominantly rural society; eighty-five percent of the population lives in the countryside. Prior to the war years, peasants owned sufficient amounts of land through family inheritance to meet their basic subsistence needs. Peasants without land accounted for less than ten per cent of the total rural population in the early 1960s and grew up to twenty per cent by 1970. While peasant impoverishment was certainly increasing in Cambodia during the 1960s, it did not reach the brink of disaster which several scholars of revolution argue is the spark necessary to ignite peasant revolutionary potential.

A second important feature of Khmer rural society which had important implications for peasant responses to the Red Khmers is that beyond the family household there are no well-defined groups. The family household constituted the basic social and economic unit in village life. The lack of distinct social groupings beyond individual families partly explains why peasant grievances and uprisings never translated into nation-wide movements against the state prior to the 1970s. This anarchic quality in village Cambodia permitted extensive personal freedom, which as Michael Vickery has pointed out, "prevailed in a society in which there was no formal freedom at all."[2] Cambodian rulers at all political levels were oppressive and demanding. Yet within the village there existed individual freedom which was a widely enjoyed aspect of rural life. In their descriptions of village life before the war, Cambodians have remarked "We worked at whatever we wanted and we were happy because we didn't have anyone telling us what to do." Indeed this individual freedom, expressed literally as "go and play," began as soon as their labor obligations had been fulfilled.

The relatively anarchic nature of Khmer peasant society and the lack of severe economic grievances were formidable obstacles in the way of Red Khmer recruitment drives prior to 1970. And aside from localized pockets of rural unrest, the Red Khmers attracted very few supporters during their first seven years in the countryside, from 1963 to 1970. In the beginning of 1970, the Red Khmer regular units totaled only 4,000 fighters for the whole country and of these less than half were armed.

What the Red Khmers required to make political inroads into the countryside was a combination of economic catastrophe and political opportunity. Both conditions were provided by the coup d'état of March 1970, after which civil war, foreign invasion, and bombing tore much of village society to pieces. The coup marked a watershed in Cambodian history: the end of the Prince Sihanouk's rule and the spread of the Vietnam war to Cambodia. Sihanouk formed an alliance with the Red Khmers to overthrow the Republican government led by Lon Nol. This alliance provided the political opportunity for Red Khmers to exploit Sihanouk's popularity by rallying forces behind his leadership in a national united front against Lon Nol and his U.S. allies. Of significance, however, is that the Red Khmers did not dare risk popular rejection by revealing their communist identity. A Red Khmer in his early twenties at the time, based in Kompong Tralach in the southwest, later recalled that the coup was interpreted by the Party as a good opportunity to gather supporters; "After Sihanouk's March 23 speech, we didn't have to do any fighting. We just made appeals to soldiers and people, civil servants, village officials. When they came over from big market areas they were sent to the rear of liberated zones to work in fields. When they were already in the countryside they were allowed to stay where they were. We immediately stopped attacking Sihanouk and started pointing out that he was Chairman of our Front and 80-90% supported Sihanouk and the Party."[3]

Thach Diem, a 23 year-old man from Bakan, Pursat province, who joined the United Front immediately after the coup corroborates this:

> The Red Khmers appeared with Vietnamese. They told the people they had come to help liberate Sihanouk and that they were there to help Sihanouk fight Lon Nol so that Sihanouk would win back his country. When Lon Nol overthrew Samdech [Prince] Sihanouk they made that propaganda.[4]

According to Pung Kuong, a minor government official in western Battambang, "Samdech Sihanouk asked the people to run into the forest and young people went into the forest to fight the traitorous group of Lon Nol. At that time people ran quietly into the forest...After that the local commander went to persuade people to come back again and I saw that some came back and some of them didn't come back."[5] Pung Kuong's impression from the time was that the young people in his district decided to slip into the maquis because they were angry at Lon Nol for overthrowing Sihanouk; they were unaware, however, of the CPK's plan for revolution in Cambodia.

Propaganda leaflets calling Cambodians to join the NUFK stressed Sihanouk's leadership role and reminded people of the contrast between the "clique of Lon Nol, Sirik Matak, and Cheng Heng, the faithful servants of the American imperialists... who force Cambodians to fight Cambodians" and the previous reign of the monarchy where "peace, prosperity and well-being were due to the leadership of Prince Norodom Sihanouk."[6] Another young recruit at the time recalled the persuasive message of the Red Khmers:

> When the Red Khmers came they talked to us, saying, "Now my friend, our country is at war. Lon Nol is a traitor. He overthrew Samdech Euv [Prince Papa]. Now, my friend, don't run away to Thailand. [The recruit lived close to the Thai border.] Become a soldier in order to give state power back to Sihanouk." They asked us to please stand up and fight against the national traitor Lon Nol who made the coup against Sihanouk. This was before the area was liberated. When the soldiers came into the area from the national highway the Red Khmers would withdraw into the forest. After the [Lon Nol] soldiers had finished their basic camp training they

withdrew. Then the Red Khmers would come out of the forest and prepare to govern the village secretly. They spread groups within the village and the cadre were there secretly at first.[7]

The secrecy was carried on once the party was able to work openly in the post-coup period.[8] The CPK cultivated peasant ignorance and confusion of its beliefs and intentions with its united front association with Sihanoukists, nationalists, intellectuals and its vague terms of self-reference: *Angkar* ("organization") or *Khmer Romdas* ("Khmer Liberation") while simultaneously demanding peasant support for its programs and war objectives.[9] Thach Diem also recalled the party's practice of keeping its identity and aims well hidden from the people during the civil war years:

> I would like to tell you that they [the people] didn't know at all [about the Red Khmer ideas]. Even the students, school teachers and intellectuals didn't know. The people who knew were those who were working with the communists. They hid this information and even the people who were working for them didn't know about it. They didn't tell anyone about communism. Even the teachers, the Buddhist *sangha*, the intellectuals who politicized their students and told them to leave school. The teachers abandoned their classes and told their students to do the same and go join the Red Khmers. But at that time no one knew that Cambodia would become communist. The teachers didn't think about this.[10]

The united front political program which was widely publicized in 1970 did not even mention the existence of the Communist Party of Kampuchea (CPK), the political party of the Red Khmers, or its goals which were "to lead the people to succeed in the national democratic revolution, to exterminate the imperialists, feudalists, and capitalists, and to form a national revolutionary state in Cambodia."[11] There were several reasons for secrecy. For one thing, secrecy was in keeping with standard united front tactics first advocated by Lenin in 1902 and subsequently used by communist parties elsewhere.[12] The CPK chose to keep its existence secret in order to rally as many people as possible to its cause during the stage of the national democratic revolution. Further, Sihanouk's past invective against the "Red Khmers" was well known and the sudden political union of the two was cause for caution. Sihanouk's longtime praise and support for Vietnamese communists, on the other hand, made their visibility in United Front activities less problematic, and for this reason, as well as for logistical ones, Vietnamese cadre took the initiative in promoting the United Front at the village level for the first several months. But the label of "communist" so strongly associated with the Vietnamese, and one the CPK wanted to avoid by concealing itself in the folds of a united front, still had to be overcome in Cambodia. Vietnamese and Khmer cadre stressed their nationalist credentials and their obedience to Sihanouk during their public rallies and never mentioned socialism or communism.

Finally, the CPK opted for secrecy because it knew it was unpopular. Decades of political work had accomplished little in the way of building support in the countryside. The party had attracted a small and dedicated following among urban, educated, middle class men and women, former monks, who had prepared themselves intellectually for making revolution, and among some rural poor. With the exception of some young, unattached men, and to a lesser extent, women, Khmer peasants displayed little interest in abandoning their families and farms for the sake of elusive political ideals. When the political inertia of village life during the Sihanouk era was shattered first by the coup, and then by the war which spilled over into Cambodia from Vietnam, peasant disinterest in Red Khmer recruiters was not always a prudent response.

Pretending to fight for the return of Sihanouk was the first deception the CPK made in order to rally popular support for its revolution. The second deception used by the CPK to gather supporters was to hide the party's goal of social revolution.

The CPK's Agitation Campaigns Among the Peasantry

Once the furor over Prince Sihanouk's overthrow had died down, the party introduced new issues to win peasant support. These covered the areas of nationalism and class struggle. In the first, the propaganda sessions focused on the need for everyone to fight the Lon Nol regime, and its supporters, the United States and South Vietnam, which were intent on taking away the country's independence and oppressing the people. The second issue introduced to villagers was the concept and practice of class struggle between peasants and workers against feudalists and capitalists. Pressing ahead with new, intimidating political ideas in rural areas taken over or under sporadic united front control proved difficult, however.

Negative, passive, or indifferent rural responses to Red Khmer propaganda obtained for two reasons. The first was that the peasantry lacked an understanding of the party and its policies. The second, and more compelling reason was the cultural context of power relations in Cambodian society. Khmer peasants had a centuries-old inferiority complex which centered on the powerlessness of the individual.

To take up the first point, the peasantry's ignorance of the CPK, as previously discussed, stemmed from the party's underground activities and need for secrecy during the Sihanouk years. The facelessness of *Angkar* was upheld by the CPK's policy of keeping itself and its leaders secret. But the party could do this because of the humbling deference displayed by peasants to figures of authority. The peasantry's reluctance to ask questions of the Red Khmers was neatly summarized to me by one elderly woman who remarked: "We don't remember the names of the Red Khmer leaders. We didn't *dare* look at the faces of the top leaders. We only worked hard."[13] When Cambodian villagers speak of their relationship to Red Khmer cadres or any other political group they use a word which infers indebtedness- the word is *bomrer,* which means to serve. This reveals a central aspect of rural political culture in which peasants were regarded and viewed themselves as subjects who remained at the bottom of the social and political hierarchy, and who served and obeyed the rulers. These attitudes prevailed among peasants who saw Red Khmer leaders replace traditional village and regional authorities. The fact that the Red Khmers were fighting to obliterate class relations was insignificant to villagers because they were still forced to comply with rules imposed from above just as they had done in the past for other rulers.

Thus while peasants were organized by *Angkar* to attend frequent propaganda sessions, attendance by itself did not show their "support" for the revolution as much as it did their fear of punishment, deference to authority, respect for Sihanouk's orders, and mild curiosity in the black-clothed cadre. Peasants memorized the slogans or key words of the propaganda sessions during the war but their meaning or significance often eluded them. For instance, Sem Pal remembers that: "The Red Khmers only told us that the war was being made to destroy imperialism and feudalism, American imperialism and Vietnamese fascism...But I didn't know what the goal of this thinking was for the life of the people."[14]   *Angkar* demanded complete obedience and loyalty of the peasantry as its 1971 slogan makes clear:

> Love *Angkar*,
> Hate *Angkar*'s Enemies;
> Tell the Truth to *Angkar*[15]

There was no discussion of *Angkar*'s policies, much less its power in the village. Phim Kun, a Khmer communist who rallied to the Republican side reported the following situation in 1971: "I saw that there was no one who dared to open their mouth to talk about important subjects of *Angkar* or of matters relating to the life that had come about...The people could only open their mouths to offer praise."[16] To peasants *Angkar* represented the new political authority in their lives which displayed the same bossy character of former leaders.

The party developed special agitation sessions, as they were called, to counter these obstacles and arouse class consciousness among peasants. Pol Pot spoke of these sessions in 1977, referring to the period of the United Front (1970-1975):

> The people had to understand our reasoning. Our policy had to conform with their interests for them to give us their support. We talked to them, had meetings with them. Sometimes they agreed with us, sometimes they didn't. We came back again and again.[17]

The CPK was convinced that once it had awakened the peasantry's class consciousness, it would have little else to do, for the peasants would rise up *en masse* and overthrow their oppressors, the "landlord class," as the peasants in the 1967 Samlaut revolt had attempted to do. But this did not happen. The emphasis on the "landlord class" as the target of the party's rural policy was put in a CPK document of 1970, titled, *Strategy and Rural Policy of the Party* : "If we can materialize the slogan "Land for Farmers," we can then settle the fundamental problem and can succeed in our Revolution. *The land problem is considered to be the essential and basic concern of the farmers.* By solving this problem, the Party of the workers can succeed in gaining the leadership of the farmer class."[18] It was restated with equal authority in Pol Pot's 1977 speech in which he refers to a decision apparently taken at the CPK's congress in 1960 that "85% of the population, that is, the peasants, were in contradiction with the exploiting class which oppressed them directly, the landowners...It had to be a priority to resolve this principal contradiction in order to mobilize the forces of the peasantry, who were the greatest force."[19]

The party's first mistake was to believe that peasants only needed some politicization to turn them into revolutionaries. The party's second mistake, more serious in its ramifications, was to base its rural policy on the overthrow of the "landlord class."[20] This policy could not reflect the interests of peasants because the majority of peasants owned land (Samlaut was an exception). This fact was never addressed by the party. By choosing the "landlord class" as the target on which peasants were to vent their anger the CPK invented an institution of oppression that was invisible to most peasants, and therefore difficult for them to understand. Yet the party forged ahead with the Chinese and Vietnamese models of social revolution to guide it.[21]

A starting point in Red Khmer propaganda campaigns according to one recruit was to focus on the exploitation of the peasantry. According to Thach Diem who joined the Red Khmers in 1970:

> They [the Red Khmers] also spoke in depth about one political aspect concerning exploitation. They said "I have anger against the capitalists and American imperialists," for example. They said that the capitalist and imperialist method was to oppress the people, to mistreat the people, to draw blood from the people. That was what they talked about first of all.[22]

According to another former Red Khmer cadre from Siem Reap, the party's recruiting propaganda emphasized a nationalist objective: fighting the Americans who threatened to take over the country. In Chhit Do's words:

> The Yuon [pejorative term for Vietnamese] were responsible for fighting with the [enemy] soldiers, and the Khmer Rouge were responsible for political education among the people, teaching them to hate Lon Nol and to fight with the Lon Nol soldiers...But they didn't really say anything about fighting against the Lon Nol soldiers. They said we were fighting with American imperialism. If it had been a matter of fighting with Lon Nol, the Khmers wouldn't have had the heart to do it, because they felt that if it was a war between Khmers, they wouldn't fight. This was because back then, the Khmers still loved one another...So they [the Red Khmers] said, "if you don't fight Lon Nol, then Lon Nol will go over to the Americans...if you don't go and fight them, if you don't have the guts

to shoot them, these guys will certainly go over to the Americans, and, in the days to come, the Americans will rule over our entire country. This was the education they gave.[23]

To attract followers, cadre were instructed to explain Angkar's commitment to greater material wealth and a higher standard of living for peasants.[24] The party promised that once feudalism and capitalism were overturned everyone would automatically enjoy a higher standard of living. For peasants, then, the incentive to join the revolution, or to lend it moral support, stemmed from the promise of rewards when the war ended. This was not a ploy on the part of the CPK to win the trust of the peasantry. Most of its leaders shared a profound faith in the ability of a socialist political system to lift Cambodia out of its archaic poverty. This message was drummed into villagers during the first years of the war. One Red Khmer woman cadre, Prum Pal, whose responsibilities included propaganda work in 1972 among the peasantry of Kreng Beng village in Kandal explained her activities there in her 1978 "confession:"

> My activities to train the people to fight [for] the revolution were to talk to them and say, "Uncle, you have worked in the rice fields since you were a child; Uncle you don't have enough food; [they] control things and you still don't have enough and you work alone and the food is not enough to satisfy your hunger. Uncle you work for the [Republic] but you do not have a high rank and after winning you will only work in the ricefields. You won't be given a high rank. Your children will only remain rice farmers, too. But if uncle wants to become a big man he will have to fight the [Republic]. That was the only way he could become a big man. If he went with me he could have money and would have a higher position. In this way he agreed. But only after a long while, a long time of training.[25]

Informants who had faith in the Red Khmers and believed in the revolution insofar as they could understand it, support Prum Pal's testimony. Im Oeun, a poor peasant from Tramkak village, Bakan district, Pursat province lived under Red Khmer control after 1972. He was attracted by the propaganda of the Red Khmers which criticized corruption in society and the system of exploitation in which poor peasants such as himself suffered the most. As Im Oeun explained:

We were poor, we wanted to have a better life. What they said seemed reasonable so we believed them. When they came to the village we gave them food to eat.[26]

A poor peasant told a Chinese journalist at the start of the war:

To tell you the truth, my entire possessions were a pair of pants. The coat I am wearing was given by a commander of the liberation army. Several days ago, when the liberation army passed by my house, the commander saw that I had no clothes on, he took off his coat and gave it to me.[27]

Kang Koeun, a monk during the Republican period, based in Kompong Som, was impressed not only by the *actions* of the Red Khmers but also by their teachings. They "believed in equality, no one richer than anyone else. These were good ideas but the practice of them was bad."[28]

The pattern of propaganda sessions was for cadre to criticize the corrupt ways in which wealth was created in Cambodia, particularly those spawned by the influx of American aid for the war effort, and then to emphasize the material benefits and physical security that would flow from the audience's participation in the revolution.[29] Difficulties arose when cadre parroted political concepts they had picked up during study sessions. Noeun Chhean, a poor peasant from Kampot recalled that he and other villagers assembled at the central *sala* (open air meeting hall) as they were instructed to do by the local Red Khmer leaders, but they "just sat and pretended to listen. I didn't understand what they were talking about. They would talk for hours and we were tired."[30] Hoeung Yat, an elderly market seller from Kompong Thom in the north, has recalled that the new political vocabulary introduced by Red Khmers was alien and confusing:

They would come and *not do much* but talk about feudalism and capitalism. I had never heard those words before and did not know what they meant. I asked the Red Khmers what the words meant but they did not tell me. Only that I was a capitalist because I sold goods in the market. And I asked my husband "Hey, what does this feudalism mean? And he said he didn't know. Then I asked the Red Khmers, hey what does this "feudalism" mean, and they didn't tell me. We didn't know what they were talking about.[31]

The CPK was less successful in persuading Khmer peasants to abandon their belief in the Buddhist notions of *karma* than it was in generating hatred of the ruling class. Peasants will say in one breath how their lives are miserable, tiring, onerous, taxing, and lowly, and that they are this way because of fate. It was this belief, for example, that led a cyclo driver to tell me in 1990: "What can I do about it, I'm born into this life as a poor person and I can't have the opportunity to become educated like other people. I really pity myself!"[32] It would have taken decades for cadre to convince peasants to give up their belief in the spiritual world and the law of *karma* rather than the few years the war lasted, as later party history boasted.[33]

Confronting this peasant view of the world, its forces of good and evil, was a challenge for the CPK. The party could not risk alienating villagers by castigating them for their beliefs in spirits, nor could it publicly spurn spiritual leaders during the early stages of agitation. But mid-way through the war, with half the rural population under its control, the CPK began its transformation of society. Red Khmer strategies lacked nuance and delicacy and depended upon force for their implementation. Land collectivization was imposed in some regions in 1973, whole village populations were kidnapped in the north and southwest and forcibly relocated in remote areas; markets, religious practices, and even traditional styles of dress were forbidden. Many Cambodians did not understand or appreciate the "new society" being foisted upon them. Their response to the Red Khmers, by and large, was designed for survival and consisted of public deference to the black-clothed cadres but private irreverence.

Rural Voices in 1973

Khmer peasants, including some 200,000 of the CPK's followers, faced their worst year in 1973 with severe food shortages in the north leading to starvation in some areas; devastation of crops, livestock and houses in the central and southwest regions which were pummeled by bombs; and a change in the CPK's behavior, leading to violent clashes with villagers. Further, the nature of the war had changed. Red Khmer soldiers and cadre suffered from low morale due to the fact that they were no longer fighting South Vietnamese and American armies, but fellow Khmers, their family members, neighbors, and friends.

Most regions, with the exception of Battambang and the sparsely populated northeast suffered from shortages in basic food items such as rice and salt. Frustrations over hunger were exacerbated by the party's rule forbidding peasants trade in government-held areas. Cadre who took pity on hungry villagers sometimes broke the rules and allowed them to trade in the Lon Nol controlled areas. They were later likened to traitors for such actions and forced to "confess" these crimes against the party.[34] Resentment, mostly kept hidden, grew among peasants who disliked being forced to engage in food production for the army when their own families went hungry. Finally, both cadre and peasants were subject to increased physical punishment and harassment for expressions of dissent, suspicions of spying, and attempts to rally. Coercive measures were used to persuade villagers to accept *Angkar*'s authority, a contrast to the use of propaganda mostly in earlier years. Killings were not uncommon.

While the bombing may have strengthened Red Khmer forces with young, angry recruits, the CPK was not always successful in keeping them. Nuon Chea spoke of the problem of building up the right revolutionary viewpoint in cadre, who were not paid wages, or given rankings, and instructed to "serve the party":

> During the struggle, we encountered many difficulties. For example, cadre separated from their families and not ideologically firm would sometimes decide to run back to their families and away from the revolution. And sometimes cadre were working underground within the enemy administration and receiving very high wages. Lacking a firm revolutionary standpoint, they would be bought.[35]

As the hardships imposed by wartime conditions increased in the latter half of 1973, so too did the coercive tactics of Red Khmers over villagers, resulting in a peasant resentment, distrust and, when possible, breakaways from liberated zones. Chhit Do explained the situation in his area:

> The peasants and the Khmer Rouge split in the latter half of 1973 and the beginning of 1974, because the peasants...didn't have any faith in the Khmer Rouge anymore, the Khmer Rouge lost credibility. They said that if things went on like they were the people wouldn't get anything out of it. All they were getting was death, the death's of their children, who were going off to war, going off to the battlefield and all getting killed. What's more it wasn't any Americans that they

were fighting. It was other Khmers just like themselves. They're weren't any Americans to be seen among the troops on the Lon Nol side. There were just the Lon Nol troops themselves, and so they saw that we were fighting among ourselves. Meanwhile, there wasn't any rice, there wasn't anything to eat. Out there in the countryside there wasn't any salt, there was nothing to wear. There wasn't anything at all. The longer we fought, the poorer we got, and so the people lost faith and started going over to the Lon Nol side whole villages at a time.[36]

Another Red Khmer from the Pursat area specified that 1973 was the year that conditions worsened, Red Khmer behavior turned violent, and people responded by suspending their support for the Red Khmers. The increased incidence of killing as a punishment inflicted on villagers by Red Khmers was, in Thach Diem's opinion, the most serious cause of the split:

> From 1970 to 1973 the Red Khmers didn't kill people. Anyone who did something wrong was put in jail. By 1973 this policy had changed and if someone did something wrong they were killed. The killing was done secretly so no one knew about it. They told people to come and study and then that's when they killed them.[37]

The hallmarks of the Democratic Kampuchea regime—forced evacuations, food deprivation, and rigid authoritarianism and widespread killings, were policies with antecedents in the pre-1975 period. These were policies which turned Cambodian peasants against the revolution and its leaders.

In conclusion, Khmer peasant politics were not bridged successfully to those of the Red Khmers. The gulf that separated Khmer peasantry from the party had three major causes. The first was that the party never showed its true face to the peasantry, who it claimed were the main beneficiaries of the revolution. Second, the discipline of the party which its cadre were to rigidly obey, was foreign to and disliked by many peasants. The party did not succeed in convincing peasants that hard work and no play was good for them and the country. The tedious work, long hours, restrictive trade, ban on travel, bland food in insufficient quantities—all were the trademarks of a "crazy" regime from which peasants did not perceive benefits. While the extraction of peasants by Red Khmers were excessive, and peasant response was to resist by whatever means were available to them, the pattern is not unique to the Cambodian revolution. Peasants under less severe revolutionary regimes have also resisted the demands made of them when they did not conform to peasant interests.

The findings demonstrate that the Red Khmers did not successfully convince the majority of Cambodians that their interests were well represented by the movement. This accounts, in part, for middle and rich peasant strategies of passive support for the Red Khmers under conditions of extreme duress, and the mass defections of peasants from base areas in some parts of the country in 1973 and 1974. The Red Khmers did, however, build up a solid base of support among the poor peasant class, whose interests were served well by the Party's narrow focus on the question of land ownership in its rural policy. The CPK's analysis of rural society led it to single out landlordism as the single most important concern of eighty-five per cent of Khmer peasants when in reality only twenty per cent of peasants were landless. The policies of collectivization that resulted from this analysis alienated the landed rural supporters by late 1972 and early 1973, who had been drawn to the movement out of duty to reinstate Prince Sihanouk. Cambodian peasants were not particularly keen to have social and economic relationships which existed prior to the war years *radically* altered, although they would have probably put up with the Red Khmers for much longer if their cruelties had not been so excessive.

Without in-depth political training it was not possible for uneducated rural people to comprehend the structural imbalances in their society and how a new, communist system would correct them. Yet the Red Khmers lacked sufficient time and personnel to undertake this task; moreover, their leaders made the calamitous decision to ignore it in some regions altogether. Coercion, force, violence, threats, these were the tactics used to obtain the peasantry's submission to the Red Khmer movement, particularly after 1973, when most of the Vietnamese forces were withdrawn, and Red Khmers shouldered the responsibility for military initiatives.

Red Khmer gains were not entirely of their own making, and indeed, without the military prowess of the North Vietnamese and Viet Cong armies which set the course of the war firmly on the side of the Red Khmers during the first two years of the war, it is doubtful the Red Khmers could have won the war so quickly, if at all. As the Lon Nol government floundered under the pressures of fighting a war for which it was not prepared, the Red Khmers, with their militarily powerful North Vietnamese allies, easily gained the military advantage within the first few weeks of the hostilities. The Red Khmers steadily gained strength while the Lon Nol regime became progressively factionalized, corrupt, mismanaged, and short-sighted.

The conditions under which the Red Khmers succeeded in coming to power in 1975 explains, to some extent, why they were unable to hang onto it for very long. Red Khmer domestic policies, which began to be implemented in the early 1970s, were not popular because they created hardship and cruelty for the people in whose name the revolution was made. Cambodians were simply not willing to defend the Red Khmers once they were at war with the Vietnamese in late 1978 and the regime quickly collapsed. One of my respondents voiced the following observation: "They [Red Khmers] didn't think about the people, they only thought about how to use the strength of the people. They didn't give the people peace. That's why all the people declared that they had no faith [in them]. But we didn't dare let this thought out. We personally struggled in our hearts to endure, to survive."[38]

The oral histories which have been highlighted in this paper reveal an important paradox: that the Khmer Rouge could lose the revolution while they were in the process of winning the war. The revolution failed in no small measure due to people's unwillingness to support a movement that didn't look after them. The oral histories and Khmer Rouge documents during the early years of the revolution's making, suggest a disparity of views between Cambodian communist leaders, who regarded themselves as the vanguard of peasants (and workers), and peasants themselves, in whose interests the revolution was apparently made.

---

[1]   V. I. Lenin, 'Left Wing Communism,' in *Selected Works,* Vol. 2: 629.

[2]   Michael Vickery, *Cambodia 1975-1982* (Boston: South End Press, 1984):14.

[3]   Lonh a.k.a Lorn, interviewed by Stephen Heder, March 11, 1980, Chantaburi, Thailand.

[4]   Author's interview with Thach Diem, June 29, 1989, Montreal.

[5]   Author's interview with Pung Kuong, April 28, 1989, Tacoma, Washington.

[6]   NUFK propaganda leaflet (captured July 5, 1970) translated by the United States Embassy, Phnom Penh, CDEC Log. No. 08-1250-70.

[7]   Thach Diem interview.

[8]   See Teri L. Caraway, *The United Front Strategies of the Khmer Rouge* (B.A. Thesis, Pomona College, 1989). I am grateful to Teri for giving me a copy of her thesis.

[9] Author's interview with Tep Khunnal, First Secretary of the Democratic Kampuchea Mission, United Nations, New York, December 2,1988, New York.

[10] Author's interview with Thach Diem, June 29, 1989, Montreal.

[11] See CPK document, "A Short Guide for Application of Party Statutes," Translated captured document, Phnom Penh 1975, published in Timothy Carney, *Communist Party Power in Kampuchea (Cambodia): Documents and Discussion,* (Data Paper 106, Southeast Asia Program, Cornell University, Ithaca, New York, 1977): 56.

[12] Lenin believed that the keeping the Party secret would increase the numbers of public organizations that could be organized by communist party members. Speaking of these united front organizations, he warned, "but it would be absurd and dangerous to confuse them with the organization of revolutionaries, to obliterate the border line between them, to dim still more the...already incredibly hazy appreciation of the fact that in order to 'serve' the masses we must have people who will devote themselves exclusively to [Communist] activities, and that such people must train themselves patiently and steadfastly to be professional revolutionaries. See *Lenin, What is to be Done?* (1902) cited in Robert V. Daniels (ed.), *A Documentary History of Communism,* (Vol. 1, Vintage Books, 1960): 17. The Thai Communist Party's open association with its front organizations in the 1970s is one exception, and may have accounted in part for its failure to attract broad based support. Personal communication, Somsak Jeamteeraskul.

[13] Kate Frieson, "The Pol Pot Legacy in Village Life," *Cultural Survival Quarterly,* 14 (1990): 72. Author's interview with elderly peasant woman, Svay village, Kandal province, Cambodia, January 1990.

[14] Author's interview with Sem Pal, March 1987, Phanat Nikom, Thailand.

[15] National radio broadcast transcript of Hanoi-trained Khmer communist, Phim Kun, December 1971, Phnom Penh: 22.

[16] Phim Kun: 23.

[17] Pol Pot, "Long Live:" 32.

[18] Strategy and Rural Policy of the [Cambodian Communist] Party (1970) CDEC 6 028 0177 71: 4. Italics added.

[19] "Long Live:" 26.

[20] The term "landlord" commonly refers in Khmer to house owners rather than land owners.

[21] The same could not be said for Laotian revolutionaries who, like the Red Khmers, found themselves promoting revolution in a country of largely landed peasants. In fact, Kaysone Phomvihane wrote in *La révolution lao* that while in most countries, the liberation of the peasantry could only come about when the policy of "land to the tillers" [the same slogan used by the Red Khmers] was practiced, Laos was an exception since the farmers practiced a pre-feudal form of production. Cited in Grant Evans' excellent study, *Lao Peasants Under Socialism,* (New Haven and London: Yale University Press, 1991): 41. The Chinese Communist Party's experience of heating up class

conflicts must also have been of the minds of the CPK leaders. For Chinese communist approaches to the politicization of the peasantry see, R.P. Madsen, "Harnessing the Political Power of Peasant Youth," in David Mozingo and Victor Nee (editors) *State and Society in Contemporary China* (Ithaca, New York: Cornell University Press, 1983): 244-264.

[22] Author's interview with Thach Diem, June 29, 1989, Montreal.

[23] Transcript of interview with Chhit Do by François Ponchaud and Bruce Palling, January 1982, Paris. I am grateful to Ben Kiernan for a copy of the interview transcript.

[24] *Angkar*, meaning 'organization' in Khmer, was the name used by the CPK to refer to itself during the civil war period and also during the time it ruled the country, 1975-1978.

[25] Prum Pal, "confession" C168, Tuol Sleng, 1978, Phnom Penh. Since the nature of this document was to "prove" her infidelity to the CPK dating from the early 1960s, she neatly converted all her work for the party into work for the "CIA party" whose mission was to sabotage the revolution. This is a party that recurs through many of the confessions I have consulted, linking party members accused of opposition to the central control of Pol Pot and Nuon Chea to an imaginary "CIA party" or "CIA-KGB Marxist-Leninist Party." Why the factionalism within the party, and more importantly, opposition to Pol Pot and Nuon Chea had to be masked by such absurd allegations remains a vexing question. Prum Pal was married to Vorn Vet, Vice-Premier of Democratic Kampuchea who was arrested as she was in late 1978 and killed. Tiv Ol was Vice-Premier of Information and Propaganda in GRUNK. The words in the text which appear in brackets are the opposite of those used by Prum Pal in the "confession," since there was no such CIA party. She was 'CIA' because she was Vorn Vet's wife. Thus if we substitute the following words [against=for], [we=they], [Republic=revolution] the likely reality of the situation in 1972 becomes clear.

[26] Im Oeun, interviewed by Pratin Dharmarak, Melbourne, 1989. All of Im Oeun's quotations derive from this interview. I am grateful to Pratin for sharing this interview with me, parts of which are included in her Master's thesis, *Cambodian Refugee Youth and Schooling in Australia* (Education Faculty, Monash University, 1990): 53-55, and Appendix B: 89-93.

[27] U.S. Central Intelligence Agency, *Foreign Broadcast Information Service (FBIS)*, June 30, 1970, H3.

[28] Author's interview with Kang Koeun, November 1987, Vancouver, BC.

[29] Prum Pal confession. This pattern was also discerned from a number of captured documents including, NUFK pamphlet, "Short Explanation of the Policy Line of the National United Front of the Khmers," Undated, CDEC No. 03-1095-72, 23; *A Red Khmer's Notebook*, 1970; NUFK leaflet, "To All Our Fellow Countrymen," Kandal Province, July 5, 1970, CDEC No. 08-1250-70; Notice of NUFK, June 18, 1971, Mondulkiri province, CDEC No. 06-1767-71; FBIS, Hu Nim Statement on Situation of Cambodia, December 31, 1972. One NUFK radio broadcast warned residents of Phnom Penh that if they did not

leave the city for liberated areas they would "suffer starvation since Phnom Penh has already been completely cut off from the provinces." *FBIS*, December 25, 1971.

[30] Author's interview with Noeun Chhean, July 7, 1990, Melbourne.

[31] Author's interview with Hoeung Yat, February 9, 1989, Vancouver, B.C.

[32] Author's conversation with cyclo driver in Phnom Penh, January 1990. Frank Smith observes that belief in karma and predestination were common frameworks through which peasants explained the misery of the DK period. See his *Interpretive Accounts of the Khmer Rouge Years: Personal Experience in Cambodian Peasant World View* (University of Wisconsin-Madison, Wisconsin Papers on Southeast Asia, Occasional Paper No. 18, 1989).

[33] The incompatibilities of the Southeast Asian peasant belief system in animism and Buddhism with a political ideology such as Marxism stressing materialism as the source of oppression is examined by Charles Keyes, *The Golden Peninsula: Culture and Adaptation in Mainland Southeast Asia*. See also Charles Keys, "Buddhism and Revolution in Cambodia," *Cultural Survival 14* (1990): 60-63; Yang Sam, *Khmer Buddhism and Politics 1954-1984* (Newington, CT: Khmer Studies Institute 1987); and Frank Smith, "Cambodian Peasant World View."

[34] The rule forbidding trade was strictly enforced and anyone bending it, regardless of party membership and rank were taken to task if caught. See Tuol Sleng confession No. A3, An Seng Hang, cadre of sector 13, Division 310, ("Biography of An Seng Hang, a.k.a. Chhun from 1967 to 74 before making the connection with Khuon," January 23, 1977: 19).

[35] Nuon Chea, Statement: 24.

[36] Chhit Do interview: 9,10.

[37] Thach Diem interview.

[38] On the intersection of biography and history, see C. Wright Mills, *The Sociological Imagination*, 1960, cited by Hugh Stretton, "George Rudé," *History From Below: Studies in Popular Protest and Popular Ideology in Honour of George Rudé* edited by Frederick Krantz, Montreal: Concordia University, 1985: 51. Author's interview with Sem Pal, Phanat Nikom, April 1987.

A Cambodian Village under the Khmer Rouge, 1975-1979

May Ebihara

In southern Kandal province are the crumbling remains of a former school that was turned into a Khmer Rouge regional headquarters, prison, and execution center during the Pol Pot regime. After the Khmer Rouge were routed, mass graves were uncovered as rains washed away soil. As one villager recounted, "They found lots of corpses in a ditch; some of them still had ropes on their hands and feet, and blindfolds on their eyes." A woman who saw some burials being excavated said that as she bent to look more closely at a skull, her tears fell on the bones.

Similar to local memorials elsewhere in Cambodia, a large mound of skulls and bones has been piled on a ledge in one of the rooms as testimony and reminder of this local "killing field."[1] A villager who accompanied me to this site softly recited the names of his kinsmen and friends who had probably been killed here. Gazing at the pile of skulls, it was devastating to think that some of the remains might be of people we had personally known. At one corner of the platform stand a small statue of Buddha and offerings of incense, expressions of compassion and mourning in this grim scene. A wooden sign on a pole in the midst of the skulls states simply but starkly that 18,318 people had been imprisoned here, of whom 5,111 died.

Several kilometers north of this former prison is a village named Sobay (a pseudonym) that I know well from anthropological fieldwork in 1959-1960 and revisits in 1990 and 1991.[2] Following upon Kate Frieson's general overview of peasantry and the Khmer Rouge from 1970-1975, this chapter offers a more specific account of the mortality suffered by inhabitants of one peasant village just prior to and during the Democratic Kampuchea (DK) regime. While executions were, perhaps, the most shocking and terrifying causes of death, DK's radical attempts to create a new social order also led to less dramatic but no less horrifying mortality from starvation, illness, and physical and emotional exhaustion.

The Village

My original research on Khmer peasant society and culture concentrated on one of three hamlets in the village, West Hamlet Sobay, which had about 159 inhabitants in 1960.[3] On a brief visit to Cambodia in 1989, after three decades of absence, I was astonished and grateful to find that the village and several dozen of my former friends and neighbors had managed to survive the devastating upheavals of the intervening years.[4] In 1990 and 1991 I collected oral histories from surviving West Hamlet villagers of their lives after 1960, with particular attention to the Pol Pot period when their existence was so drastically changed. Their experiences largely parallel (and substantiate) the harrowing and eloquent accounts by Teeda Butt Mam and other literate Khmer refugees.[5] But the villagers' accounts serve to emphasize and remind us of the important point, sometimes overlooked, that so-called "New People" who suffered so grievously during DK included not only educated, middle and upper class city dwellers, but rural peasants as well.

West Hamlet Sobay as I initially knew it in 1959-1960 was comprised of thirty-two households, mostly peasant cultivators with small landholdings (averaging about one hectare of rice fields per family) who cultivated rice more for subsistence than the market. Most households were fairly poor but not poverty-stricken, earning additional income when necessary with side pursuits such as making palm sugar or raising pigs for sale. The critical social and economic unit in village life was the household, either a nuclear or extended family. A larger circle of relatives on both sides of the family was also important in terms of mutual affection and aid. Another crucial feature of village life was, of course, religion. Sobay had its own Buddhist temple, and most adult men had been monks at some time in their lives.

The Beginnings of Upheaval

According to the villagers, their lives continued to be much the same into the late 1960s. The first tremors of upheaval began in the early 1970s as the Khmer Rouge began to build strength and make forays into this area from their early bases in southwestern Cambodia.[6] Because some Lon Nol government soldiers had been stationed near

Sobay, villagers became trapped in the fighting between these troops and the Khmer Rouge insurgents. In 1970-1971, two respected elders were accidentally shot; several houses were destroyed by artillery fire; and some villagers were kidnapped by the Khmer Rouge and taken south to rebel bases. As it became increasingly dangerous to remain in the area, West Hamlet residents began fleeing Sobay in the early 1970s. Most escaped to what they thought was the safety of Phnom Penh, although some twenty-five families from other Sobay hamlets opted to join Khmer Rouge base communities to the south because they thought they would not be able to subsist in the city. Thus, Sobay was largely abandoned during the Nixon-Kissinger "strategic bombing" of the Cambodian countryside in the summer of 1973 that was meant to destroy Khmer Rouge bases.[7] At one point the area around a market town two kilometers from Sobay, that had been the scene of intense fighting between rebel and government forces, was bombed every day for an entire week. Ironically, however, as villagers frantically fled to Phnom Penh, the Khmer Rouge were able to move into the devastated region.

In Phnom Penh, crammed with other refugees from the countryside, Sobay villagers survived with various odd jobs, and a number of able-bodied men were either conscripted into or voluntarily joined the army to assure some kind of livelihood. But the presumed security of Phnom Penh vanished as the city itself came under attack from the encircling Khmer Rouge. One villager lost all of her four children when her house was hit by a shell, and an elderly man from Sobay was mortally wounded in an artillery attack.

The Ordeal of Democratic Kampuchea

Eventually, on April 17, 1975, the Khmer Rouge captured Phnom Penh, and no further escape was possible. The villagers, along with other city residents, were expelled into the countryside. Most of the former residents of West Hamlet set out for Sobay, although some were forced by Khmer Rouge soldiers to go in other directions and were never seen again. Those who succeeded, after sometimes protracted and arduous journeys, in reaching what had once been their home village were shocked to find an overgrown and bombed-out landscape—as well as Khmer Rouge cadre who ordered them to continue further south to an uninhabited and barren wilderness. Here they were held for several months, jammed together with hundreds of other evacuees in makeshift shelters without adequate water, food, or medicine. And here the first wave of deaths from starvation and illness began. Villagers say that the elderly and children were least able to survive lack of food, but even young adults died.

When people were eventually permitted to return to the Sobay area, it had been renamed "New Village," and its former residents were labeled "New People," "April 17 people," "Lon Nol people," or simply "the enemy."[8] Although the villagers had been relatively poor peasants (and hence presumably from "politically correct" social strata), they were suspected of lying about their backgrounds and accused of having been urbanites from higher social classes or even "CIA." But even if they were indeed former peasants, they were still "the enemy" because they had fled the countryside rather than join the Khmer Rouge.[9] Such New People, said one villager, were considered to be "of no value....People's worth was measured in terms of how many cubic meters of dirt they moved...We watched our children become beasts of burden...They used us without a thought as to whether we lived or died."

Comments by some writers suggest that former peasants would have adapted to conditions in DK more easily than did city dwellers because villagers were already accustomed to a simple diet, manual labor, and agricultural work.[10] This assumption, however, ignores the fact that living conditions and labor requirements in DK were far more severe than in pre-revolutionary times, that many fundamental aspects of traditional peasant life were drastically altered or crushed during DK, and that villagers lost control over their own lives. As a villager said, "We had no freedom to do anything: to eat, to sleep, to speak...We [even] had to hide our crying and wept into a pillow at night." Thus Sobay villagers, no less than middle and upper class urbanites, regard the Pol Pot period as a time of such exceptional and intense misery that, in the words of one woman, "It was beyond suffering."

During the DK period, Cambodia was divided into a number of territorial units called "zones." While conditions varied regionally, "New Village" was located in the so-called "Southwest Zone" that was a stronghold of the Pol Pot faction of the Kampuchean Communist Party and an area said to have had more stringent controls than some other zones administered by more moderate Khmer Rouge cadre.[11] Some of Sobay's former residents were kept in "New Village" along with other evacuees from Phnom Penh, but a number were dispersed to various communes to the south (still within the Southwest Zone). Others were later sent northwest to Pursat province, a region noted for particularly harsh conditions—rampant malaria, back-breaking labor, and insufficient food —that left few survivors.

Villagers speak with bewilderment, anger, and hatred of the various ways in which their customary existence was overturned. The solidarity of the family as a primary social unit of economic cooperation and emotional bonds was shattered by communal organization into labor teams segregated on the basis of age and gender,[12] dispersal of family members and kinfolk into different work groups and communes, and suppression of familial sentiments. The separation of parents and children caused anguish, as did seeing family members die in terrible circumstances without being able to save them or even openly grieve their deaths.[13] Personal loyalties were now supposed to be directed toward the revolutionary regime, and DK cadre (who were often very young) replaced parents and the elderly as authority figures.

Buddhism was also demolished both symbolically and literally when the Khmer Rouge blew up the village temple. Religion was replaced with revolutionary political ideology as DK tried to instill new values and rules of behavior through political meetings, criticism sessions, stringent discipline, and severe punishments for misbehavior. Particular attention was paid to indoctrinating youth, but efforts were made also to "build" (in the sense of remake) adults.[14] Love, sorrow, anger, and other emotions could no longer be openly expressed, and the normally lively villagers were turned into silent automatons. Contrary to Buddhist codes of conduct in pre-revolutionary village life, people sometimes found themselves driven to lying about themselves and others, stealing food, and other acts of subterfuge in order to survive the extraordinary pressures and constraints on their lives.

The work demands of DK were overwhelming, even for peasants accustomed to manual labor. In the past, villagers had determined their own work schedules, with time for rest in even the busiest seasons and periods of relative leisure during the year. Now they were now driven to unrelenting labor that was arduous and exhausting even for country folk. While precise work hours could vary according to the type of labor team and its specific tasks, labor often started at dawn and sometimes extended into the night, with brief breaks for midday and evening meals. Some groups received one day of rest for every ten days of labor, but others were not allowed even that. Work was also subject to daily quotas (digging so many cubic feet of earth, producing so much fertilizer, harvesting so many bundles of rice) that were sometimes totally unrealistic or could be filled only by dint of enormous exertion. People were also constantly harassed and criticized. A villager, for example, told of an instance when she was transplanting rice seedlings (a task at which she was very experienced). The work team supervisor followed behind her, said she was transplanting incorrectly, ripped out all the seedlings, and made her replant them. But since accusations of "laziness" and inadequate performance meant beatings, withholding of food, and even execution, people struggled to work even when they were ill.[15]

Sobay's villagers labored at a variety of tasks: building large irrigation systems with hand labor, reshaping paddy fields into huge plots of uniform size, serving as human draft animals to pull plows when oxen were not available, growing successive crops of rice in regions where irrigation enabled multiple cropping (in contrast to the mono-cropping that had been typical of pre-revolutionary Sobay), making fertilizer from a mixture of human excrement, cow dung, and other ingredients, cultivating vegetables and fruit trees, tending animals and poultry, making mats and thatch, and so on.[16] No sooner was one task finished than people were dispatched to other work.

Exhausting labor was coupled, in a literally deadly combination, with lack of adequate nourishment. This was particularly the case after 1976-1977 when DK instituted communal dining halls, forbidding individuals to collect and prepare food on their own.[17] Although rice and other produce were indeed available, only minimal food was given to New People while local DK cadre and Old People ate well, and huge amounts of rice were appropriated by the state. Villagers say repeatedly, "You could see food, but you weren't allowed to eat it," and "There were piles of rice as big as this house, but it was taken away in trucks." Living primarily on thin rice gruel that was mostly water and soups made from wild plants, with occasional handouts of corn or beans, people were constantly famished and driven to scavenging or stealing food despite the risk of beatings or even death if they were caught. One man who had hauled sacks of rice onto trucks said he sneaked out that night to look for any grains of rice that might have fallen on the ground; and others report grabbing and hiding tiny crabs that were found in the fields. People craved the taste of salt and sugar, seasonings that were denied them, and were reduced to eating even rice husks that were formerly considered "food for pigs."

Given such lack of food, it is not surprising that illness was endemic. People would collapse, sicken, or die of exhaustion and malnutrition, compounded by malaria, dysentery, "swelling," infections, and other illnesses. Women often ceased to menstruate, their breasts shriveled, and some report that their uteruses collapsed and fell out from overwork. A building on the former temple grounds was turned into a hospital, but villagers deeply distrusted its homemade medicines (as one villager said, "It looked like shit") and usually avoided hospitalization unless totally incapacitated.

Last but by no means least, death became commonplace. Villagers were familiar with deaths due to old age or illness, but they now saw family, kinsmen, and friends die also from starvation, overwork, total demoralization, and—most chilling of all—execution. While some executions seemed to have a definite reason (such as infraction of rules or having the wrong background), in many cases it was not at all clear why some people were "taken away" while others were not. This inexplicability made the killings all the more terrifying, and people lived in perpetual fear, not knowing when DK cadre might come to call you away "to work"—a ruse for taking people to be executed—or seize you in the middle of the night. As one woman said, "Every morning you were grateful to have survived another night, and on the way to work you stole glances at the other work teams to see if your children were still alive."

The death toll among the former residents of West Sobay was startlingly high. As noted earlier, in 1960 West Hamlet had some 159 inhabitants. Speaking now only of these people, sixteen died during the 1960s of old age or illness. Four died in the early 1970s because of the civil war. Thus, in 1975 at the beginning of DK, 139 persons were left—of whom seventy (fifty percent) died during DK.[18] There were an additional five deaths either just before or during DK for which exact dates are not known because family members were separated. The fate of three other villagers is uncertain, but they are presumed dead because no one has seen or heard of them.

The precise causes of deaths cannot always be ascertained. In many instances it is impossible to say whether a particular death was due to malnutrition, overwork, or illness because there was an obvious interaction among these factors. However, villagers attributed eleven deaths at the outset of DK (when villagers were herded into the wilderness area and then permitted to return to "New Village") to starvation. Eight persons (including one woman) were executed. In a number of other cases, the cause of death is not known because people were in different communes. I was also sometimes reluctant to press villagers to specify how a family member died because memories of DK are painful to recall. As one man impatiently chided me, "Death is death, whether it's starvation or execution."

In sum, then, only sixty-four out of 139 people managed to survive the Pol Pot period. Of the West Sobay families that existed in 1975, some were totally decimated during DK, while others were left with only one or a few survivors. Everyone in Sobay has suffered the deaths of some close family members during the civil war or DK, whether parents, grandparents, siblings, or children.

The Aftermath of DK

Now, more than a decade after DK, Sobay's survivors have reconstructed the community and their lives. In early 1979 the Vietnamese pushed the Pol Pot forces toward the northwest border region and installed a new government, the People's Republic of Kampuchea (PRK). Various former residents of Sobay returned to the village and reestablished whatever remnants of families remained. After a brief period of partial collectivization at the PRK's outset because there were shortages of male labor and draft animals, household production and private property were reinstituted in 1986 and formally recognized in 1989 by the newly renamed State of Cambodia, whose constitution also reinstated Buddhism as the national religion.

On the surface, village life in present day Sobay echoes what I knew thirty years ago. There are once again nuclear and extended families; households cultivate rice, fruits, and vegetables on privately owned land; there are monks and ceremonies at the Buddhist *wat* where the central temple is being rebuilt; weddings are festive and joyous occasions; children are going to school; almost everyone has adequate food, clothing, and shelter. Clearly, however, people have been indelibly scarred by their experiences during the DK regime and still suffer its lingering aftereffects. I will note just two examples.

First, there is a skewed sex ratio in the current adult population of Cambodia that is estimated as sixty-four percent female.[19] Men had higher mortality during the years of civil war and DK because they were more likely to die in combat and from starvation or executions.[20] Of the former residents of West Sobay who were still alive in 1975 but died during DK, fifty-six percent were males. There is now a disproportionate number of widows and female-headed households in various parts of the country, and the present day village of West Sobay[21] is no exception in this regard. According to the local district office's figures for 1990, there were 339 females (80.5 percent) and eighty-two males in the village.[22]

Compared to my 1960 census of West Hamlet families, many more households are now headed by or include widows, or consist of a lone couple or single person who lost family members.[23] Such households are usually at an economic disadvantage. Because paddy fields were redistributed on a per capita basis, small families have very little land to cultivate. Moreover, those without able-bodied males and oxen (essential for plowing fields) in the household or among close kin must now enter into sharecropping agreements, hire wage labor, or reciprocate with hours of female labor.[24] Such arrangements also existed in pre-revolutionary village life, but they now occur more frequently because of the shortage of male labor power. Thus, more families face the economic problems of reduced subsistence with sharecropping, the need to earn cash to pay hired workers, or increased work for women with labor exchange.

Another legacy of DK is persistent medical problems. Villagers attribute the deaths of five West Sobay residents after 1979 to illnesses caused by conditions in DK; and many people explain disabilities such as weak limbs, difficulty walking, constant fatigue, impaired vision, and faulty memory as due to beatings or overwork suffered during DK.[25] Only one person says explicitly that DK made her emotionally unstable, but she holds a job and otherwise functions capably.[26] While other villagers must also bear deep psychic wounds, I have not encountered other examples of mental instability in West Sobay. It is quite possible that psychological aftereffects of DK are being somaticized as various ailments reported by the villagers, but it is also the case that physical problems are endemic in a peasant population.

Finally, villagers live with the knowledge and fear that Democratic Kampuchea forces still exist. While there are no Khmer Rouge in the immediate area, people have sometimes heard distant explosions from mountain regions where DK troops take refuge, and they are aware of Khmer Rouge attacks in other parts of the country. On my last visit to Sobay in the summer of 1991 when it seemed as if a settlement might actually be reached among the various contenders for political power, villagers were guardedly hopeful that peace might finally be at hand. At the time of writing, the United Nations Transitional Authority in Cambodia is attempting to prepare the country for national elections for a coalition government. Thus far, however, the Khmer Rouge have refused to disarm their troops and are once again trying to seize control of various parts of the country. It is tragic to think that the villagers' hopes for peace must be diluted with the terrible apprehension that the Khmer Rouge are not yet a thing of the past.

---

[1] See David Hawk, "The Photographic Record," in Karl Jackson, ed., *Cambodia 1975-1978* (Princeton, NJ: Princeton University Press) 1989:, for photographs of two early memorials. Executions also took place in a village near Sobay where the sub-district office was located during Democratic Kampuchea. Some skeletal remains and tattered remnants of clothing have been found here and are kept stored in a shed but not displayed.

[2] The original research in 1959-60 was supported by a Ford Foundation Foreign Area Training Fellowship. Fieldwork in 1990 was funded by the PSC-CUNY Faculty Research Awards Program, and in 1991 by the Wenner-Gren Foundation for Anthropological Research. I express my deep appreciation to the preceding, as well as to Dr. Judy Ledgerwood who assisted my later research in numerous ways. I also thank Ms. Siwanny Roy, Ms. Mora Chan Tho, and Mr. Kheang Ung for their help with translations and transcriptions.

[3] May Ebihara, *A Khmer Village in Cambodia*, Ph.D. dissertation, Columbia University, 1968 (Ann Arbor: University Microfilms).

[4] May Ebihara, "Return to a Khmer Village," *Cultural Survival Quarterly*, 14:3: 67-70.

[5] See Joan Criddle and Teeda Butt Mam, *To Destroy You Is No Loss* (New York: Atlantic Monthly Press) 1987; Someth May, (James Fenton, ed.), *Cambodian Witness: The Autobiography of Someth May* (New York: Random House) 1986; Haing Ngor (with Roger Warner), *A Cambodian Odyssey* (New York: Macmillan) 1987; and, Pin Yathay, *Stay Alive, My Son* (New York: Free Press) 1987.

[6] Ben Kiernan, *How Pol Pot Came to Power* (London: Verso) 1985; and, Michael Vickery, *Cambodia 1975-1982* (Boston: South End Press) 1984.

[7] William Shawcross, *Sideshow: Kissinger, Nixon and the Destruction of Cambodia* (New York: Simon & Schuster) 1979; and, Ben Kiernan, "Roots of Genocide: New Evidence on the US Bombardment of Cambodia," *Cultural Survival Quarterly* 14:3: 20-22.

[8] The Khmer Rouge distinguished between "Base People"/"Old People" and "New People." The former were Khmer Rouge cadre, persons from areas that had been taken over by the Khmer Rouge before 1975, or those from the "basic classes" of poor and lower-middle strata peasants. "New people" came from regions that were "liberated" by the Khmer Rouge only as of April 17,1975. New People were generally treated more harshly than Old People. There was also a tripartite categorization into those with "full rights," "candidates," and "depositees," but Sobay villagers were not clear as to these distinctions. On these points, see also Stephen Heder, *Kampuchean Occupation and Resistance* (Bangkok: Institute of Asian Studies, Chulalongkorn University) Asian Studies Monograph Number 27, 1980: 4-7; and Tim Carney, "The Organization of Power," in Karl Jackson, ed., *Cambodia 1975-1978* (Princeton: Princeton University Press) 1989: 80-84.

[9] Kate Frieson, "The Pol Pot Legacy in Village Life," *Cultural Survival Quarterly* 14:3: 71-73.

[10] Michael Vickery, "Democratic Kampuchea: Themes and Variations," in David Chandler and Ben Kiernan, eds., *Revolution and its Aftermath in Kampuchea: Eight Essays* (New Haven: Yale University Southeast Asian Studies, Monograph Series Number 25) 1983: 12; Vickery, "Democratic Kampuchea": 16, 24; Charles Twining, "The Economy," in Karl Jackson, ed., *Cambodia 1975-1978* (Princeton: Princeton University Press) 1990: 131.

[11] Ben Kiernan, "Conflict in the Kampuchean Communist Movement," *Journal of Contemporary Asia* 10 (1980): 75-118, and *How Pol Pot Came To Power*, Vickery, "Democratic Kampuchea," and *Cambodia 1975-1982*; and, David P. Chandler, *The Tragedy of Cambodian History* (New Haven: Yale University Press) 1991.

[12] There were distinct labor teams for children, adolescents and young adults, married (or widowed) adults, and the elderly, each of which was further divided into male and female groups. Hardy young people were placed in mobile work groups sent to different locations, wherever labor was needed, and saw their parents only rarely.

[13] One woman managed to remain stoically silent when her husband was "taken away" for execution. When her baby died some months later, however, she could not contain herself and howled and wept in grief. The cadre said, "You're crying over that little thing? We lost all those people [in our revolutionary struggle], and we're not crying."

[14] The term *kosang* means literally "to build," but was used during DK in the sense of remolding an individual to proper revolutionary standards of thought and behavior. The word was also used to refer to criticism sessions for improper behavior. (See also Chandler: 256; and, John Marston, "Metaphors of the Khmer Rouge," paper presented in a panel on "Khmer Culture: Persistence and Process" at the annual meetings of the Association for Asian Studies, 1989.)

[15] People could also be imprisoned. Two West Sobay women were put in prisons — one in the regional prison described at the outset of this paper and the other in Pursat province — for reasons never made clear to them. Neither was executed but both were made to labor during their prison terms.

[16] A person's work could vary according to the type of labor team one was assigned to (e.g., the elderly generally performed less arduous tasks such as women tending babies and men herding cattle), seasonal and other demands of rice cultivation, and individual assignments that might change over time. The type and amount of work demanded could also vary according to one's personal background: e.g., in one labor group, men who were known to have been soldiers during the Lon Nol regime were placed in a distinct unit and made to work harder than others.

[17] Food rations varied in different places and over time (see Ben Kiernan, "Conflict in the Kampuchean Communist Movement," *Journal of Contemporary Asia* 10 (1980): 75-118; and, Vickery, *Cambodia 1975-1982*). Villagers report that one commune to the south had adequate food at the beginning of DK, but in New Village/Sobay there was a spate of deaths from starvation in 1975 and limited food from the outset. During DK some work groups received small amounts of rice at harvest time, but others did not.

[18] These figures take into account only the West Sobay villagers I knew in 1960. The death toll would be much higher if I included marriages and children born after I left Sobay, but my data on the latter are still incomplete.

[19] UNICEF, *Cambodia: The Situation of Women and Children* (Phnom Penh: UNICEF, Office of the Special Representative) 1990: 7.

[20] Chanthou Boua, "Women in Today's Cambodia," *New Left Review* 131 (1982):45-61; and, Judy Ledgerwood, *Analysis of the Situation of Women in Cambodia*. Report for UNICEF (unpublished manuscript) 1992.

[21] In pre-revolutionary times, the village of Sobay was informally divided into three hamlets: West, Middle, and East. At the outset of the PRK, an administrative reorganization split Sobay into two separate villages: East Sobay and West Sobay, with the latter merging what had formerly been called the West and Middle hamlets of the village.

[22] In 1992 the village chief gave a different estimate of 320 females (seventy-three percent) and 120 males in West Sobay. Note that the figures given by both the district office and the village chief are for the total population of West Sobay, including both adults and children.

[23] Ledgerwood (7) notes that the number of widow-headed households varies from about twenty-five percent to fifty percent in different communities in Cambodia. The national average is estimated at thirty-five percent female-headed households (UNICEF: 111). In a survey of West Sobay conducted by Ledgerwood, forty-one percent of one hundred households contacted were headed by widows (Ledgerwood: 25).

[24] That is, rather than paying for male labor with cash, one can provide hours of female labor instead. In such arrangements it is common that women must reciprocate with more work hours than a man gives: e.g., a household that engages a man to do five hours of plowing might have to provide ten to fifteen hours of female labor for transplanting, depending on what is negotiated. See also Ledgerwood.

[25] This impaired vision is not the hysterical blindness reported for Cambodian refugees in the U.S. Eye ailments are common (as they were also in pre-revolutionary Sobay), and some of the current vision problems are due to aging. There is also one case of what I guess to be detached or deteriorating retina.

[26] As she herself says, "Sometimes I laugh or cry for no reason." During DK she was sent to Pursat province and suffered the deaths of her parents, husband, four children, and siblings. Villagers have heard that she went "crazy" at some point, weeping and refusing to get up despite threats from DK cadre who accused her of "laziness" and malingering.

After the Nightmare: The Population of Cambodia

Judith Banister and Paige Johnson

Summary

This chapter is an overview of population trends in Cambodia and of the numbers and locations of Cambodians now living outside the country. Because the 1962 census of Cambodia is the most recent actual census taken, and serious multiple catastrophes have befallen the Cambodian people since that census, it is not possible today to provide firm, accurate figures for Cambodia's population size and characteristics. Accordingly, we explore here those generalizations that can be made about Cambodia's population with reasonable confidence and suggest which commonly-repeated observations or figures may be incorrect.

The basic population model presented here reconstructs a plausible scenario for Cambodia's demographic trends from the 1962 census to 1980, when an administrative population count was taken, recreating to the extent possible the total population, age structure, and sex ratio data reported from that survey. This "Survey-based" scenario takes as correct not only the 1980 population survey data but also the national birth rate and death rate reported from a 1982 demographic survey. We have incorporated into the reconstruction annual estimates of net international migration from all available sources. These results form the basis for long-term projections to the year 2050, which we use to assess the age and sex structures of Cambodia in the future. The Survey-based scenario includes the following midyear population size and sex ratio estimates.

Population growth was slow between the 1962 census and the 1980 survey because of civil and international warfare in the early 1970s and the turmoil of the Khmer Rouge ("Red Khmer") reign in the late 1970s. These political and military catastrophes, and their accompanying economic and social destruction, took a great toll. Without the excess deaths, reduced births, and international migration that resulted from these conditions, the midyear 1980 population would have been about 9.3 million, 2.8 million more than the reported figure.

Year	Midyear population (millions)	Males per hundred females	Average annual population growth (percent)
1962	5.76	100	
			0.7
1980	6.50	86	
			3.2
1993	9.90	92	
			2.9
2000	12.10	94	

Based on all the information we now have, we conclude that the population shortfall in 1980 was caused by the following factors:

♦ Net emigration of 567,000 people during the years 1970 through mid-1980.

♦ About 70,000 fewer births than expected during the warfare of the 1970-1974 period, because of losses of women in childbearing ages.

♦ A dearth of approximately 570,000 births during the Khmer Rouge years 1975-1978. This was caused by famine, family dislocation, and massive losses of women and men in reproductive ages.

♦ About 216,000 fewer births in 1979 and the first half of 1980 than would have been the case had not so many reproductive-age women died or left.

♦ About 275,000 excess deaths during 1970-1974, caused by civil war, bombing, and growing food shortages.

♦ About 1.05 million excess deaths during Khmer Rouge rule, 1975-1978, nearly two-thirds male and over one-third female. The high mortality was caused by famine, the near-complete breakdown of public health and medical systems, and the apparent targeted slaughter of adults from the mid-teens through middle age. For each of these four years, in addition to high underlying mortality conditions, about ten percent of men and almost three percent of women in these ages were killed.

According to the 1980 survey, Cambodia's population had only eighty-six males per hundred females, presumably because of the loss of men through extra male deaths and emigration. The dearth of male adults and the general loss of population and agricultural draft animals has created a labor shortage in relation to the need for workers in this subsistence, labor-intensive economy. We show that the size of the population in young work force ages 15-29 grew rapidly in the last decade, but will grow only slowly between 1993 and the turn of the century. The numbers of people in middle and older labor force ages 30-64 have increased rapidly in the 1980s and will continue to do so in the 1990s.

In addition to the Survey-based model which we reconstruct and project from 1962 to 2050, we present a "High" scenario and a "Low" scenario from 1980 to 2010. We show that the Low scenario may be the more correct one because local and provincial officials had financial reasons to exaggerate the numbers of people in their jurisdictions in the 1980 survey. On the other hand, the High alternative may be closer to reality because it is so easy and common to under-count populations in censuses and surveys the world over, especially in a poor and traumatized developing country. In creating the High, Survey-based, and Low reconstructions and projections, we have assigned plausible but different levels of birth and death rates to illustrate an entirely reasonable range of population sizes and vital rates. From a midyear 1993 population estimated at 9.9 million (range: 9.0 to 11.2 million), we project rapid population growth to 12.1 million in the year 2000 (range: 10.7 to 14.2 million). We discuss why even this wide range of estimates does not exhaust all possibilities.

After reviewing political and economic trends in the 1970s and 1980s, we focus on the demographic and social information that is available for Cambodia. The main features of Cambodia's population that can be discerned from the available sources include:

Population distribution and density:

The 1980 survey showed that there were thirty-six persons per square kilometer in Cambodia, but density was extremely uneven, as had historically been the case. In the hilly northern and northeastern provinces, there were only 1-5 persons per square kilometer, in contrast to the densely populated southeastern plains region, with 97-175 persons per square kilometer. Today Cambodia has a density of about fifty-four persons per square kilometer, which is still low by international, especially Asian, standards.

Urbanization:

The urban proportion of Cambodia's population was reduced to nearly zero by the Khmer Rouge policy of forcing urban residents to evacuate the cities and towns. But in 1979, after a Vietnamese invasion overthrew Pol Pot's government, many Cambodians moved to urban places. In the year-end 1980 count, a reported 12.6 percent of the country's population lived in the two leading municipalities and the provincial capital cities. Since then, the population of the capital Phnom Penh has grown from 368,000 to today's 800,000 in the rainy season, which swells to one million in the dry season.

Ethnic composition:

In the mid-1960s, an estimated 16-17 percent of Cambodia's population was members of minority groups and eighty-three or eighty-four percent was the dominant Khmer ethnic group. But the Vietnamese, Chinese, and Muslim ethnic groups were brutally treated and driven out by the Lon Nol government of the early 1970s and the Pol Pot government of the late 1970s. After 1978, Vietnamese settlers followed the Vietnamese military invasion into Cambodia. Today, there are probably more Vietnamese in Cambodia than before the upheavals of the 1970s, but far fewer of the Chinese ethnic group than in earlier decades. The population of Cambodia's various hill tribe groups can only be estimated because these groups have never been counted separately in a national census.

Fertility:

The Phnom Penh administration adopted a pronatalist policy when it took over from the Khmer Rouge in 1979; there are signs, though, that this may change, with recent mention of family planning education and child spacing. The average number of births per woman is high but the exact level is unknown. We estimate a total fertility rate of about 5.8 births per woman today (range: 5.5 to 6.1).

Health:

Health conditions are poor. A rudimentary public health system has been set up from the ashes of Khmer Rouge destruction, staffed by newly and minimally trained health workers. Hospitals have been established at district and provincial levels. But the dangers from active warfare and from mine explosions have continued. Environmental conditions, including the water supply, are unsafe and unsanitary. Food supply is precarious. Certain virulent diseases, such as falciparum malaria, tuberculosis, and dengue hemorrhagic fever, are unchecked. One bright spot in the health and mortality situation is a nationwide child immunization program supported by the United Nations Children's Fund. Working with international organizations, the Phnom Penh administration has developed an ambitious plan for the improvement of Cambodia's health care system.

Mortality:

Data are poor but indications are that mortality conditions have rebounded to the levels achieved in the 1960s and perhaps have improved further. But infant, child, and maternal mortality are reported to be high. We estimate that life expectancy at birth may be about forty-nine years today (range: forty-eight to fifty-seven years) and that the infant mortality rate is approximately 111 deaths in the first year of life per thousand live births (range: seventy-six to 119).

Education:

We discuss the rejuvenation and expansion of the basic educational system in the 1980s in the context of the low level of human capital in Cambodia's population after Khmer Rouge rule. During the 1980s there were reported to be 1.3 to 1.5 million primary school students and 148,000 to 350,000 secondary school students in the country. These enrollment figures constitute about three-quarters of the children in relevant ages. But teachers are minimally trained, school buildings are inadequate and unsanitary, and only one-quarter of the needed textbooks have been produced.

Cambodians outside Cambodia:

In March 1992, the United Nations High Commissioner for Refugees (UNHCR) began repatriating the 370,000 Cambodian refugees in Thailand to Cambodia. Most of them have stated that they wish to move to one of three provinces adjacent to the Thai border where the refugee camps are. In addition, there are reported to be 25,000 refugees from Cambodia living in Vietnam, 152,000 Cambodians in the United States, and 90,000 in other countries. Some of these Cambodians abroad may return to live or conduct business, and many will send remittances to help their remaining relatives or friends in Cambodia.

In conclusion, we note that Cambodia's current situation is indeed grim, but nowhere near as terrible as under Khmer Rouge rule in the late 1970s. Some progress has been made in the 1980s, especially in basic education and certain public health measures. However, the reliability of Cambodian population projections into the future is clouded by the lack of certainty that the current fragile moves toward peace will succeed.*

* The analysis, opinions, and conclusions in this report are solely the responsibility of the authors, and do not represent the policies of the United States Government or the U.S. Bureau of the Census. The authors would like to thank Andrea Miles for organizing and carrying out the arduous task of soliciting, locating, scanning, and copying information relevant to population trends in Cambodia. Grace Barnas was extraordinarily helpful to us in procuring books and articles on Cambodia. Peter Johnson provided essential computer programming assistance. Steve Ho digitized the map of Cambodia and its provinces, and Richard Turnage provided expert assistance with the provincial maps.

The following persons and organizations graciously responded to our requests for information with copies of their papers, reports, and citations to relevant sources: Michael Vickery, noted author of books on Cambodia; James M. Robey, World Health Organization, Regional Office for the Western Pacific, Manila; Naoko Amakawa and Yasuko Hayase, Institute of Developing Economies, Tokyo; Jerrold W. Huguet, Population Division, United Nations Economic and Social Commission for Asia and the Pacific, Bangkok; Court Robinson, U.S. Committee for Refugees, Washington; Carol Levin, Asia-Pacific Rim Branch, Agriculture and Trade Analysis Division, Economic Research Service, U.S. Department of Agriculture; R.H.F. Austin, Director of the Electoral Component, UNTAC, Phnom Penh. We appreciate the criticisms and suggestions of the following persons who reviewed an earlier draft: Barbara Boyle Torrey, Barry Kostinsky, Sylvia Quick, Eduardo Arriaga, Kheang Hang, Christina Harbaugh, and Ben Kiernan.

Background

Cambodia was and is a poor, rural, agricultural country in southeast Asia, bounded by Vietnam to the east and south, Laos to the northeast, Thailand to the north and west, and the Gulf of Thailand to the southwest (see Map 1).[1]   Though it had a historical period of comparative splendor during the Angkor Empire (ninth through fourteenth centuries), in recent centuries Cambodia has been under French colonial control and threatened by more powerful neighbors. Cambodian leaders have had to compromise and acquiesce to the demands of the Thai, Vietnamese, and French governments at different times.

The staple food of Cambodia is rice, which is grown in the lowland areas around the rivers in the southeastern portion of the country and in a region extending north and west along the huge Tonle Sap lake. Most of the population has been concentrated in this delta and plains core of Cambodia. The dominant ethnic group in Cambodia, the Khmer, are Buddhists and are culturally linked to Thailand and India. People of both Khmer and hill tribe origins living in the mountainous regions to the northeast and southwest of the country have generally led more primitive and isolated lives.

Cambodia's census of April 1962 counted 5.73 million people, balanced between the sexes and with a national population density of only thirty-two persons per square kilometer. Of the total population, 10.3 percent was classified as urban. There were four municipalities and fourteen other urban centers; Phnom Penh Municipality included 394,000 people, who constituted two-thirds of the entire urban population of Cambodia. Fertility was high, with the total fertility rate over seven births per woman.[2]

By 1962, there had been considerable improvement in mortality rates from high levels in the past. The United Nations estimated a crude death rate of about twenty deaths per thousand population and life expectancy of forty-three years for the early 1960s.[3] Had mortality and fertility conditions been unchanged from 1962 to 1980, with no catastrophic loss of life or mass emigration, we project that Cambodia's population would have grown to about 9.3 million by midyear 1980; this is in sharp contrast to the official figure of 6.5 million.

In the 1960s, Prince Sihanouk of Cambodia attempted to keep the escalating Vietnam war from spilling over into his country, but eventually supply lines of North Vietnamese troops and Viet Cong guerrillas were allowed to move through Cambodia's eastern provinces. Sihanouk's government was opposed by both the left and the right in the late 1960s. On the left were the insurgents associated with the Communist Party of Kampuchea; Sihanouk labeled them the "Khmers rouges" (Red Khmer). On the right were the anti-Communist, pro-American members of the elite who were impatient with Sihanouk and angered by the leftist character of his policies. Circumstance forced Sihanouk, as the economy, insurgency, and spill-over into Cambodia of the Vietnam War continued to worsen, to ask Lieutenant-General (later Marshal) Lon Nol to form a new government in 1969. In early 1970, the National Assembly withdrew its confidence from Prince Sihanouk and declared a state of emergency, giving power to Lon Nol.[4]

Demographic Disasters of 1970-1980

During 1970-1974, warfare escalated between the Khmer Rouge (Pol Pot's peasant army) and Vietnamese Communist forces, on one side, and the army of the Khmer Republic (Lon Nol's government) supported by United States dollars, troops, and bombing on the other side. Excess deaths in this period have been estimated in various sources at 600,000-800,000.[5]

Because the government of Lon Nol perceived Cambodia's Vietnamese minority as a security threat, many thousands were massacred and about 200,000 were expelled south and east to Vietnam in 1970.[6] During 1971-1974, a further 120,000 Vietnamese reportedly fled to Vietnam[7] and 34,000 refugees emigrated to Thailand and the West.[8] Within Cambodia, an estimated two million displaced people filled the cities to escape warfare and bombing.[9]

The Khmer Rouge completed their takeover of Cambodia with the capture of Phnom Penh in April 1975. Their policies resulted in excess deaths estimated by various observers at between one and three million before the Khmer Rouge were ousted in January 1979 by a Vietnamese invasion.[10] The first move of the Pol Pot regime in 1975 was to force the several million people living in cities and towns to immediately evacuate urban areas and move to the countryside without any food or water and with no preparation. During 1975-1978, the Cambodian people were subjected to starvation rations, heavy labor, lack of medical care, and brutality by Khmer Rouge soldiers and cadres.[11] Many who tried to flee died before reaching Thailand or Vietnam.[12]

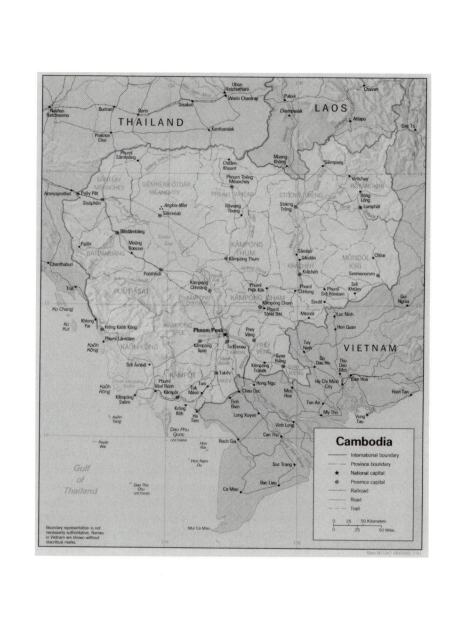

THAILAND

LAOS

Ubon Ratchethani
Warin Chamrap
Chavan
Sisaket
Pakxé
Champasak
Attapu
Dac To

Nakhon Ratchasima
Burirum
Surin
Kantharalak

Prakhon Chai

Phumi Sämröng
Chôm Khsant
Phnum Tbêng Méanchey
Muang Không
Sämpang
Virôchey
ROăKANOKIRI

BANTEAY MEANCHEY
SIEMREAB-OTDAR MEANCHEY
PREAH VIHEAR
STOENG TRENG
Bông Lông
Lumphăt

Aranyaprathet
Poay Pêt
Sisôphôn
Angkor Wat
Siĕmréab
Rôviĕng Thong
Stoĕng Trêng

Bătdâmbâng
Moŭng Roăssei
Tônlé Sab
KÂMPÔNG THUM
Kâmpông Thum
Sâmbôr
Sândân
Krâchéh
MÔNDÔL KIRI
Chhar

Pailin
BATDÂMBÂNG
POŬTHISAT
Pouthĭsăt
KÂMPÔNG CHHNANG
Kâmpông Chhnăng
KRÂCHÉH
Krâchéh
Senmonorom
Srê Khtŭm

Chanthaburi

Trat
Ko Chang

Ko Kut
Khlong Yai
Krŏng Kaôh Kŏng
KÂMPÔNG SPOE
Phnom Penh
Phumi Lâmdăm
KAÔH KŎNG
Srê Âmbĕl
Kaôh Rŭng
Kâmpông Saôm
KÂMPÔT
Phumi Vŏal Rénh
Kâmpôt
Krŏng Kêb
Kaôh Tang
Dao Phu Quoc
(VIETNAM)

Phumi Prêk Kak
Phumi Tônlé Bêt
Kâmpông Cham
KÂMPÔNG CHAM
Phumi Chhlong
Phumi Srê Rôniem
Snuŏl
Memot
Loc Ninh
Hon Quan

Prey Vêng
PREY VÊNG
Ta Khmau
KANDAL
Svay Riĕng
SVAY RIĔNG
Kâmpông Trâbêk
Tay Ninh
VIETNAM
Bô Dau Ha
Thu Dau Mot
Tân An
My Tho
Ham Tan
Bien Hoa
Hô Chi Minh City

Tani
TAKÊV
Ta Kêv
Tuk Méas
Hong Ngu
Chau Doc
Moc Hoa
Vung Tau

Tinh Bien
Long Xuyen
Vinh Long
Ha Tien
Can Tho
Soc Trang
Rach Gia
Bac Lieu
Ca Mau

Hon Rai
Hon Nam Du
Dao Tho Chu (VIETNAM)
Poulo Wai

Gulf of Thailand

Mui Ca Mau

Cambodia

	International boundary
	Province boundary
★	National capital
⊛	Province capital
	Railroad
	Road
	Trail

0   25   50 Kilometers
0   25   50 Miles

Boundary representation is not necessarily authoritative. Names in Vietnam are shown without diacritical marks.

Base 801647 (800928) 2-91

Although the two victorious Communist regimes in Cambodia and Vietnam had been allied during their revolutionary struggles, this alliance did not survive. Khmer Rouge policies evidenced strong xenophobia, directed most virulently against perceived Vietnamese territorial ambitions in Cambodia; border clashes began in 1975. Also in 1975, the Khmer Rouge expelled or drove thousands of Vietnamese from Cambodia.

Border clashes continued until the large-scale Vietnamese invasion, begun on December 25, 1978, finally ousted the Khmer Rouge. This did not end conditions leading to excess mortality, however. Warfare continued between the Khmer Rouge and Vietnamese troops; severe regional food shortages occurred. Instead of trying to plant crops, many people, who had been forcibly displaced by the Khmer Rouge, left to return to their previous homes or to search for missing relatives. There was a major shortfall in rice production in 1979-1980 leading to fears of nationwide famine.[13]

Political Developments Since 1979

In the wake of the Vietnamese invasion of Cambodia in 1978, Southeast Asia and the major powers were polarized. The People's Republic of Kampuchea,[14] the Vietnamese-installed regime, was recognized by only a small number of nations including Vietnam, the Soviet Union, the nations of Eastern Europe, and a few non-aligned states such as India. Opposing the Vietnamese were the remnants of the Khmer Rouge supported by the People's Republic of China. The nations of non-Communist Southeast Asia, perceiving an expansionist Vietnam as a threat, sided with the resistance and set about constructing a more viable, globally presentable resistance coalition. The result of the brokering of the ASEAN states and China was the Coalition Government of Democratic Kampuchea, Cambodia's "government in exile," composed of three factions: the Khmer Rouge, the Party of Democratic Kampuchea (PDK); those loyal to Prince Norodom Sihanouk, FUNCINPEC (the French acronym for the National United Front for an Independent, Neutral, Peaceful, and Cooperative Cambodia); and the followers of the former Prime Minister Son Sann, called the Khmer People's National Liberation Front (KPNLF). The United States followed the lead of ASEAN and the People's Republic of China on Cambodia policy.[15]

This international polarization over Cambodia had negative effects on Cambodia's development. Perceived as a puppet regime of the Vietnamese, the Phnom Penh administration was isolated and boycotted by the West.

In the late 1980s, changes in the Communist world presented a variety of options for solution of the Cambodian conflict. The Vietnamese withdrew the last of their forces in September 1989.[16] Agreement by the Permanent Five members of the United Nations Security Council in the summer of 1990 on a framework peace plan allowed the Cambodian factions to move toward ending the civil war. In the words of Douglas Pike, "the center of gravity for the peace process . . . shifted from outside to inside Cambodia."[17] By October of 1991, the Comprehensive Settlement to the Cambodian Conflict was signed in Paris and the U.S. trade embargo was being lifted. In November, Prince Sihanouk returned to Cambodia in his capacity as Chairman of the Supreme National Council (SNC), which embodies Cambodia's sovereignty until UN-supervised elections are held in May of 1993.

One consequence of the Peace Agreement is the repatriation of an estimated 370,000 Cambodian refugees in Thailand.[18] The repatriation program, begun in March of 1992 and undertaken by the United Nations High Commissioner for Refugees (UNHCR), is scheduled to return all of the refugees to Cambodia before the elections in 1993.[19]

In addition to changes in the international environment, numerous changes have been taking place within Cambodia as well. Since 1989, the ruling regime has initiated a number of political reforms. In 1991, Prime Minister Hun Sen called on his Party to support former rebel leader Sihanouk as the next President of Cambodia.[20] The name of the ruling party was changed from the Kampuchean People's Revolutionary Party to the Cambodian People's Party. Heng Samrin, long-time leader of the Party was removed to the largely ceremonial position of Honorary Party President.[21] Multi-party democracy and a free-market economy were accepted in principle and all references to Marxism-Leninism deleted from the Party platform. These recent reforms are widely believed to be designed to boost the Party's chances in the UN-sponsored elections.

Despite the official transfer of sovereignty to Cambodia's Supreme National Council in the wake of the signing of the Paris Peace Accords, actual administrative control of eighty to ninety percent of Cambodia's territory remains in the hands of the State of Cambodia.[22] Administration of the country has only been supervised by the United Nations in order to ensure a neutral political environment in which the elections can be held.

In May 1993, Cambodians will elect a Constituent Assembly. The Assembly will first draft a constitution, and then the elected officials are to become representatives in the new government of the provinces from which they were selected.[23]   According to the Director of UNTAC's Electoral Component, R.H.F. Austin:

> The Electoral Component is proceeding on the following basis. First, we carry out a preliminary survey to get an estimate of the population and its distribution, based on existing statistics held by various authorities to whom we have access. Second, (and ultimately more important) we will conduct throughout the country, at an estimated 800 registration points, a registration of persons who come forward to claim the vote. This process will proceed for three months, from the beginning of October until the end of December 1992. At the end of it, we will publish a verified list of voters, which will also be the basis for the allocation of seats . . . in the Constituent Assembly, to be elected [in] . . . May.[24]

Important to the study of Cambodia's population from Mr. Austin's description of the registration process is that only those who come forward to claim the vote will be counted. There will be no effort (beyond public education programs designed to encourage registration and voting) to seek out all those eligible to vote. Eligible voters include all those, age eighteen and above, who were born in Cambodia and who had at least one parent born in Cambodia or who were born outside of Cambodia and who had at least one parent and grandparent born in Cambodia.[25] Further, Mr. Austin describes the preliminary survey of the population as being derived from "existing statistics held by various authorities to whom we have access." Mr. Austin is suggesting that, for the eighty to ninety percent of the country under the control of the State of Cambodia, SOC estimates will serve as the UN's preliminary numbers as to population size and distribution. He is also suggesting that data are being collected from the three resistance factions as to the populations under their control; this is important because as of March 1993, the United Nations does not "have access" to areas under Khmer Rouge control. Will this leave the Khmer Rouge an option to resort at last to a military solution, claiming they were not given fair treatment in the conduct of the elections?[26] Will the country be effectively partitioned by Khmer Rouge non-participation in the elections?

The electoral law, drafted by UNTAC and passed on September 13, 1992, has been widely criticized by all of the four Cambodian factions. The KPNLF's Son Sann argues that overseas Cambodians must be given an opportunity to participate in the elections. Both the Khmer Rouge and KPNLF factions maintain that registration of Vietnamese voters, even those born in Cambodia, will allow the Vietnamese to "vote for the regime they have installed in the country."[27] The SOC Foreign Minister has said that those who are not ethnic Khmer should not vote in the election even if they were born in Cambodia and technically qualified under the current electoral regulations.[28]

All four factions have adopted an anti-Vietnamese stance for the coming elections; these groups are both tapping and fueling the strong current of anti-Vietnamese feeling among the Khmer populace. No matter which faction emerges victorious from the elections, a unified Cambodian government is likely to attempt to clamp down stringently on spontaneous, "illegal" immigration of Vietnamese into Cambodia, and might expel large numbers of ethnic Vietnamese from the country entirely.

The Khmer Rouge, BLDP and FUNCINPEC factions all agree that free and fair elections cannot be held until all foreign forces are out of Cambodia; "foreign forces" is the resistance code word for a continued Vietnamese military presence in Cambodia. The resistance factions claim that the Vietnamese settlers in Cambodia are Vietnamese troops in "disguise."[29]

Under the current electoral regulations, only those Vietnamese, age eighteen and above, who were born in Cambodia and had at least one parent born in Cambodia or who were born outside of Cambodia and had at least one parent and one grandparent born in Cambodia will be able to participate in the elections. It is unknown how many Vietnamese will claim the right to vote. This uncertainty comes in part from the lack of information regarding which immigrants from Vietnam were returnees—people who had been expelled or driven from Cambodia in the 1970s and subsequently returned after the Vietnamese invasion—and therefore perhaps eligible to vote. New immigrants from Vietnam in the 1980s are technically not allowed to vote.

The Phnom Penh regime fears further that elections cannot be truly free and fair in the absence of complete security for villagers from Khmer Rouge reprisals. The regime favors mixing the ballots collected in various locales so that the Khmer Rouge cannot isolate villages which turned against them in the elections.

The Cambodian Economy

After more than a decade of destruction due to civil war and Khmer Rouge policies, the Cambodian economy in 1979 was, in Vickery's words, at the "year Zero."[30] There was almost no industry, due to the Khmer Rouge's policy of enforced "peasantization" of the population.[31] There was no government administration, no education, no currency.[32]

Agriculture was in disarray in the immediate post-invasion period as many survivors of the Khmer Rouge regime crisscrossed the country. Crops were not tended, seed was eaten, food stocks were taken by the military groups for their loyalists, and a serious food crisis ensued. While the food shortage was doubtless severe in several regions of the country and caused regional famine, from available demographic data we conclude that a nationwide famine did not occur in 1979-1980 (for more information on the effect of the food crisis on Cambodia's population, see Table 1: The Cambodian Population in 1980, below).

For those who stayed where they were in the post-invasion period, there was adequate food throughout the first half of 1979; some rice was harvested and people consumed fowl, pigs, and draft animals.[33] The alarm of potential food shortage was sounded early by the Phnom Penh administration and international aid of 317,000 metric tons of grains in 1979 and 132,000 metric tons in 1980 seems to have staved off nationwide famine, although regional famine did occur and suffering among the affected populace was tremendous.[34] Production increases of rice in 1980, international assistance, and quick planting of alternative crops, like manioc, white maize, and sweet potato, by Cambodia's farmers helped to avert a more serious famine.[35]

Currency, the Cambodian riel, was reestablished in March 1980.[36] The currency gradually took hold but has never completely replaced gold and the Thai baht and more recently the U.S. dollar, which also serve as media of exchange, especially for large transactions.[37]

Table 1. Cambodia, Results of Year-end 1980 Population Count

Province or City	Population	Percent of Total Population	Male	Female	Percent male	Urban population	Percent urban	Area in square kilometers	Population density (persons per sq. km.)
Cambodia	**6,589,954**		**3,049,385**	**3,540,569**	**46.27**	**831,700**	**12.62**	**181,916**	**36.23**
Plains Region	**3,563,470**	**54.07**	**1,642,382**	**1,921,088**	**46.09**	**480,432**	**13.48**	**26,024**	**136.93**
Phnom Penh	367,568	5.58	163,875	203,692	44.58	367,568	100.00	46	7,990.61
Kandal	666,999	10.12	306,180	360,819	45.90	26,880	4.03	3,813	174.93
Kampong Cham	1,054,810	16.01	494,020	560,790	46.83	26,898	2.55	10,498	100.48
Svay Rieng	287,898	4.37	129,117	158,781	44.85	7,053	2.45	2,966	97.07
Prey Veng	662,945	10.06	307,941	355,004	46.45	31,887	4.81	4,883	135.77
Takev	523,249	7.94	241,249	282,000	46.11	20,145	3.85	3,818	137.05
Tonle Sap Region	**1,943,706**	**29.49**	**906,034**	**1,037,671**	**46.61**	**248,776**	**12.80**	**60,404**	**32.18**
Kampong Thum	373,673	5.67	175,909	197,764	47.08	28,885	7.73	12,251	30.50
Siemreab–Otdar Meanchey	457,872	6.95	216,412	241,460	47.26	58,791	12.84	10,897	42.02
Batdambang	721,643	10.95	339,405	382,238	47.03	124,185	17.21	19,044	37.89
Pouthisat	172,793	2.62	77,753	95,040	45.00	17,124	9.91	12,692	13.61
Kampong Chhnang	217,725	3.30	96,554	121,171	44.35	19,791	9.09	5,520	39.44
Maritime Region	**425,807**	**6.46**	**195,211**	**230,596**	**45.84**	**76,253**	**17.91**	**21,071**	**20.21**
Sihanoukville (Kampong Saom)	51,882	.79	23,075	28,807	44.48	51,882	100.00	69	751.92
Kampot	348,738	5.29	160,790	187,948	46.11	16,983	4.87	9,862	35.36
Kaoh Kong	25,186	.38	11,345	13,841	45.05	7,387	29.33	11,140	2.26
Plateau and Forest Region	**656,972**	**9.97**	**305,757**	**351,214**	**46.54**	**26,240**	**3.99**	**68,739**	**9.56**
Kampong Spoe	335,353	5.09	153,987	181,366	45.92	23,911	7.13	7,016	47.80
Preah Vihear	68,492	1.04	32,351	36,140	47.23	N/A	N/A	14,350	4.77
Rotanokiri	44,461	.67	20,467	23,994	46.03	778	1.75	10,782	4.12
Stoeng Treng	38,722	.59	18,008	20,715	46.50	N/A	N/A	11,209	3.45
Mondol Kiri	15,363	.23	7,564	7,799	49.23	685	4.46	14,288	1.08
Kracheh	154,580	2.35	73,380	81,200	47.47	865	.56	11,094	13.93
Inland Water								5,678	
Total Land Area								176,238	37.39

Notes: The 1980 boundaries of Batdambang include today's Banteay Meachey and Batdambang provinces. The 1980 population survey appears to have been taken at the end of 1980. The data in this table are derived from reported 1990 provincial estimates that were based entirely on the 1980 survey assuming the same rate of population growth for all areas and assuming no migration. Therefore, we have derived the 1980 data from the reported 1990 estimates. Source: Hou Taing Eng, 1992.

The regime organized peasant families into solidarity groups, known as *krom samaki* and composed of ten to twenty families (depending upon local conditions), for agricultural production. By 1984, however, the Phnom Penh authorities were forced to acquiesce to reality in the countryside by recognizing that cooperativization was a disincentive to agricultural production. Individual family farming was legitimized.[38] In February 1989, the government, implementing its "land to the tiller" program, moved farther from state control over agriculture by recognizing private ownership of land and real estate and the rights to inheritance.[39] The government has also consulted with the International Rice Research Institute (IRRI) in the Philippines to develop a variety of high-yielding rice suited to Cambodian conditions.[40]

Despite a lack of fertilizer, skilled labor, draft animals and mechanization, agriculture has made some measure of recovery since 1979.[41] The annual rice harvest has increased from 565,000 metric tons in 1979 to 2.4 million metric tons in 1989.[42] Annual shortfalls are still reported, however. Due to the primitive nature of Cambodian agriculture and the lack of irrigation (only about five to seven percent of the rice fields are irrigated), agriculture is heavily dependent upon the weather.[43] A major flood in 1991 is expected to have caused a 171,000 metric ton shortfall for 1992.[44] Per hectare yields are still low. Not all of the arable land is exploited because of the labor-intensiveness of Cambodian agriculture (caused by the lack of mechanization), the lack of available labor power, and the guerrilla war which has left large areas of arable land unworkable due to the proximity of combat or mines.

By 1988, industry was still only a small part of the economy, representing five percent of Gross Domestic Product (GDP).[45] It was not until 1989 that the government restored to production most of the rice mills that had been in operation prior to 1975.[46] The loosening of state control over industry began in 1986, and by 1988, state firms were granted management autonomy and piece rates were introduced in an attempt to increase production.[47]

The effect of the resistance groups on the ability of the Phnom Penh regime to rebuild the economy has been large. Defense consumed thirty to forty percent of the government budget in the late 1980s.[48] Also, about 200,000 able-bodied males have been engaged in the fight for or against the regime throughout the 1980s and early 1990s, taking scarce labor power away from agricultural production.[49]

The Peace Agreement signed by the warring factions in October 1991 calls for a universal seventy percent reduction in military troops.[50] While there is still doubt that the demobilization will occur, even if carried out, questions remain as to the ability of the demobilized soldiers to be reintegrated into civilian production. As was Vietnam's experience with its recent demobilization, there are economic implications of large-scale demobilization. Can soldiers, accustomed to the military lifestyle, adjust to subsistence agriculture or wage labor? Do the soldiers have any skills which can be transferred to civilian production? There is some evidence that thus far some demobilized soldiers in Cambodia have not returned to agriculture as was hoped but have turned instead to banditry to feed themselves and their families.[51]

Despite its economic backwardness, throughout the 1980s, because of the political situation surrounding the Phnom Penh regime's accession to power, Cambodia was denied much United Nations assistance as well as bilateral aid from the West. In 1986, Cambodia received only US$22.8 million from United Nations and non-governmental aid organizations (NGOs).[52] Cambodia's economy was almost entirely supported by aid from and trade with the Soviet Union, Vietnam, and the Eastern European countries. In 1989, these countries provided seventy-five to eighty percent of the state budget.[53]

In the wake of the changes in Eastern Europe and the former Soviet Union, aid began to decline precipitously. As Vice-Minister in the Prime Minister's Office Cham Prasidh said, Cambodia is "handicapped by the loss of one of her crutches."[54] This compounded Cambodia's economic problems as it was concurrent with the Vietnamese troop withdrawal and the concomitant increase in defense expenditures which were borne by the Phnom Penh regime. In May 1990, Cambodia was informed by the Soviet Union that it would have to pay commercial prices for vital imports such as oil which had previously been received at heavily subsidized prices.

As the Eastern bloc role in Cambodia's economy has receded, it is being replaced by Japan and Cambodia's non-Communist Southeast Asian neighbors. Also, in light of the agreed political settlement to the conflict, the United States lifted its trade embargo of Cambodia in January 1992.[55] The nations of the ASEAN grouping (Association of Southeast Asian Nations) are eager to get in on the ground floor of Cambodia's development. Thailand, in particular, sees its business interests in Cambodia growing over the years to come.[56] Singapore has become Cambodia's top trade partner since the collapse of the Soviet Union.[57] Also, since the government's enactment of foreign investment legislation in July 1989, joint ventures have begun to spring up. By April 1992, the SOC had approved 260 investment projects with 145 foreign companies; these projects are concentrated in hotel development, light manufacturing, oil exploration, and banking.[58]

Much of the recent development, however, has not been national in scope. Phnom Penh is now a bustling city. The influx of foreign NGOs, foreign investment, and the United Nations has made Phnom Penh seem a metropolitan boomtown[59] while those in the countryside continue to engage in subsistence agriculture. The gap between the living standards and income of urban and rural Cambodians has begun to widen.[60] Further, there are fears that the boom in Phnom Penh is artificial, fueled by the United Nations presence and disrupting the economy in an "orgy of get-rich-quick activity."[61] Privatization and the opening of the economy have led to charges of widespread corruption among SOC officials. Dissatisfaction with government corruption led to large popular demonstrations in December 1991.[62]

Another problem is inflation, caused in part by financing public sector deficits through monetary expansion.[63] In 1984, the official exchange rate was four riel to the dollar; by 1992, the official rate was one thousand riel to the dollar; the unofficial (black market) exchange rate is even higher, running at 1,100 to 1,200 per dollar at the end of June 1992.[64] Inflation in 1992 was between 150 and 200 percent.[65]

According to Kong Samol, Chairman of the SOC Council of Ministers, 1989's Gross National Product (GNP) was only seventy percent of that of 1968.[66] Although rice production has reached prewar levels, other areas, such as rubber production, have yet to attain levels reached in the 1960s.[67] Production of fish and marine products stands at 12,000 tons a year, compared to 40,000 tons a year in the 1960s.[68]

Cambodia's economy remains one based on subsistence agriculture and supported by foreign aid.[69] Aid from the Eastern bloc countries sustained Cambodia during the 1980s. The collapse of the Soviet Union left Cambodia in desperate need of Western assistance. At the end of June 1992 at the Ministerial Conference on the Rehabilitation and Reconstruction of Cambodia in Tokyo, Western nations and international institutions pledged a total of US$880 million over the next two years for Cambodia's reconstruction.[70] This aid is possible now that Western nations, particularly the United States, are expected no longer to block development assistance to Cambodia by multilateral institutions. Reconstruction aid is expected to focus initially on food security; health, water, and sanitation; education and training; and infrastructure projects such as roads, railways, the ports of Phnom Penh and Sihanoukville,[71] civil aviation, electricity generation and distribution, and telecommunications.[72]

Natural and cultural factors suggest that a peaceful Cambodia could make economic gains. Vice Minister in the Prime Minister's Office, Cham Prasidh, suggested that with its available resources Cambodia could afford to feed twenty million people.[73] Increased production of phosphate for fertilizer and limestone for cement is possible. Contracts for exploration of potential off-shore oil deposits have been signed.[74] There is potential for growth in production of rubber and aquatic products as well as the generation of hydroelectric power from the Mekong river.[75] Furthermore, with its Angkor Wat, Khmer culture, and natural beauty, Cambodia could also develop a tourist industry in order to earn needed foreign exchange.[76]

The Cambodian Population in 1980

After consolidating its hold on most of Cambodia, the Phnom Penh regime reportedly carried out a population count in 1980 in coordination with international aid organizations. Most information from this count has been suppressed. Cambodia's Department of Statistics describes the count as a "general population survey," but it was probably more of an administrative count with figures compiled upward from villages to communes to districts to provinces to the national administration.[77] The count included only Cambodians within the borders of Cambodia at the time the count was taken and excluded Cambodian refugees in Thailand, Vietnam and resettled in third countries. The total population was reported to be 6.59 million at the end of 1980. Cambodia's Department of Statistics has estimated the total and provincial populations of Cambodia in 1990 based completely on the survey of 1980 extrapolated to 1990 assuming 2.8 percent a year population growth everywhere.[78] This source gives us essentially no credible information about Cambodia in 1990 but does permit calculation of provincial population distribution and national population size at the end of 1980 (see Table 1). The midyear 1980

Table 2. Cambodia Year-End Population Structure as Reported

Age	Population at the end of 1980			Percentage			Sex distribution of the population in each age group	
	Total	Male	Female	Total	Male	Female	Male	Female
All Ages	**6,589,954**	**3,049,450**	**3,540,504**	**100.00**	**100.00**	**100.00**	**46.3**	**53.7**
0-15	3,092,083	1,556,526	1,535,557	46.9	51.0	43.4	50.3	49.7
0 to exact age 1	274,764	137,833	136,931	4.2	4.5	3.9	50.2	49.8
1	216,850	109,077	107,773	3.3	3.6	3.0	50.3	49.7
2-5	600,442	302,830	297,612	9.1	9.9	8.4	50.4	49.6
6-15	2,000,027	1,006,786	993,241	30.3	33.0	28.1	50.3	49.7
Males 16-60 and females 16-55	3,112,649	1,346,107	1,766,542	47.2	44.1	49.9	43.2	56.8
16	125,893	58,569	67,324	1.9	1.9	1.9	46.5	53.5
17	121,701	52,891	68,810	1.8	1.7	1.9	43.5	56.5
Males 18-60 and females 18-55	2,865,055	1,234,647	1,630,408	43.5	40.5	46.1	43.1	56.9
Males 61 and older and females 56 and older	385,222	146,817	238,405	5.8	4.8	6.7	38.1	61.9

Source: Cambodian Department of Statistics, 1992.

population size (as we can extrapolate backward from the 1990 estimates) was officially estimated at 6.5 million.

Partial data on Cambodia's population age-sex structure in 1980 have been released and are shown in Table 2. The age groupings seem to be dictated by rough educational, labor force, and voting age categories, for example 0-15 (below working age), 2-5 (preschool), 6-15 (school ages below labor force ages), 16-60 for men and 16-55 for women (formal labor force age groups), 18-60 for men and 18-55 for women (eighteen is the age of eligibility to vote), sixty-one and above for men and fifty-six and older for women (nominal retirement ages).

Even this partial age structure is informative. The numbers of men and women counted in adult working ages are far fewer than would have been expected even from massive civil war and emigration, which means that teen and adult losses in the 1970s were extraordinary for both sexes. In addition, adult male losses were far more severe than female losses. The reported shortage of young people ages sixteen and seventeen, especially young men, is shocking compared to the numbers that would have been expected even in bad times.

In contrast, the 1980 count recorded more children and more old people than would have been expected, given the tragedies of the 1970s. What this implies is that the underlying mortality conditions of the 1970s, though atrocious, were not terrible enough to account for the excess losses among working age adults. The large count of children ages 6-15 tells us that the level of fertility in Cambodia was very high during their years of birth 1965-1974, right up to the Khmer Rouge takeover. There was apparently no reduction in the birth rate resulting from famine or dislocation in the early 1970s, in spite of the civil war and bombing. This suggests that underlying mortality conditions in the early 1970s were not dismal, though warfare and bombing may have claimed hundreds of thousands of lives. The large 1980 count of children ages 6-15 also suggests that children past infancy survived better than expected during the Khmer Rouge period. For purposes of population reconstruction, this indicates that we cannot use standard patterns of very high mortality that include extremely high child mortality. There was excess mortality at all ages under the Khmer Rouge, but beyond this generalized rise in deaths, additional excess deaths seem to have been very selective by age.

Children who were ages 2-5 at year-end 1980 were born in the Khmer Rouge years 1975-1978. The numbers counted indicate that fertility in that period was below the pre-crisis level of more than seven births per woman, but higher than famine-level fertility which would have been about half of normal (3.5 or four births per woman). We do not have enough information to determine how fertility may have varied from year to year in the late 1970s, so we assume a constant fertility level in the Khmer Rouge years, which was about 4.6 births per woman, based on the counted numbers ages 2-5 in 1980.

The year-end 1980 count of children at ages zero and one is higher than expected, given reports of widespread famine in Cambodia during 1979 and 1980. The fertility level was 5.8 births per woman in 1979 and 6.3 in 1980, which does not suggest that a severe famine affected most of the country. Indeed, the apparent rise in fertility in 1979 indicates that underlying mortality conditions may have improved somewhat during the latter part of 1978 and in 1979, when these children were conceived. The usual pattern in a severe famine is that the fertility level drops in half nine months after the famine strikes, and fertility rises again nine months after food supplies are restored.

The basic population model presented here reconstructs a plausible scenario for Cambodia's demographic trends from the 1962 census to the 1980 population survey, matching to the extent possible the total population, age structure, and sex ratio data reported in fragments from that survey. This Survey-based scenario then projects Cambodia's population to 1993, taking into consideration reported emigration from and immigration into Cambodia as well as plausible fertility and mortality estimates. We then project Cambodia's population to the year 2050 to see what the age-sex structure is likely to be in the future.[79]

Map 2 displays provincial population densities in 1980 based on the official survey (data in Table 1). The survey confirmed that Cambodia's population remained extremely unevenly distributed, with very low population densities in the northeastern hilly areas, and higher but still low densities in provinces adjacent to the plains and in the Tonle Sap lake region. The greatest provincial population densities outside the province-level municipalities, 94-170 persons per square kilometer, were found in the southeastern plains area, but these densities were still low by Asian standards.

The Cambodian Department of Statistics reported that according to the 1980 count, the sex ratio of the total population was only eighty-six males per hundred females, in striking contrast to the equal numbers of males and females that had been counted in Cambodia's 1962 census. As shown in Table 2, in 1980 at ages 0-15 there were reported to be 101 boys per hundred girls, while the dearth of men over age fifteen was severe.[80] In our Survey-based scenario, we have approximately replicated the 1980 age-sex structure and total population as given in Table 2.

Map 3 shows the male percentage of each province's recorded population in 1980 (see Table 1 for data). All provinces recorded a shortage of males, but the dearth of males was most pronounced in the two municipalities Phnom Penh and Kampong Saom (now Sihanoukville), and in the southern and southwestern coastal provinces. The province with the most normal ratio between the sexes was Mondol Kiri, Cambodia's least populous and least densely populated province.

Implications of 1980 Population Data

We have modeled Cambodia's population change from the 1962 census to the 1980 survey and compared our reconstruction to what would have been the case with no disasters and no change in the fertility and mortality levels of the 1960s. Cambodia's population grew at the rapid rate of about 2.6-2.7 percent a year during the 1960s. By 1970 the country had about seven million people. Had it not been for the civil war, bombing, disruption of food production, and the expulsion of the Vietnamese minority by the Lon Nol government, there would have been about 8 million people in the country by the beginning of 1975 when the Khmer Rouge took over. Instead, we estimate that there were about 7.3 million. Components of the reduced population growth of the early 1970s were:

♦ net emigration of about 349,000 people.

♦ 70,000 fewer births than expected because more women of childbearing age died or left than would normally have been the case.

♦ An estimated 275,000 excess deaths. We have modeled the highest mortality that we can justify for the early 1970s.

Map 2. Population Density by Province, 1980 Survey of Cambodia

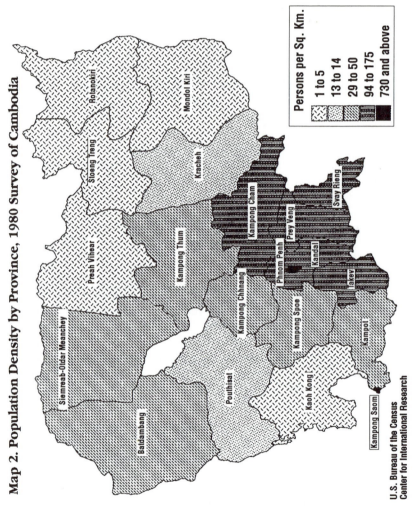

Persons per Sq. Km.

- 1 to 5
- 13 to 14
- 29 to 50
- 94 to 175
- 730 and above

Rolanokiri

Stoeng Treng

Mondol Kiri

Kracheh

Kampong Cham

Preah Vihear

Kampong Thum

Svay Rieng

Prey Vang

Siemreab-Oldar Meanchey

Kampong Chhnang

Phnom Penh

Kandal

Takev

Baidambang

Pouthisat

Kampong Spoe

Kampot

Kaoh Kong

Kampong Saom

U.S. Bureau of the Census
Center for International Research

Map 3. Population Percent Male by Province, 1980 Survey of Cambodia

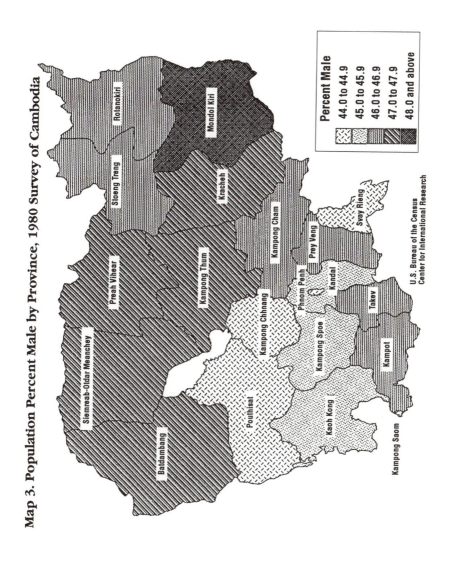

Percent Male

- 44.0 to 44.9
- 45.0 to 45.9
- 46.0 to 46.9
- 47.0 to 47.9
- 48.0 and above

Rotanokiri

Mondol Kiri

Stoeng Treng

Kracheh

Preah Vihear

Kampong Thum

Kampong Cham

Prey Veng

Svay Rieng

Siemreab–Otdar Meanchey

Batdambang

Pouthisat

Kampong Chhnang

Phnom Penh

Kandal

Kampong Spoe

Takev

Kaoh Kong

Kampot

Kampong Saom

U. S. Bureau of the Census
Center for International Research

Because fertility was not reduced at all, we conclude that mortality conditions did not deteriorate to famine levels. Our analysis concludes that the usual estimates of 600,000 to 800,000 excess deaths in the early 1970s are greatly exaggerated. These figures seem to refer instead to the total population shortfall from all causes—excess mortality, fewer births, and net emigration.

Under Khmer Rouge rule, we estimate that Cambodia's population declined from around 7.3 million at the beginning of 1975 to around 6.36 million at the end of 1978. Under a no-disaster scenario in the last half of the 1970s, the population would have grown from 7.3 million to 8.2 million in the same period. The loss of 1.8 million people in four years had the following components:

♦ Net emigration of 218,000 people.

♦ A dearth of 570,000 births compared to the expected level.

♦ Excess deaths totaling about 1.05 million.

The high mortality of the Khmer Rouge years had several causes. First, the general mortality conditions of the population deteriorated to high traditional historical levels. This happened because of the destruction of the meager existing public health and medical system, shortages of food available for or given to the population, and callous mobilization of the people for geographical moves and heavy physical labor. But these factors do not fully explain the extremely high mortality among adults from the mid-teen years through middle age. Our estimates of adult mortality in the late 1970s are based on the reported age-sex structure in the 1980 count (Table 2), combined with all the other available information on Cambodia's age structure, total population size, fertility, mortality, and migration prior to the period of Khmer Rouge rule. We conclude that most of the missing adults died rather than emigrated, based on reported data on refugees from Cambodia. Utilizing all this information, we calculate that on average, during each year of the four Khmer Rouge years, ten percent of men and almost three percent of women in young adult and middle age years were killed, above and beyond those who died due to the general mortality situation.

Alternative Population Projections

There is much uncertainty about the accuracy of the 1980 administrative count. Ea Meng-Try noted that under the Vietnam-backed government, the heads of solidarity groups in the countryside keep household records. He claimed that in 1980 it was in their interest to exaggerate the numbers of households and people in their jurisdictions, especially in those areas where the population suffered from food shortages 1979-1980; this subsistence crisis reflected poorly on the Vietnam-backed leadership.[81] Others argue that the 1980 provincial population figures may well have been inflated by local officials because access to resources distributed by Phnom Penh was based in part on the population in their jurisdiction.[82] The local population figures were also to be used for planning United Nations assistance, a factor that could have led to excessively high population numbers.[83] For our Low population scenario, we have assigned a midyear 1980 population of six million rather than the official estimate of 6.5 million, because it is entirely possible that officials intentionally erred on the side of overestimating their local populations.

On the other hand, even carefully prepared censuses the world over tend to undercount their populations, especially mobile or marginal age-sex groups. A 1964 survey in Cambodia indicated that the 1962 census may have missed about four percent of the population.[84] If so, then our reconstruction of demographic trends since 1962 may have underestimated the population each year as well. Migozzi's study of Cambodia's population, done in the early 1970s, posits a 1970 total population of 7.3 million; this is four percent higher than the seven million figure reconstructed here.[85] Similarly, various sources have suggested that Cambodia had a population of 7.89 million in April 1975 (nine percent higher than our estimate of 7.25 million) and 7.74 million in 1976.[86] Even if true, this does not prove that losses were greater in the Khmer Rouge period than we have modeled here. Rather, it is just as likely that the count in 1980 was an undercount. Cambodia was chaotic; warfare was continuing; there were at least local food shortages; and people were on the move all over the country. To count such a traumatized population was a major challenge, and it is likely that many people were simply overlooked. For our High reconstruction, we estimate a midyear 1980 total population of seven million rather than the official 6.5 million.

This would constitute a seven percent net undercount, quite possible under such conditions.

For these reasons, in addition to the Survey-based scenario which we reconstruct and project from 1962 to 2050, we present a "High" scenario and a "Low" scenario from 1980 to 2010. In developing the High and Low scenarios, we assign plausible but different levels of birth and death rates to illustrate an entirely reasonable range of population sizes and vital rates. For the Low projection, we arbitrarily choose lower fertility, higher mortality, and therefore a lower population growth rate than the Survey-based scenario. This technique produces a widening gap between the Survey-based and Low scenario population estimates over time. Similarly, we assign higher fertility, lower mortality, and therefore higher population growth to the High scenario, which also widens the range of estimates over time. These three scenarios serve to emphasize the general truth that population estimates can incorporate increasing error the longer the time that has elapsed since the last enumeration.

Even our High and Low estimates do not really encompass all plausible scenarios. Whenever Cambodia takes its next real census, we may all be in for some major surprises, and there is no predicting in what direction those revelations might lead. The true population size may be lower than our Low scenario or higher than the High projection. The sex ratio of the population may be quite different from what was reported from the 1980 count and what we have reconstructed and projected here. For example, suppose in 1980 that military age males strenuously avoided being counted because they feared conscription or perhaps retribution for their previous military roles. In that case, the dearth of men in Cambodia, though severe, may not be as extreme as now thought. Caution is required in using any population figures for Cambodia until a better enumeration can be conducted.

Caution is also advised in using the population count which was conducted in 1992-1993 in preparation for the planned election of May 1993. If the United Nations representatives made use of local registration records and reports, instead of enumerating each individual household, it is possible that local officials overreported the numbers of people, especially potential voters, in their jurisdictions. But it is equally possible that registration records are missing plenty of inhabitants of Cambodia. Population modeling that uses the results of the enumeration will be "Survey-based," like the model we use in this report, and will probably be more accurate than if there were no information at all. But the total count could easily be too high or too low.

At the close of voter registration on 31 January 1993, the UN had counted an estimated 4.7 million eligible voters;[87] this figure may exclude most of the adult population of the Khmer Rouge-controlled areas (to which the United Nations does not have unimpeded access) and many of the post-1979 Vietnamese immigrants who may not meet the voting qualifications.[88] This figure may or may not include overseas Cambodians registered to vote.[89] Our Survey-based reconstruction/projection estimates that there were 4.9 million persons age eighteen and older at midyear 1992 (including Vietnamese immigrants) and five million by March 1993, to which we must add about 60,000 eligible voters who have been counted at the Thai-Cambodian border but are being repatriated in our model throughout the rest of 1993. In other words, our Survey-based reconstruction is reasonably consistent with the United Nations count of eligible voters. This reconstruction implies that the total population of Cambodia in March 1993, including refugees being repatriated from the border, was about 9.9 million.

Plausible Fertility and Mortality Trends, 1981-1993

The Cambodian Department of Statistics assumes a steady population growth rate of 2.8 percent per year for the period 1980-1990.[90] "The basis for the growth rate of 2.8 percent assumed for the period 1980-1990 is a demographic survey conducted by the Ministry of Health in 1982 that showed a crude birth rate (CBR) of 45.6 and a crude death rate (CDR) of 17.6, but no documentation for these rates or the methodology of the survey had been provided to the Mission."[91] For our Survey-based scenario, we assume that these birth and death rates were correct in 1982. Those rates imply a fertility level of 5.8 births per woman and an expectation of life at birth of about forty-seven years. In the Survey-based reconstruction, we assume that fertility has been constant during 1982-1993, and that life expectancy at birth has improved only slowly to forty-nine years.

For our Low scenario since 1980, we assume that the death rate in 1982 was underreported, a common occurrence in developing countries, and that actual life expectancy at birth was forty-four years.

We also assume that the high fertility level detected in 1982 declined slightly in subsequent years.

State of Cambodia policy has been to increase the size of the population as rapidly as possible. The population has been viewed as too small to exploit efficiently the nation's resources and to defend the territorial integrity of the country. Fertility policy has been pronatalist. In order to reduce mortality and increase population growth, "the government is striving to improve the network of health clinics and rural maternity centers, to organize immunization campaigns, and to improve sanitation and the supply of drinking water"[92]

Consistent with these policies, our High scenario assumes that fertility was higher than reported in 1982, and has remained above six births per woman since then, a phenomenon seen in recent decades in many of the world's poorest developing countries. We also assume that mortality has declined rapidly due to public health policies. Some official Cambodian sources suggest that true population growth in Cambodia is now between three and four percent per year,[93] which we replicate in our High scenario, net of international migration flows.

Although the pronatalist position has dominated SOC policy throughout the 1980s and into the 1990s, there are now small signs of change. According to the Director of Phnom Penh's Ministry of Health, a comprehensive health care plan was devised in 1991 with the assistance of UNICEF.[94] One component of the plan emphasizes "family planning education for all couples (both husband and wife with emphasis on child spacing)."[95] Sarah Newhall, a resident of Phnom Penh working with the non-governmental organization PACT, also cited the administration's recent emphasis on child spacing.[96] If the regime truly intends to implement any family planning program in Cambodia, this represents a major departure from the pronatalist policy of the past. It is difficult to ascertain the degree to which the Phnom Penh administration is truly committed to implementing a family planning program.

A further problem is that the government may be unable to carry out a program of this kind on such a traumatized population. Experience with family planning programs among the Cambodians in the refugee camps in Thailand suggests that when confronted with an attempt to limit population growth, the Cambodians feared that "the Thai people . . . may have wanted to destroy our race, which was already partly massacred," referring to the massive deaths under the

Khmer Rouge regime.[97] Gaining acceptance for a family planning program regardless of the sincerity of the government's implementation may be difficult, although a recent observer has noted that many Cambodians, both men and women, were now seeking access to contraception.[98]

Age Structure of the Population Today

Like other countries that have experienced massive warfare and have begun their recovery, Cambodia has a population age structure that reflects those tragedies and recent improvements. Figure 1 presents our projected age structure for Cambodia in 1993 from the Survey-based reconstruction. Certain aspects of this age structure are somewhat speculative, but we can be confident about some of the characteristics seen in Figure 1. The greatest uncertainties are:

◆ Is the dearth of men now at ages 30-34 and older really as severe as has been reported and as shown in the left half of the population pyramid?

◆ Is the contraction in the age structure at ages 15-19 really as pronounced as shown in Figure 1, or was fertility during the Khmer Rouge period actually higher than the fertility level we have reconstructed from the reported 1980 age-sex structure?

Much of what we think we "know" about Cambodia's population today may turn out to be wrong, but certain characteristics are very likely to be true:

◆ Cambodia's total population size and the numbers of people in each age group are much smaller than would have been the case without the crises of the 1970s and warfare in the 1980s.

◆ Some dearth of adult males has been so widely reported that this impression must have some validity. At least twenty percent of adult females are estimated to be single, widowed, separated or divorced.[99]

♦ Cambodia still has a young population. Fertility was high
through 1974 and has been high since 1979. There are large
cohorts of children under age fourteen. We estimate that half
the total population is now under age nineteen.

**Figure 1. Cambodia 1993 Population Structure
Survey-Based Model**

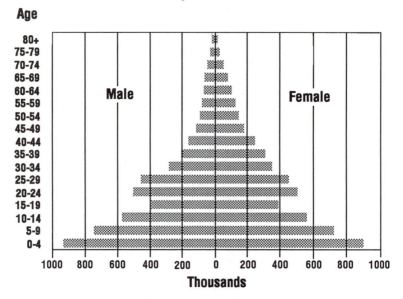

Source: Modeled at the Center for International Research, U.S. Bureau of the Census

Ethnic Composition

The ethnic makeup of the population has shifted radically over the
years, but documentation of numbers in each ethnic group is poor.
The 1962 census did not count ethnic groups as such but rather
reported the "nationality" of the population; this category was far too
broad to have adequately enumerated the populations of Cambodia's
many ethnic groups. In fact, the populations of the minority Cham
and various hill peoples were not reported at all; they were included
under the nationality "Khmer."[100]

The population as reported in the census was ninety-three percent Khmer, four percent Vietnamese (218,000), and three percent Chinese (163,000), with tiny numbers of other nationalities.[101] However, at a press conference in 1965, Sihanouk said there were 400,000 Vietnamese in Cambodia.[102] Estimates of the actual number of Chinese in Cambodia during the 1960s ranged from 300,000 to 435,000.[103] A 1968 estimate of other minority groups put the Cham population at 150,000 and the population of the various hill tribes at 90,000.[104] These later revisions of the numbers of minorities in Cambodia reflect the fact that the citizenship-based definition of the 1962 census was inadequate for developing an accurate picture of Cambodia's ethnic make-up. The revised figures suggest that in the mid-1960s, Cambodia's population included over one million members of minority groups, constituting about sixteen or seventeen percent of the total population.

The Vietnamese population in Cambodia has fluctuated with expulsion and invasion. Sources differ as to when and how many ethnic Vietnamese residents of Cambodia were driven out to Vietnam. Most sources agree that Lon Nol expelled most Vietnamese in the early 1970s, and of those still in Cambodia, the Khmer Rouge killed or drove out the remainder. Therefore, there were few ethnic Vietnamese living in Cambodia by 1978.[105]

Following the Vietnamese invasion, a steady stream of Vietnamese immigrants entered Cambodia. In addition to the approximately 200,000 Vietnamese soldiers, about 500,000 Vietnamese settlers have reportedly entered the country since 1978. There is considerable controversy over the number of Vietnamese in Cambodia as the various factions attempt to use the number to their political advantage. Estimates of the number of Vietnamese settlers in Cambodia range from 90,000 (SOC figure) to two million (Khmer Rouge estimate). We have chosen a figure of 500,000 because it is in the range (300,000-700,000) of most estimates by less interested observers and was admitted by Phnom Penh officials to the Economist Intelligence Unit.[106] Ben Kiernan estimates a national total of approximately 350,000 Vietnamese in Cambodia,[107] while a 1993 article in *Le Monde* gave an estimate of 600,000 to 800,000.[108] Given the wide range of estimates for Vietnamese settlers in Cambodia, our arbitrary estimate is reasonable. Vietnamese settlers are still in Cambodia, though the soldiers were reportedly withdrawn back to Vietnam by the end of 1989.

Whether the Vietnamese will be allowed to participate in the 1993 elections or whether the group will be allowed to remain in Cambodia at all is a hotly contested political issue. All of Cambodia's contending factions have adopted an anti-Vietnamese posture. Anti-Vietnamese sentiment is high among Khmer Cambodians, and all four factions perceive being anti-Vietnamese as a necessity for winning the support of the ethnic Khmer in the elections. Ethnically motivated attacks against Vietnamese have begun to occur; more than thirty-five Vietnamese were murdered in separate incidents in 1992.[109]

After the elections, a unified Cambodian government is likely to clamp down on spontaneous immigration of Vietnamese into Cambodia or expel "illegal" immigrants outright. The Khmer Rouge have suggested that UN-supervised withdrawal of the Vietnamese settlers is a precondition for further implementation of the peace accord. All three resistance factions (the Khmer Rouge, KPNLF, and FUNCINPEC) have claimed that at least some of the illegal Vietnamese immigrants are Vietnamese soldiers; FUNCINPEC and the KPNLF differ with the Khmer Rouge as to whether this should be allowed to delay implementation of the peace accord.

The Chinese minority, probably numbering at least 400,000 in the late 1960s, worked primarily as traders, shopkeepers, and money-lenders in the cities and rural towns. As Willmott states, "[a]bout 90 percent of the Chinese were involved in commerce, and 92 percent of those involved in commerce were Chinese."[110]

Under the Khmer Rouge, members of the Chinese minority were badly abused.[111] Kiernan suggests that the Chinese were not targeted as an ethnic group but rather because of their urban, "exploiter" backgrounds.[112] Further, he suggests that because of their lack of experience in farming, the Chinese suffered disproportionately from the rigors of forced agricultural labor to which all Cambodians were subjected.[113]

Chinese in Cambodia who survived the Khmer Rouge years were treated with suspicion by the new regime after the 1978 Vietnamese invasion; they were seen as natural allies of China, which supported the Khmer Rouge. At that time, Vietnam was expelling many of its own ethnic Chinese residents (who comprised much of the post-1978 boat people outflow), and there is some evidence of the expulsion of ethnic Chinese residents of Cambodia by Vietnamese troops as well.[114] Recent estimates of the number of ethnic Chinese in Cambodia range from 100,000 to 130,000.[115]

The Cham were not counted separately in the 1962 census of Cambodia, so estimates of their number have been speculative. In addition, some scholars have estimated that under the Khmer Rouge the Cham suffered particularly harsh treatment, large numbers being killed.[116] Kiernan estimates that 90,000 or more than one third of the Cham perished during the years of Khmer Rouge rule.[117] Vickery estimates that the Cham suffered far fewer deaths. To determine accurately the number of Cham in Cambodia today would require a census which specifically enumerates this group or a more reliable system of population registration.

The numbers of hill tribal people are unknown as well. These tribal peoples are generally found in Rotanokiri, Stoeng Treng, Kracheh, and Mondol Kiri provinces.[118] Major hill tribal groups include the Kuy, Mnong, Stieng, Brao, Pear, Jarai, and Rade.

Human Capital

One of the most tragic aspects of Cambodia's current situation is the striking lack of people with education above primary level, skills in technical fields, or professional training. Before the 1970s, Cambodia had a small cadre of trained personnel and workers in nonagricultural fields. According to the 1962 census, of the economically active population age ten and above, eighty percent was engaged in agriculture and forestry. There were 65,000 professional and technical workers, who constituted 2.6 percent of the country's work force. Artisans and factory workers made up another 4.1 percent. There were also small numbers of transport, mining, and retail trade workers. Government and military employees and religious leaders made up the rest.[119] Of the entire population of Cambodia age ten and above in 1962, fifty-seven percent reported themselves unable to read or write (that is, illiterate) and five percent said they could read but not write (semi-literate); thirty-eight percent claimed to be able to read and write (literate). Only two percent had graduated from primary school but not gone on to secondary, 0.4 percent had graduated from secondary school and stopped there, and merely 761 people claimed any advanced degree. Of those literate or with any education, the vast majority were males.[120]

Even these small numbers of trained people were decimated by the Khmer Rouge's targeting of the urban and the educated. Many died or fled abroad. After the Khmer Rouge regime was deposed, Cambodia had to begin building from a very weak base at the beginning of the 1980s. Skilled immigrants from Vietnam have answered some of the country's needs. By any definition, be it educational level, number of skilled workers, or professional leadership, the human capital embodied in Cambodia's population is still rudimentary.

Education

Professionals and teachers were and are in short supply, but the system of basic education is now far more widespread than in the past. UNICEF describes the changes in the 1980s and the current situation as follows:

> The deliberate eradication of the educational system between 1975 and 1979 resulted in the death or escape abroad of between 15,000 and 20,000 teachers and the destruction of books, equipment and facilities. By 1979 most children between 8 and 14 years of age had either never been to school or had forgotten what they previously knew. The Government has set a high priority on education and a measure of its achievements is that about one in every four Cambodians is enrolled in some type of schooling, whether it be in the formal sector, or in a non-formal adult education program or in vocational training. Five years of primary education are free and compulsory and close to 90 percent of school-age children are believed to be in school, although significant regional variations exist and drop-out rates, especially among girls, are high. Between 1979 and 1983, 42,600 teachers, many of whom had to be recruited with very low basic education skills, received short-term training and refresher training....In general, schools are inadequate and ill-equipped, many of them without any water or sanitation facilities....The present production levels of the Ministry of Education printing house and other presses are estimated to meet only 25 percent of the actual requirements for text books. Each text book is expected to be shared by four students and last for four years.[121]

Eradication of illiteracy has been a major goal of the Phnom Penh authorities. Through national literacy campaigns, the regime has attempted to increase literacy, particularly among the target age groups, men 13-45 and women 13-40. The government claims great success in its programs, reporting the attainment of a literacy rate of 93 percent in these target groups.[122] The literacy rates are based upon attendance in the literacy classes rather than measurable achievement and refer only to the target age group and thus provide little information on overall literacy in the country. UNICEF estimates a national adult literacy rate of seventy percent .[123] A more recent estimate by four international organizations evaluating Cambodia's current situation and development needs offers an adult literacy figure of thirty-five percent .[124]

Fragmentary data are available on school enrollments during the 1980s. In 1984, there were reported to be 1,504,840 pupils in primary schools, 147,730 in secondary schools and 7,334 in vocational establishments.[125] By the 1988-1989 academic year, there were reported to be 50,000 teachers, 1.3 million primary school students, and 350,000 secondary school students in Cambodia.[126] In 1984, we project that there were only about 989,000 children in the primary school ages 6-11 and 1,192,000 children of secondary school ages 12-17, totaling 2,181,000 children ages 6-17, compared to a total of 1,653,000 reported enrolled in primary and secondary schools, suggesting that seventy-six percent of school-age children may have been attending school. As of year-end 1988, we project that Cambodia had about 1,196,830 children in the primary school ages 6-11 and 1,060,113 in the secondary school ages 12-17, totaling 2,256,943 at ages 6-17. The total number of primary and secondary school students in 1988-1989, 1,650,000, was the equivalent of seventy-three percent of young people in the relevant ages. Due to past lack of opportunity for primary school, however, it appears that throughout the 1980s, many people older than 6-11 were trying to get a primary school education. This is a common occurrence in developing countries and is the reason why Cambodia could have had 1.5 million primary school students in 1984 and 1.3 million in 1988-1989 but only 989,000 in the prescribed primary school ages in 1984 and 1.2 million in 1988-89.

Further, enrollment rate figures must be viewed with caution as regional variation exists. Phnom Penh's enrollment rate is probably more than ninety percent while in some of the nation's more isolated areas enrollment is likely as low as thirty percent of the school age population.[127] According to a recent study, the Northeast of the country is not even covered by the national primary school network.[128]

Throughout the 1980s, Cambodia was heavily dependent upon the Soviet Union and Vietnam for higher education. Russian and Vietnamese were the languages of instruction at Cambodian schools of higher education (most of the instructors were themselves Russian and Vietnamese). By 1993, the government hopes to have trained enough teachers to conduct Cambodia's higher education in Khmer.[129] In the 1990-1991 school year, there were forty postgraduate students and 6,700 undergraduates in Cambodia.[130] From 1980 to 1991, Cambodia sent eight-thousand students abroad (mainly to Vietnam and countries of the former Eastern Bloc) for advanced studies.[131]

Health

During the Khmer Rouge period of the late 1970s, the health and survival chances of the Cambodian people were reduced to a primitive level devoid of modern medical inputs. The Pol Pot regime intentionally killed the doctors and pharmacists, laid waste the hospitals and clinics, and almost completely destroyed what little preventive and primary health infrastructure had existed before their rule. Under the Khmer Rouge, "[s]o-called medical care was given by 'the barefoot doctors,' teenagers from 12 to 15 years old who had three months of training."[132]

Compared to these dismal beginnings, much progress has been reported in the 1980s. A simple health system has been set up in much of the country, but facilities are very poor, security is problematic and transport weak; so utilization rates are very low.[133] Medical workers in most provinces are only minimally trained. Beginning with only the forty-five doctors who remained in Cambodia in 1979 (there had been five hundred in 1975), there were 705 physicians in 1990.[134] There are a further 15,180 medical support personnel, including medical assistants, nurses, midwives, and pharmacists.[135]

Despite the destruction of Cambodia's medical facilities during the Khmer Rouge period, reconstruction has made progress. Today, there are 1,360 sub-district level health centers and dispensaries and 175 district hospitals;[136] these facilities are backed up by one main hospital in each provincial capital, except for Kampong Cham, which has four, and Phnom Penh, which has nine.[137] Health services are best in Phnom Penh and deteriorate in terms of quality of staff and equipment as one moves downward to the sub-district level health centers.

Access to medicine, even in hospitals, is a major problem. According to the Director of Phnom Penh's Health Ministry, Dr. Abdul Coyaume, only the National Pediatric Hospital, supported by World Vision International, has enough drugs for its needs. In the nation's other hospitals, patients must purchase drugs at outside, private pharmacies.[138] To improve the availability and provision of medication in the country, the authorities hope to regulate private pharmacies more effectively in the future as well as increase the number and amount of pharmaceuticals produced domestically.[139]

Much of the illness and death in Cambodia is caused by continuing lack of security from conflict and by primitive environmental conditions. A majority of children are born in unhygienic conditions, so neonatal tetanus followed by death is widespread. Maternal mortality is reported to be high and is caused primarily by lack of adequate prenatal care, complications during delivery, and unsafe abortions.[140] Child mortality is thought to be so high that Cambodia ranks among the twenty worst countries in the world.[141] High rates of child illness and death are due to diarrhea, acute respiratory infections, and a host of preventable diseases. The great lack of potable water (only twenty-one percent of those in urban areas and twelve percent of those in rural areas have access to safe water) and adequate sanitation leads to frequent illness for the population and to untimely deaths particularly among children under age five.[142]

Some of the most serious disease problems in Cambodia are falciparum malaria, which is resistant to chloroquine and endemic in most provinces; tuberculosis, 150,000 cases with only 20,000 receiving treatment in 1990; and dengue hemorrhagic fever, epidemics of which occur every two or three years and which kills five to ten percent of those who contract the disease.[143]

Cambodia's international isolation of the past decade may or may not have insulated the country from the spread of Acquired Immune Deficiency Syndrome (AIDS).[144] Dr. Oum Sophal of Phnom Penh's Health Ministry described Cambodia's concern this way: "On the surface, it seems that AIDS is not yet a problem in our country. But in reality it may already be."[145] The Phnom Penh authorities recognize the potential danger of the introduction and spread of AIDS and in 1991 began a program of public education (for prevention) and training of medical personnel (for care of HIV-positive persons). A 1992 study by Phnom Penh's Ministry of Health reported forty-five cases of HIV infection (up from two in 1992); the infection rate among prostitutes is said to be high, fourteen percent in one of Phnom Penh's red light districts.[146]

A recent bright spot in Cambodia's health picture is that a child immunization program was launched in the Phnom Penh region in October 1986 and has since been gradually expanded to all twenty-one provinces. It is supported by UNICEF and seeks to immunize eighty percent of children under age one against six major diseases of childhood. A 1989 survey reported good progress in thirteen provinces.[147]

The high morbidity and mortality in Cambodia is caused partly by the uncertain food supply. Hunger and malnutrition are common. People in many parts of the country still forage for part of their food intake. International food aid is selectively used to avert famine. Distribution of food from surplus to deficit areas is, in general, not working. Recent severe drought as well as floods in 1991 have compromised food availability.[148]

The continued presence of mines, spread by both Phnom Penh and anti-government forces, is a constant threat to the safety of the population. A recent report by Asia Watch and the Physicians for Human Rights said "[m]ine accidents now rank with malaria and tuberculosis as one of Cambodia's three greatest public health hazards."[149] Even where mine locations are known by one of the factions, until the outcome of the peace process is known, the factions are reticent to reveal their locations because they believe the mines are still required for tactical purposes.[150]

The number of amputees in Cambodia is variously estimated at between 22,000 and 30,000. Fifty percent of these are estimated to be civilians.[151] The number of amputees in the refugee camps in Thailand is estimated at 5,000-6,000.[152] These numbers do not tell the entire story, though, as only one in two mine victims is estimated to survive at all.[153] Further, Handicap International estimates that these numbers increase at a rate of 200-300 new amputees a month.[154]

In addition to the physical limitations imposed by the loss of a limb, Cambodian amputees are hampered by the prevalent view that the disabled are a burden, "no use to anyone."[155] Although the government has conducted public education campaigns to change this attitude, recent visitors to Cambodia have suggested it is still prevalent.[156] Unable to participate actively in agriculture, many amputees resort to begging and petty thievery in order to support themselves.[157]

Working with UNICEF, the Phnom Penh administration has set out an ambitious plan for the nation's health care system.[158] This plan envisions future improvement in disease prevention, nutrition, curative medicine, and medication.[159] The regime had been hampered in the past in improving the health care system by international isolation, economic backwardness and the perceived necessity of devoting a high percentage of the government budget to defense.[160] With the peace process underway and with the assistance of the international community in the reconstruction of Cambodia's economy and the upgrading of its health care system, perhaps Cambodia can come closer to reaching its health care goals.

Working-age Population and Labor Force

There are few opportunities in Cambodia today for work outside of agriculture. Different sources estimate that seventy to eighty percent of an economically active population of about 3.7 million are engaged in agriculture, forestry, or fishing.[161] One source says that fifteen percent are engaged in services, and another estimates that thirty percent of the labor force work in nonagricultural pursuits.[162] In the primary sector, the level of mechanization is low, and even simple agricultural implements are in short supply due to a lack of metal parts. Many of the draft animals used for agricultural work were killed during the 1970s.[163] All of this means that labor needs are large in agriculture today. There is a relative shortage of agricultural laborers because of the labor-intensive nature of Cambodian agriculture, the heavy adult male losses from the 1970s, large numbers of disabled persons, and the siphoning off of many men into military or guerrilla roles.[164] Heng Samrin, then President of the People's Republic of Kampuchea, in a speech to the Fifth Party Congress, recognized the labor shortage as an impediment to Cambodia's economic development.[165] It is thought that women head thirty-five percent of the households in Cambodia and that over sixty percent of farmers are women.[166] In most developing countries experiencing rapid population growth as Cambodia is today, the problems are unemployment and excess labor power rather than labor shortage. Perhaps as demographic recovery proceeds, Cambodia's labor shortage will be short-lived.

Figure 2 shows our projected number of persons in the young working ages 15-29 and the middle and older working ages 30-64 between now and the year 2010, from the Survey-based scenario. Between 1980 and 1993, the numbers of young adults 15-29 increased from 1.8 to 2.7 million, averaging 3.1 percent a year growth. This constitutes rapid recovery of the numbers in the young adult ages, though by 1993 there would have been at least 3.5 million ages 15-29 without the catastrophes. We project that the number at ages 15-29 will grow from 2.7 million in 1993 to only three million by the year 2000, at a modest growth rate of 1.5 percent a year. The comparatively slow growth of the young working age population during the 1993-2000 period is attributable to the loss of reproductive-age women during the Khmer Rouge years and the massive loss of men that left many living women without partners. Births in the early 1980s were therefore fewer than would normally have been expected. These smaller cohorts will enter the 15-29 age group in the 1990s.

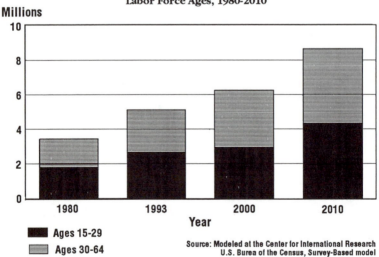

Figure 2. Cambodia, Projected Population of Labor Force Ages, 1980-2010

Source: Modeled at the Center for International Research
U.S. Burea of the Census, Survey-Based model

As shown in Figure 2, the 1980 population ages 30-64, having survived the shocking level of excess mortality in the 1970s, was estimated to be even smaller than the 15-29 group who were also hard hit. Since then, however, the 30-64 age group has grown rapidly in size to 2.4 million in 1993. This trend will accelerate, with the population ages 30-64 growing to about 3.3 million at the turn of the century while the 15-29 group will increase to only about three million. After that, both segments of the working ages will grow in number.

During the rest of the 1990s, how will Cambodia cope with the perceived scarcity of labor power? First, demobilization of the various military forces could free up many men for civilian work. Second, the continuing shortage of people in the young working ages can be partly compensated for by looking toward the growing numbers of people in the middle and older working ages. Third, replenishment of draft animals and simple forms of agricultural mechanization could greatly raise the productivity of the average agricultural worker. Fourth, the expansion of the educational system that has already taken place, strengthened by attention to raising its quality, could enhance the effectiveness of the future work force.

Urbanization and De-urbanization

Before the decade of demographic catastrophes, Cambodia was already experiencing some urbanization. By about 1967, the country's urban population had reportedly reached 880,000 (thirteen percent of the population), compared to 590,000 and ten percent of the population in 1962.[167] The warfare and bombing of the early 1970s caused a flight of refugees to the cities and towns. It has been estimated that an additional two million urban in-migrants were added to the one million former urban residents, totaling three million or over forty percent of Cambodia's population in April 1975.[168] Phnom Penh's population alone reportedly reached 1.5-2.6 million by then.[169]

The Khmer Rouge, however, required virtually all of the urban residents to move to the countryside from the cities and towns. Phnom Penh was depopulated, after which the Khmer Rouge transferred into the city about twenty-thousand cadres and workers considered loyal to the regime.[170] Starting in early 1979, after the Vietnamese invasion, people were allowed to move from rural to urban areas.

By the time of the demographic survey in late 1980, 12.6 percent of the population was said to be living in urban areas, based on a "provisional definition" of urban places that included only Phnom

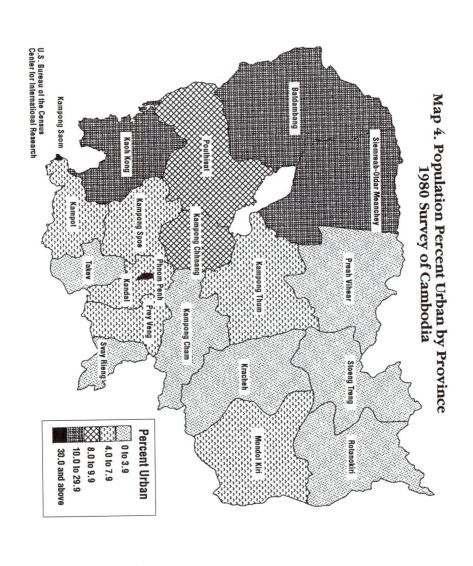

Map 4. Population Percent Urban by Province
1980 Survey of Cambodia

U.S. Bureau of the Census
Center for International Research

Kampong Saom

Battambang

Siemreab-Oddar Meanchey

Kaoh Kong

Pouthisat

Kampong Chhnang

Kampong Thum

Preah Vihear

Kampot

Kampong Spoe

Pnom Penh

Kandal

Prey Veng

Kampong Cham

Takev

Svay Rieng

Kracheh

Stoeng Treng

Mondol Kiri

Rotanokiri

Percent Urban

0 to 3.9
4.0 to 7.9
8.0 to 9.9
10.0 to 29.9
30.0 and above

Penh, Kampong Saom (now Sihanoukville), and the chief urban place in each province such as the provincial capital or biggest town.[171] As shown in Map 4, the eastern three-fifths of Cambodia was extremely lightly urbanized except for Phnom Penh. In seven provinces of the northeast and east, less than four percent of the provincial population lived in the provincial capital. In a total of thirteen eastern provinces, less than eight percent of the population was urban by this provisional definition. The western provinces had a higher proportion of their populations in the leading city or town (Table 1). For example, seventeen percent of the population of Batdambang province on the border with Thailand lived in the provincial capital. (Batdambang has now been divided into two provinces; in 1980, 18.6 percent of the population in the area that is now Batdambang was called urban, and 16.1 percent in the area that is today Banteay Meanchey province.) In 1980, the populations within the boundaries of Phnom Penh and Kampong Saom province-level municipalities were defined as one hundred percent urban. Otherwise, the most urbanized province in the country at that time was Kaoh Kong province on the Gulf of Thailand, where twenty-nine percent of the population lived in the provincial capital.

As of 1988-1989, the urban population of Cambodia was reportedly 959,000, about twelve percent of the country's estimated total population.[172] The twelve percent figure was also reported for 1991.[173] However, it is possible that "twelve percent" is derived completely from the 1980 survey, and that no new nationwide urban data have actually been compiled since then.[174] For instance, the 12.6 percent figure for 1990 given by the Cambodian Department of Statistics is based entirely on 1980 data.[175]

Because of Phnom Penh's huge transient and squatter population, estimates of the population of the city vary widely. The official figure for Phnom Penh's total population as of midyear 1990 was 620,000, as estimated by the city's Planning Commission.[176] As of 1991, "the Popular Committee of Phnom Penh Municipality estimates that the city's population equals 800,000 in the rainy season and reaches 1.0 million in the dry season, when farmers have less work to do in rural areas."[177] There is a severe shortage of housing in the city, so its government is promoting the building of housing and economic development zones with international financial assistance.[178] Compounding the problems of Phnom Penh's sudden urbanization since 1979 has been the fact that an estimated seventy percent of the new residents are originally from the countryside, "importing rural ways in the densely built central parts of the city."[179]

Aside from Phnom Penh, concentrations of Cambodians outside Cambodia have rivaled in size urban places in Cambodia. For example, the population of Site 2, a Cambodian refugee camp on the Thai side of the border, was more than 209,000, reported to be the largest town of Cambodians after Phnom Penh, before repatriation began.[180]

Urbanization could increase following the repatriation of the 370,000 refugees from Thailand. Although it is generally planned that refugees will be returned to farming in the rural areas of Cambodia, there is no guarantee that the returnees will remain in the countryside if their readjustment to subsistence farming proves too difficult. The United Nations' recent attempts to speed up the repatriation process by providing money rather than land to returning refugees willing to make their own post-repatriation arrangements will probably also increase urbanization. James Lynch, in his 1989 demographic study of the Cambodian refugees in Thailand, suggests that some of those who have acquired technical skills during their time in the refugee camps would prefer to return to an urban location.[181]

Population Distribution and Internally Displaced Persons

Most figures given for Cambodia's provinces today are extrapolated in some way from the 1980 population distribution. These estimates take little account of events since 1980, such as population movement within the country or international migration streams since early 1980. Therefore they are not very informative. For example, in provinces that have experienced considerable in-migration during the 1980s and early 1990s, such as the municipalities of Phnom Penh and Sihanoukville and the provinces of Kaoh Kong and Kandal, provincial totals extrapolated from 1980 would be too low today.[182] Huguet reports that "provincial offices estimate the population of their province by requesting village heads to report the total by sex to the commune, which reports to the district, which reports to the province." As of year-end 1990, he stated, three southeastern provinces near Phnom Penh provided the following figures for their total populations: Prey Veng, 850,000; Takev, 598,465; Kampong Spoe, 420,000. The Takev figure is much less than projected from the 1980 count,[183] which suggests that there may have been net out-migration from Takev during 1980-1990. In contrast, Phnom Penh has grown much faster than would have been expected from natural population increase (births minus deaths) alone.

Table 3 gives recent figures for the populations of nine provinces in Cambodia; these totals are apparently not extrapolated from the 1980 data, so perhaps they come from recent provincial compilations. Of Cambodia's twenty-one provinces, there are still nine provinces for which no recent figures are available.[184]

Table 3. Total and Displaced Population for Selected Provinces, September 1991

Province or City	Population		Displaced Persons	
	Persons	Families	Persons	Families
Nine Provinces	—	—	169,727	33,069
Siemreab-Otdar Meanchey	547,972	96,504	27,399	4,904
Banteay Meanchey	349,587	65,499	47,049	8,840
Batdambang	484,890	94,174	31,859	6,452
Pouthisat	228,155	45,357	5,328	1,016
Kampong Chhnang	277,357	55,302	7,126	1,564
Kampot	437,822	84,094	10,725	2,006
Kampong Spoe	426,955	79,974	30,779	6,311
Kampong Thum	446,395	77,930	8,329	1,537
Preah Vihear	80,000	N/A	1,133	439

Source: Huguet, 1991: 87. Data provided by the Cambodian Displaced Persons Working Group, Phnom Penh.

Table 3 also gives the reported number of "internally displaced people and families in Cambodia" as of September 1991. This term does not include Cambodians in refugee camps on the Thai side of the border. The internally displaced population was reported from nine provinces only, not including the two province-level municipalities. This suggests that people who voluntarily migrate somewhere, such as from a rural to an urban place, are not considered "displaced." The term appears to refer to people who have fled from active fighting in

their localities and live in "displaced persons camps."[185] Banteay
Meanchey province (see Map 1), a northwestern border province,
reports the largest number of internally displaced persons, followed
by the two adjacent provinces Siemreab-Otdar Meanchey and
Batdambang, and the southern province of Kampong Spoe.

Cambodians and Khmer Outside Cambodia

Because of Cambodia's two recent decades of crises and the massive
population movements they have caused, more than 630,000
Cambodians were outside their native country as of 1991-1992 (for a
more detailed examination of population movements, refer to
Appendix A and Table A-1). These Cambodians abroad can be found
in Thailand or Vietnam, or resettled in third countries like the United
States, Canada, France, and Australia, as documented in Table 4. In
general, Cambodians now living in third countries originally left
Cambodia for Thailand and were admitted to their countries of
resettlement from Thai camps.

James Lynch discussed the characteristics of the Cambodian
population of three of the refugee camps in Thailand which he
surveyed for his 1989 demographic study.[186] Lynch projected that
rough sexual parity existed in the camps, males comprising 51.1
percent of the population and females 48.9 percent.[187] Lynch's
estimates of the age-sex structure of the three camps follow:

Years of Age	Total	Male	Female	Sex Ratio[188]
0-9	89,968	47,770	42,198	113
10-19	39,811	22,022	17,789	123
20-29	45,653	21,240	24,413	87
30-39	39,522	19,762	19,760	100
40-49	14,655	6,854	7,801	88
50-59	9,383	4,558	4,825	94
60-69	4,978	2,363	2,615	90
70-79	1,181	567	614	92
80-89	99	71	28	254
Total	245,250	125,207	120,043	104

Table 4. Cambodians Outside Cambodia, 1991-1992 Data

Location	Number of Cambodians
Asia	
China	65
Indonesia	1,370*
Japan	970
Thailand	367,842 to 386,866*
Vietnam	25,000*
Europe	
Austria	339
Belgium	732
France	34,205
Germany	874
Italy	321
Netherlands	457
Norway	126
Switzerland	1,993
United Kingdom	263
Oceania	
Australia	16,240
New Zealand	4,000
North America	
Canada	20,209
United States	152,000
Other countries	7,395
Total	634,401 to 653,425

Notes: Asterisk indicates numbers of refugees. All other data refer to those admitted for resettlement.

Sources: FBIS, 1992d, p.34; FBIS, 1992e: 52; Court Robinson, 1992, personal communication; Brian Johnson, 1992, personal communication; Linda Gordon, 1992, personal communication; Federal Aliens Office (Switzerland), 1992, personal communication; Mazel, 1992; Grazer and Lowman, 1992: 3; UNHCR mimeograph on Indochinese refugees, 1992.

The age-sex structure of the camps was very roughly comparable to that of a stable population, although numbers were higher in the 20-29 and 30-39 age groups than would be anticipated. The structure suggests that, generally, whole families migrated from Cambodia to Thailand; in addition, of those who came alone to the border camps, large numbers were those who are now in their twenties and thirties.

Lynch found that natural increase in the camps was high, with the result that thirty-seven percent of the total camp population was under ten years of age; this was likely due to an extremely high birth rate as well as improved health and mortality conditions in the camps and despite the fact that twenty percent of all camp females were widowed.[189]

As to the education level of those in the camps, Lynch found that being from rural backgrounds, most refugees had received little education in Cambodia, seventy-eight percent having had three years of schooling or less.[190] Opportunities existed at the camps for education but quality was poor, up to eighty students per teacher in some cases. Secondary education was not even offered in the camps until 1988. The United Nations Border Relief Operation (UNBRO), which has been responsible for the care of the displaced Cambodians in Thailand, has trained numbers of Cambodian teachers but those trained generally prefer taking other jobs outside of education with the NGOs in the camps.[191]

For this study, we have accepted a year-end 1991 figure of 370,000 Cambodian refugees in Thailand, although estimates vary.[192] These refugees were scheduled to be repatriated in 1992 and 1993 under the terms of the 1991 Memorandum of Understanding reached among Thailand, Cambodia's Supreme National Council, and the United Nations High Commissioner for Refugees. We have used Lynch's estimates of the composition of the border camp population in order to model the age-sex structure of the repatriates.[193]

Of the 370,000 refugees, 160,000 expressed a preference for moving to Batdambang province, long considered Cambodia's ricebowl; 42,000 hoped to be repatriated to neighboring Banteay Meanchey province and 18,000 to Siemreab-Otdar Meanchey (see Map 1). Other Cambodian provinces were selected by refugees in smaller numbers. Some refugees left the decision of where they would be returned to the United Nations. These figures were based on a preregistration, supervised by the United Nations High Commissioner for Refugees, of the refugees in the border camps.

"Most Cambodians wanted to repatriate to areas more or less adjacent to where they are now encamped."[194] An NGO worker suggested that the border provinces were not chosen because of the supposed fertility of the land[195] but rather so that flight to Thailand would be easier if the peace process takes a turn for the worse. Other problems with the repatriation process include the difficulty of reintegrating the returnees with the local population. It was feared that the refugees would be resented because of the assistance package provided by the United Nations for their return. A recent Cambodia trip report by Walter Grazer and Shep Lowman suggests further problems:

> [T]he populations of the camps have lived in an artificial environment with clean water, good health care, and other services. The camp populations are almost 50 percent young people who lack farming and general coping skills, are not used to taking the initiative to help themselves, and lack the natural immunities and tolerances to disease which the native population in-country may have built up.[196]

In addition to the refugees in Thailand, most of whom have now been repatriated to Cambodia, there are 25,000 "mainly Chinese" Cambodian refugees in Vietnam.[197] Information on these refugees is limited, but one source does mention these refugees as "settling" in Vietnam.[198] It is unknown whether many of these refugees have returned or plan to return to Cambodia.

There is also an indigenous Khmer population (known in Khmer as Khmer Krom) numbering 872,000 in southern Vietnam.[199] These ethnic Khmer are not refugees from Cambodia. Their ancestors began settling in the region in the first century AD and have been living under Vietnamese dominion since the Vietnamese gained control of the region three centuries ago. The Khmer Krom are not expected to provide Cambodia with remittances from abroad or to move in large numbers to Cambodia, although there is a history of Khmer Krom activity in Cambodian politics.

Many of the Cambodians abroad are expected to play a role in their country's political and economic development following the UN-supervised elections. Some will doubtless return permanently to Cambodia although the numbers of returnees from third countries are likely to remain small until a stable future for Cambodia is more assured. Two Cambodian-Americans, Vanna Om Strinko and Kethavy

Kim, have returned to Cambodia and announced the formation of new political parties, the New Life Democratic Party and the Republic Democracy Party of Kampuchea, independent of the four warring factions that compose Cambodia's Supreme National Council.[200] Thida Khus, Director of the Cambodian Network Council, a Cambodian-American Association, has called returning Cambodian-Americans a "natural transmitter" of democracy.[201]

Other Cambodians may return to seek business opportunities. Both the United Nations Development Program (TOKTEN) and the International Organization for Migration (Return of Talent Program) are attempting to assist skilled Cambodians abroad to return to their country either permanently or on a short-term basis.[202] Also, "with the lure of money to be made, those Chinese-Cambodians who took refuge in Hong Kong, Thailand, Taiwan and Singapore—and made fortunes in the meantime—are returning with full pockets" to take part in Cambodia's development.[203] Other Cambodians who do not elect to return may provide needed foreign exchange by providing remittances to relatives who have remained in the country.[204]

Future Population of Cambodia

At midyear 1993, we estimate that Cambodia's population is in the range 9.0-11.2 million, based on the Low and High reconstructions; our Survey-based reconstruction gives an estimate of 9.9 million.[205]

In projecting Cambodia's population into the future, we have assumed no escalation of the current civil war and gradual improvement in the health and mortality situation in the coming years. As shown in Figure 3, the population will continue its rapid growth in the near future, and by the year 2000, we project that there will be between 10.7 and 14.2 million people in the country; in the Survey-based scenario we project 12.1 million. The average annual population growth rate from 1993 to 2000 is projected in each scenario as follows: Low, 2.5 percent; Survey-based, 2.9 percent; High, 3.4 percent.

In the coming decades, the extreme dearth of men in the Cambodian population will gradually modulate. From a sex ratio of only eighty-six males per hundred females in the total population counted in 1980, we project that in 1993 the total population sex ratio has risen to ninety-two males per hundred females. By the year 2000, there will be about ninety-four males per hundred females. What is happening is that the shortage of men in age groups affected by warfare and slaughter in the 1970s and 1980s persists, but younger cohorts and those being born now have relatively balanced numbers of boys and girls. As they grow up, over time more age groups in the population will have a normal sex ratio.

Figure 3. Total Population of Cambodia, 1980-2010 Low, Survey-Based, and High Scenarios

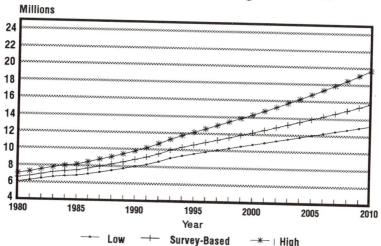

Source: Modeled at the Center for International Research
U.S. Bureau of the Census

Conclusions

In this chapter, we have attempted to compile and assess what little is known about the current population of Cambodia. This is clearly an interim, temporary set of estimates. Our estimates and everyone else's estimates will someday be superseded by a census or by demographic surveys that give us better data on the size, age-sex structure, growth rate, and geographical distribution of Cambodia's population. The 1992-1993 attempt to gather data on the size, age-sex structure, geographical distribution, and voter eligibility of Cambodia's population is an important step in the right direction, but its accuracy may be hurt by politically-motivated error or other problems.

Meanwhile, we have created a basic reconstruction of the nation's population trends from the 1962 census to the 1980 population count as reported. This is the Survey-based scenario, because we use these official counts without adjusting them for underreporting or overcounting. In this scenario, we have tried to incorporate reasonable fertility and mortality assumptions that adequately connect these two enumerations and project from the 1962 census to the 1980 population size, age structure, and sex ratio. The Survey-based reconstruction also assumes correct the 1982 demographic survey crude birth and death rates reported for Cambodia. Beyond 1982 to 1993, fertility is assumed constant and a slow reduction in mortality is assumed. We project continued high fertility to the turn of the century, followed by slow fertility decline, and continuing moderate declines in mortality. The Survey-based scenario is plausible and consistent with the small amount of demographic data that has been collected and reported for Cambodia.

But that does not prove that our Survey-based scenario is correct. We have also created Low and High reconstructions and projections to illustrate alternative scenarios for Cambodia's population size and growth that are quite reasonable and possible, given the information we have to work with. In future, we may discover that the Low or High reconstruction was closer to correct than the Survey-based scenario.

In all three scenarios, we have incorporated the information we have collected on international migration out of and into Cambodia. For most years, we have no more knowledge than an estimated total number of refugees leaving Cambodia or immigrants entering Cambodia. Sometimes the available sources report that it is members of a certain ethnic group that are being expelled, are fleeing, or are returning to Cambodia by the tens or even hundreds of thousands. Details are given in Appendix A and compiled in Table A-1.

Our chapter includes background information on historical, political, and economic trends so that population trends may be better understood. We note that the political chaos and misrule that have engulfed Cambodia have adversely affected people's survival chances, their physical and mental health, their marital and family situation, their reproductive health, and their overall quality of life. The economy was a disaster in the 1970s and now is limping toward a more normal condition of underdevelopment. Cambodia's international isolation and orientation toward the Soviet bloc has meant that desperately needed Western multilateral and bilateral assistance has barely been forthcoming. If current attempts at a political solution to Cambodia's tragic situation do succeed, the biggest barrier to the country's recovery and development will be removed.

On a more demographic note, we explore here the available information on health and mortality conditions of the Cambodian people. We rely heavily on the assessments made by international organizations working in Cambodia, such as the United Nations Children's Fund (UNICEF). Our chapter describes the poor environmental sanitation and unsafe water supply, the unsanitary conditions in which women give birth, the precarious food supply, and the most widespread and devastating diseases. Added to all these serious causes of ill health and early death have been disabilities and deaths caused by mine explosions and civil warfare. Our chapter also focuses on the improvements in the system of health care and disease prevention. We describe the rudimentary but growing health delivery system with its local health stations, district and provincial hospitals, and minimally trained health personnel. Finally, we mention the national immunization program, which is reducing the incidence of and mortality from six major diseases of childhood.

We observe that fertility is high in Cambodia, and that the Phnom Penh administration's policy has been pronatalist. While contraceptives and abortion are hardly available in the country, there are now signs of a possible change in policy that would include family planning education and support for the concept of child spacing. Fertility would probably be higher than it is now if more of the adult women were currently married. It has been estimated that about twenty percent of adult women are without husbands.[206]

Our chapter discusses the ethnic composition of Cambodia's population today. The Khmer remain by far the dominant ethnic group. It is thought that there are more Vietnamese in Cambodia today than there were before the catastrophes of the 1970s, because of a huge influx of Vietnamese settlers following the Vietnamese invasion of 1978. Khmer hatred of the Vietnamese settlers proved a major political issue in the preparations for the elections. Increased violence against the Vietnamese minority as well as expulsion of large numbers of Vietnamese are entirely possible. Members of the Chinese minority in Cambodia are now thought to be far less numerous than in the 1960s. Figures for other minorities are nonexistent or very problematic.

We discuss the age structure of Cambodia's population today and in the future. Prominent features of the age-sex pyramid today are a striking shortage of men, comparatively small cohorts of children born during the Khmer Rouge period, and larger cohorts of children born during and since 1979 and since then who are now age fourteen or younger. We show that the shortage of people in the young working ages (relative to the need for them in a subsistence, labor-intensive economy) will continue through the turn of the century. Meanwhile, however, the numbers of adults in the middle and older working ages 30-64 have increased and will increase rapidly.

We show that the administration in power since early 1979 has emphasized the provision of education, and we provide fragmentary figures on school enrollments. Comparing enrollments to children of school ages, we note that the whole educational system is playing catch-up, attempting to provide a primary education to those who had no opportunity for education in the 1970s.

Our chapter provides details from the 1980 population count on provincial population size and density, population sex ratios by province, and urban populations by province. We look at recent urbanization trends, to the extent that any can be discerned, and we discuss the locations of internally displaced persons. We report where the returnees planned to go as they reentered Cambodia during 1992 and 1993 under United Nations supervision. Finally, we document the numbers of Cambodians abroad by country, and discuss the roles they might play in Cambodia's future.

Our overall assessment is that Cambodia's current situation is indeed grim, but nowhere near as terrible as under the Khmer Rouge regime in the late 1970s. Some progress has been made in the 1980s, especially in basic education and certain public health measures. However, the reliability of Cambodian population projections into the future is clouded by the lack of certainty that the current fragile moves toward peace will succeed.

Appendix A

International Migration Assumptions

Year or years	Assumptions
1962-1969	None
1970	200,000 Vietnamese citizens of Cambodia were expelled to Vietnam by the Lon Nol government.[207] It was reported that 5,000 Khmer communists, taken to Hanoi in 1954 following the Geneva Conference, returned to Cambodia after Sihanouk's overthrow.[208] (Ben Kiernan suggests that there were only 1,000 such Khmer Communist returnees. We continue to use the arbitrary figure of 5,000, but note the uncertainty surrounding this estimate.)
1971-1974	34,000 refugees fled to Thailand and another 120,000 (mostly Vietnamese residents of Cambodia) to Vietnam.[209] We have divided the refugees equally among the four years.
1975-1978	34,039 Cambodians made it to Thailand and 150,000, predominantly Chinese and Khmer Cambodians, fled to Vietnam from the Pol Pot regime.[210] Year-by-year data for those fleeing to Thailand was available from UNHCR; for those fleeing to Vietnam, we have divided the refugees equally among the four years. 10,400 Cambodians fled to Laos in 1975 when the Khmer Rouge came to power.[211] These refugees were returned to Cambodia under an agreement between the Lao People's Democratic Republic and the People's Republic of Kampuchea. All were returned to Cambodia by 1987.[212] Because the number of refugees was small (relative to flows to and from Thailand and Vietnam) and all were

returned to Cambodia, they have been excluded from the international migration stream used in our reconstruction.

1978   The Vietnamese army which invaded Cambodia on 25 December 1978 and which remained in Cambodia at various force levels until September 1989, has not been included in the migration streams.

1979-1980   100,000 Cambodian refugees return to Cambodia from Vietnam.[213] From 1979 to 1980, 172,380 Cambodian refugees, fleeing serious regional food crises, traveled to Thailand.[214] Of this number, there were at least 12,000 ethnic Chinese fleeing feared persecution by the Vietnamese or the Phnom Penh regime.[215]

1980   It is believed that once the situation in Cambodia stabilized large-scale Vietnamese immigration into Cambodia began.   These new immigrants are believed to include many of those who had migrated to Vietnam 1970-1978.[216] To arrive at our estimation of 500,000 Vietnamese currently in Cambodia, we have annually (from 1980 to 1991) migrated 41,666 Vietnamese into Cambodia. We have chosen a figure of 500,000 Vietnamese currently in Cambodia because it is in the range (300,000-600,000) of most estimates by less interested observers and is admitted by Phnom Penh officials to the Economist Intelligence Unit.[217]

1981-1983   Few arrivals to Thai camps were documented during the period.[218]

1984-1985   At the end of 1984, 208,995 Cambodians were pushed into Thailand from their camps on the Cambodian side of the border; this followed the offensive launched by the Vietnamese in November 1984.[219] In early 1985, toward the end of the Vietnamese offensive, we have assumed that Khmer Rouge military and associated civilian populations crossed into Thailand. Estimates of this "hidden population" vary widely, but generally range from 50,000 to 100,000.[220] We have assumed a figure of 70,000.

From 1984-1991, natural increase in the camps is estimated to be high, three percent; this accounts for increase in the population of the camps of almost 57,000 from 1984-1991, exclusive of migration.

1986-1989   Our figures for refugee movements during this period are rough estimates. There was a great deal of movement from Cambodia to the Thai border and back, Cambodians engaged in trade or the guerrilla struggle or just seeking UN-provided food. To arrive at our estimates, we have extrapolated to the total camp population from "date of arrival data" from James Lynch's *Demographic Study of the Border Khmer*.[221] We then combined these estimates with documented arrival data from the UNHCR which covers arrival of refugees only (genuine refugees are housed separately from the displaced persons making up the bulk of the Cambodian refugee population in Thailand; refugees under the care of the UNHCR were not included in Lynch's study).[222]

1990-1991   Data for these years include only UNHCR registered arrivals of refugees.[223]

1992   UN officials acknowledged in early 1992 that there had been a considerable number of new migrants to the Thai camps in early 1992; this was likely caused by the pull of the announced UNHCR Repatriation Plan which provides substantial benefits, valued at US$570, to those repatriated under UN auspices.[224] But, on the other hand, many Cambodians returned to Cambodia ahead of plan to lay claim to unoccupied land or were encouraged to return to "liberated areas" by the Khmer Rouge.[225] We have assumed that these movements canceled each other, resulting in zero net international migration prior to the UN-sponsored repatriation.

Although the repatriation plan reportedly fell behind schedule, UNHCR endeavored to return to Cambodian territory all Cambodian refugees in time for the elections (May 1993) even if this was done outside of the original repatriation and resettlement plan. Under the revised UNHCR estimates, about 220,000 refugees were to be returned in 1992.[226]

Small numbers of Cambodians are also beginning to return from third countries; these returnees have been excluded from the migration streams.

In order to model the age-sex structure of those being repatriated from Thailand, we have used Lynch's estimates of the composition of the border camp population[227] applied to the estimated number of returnees for both 1992 and 1993.

1993   Under the revised UNHCR plan, about 150,000 refugees were to be repatriated in 1993. The United Nations hoped to have all but "negligible" numbers returned before the elections in May 1993.[228]

Table A-1.   Cambodia Assumed International Migration

Year	To/From Thailand	To/From Vietnam	Cambodia net intl. migration
1970	0	-195,000	-195,000
1971	-8,500	-30,000	-38,500
1972	-8,500	-30,000	-38,500
1973	-8,500	-30,000	-38,500
1974	-8,500	-30,000	-38,500
1975	-17,038	-37,500	-54,538
1976	-6,428	-37,500	-43,928
1977	-7,045	-37,500	-44,545
1978	-3,528	-37,500	-41,028
1979	-137,894	100,000	-37,894
1980	-34,586	41,666	7,080
1981	-16	41,666	41,650
1982	-14	41,666	41,652
1983	0	41,666	41,666
1984	-208,995		
		41,666	
			-167,329
1985	-70,000	41,666	-28,334
1986	-4,997	41,666	36,669
1987	-5,769	41,666	35,897
1988	-4,410	41,666	37,256
1989	-6,936	41,666	34,730
1990	-1,551	41,666	40,115
1991	-1,157	41,666	40,509
1992	220,000	0	220,000
1993	150,000	0	150,000
Net Migration	-174,364	134,992	-39,372

Note: A positive number indicates migration into Cambodia. A negative number indicates migration from Cambodia to other countries.

---

[1] Our spelling of Cambodian place-names in this report is based on the standardized U.S. government transcription system.

[2] George S. Siampos. 1970. "The Population of Cambodia 1945-1980." *Milbank Memorial Fund Quarterly*, Vol. XLVIII, No. 3, July 1970: 317-360: 337.

[3] United Nations. 1981. *World Population Prospects as Assessed in 1980*. New York: Tables A-9, A-15.

[4] U.S. Department of State. 1987. "Background Notes—Cambodia." Washington, D.C.: 5-7.

[5] FBIS. 1976. Foreign Broadcast Information Service. *Asia and Pacific Daily Report*, Vol. IV, No. 63; CIA. 1980. Central Intelligence Agency. *Kampuchea: A Demographic Catastrophe*. Washington, D.C.; Ea, Meng-Try. 1987. "Recent Population Trends in Kampuchea." In David A. Ablin and Marlowe Hood, eds. *The Cambodian Agony*. Armonk: M.E. Sharpe: 3-15: 5.

[6] Ea Meng-Try, 1987: 7.

[7] *Ibid.*: 7, 10.

[8] Eva Mysliwiec. 1988. *Punishing the Poor: The International Isolation of Kampuchea*. Oxford: Oxfam: 95.

[9] U.S. Department of State, 1987: 6.

[10] Ea Meng-Try, 1987: 6; Michael Vickery. 1986. *Kampuchea: Politics, Economics and Society*. Boulder: Lynne Rienner, 1986: 2-3.

[11] Linda Mason and Roger Brown. 1983. *Rice, Rivalry and Politics: Managing Cambodian Relief*. Notre Dame: University of Notre Dame Press: 6-10; Russell R. Ross, ed. 1990. *Cambodia: A Country Study*. Washington, D.C.: Library of Congress Federal Research Division: 48-70; François Ponchaud. 1977. *Cambodge Annee Zero. [Cambodia: Year Zero]. Joint Publications Research Service*, No. JPRS L/7334, Aug. 23, 1977; Hurst Hannum. 1989. "International Law and Cambodian Genocide: The Sounds of Silence." *Human Rights Quarterly*, No. 11: 82-138. There was considerable regional variation in suffering under the Khmer Rouge due to differences in the style of rule of the Khmer Rouge zone (regional) authorities and productivity of the land. For more information, see Michael Vickery. 1984. *Cambodia: 1975-982*. Singapore: South End Press.

[12] For histories of the Khmer Republic (Lon Nol period) and Democratic Kampuchea (Pol Pot era), see John Barron and Anthony Paul. 1977. *Murder of a Gentle Land*. New York: Thomas Y. Crowell Company; Ponchaud, 1977; William Shawcross. 1980. *Sideshow: Kissinger, Nixon, and the Destruction of Cambodia*. London: Fontana; David P. Chandler and Ben Kiernan, eds. 1983. *Revolution and Its Aftermath in Kampuchea: Eight Essays*. New Haven: Yale University Southeast Asia Studies; Craig Etcheson. 1984. *The Rise and Demise of Democratic Kampuchea*. Boulder: Westview; David A. Ablin and Marlowe Hood, eds. 1987. *The Cambodian Agony*. Armonk: M.E. Sharpe; and David P. Chandler. 1991. *The Tragedy of Cambodian History: Politics, War and Revolution Since 1945*. New Haven: Yale University Press.

[13] Mason and Brown: 11-12; Orlin Scoville. 1987. "Rebuilding Kampuchea's Food Supply." In David A. Ablin and Marlowe Hood, eds. *The Cambodian Agony*. Armonk: M.E. Sharpe: 263-290: 268-269.

[14] Throughout the study, we refer to the People's Republic of Kampuchea by a variety of commonly used names: State of Cambodia (SOC), to which the name was formally changed in 1989; "the Vietnamese-backed regime" or "the Vietnamese-installed regime," because the government came to power in the wake of the Vietnamese invasion; as well as "the Phnom Penh regime" and "the Phnom Penh administration."

[15] E. Paige Johnson. 1990. "International Law or International Politics? Recognition and Intervention: The Case of Cambodia." *Monterey Review*, 11:3, Fall 1990: 35-44.

[16] Since the Vietnamese withdrawal, there have been numerous reports of sightings of Vietnamese troops still in Cambodia (Hong Kong AFP. 1992b, "UNTAC Deputy Says No SRV Troops Discovered." *Foreign Broadcast Information Service Daily Report*, No. FBIS-EAS-92-092, May 12, 1992: 26). UNTAC officials have discovered three Vietnamese soldiers and have suggested that "[t]here are some more left" ("Akashi: 'More' Vietnamese Troops in Cambodia." 1993. Agence France Presse [Hong Kong]. *Foreign Broadcast Information Service Daily Report*, No. FBIS-EAS-93-043, Mar. 8, 1992:46). These three soldiers had married Cambodian women and were given citizenship cards by the Phnom Penh administration (Hong Kong AFP. 1993. "SRV Says Soldiers Left Behind Are Cambodians." *Foreign Broadcast Information Service Daily Report*, No. FBIS-EAS-93-039, Mar. 2, 1993: 37).

[17] Douglas Pike. 1991. "U.S. Policy Toward Indochina." Presented at the International Symposium on Indochinese Economic Reconstruction and International Economic Co-operation, Institute of Developing Economies, Tokyo, Nov. 13 -14, 1991: 9.

[18] UNHCR. 1991. United Nations High Commissioner for Refugees. "Information Bulletin No. 1—On Cambodia Repatriation Plan." Geneva: UNHCR Public Information, Oct. 7, 1991: 25; FBIS. 1992g. "Refugee Repatriation Centers 'Almost Completed'." SPK (Phnom Penh). *Foreign Broadcast Information Service Daily Report*, No. FBIS-EAS-92-057, Mar. 24, 1992: 23-24; FBIS. 1992h. "Thai, Indonesian Ministers on Cambodian Refugees." Voice of Free Asia, in Thai (Bangkok). *Foreign Broadcast Information Service Daily Report*, No. FBIS-EAS-92-046, Mar. 9, 1992: 46.

[19] As of July 20, 1992, 56,568 refugees had been returned to Cambodia (Bangkok Radio Thailand. 1992. "56,568 Cambodian Refugees Repatriated Since March." Bangkok [in Thai]. *Foreign Broadcast Information Service Daily Report*, No. FBIS-EAS-92-146, July 29, 1992: 35). Although the repatriation plan is reportedly falling behind schedule, UNHCR will endeavor to return to Cambodian territory all Cambodian refugees in time for the elections even if this is done outside of the original repatriation and resettlement plan. Delaying the process has been the lack of available (vacant and mine-free)

land for returning refugees in the Western part of Cambodia to which they wish to return. The United Nations has shifted emphasis from first locating land for the refugees to moving the returnees into Cambodia and then either finding land for them or providing them with a lump sum of money to enable them to make their own arrangements with relatives, etc. Those who elect to wait for available land will become, in effect, internally displaced persons until enough land can be found. Several thousand refugees have refused to register to return, still hoping for resettlement in a third country (Jay Solomon. 1992. "Going Nowhere." *Far Eastern Economic Review*, Sept. 17, 1992: 56).

[20] Murray Hiebert. 1991b. "Exit Heng Samrin." *Far Eastern Economic Review*, Oct. 31, 1991: 11-13: 11.

[21] *Ibid.*: 11.

[22] The remaining 10-20 percent of Cambodia is controlled by the various resistance factions. Resistance control is concentrated in Batdambang, Banteay Meanchey and Siemreab-Otdar Meanchey provinces; see Map 1 (Frederick Z. Brown. 1992. "Cambodia in 1991." *Asian Survey*, Vol. 32, No. 1, Jan. 1992: 88-96: 93). Since the Peace Agreement was signed, however, there have been continued clashes between Phnom Penh and Khmer Rouge forces for control of territory (Nayan Chanda. 1992b. "Hun Sen Warns That a Failure to Implement Cambodia Peace Plan May Benefit Khmer Rouge." *The Asian Wall Street Journal Weekly*, Apr. 6, 1992: 3, 24: 3). On July 1, 1992, in response to Khmer Rouge complaints that the SOC administration had not been dismantled as was called for in the Peace Agreement, UNTAC activated the "civil administration component" of the Peace Accord; this will allow the United Nations to exercise direct control over Cambodia's foreign affairs, defense, finance, and public security organs. The UN will reportedly also have "optional control" over a number of other aspects of administration such as public health, education, and agriculture ("UNTAC Begins Civil Administrative Control." 1992. *Bangkok Post* (Bangkok). *Foreign Broadcast Information Service Daily Report*, No. FBIS-EAS-92-129, July 6, 1992: 34). UNTAC Chief Yasushi Akashi has ruled out the complete dismantling of the Phnom Penh administrative structure as demanded by the Khmer Rouge (Sheri Prasso. 1992a. "Akashi Refuses KR Demand on Phnom Penh Regime." Agence France Presse (Hong Kong). *Foreign Broadcast Information Service Daily Report*, No. FBIS-EAS-92-149, Aug. 3, 1992: 25; "Akashi Rules Vietnamese Can Vote in Elections." 1992. Agence France Presse (Hong Kong). *Foreign Broadcast Information Service Daily Report*, No. FBIS-EAS-92-152, Aug. 6, 1992: 26).

[23] Representation in the Constituent Assembly will be proportional to the numbers of registered voters by province, and representatives will be selected on the basis of lists of candidates put forward by the political parties.

[24] R.H.F. Austin, 1992, personal communication.

[25] "UNTAC Chief Signs Cambodian Election Laws." 1992. SPK (Phnom Penh). *Foreign Broadcast Information Service Daily Report*, No. FBIS-EAS-92-161, Aug. 19, 1992: 20-21: 20.

[26] Khmer Rouge leader Khieu Samphan has said, "If the SNC remains without power or means[,] then UNTAC . . . is cooperating with the Phnom Penh regime. This means that elections will certainly be held within the framework of the regime set up by the Vietnamese . . . We will never accept this, and cannot participate in elections or political activity under such conditions" (Nate Thayer. 1992a. "Fighting Words." *Far Eastern Economic Review,* Aug. 20, 1992: 8-9: 9).

[27] Voice of the Great National Union Front of Cambodia. 1992a. "Regime Naturalizing Vietnamese Before Elections." Voice of the Great National Union Front of Cambodia (in Cambodian). *Foreign Broadcast Information Service Daily Report,* No. FBIS-EAS-92-099, May 21, 1992: 24-25: 24.

[28] "Foreign Minister on KR Stance in UN Troops." 1992. Agence France Presse (Hong Kong). *Foreign Broadcast Information Service Daily Report,* No. FBIS-EAS-92-067, Apr. 7, 1992: 24-25: 24.

[29] Voice of the Great National Union Front of Cambodia. 1992b. "Vietnamese 'Aggressors' Said Living in Phnom Penh." Voice of the Great National Union Front of Cambodia (in Cambodian). *Foreign Broadcast Information Service Daily Report,* No. FBIS-EAS-92-099, May 21, 1992: 25; Voice of the Khmer. 1992. "Son Sann on 'Very Successful' Tokyo Meeting." Voice of the Khmer (in Cambodian). *Foreign Broadcast Information Service Daily Report,* No. FBIS-EAS-92-130, July 7, 1992: 40-44: 41; "Ranariddh Discusses Tokyo Aid Conference." 1992. Voice of the Khmer (in Cambodian). *Foreign Broadcast Information Service Daily Report,* No. FBIS-EAS-92-127, July 1, 1992: 30-34: 32.

[30] Michael Vickery. 1991a. "The Cambodian Economy: Where Has It Come From, Where Is It Going?" Presented at the International Symposium on Indochinese Economic Reconstruction and International Economic Co-operation, Institute of Developing Economies, Tokyo, Nov. 1991: 7. Vickery alludes to the "year Zero" of the Khmer Rouge. The radical Communists believed that only by starting from the beginning, from the "year Zero," and destroying everything that came before could they reach their vision of utopia. Vickery implies that, after the disastrous Khmer Rouge years, developing the ruined economy truly was like starting over.

[31] *Ibid.:* 7-8.

[32] *Ibid.:* 7.

[33] Vickery, 1984: 219; Vickery, 1986: 138; François Ponchaud. 1979. "The Vietnamese Engage in Serious Acts of Plunder in Cambodia." *Le Monde* (Paris). "Refugees Report Hardship, Vietnamese Misconduct." *Joint Publications Research Service Translations on South and East Asia,* No. 828, June 19, 1979: 74-76: 76.

[34] Barry S. Levy and Daniel C. Susott. 1986. "Historical Context and Brief Overview of the Relief Operation." in *Years of Horror, Days of Hope.* Barry S. Levy and Daniel C. Susott, eds. Millwood, New York: Associated Faculty Press: xix-xxii: xx. It is clear from agricultural data that the amount of rice (production as well as imports/aid) available in Cambodia in 1980 was

comparable to levels available throughout the early 1980s; rice availability was more limited in 1979 (USDA mimeograph on annual rice production in Cambodia). Regional famine occurred, in part, due to overall food shortage as well as the difficulties of distributing the food to the most severely food-deficit areas (François Nivolon. 1980. "Aid Distribution, Services Seen as Improved." *Le Figaro* [in French]. *Joint Publications Research Service South and East Asia Report,* No. 901, June 26, 1980: 139-143: 140).

[35] Levy and Susott, 1986: xxii; Scoville, 1987: 278.

[36] Economist Intelligence Unit. 1991. *Indochina: Vietnam, Laos, Cambodia Country Profile 1991-92.* London: Business International, Ltd.: 64.

[37] Robin Davies. 1992. "Economist Explains Riel Fluctuations." *Bangkok Post* (Bangkok). *Joint Publications Research Service,* No. JPRS-SEA-92-006, Apr. 8, 1992: 4-5: 4.

[38] Vickery, 1991a: 9.

[39] Cham Prasidh. 1992b. Speech to the U.S. NGO Forum on Viet Nam, Cambodia and Laos, Stony Brook, New York, June 14, 1992.

[40] UNICEF. 1990. United Nations Children's Fund. *Cambodia: The Situation of Children and Women.* Phnom Penh: UNICEF Office of the Special Representative: 26.

[41] Richard Vokes. 1991. "Economy." *The Far East and Australasia 1991.* London: Europa: 272-275: 273.

[42] Vokes, 1991: 273; ADB. 1992. Asian Development Bank. *Cambodia: Socio-Economic Needs and Immediate Needs.* Produced jointly with the International Monetary Fund, United Nations Development Programme and the World Bank. May 1992.

[43] Vokes, 1991: 273.

[44] "Foreign Minister Asks World Help for Food Shortages." 1992. Agence France Presse (Hong Kong). May 23, 1992.

[45] Vokes, 1991: 274.

[46] *Ibid.*

[47] *Ibid.*; Vickery, 1991a: 11.

[48] Murray Hiebert. 1989. "War Against Want." *Far Eastern Economic Review,* July 13, 1989: 72-74: 72.

[49] Andrew Sherry. 1992a. "Disarming to Begin June 13, 1992." Agence France Presse (Hong Kong). *Foreign Broadcast Information Service Daily Report,* No. FBIS-EAS-92-091, May 11, 1992, pp. 31-32: 31.

[50] The demobilization, part of Phase II of the implementation of the Paris Peace Agreement, was scheduled to begin on June 13, 1992. Phase II was delayed, however, by the Khmer Rouge, who have been unwilling to participate in the cantonment (the sending of troops into United Nations-supervised military camps), disarming and demobilization of their troops. The Khmer Rouge have cited a continued Vietnamese military presence in Cambodia and foreign aid to the SOC, as well as the necessity for dismantling the Phnom Penh administration as reasons for their refusal to participate in Phase II (Nate Thayer. 1992c. "The War Party." *Far Eastern Economic*

Review, June 25, 1992: 12.). By August 3, 1992, slightly fewer than 18,000 of the troops of the other three factions had been placed under UN supervision ("Soldiers Released from Barracks to Plant Rice." 1992. Agence France Presse (Hong Kong). *Foreign Broadcast Information Service Daily Report,* No. FBIS-EAS-92-151, Aug. 5, 1992: 33.).

[51] "Cambodian Peace Prompts Banditry, 'Quick Profits'." 1991. *The Nation* (Bangkok). *Foreign Broadcast Information Service Daily Report,* No. FBIS-EAS-91-184, Sept. 11, 1991: 46-47: 46.

[52] Mysliwiec, 1988: 73.

[53] *Bangkok Post.* 1992. "Problems of Daily Life, Peace Accord Viewed." *Bangkok Post* (Bangkok). *Foreign Broadcast Information Service Daily Report,* No. FBIS-EAS-92-037, Feb. 25, 1992: 55-56: 55; Murray Hiebert. 1990a. "Hammerblow for Hanoi." *Far Eastern Economic Review,* July 5, 1990: 44-45: 44.

[54] Cham Prasidh. 1992a. Speech to the U.S. NGO Forum on Viet Nam, Cambodia and Laos, Stony Brook, New York, June 13, 1992.

[55] Harish Mehta. 1992. "Peace Dividend." *Singapore Business,* Apr. 1992: 16-23: 16.

[56] Murray Hiebert. 1992. "Baht Imperialism." *Far Eastern Economic Review,* June 25, 1992: 46-47.

[57] *Ibid.:* 46.

[58] Mehta, 1992: 18.

[59] Sarah Newhall. 1992. Speech to the U.S. NGO Forum on Viet Nam, Cambodia and Laos, Stony Brook, New York, June 13, 1992; William, Branigin. 1992c. "U.N. Influx Livens Phnom Penh Nights." *Washington Post,* June 22, 1992: A11, A14: A11.

[60] Brown, 1992: 94. The widening disparity between urban and rural lifestyles and alleged corruption of SOC officials are fueling the Khmer Rouge propaganda machine (*The Economist.* 1991. "Town and Country." *The Economist,* Nov. 23, 1991: 39).

[61] Branigin, 1992c: A11.

[62] Nate Thayer. 1992b. "Plunder of the State." *Far Eastern Economic Review,* Jan. 9, 1992: 11.

[63] Fritz Loebus. 1992. Speech to the U.S. NGO Forum on Viet Nam, Cambodia and Laos, Stony Brook, New York, June 14, 1992.

[64] "Central Bank Wants to Tie Riel Rate to Thai Baht." 1992. *Bangkok Post* (Bangkok), June 29, 1992: 13, 22.

[65] Raphael Pura. 1992a. "Cambodia Economy Nears Collapse as Funds Dry Up." *Asian Wall Street Journal Weekly,* Vol. XIV, No. 46, Nov. 16, 1992: 1, 20: 20.

[66] Hiebert, 1989: 72.

[67] *Ibid.*

[68] Anurat Maniphan. 1989. "Thai Correspondent Analyzes Economic Situation." *Bangkok Post* (Bangkok). *Foreign Broadcast Information Service Daily Report,* No. FBIS-EAS-89-244, Dec. 21, 1989: 33-35: 34.

[69] UNICEF, 1990: 17.

[70] Christopher J. Chipello. 1992. "Cambodia Gets Pledge of Aid for Rebuilding." *The Wall Street Journal,* June 23, 1992: A17. As of February 1993, however, only $94 million of the $880 million pledged had reached Cambodia (Prasso, 1993: 37).

[71] Sihanoukville was known as Kampong Saom until May of 1992.

[72] Fritz Loebus, 1992, personal communication.

[73] Cham Prasidh, 1992b.

[74] East-West Center. 1992. "Cambodia Primed for Oil Discoveries." *East-West Center Views,* May-June 1992: 3. The East-West Center's Charles Johnson, after a recent trip to Cambodia, estimates that Cambodia's reserves, based on data from neighboring countries, are in the range of 1.5 to 3.5 trillion cubic feet of gas and 50 to 100 million barrels of oil; by the year 2005, sales could reach US$600 million, creating about US$175 million in government income (East-West Center, 1992: 3).

[75] Siam Rat. 1992. "Thai Firm Surveys Investment, Economic Conditions." Bangkok (in Thai). *Joint Publications Research Service Daily Report,* No. JPRS-SEA-92-009, Apr. 23, 1992: 1-3: 3; UNDP. 1989. United Nations Development Programme. *Report of the Kampuchea Needs Assessment Study.* August 1989: xiv.

[76] UNICEF, 1990: 40; Siam Rat, 1992: 1-2.

[77] Jerrold W. Huguet. 1991. "The Demographic Situation in Cambodia." *Asia-Pacific Population Journal,* Vol. 6, No. 4, Dec. 1991: 79-91: 80.

[78] Hou Taing Eng. 1992. Data provided to the Population Reference Bureau, Washington, D.C.

[79] Our modeling of Cambodia's future population assumes no escalation of civil war.

[80] Huguet, 1991: 83.

[81] Ea Meng-Try, 1987: 11.

[82] Robert J. Muscat and Jonathan Stromseth. 1989. *Cambodia: Post Settlement Reconstruction and Development.* New York: East Asian Institute: 20; Huguet, 1991: 80.

[83] Warren Robinson. 1989. "Population Trends and Policies in Laos (Lao People's Democratic Republic) and Cambodia (Democratic Kampuchea)." *International Population Conference, New Delhi.* Vol. 1, Liège, Belgium: International Union for the Scientific Study of Population: 143-153: 148.

[84] *Ibid.*

[85] But a population table in Migozzi gives a total population figure of 7.14 million in 1970 (Jacques Migozzi. 1973. *Cambodge: Faits et Problemes de Population.* Paris: CNRS: 20, 212, 267).

[86] Ben Kiernan, 1992, personal communication.

[87] *Le Monde.* 1993. "Douze Millions d'Habitants?" *Le Monde* (Paris), Mar. 5, 1993: 5; Phnom Penh SPK. 1993. "KR Ignore Election Registration Deadline." *Foreign Broadcast Information Service Daily Report,* No. FBIS-EAS-93-018, Jan. 29, 1993: 43.

[88] *Le Monde*, 1993: 5.

[89] Hanoi Voice of Vietnam. 1992. "Cambodia Voter Registration, Khmer Rouge Viewed." *Foreign Broadcast Information Service Daily Report*, No. FBIS-EAS-92-199, Oct. 14, 1992: 41.

[90] Hou Taing Eng, 1992.

[91] Huguet, 1991: 80.

[92] Robinson, 1989: 150.

[93] Economist Intelligence Unit, 1991: 62.

[94] Abdul T.Y. Coyaume. 1992. "Health Situation in Cambodia." Presented to the Sectoral Workshop on Health, Prosthetics and Family Planning, U.S. NGO Forum on Viet Nam, Cambodia and Laos, Stony Brook, New York, June 13, 1992.

[95] *Ibid.l: 3.

[96] Newhall, 1992.

[97] Pheng Eng By. 1986. "Family Planning: The Perspective of a Cambodian Public-Health Nurse." In *Years of Horror, Days of Hope*. Barry S. Levy and Daniel C. Susott, eds. Millwood, New York: Associated Faculty Press: 214-215: 214.

[98] Newhall, 1992.

[99] Huguet, 1991: 79.

[100] Census of Cambodia. 1966. National Institute of Statistics and Economic Research. *Resultats Finals Du Recensement General De La Population 1962 [Final Results of the General Census of the Population 1962]*. Phnom Penh: 27.

[101] *Ibid.*: 7, 14, 27.

[102] Peter Kunstadter, ed. 1967. *Southeast Asian Tribes, Minorities, and Nations*: (2 volumes). Princeton: Princeton University Press: 867.

[103] *Ibid*.

[104] Economist Intelligence Unit, 1991: 62.

[105] Ea Meng-Try, 1987: 7-8.

[106] *The Nation*. 1991. "SRV Relations 'Strained' After Peace Accord." *The Nation* (Bangkok). *Foreign Broadcast Information Service Daily Report*, No. FBIS-EAS-91-226, Nov. 22, 1991: 33; Economist Intelligence Unit, 1991: 62; Branigan, 1992c: A14.

[107] Ben Kiernan, 1992, personal communication. [Independent estimates of the total ethnic Vietnamese population in Cambodia in 1992-1993 vary from 150,000 to 200,000-500,000. Sheila McNulty, AP, Phnom Penh, 26 March 1993, and Mark Dodd, Reuter, Phnom Penh, 26 March and 3 June, 1993, give the different estimates.—Ed.]

[108] *Le Monde*, 1993: 5.

[109] Frederick Z. Brown. 1993. "Cambodia in 1992." *Asian Survey*, 33:1, Jan. 1993: 83-90: 89.

[110] W.E. Willmott. 1981. "The Chinese in Kampuchea." *Journal of Southeast Asian Studies*, Vol. XII, No. 1, Mar. 1981: 38-45: 39-40.

[111] Ben Kiernan. 1986. "Kampuchea's Ethnic Chinese Under Pol Pot: A Case of Systematic Social Discrimination." *Journal of Contemporary Asia,* Vol. 16, No. 1: 18-29.

[112] *Ibid.*: 18.

[113] *Ibid.*: 19-20.

[114] Willmott, 1981: 45.

[115] Hong Kong AFP, 1989, "80,000 Civilians Reported in Cambodia." Agence France Presse (Hong Kong). *Foreign Broadcast Information Service Daily Report,* No. FBIS-EAS-91-210, Oct. 30, 1991: 37: 61. Kawi Chongkitthawon. 1991. "Postwar Political Developments Previewed." *The Nation* (Bangkok). *Foreign Broadcast Information Service Daily Report,* No. FBIS-EAS-91-215, Nov. 6, 1991: 33.

[116] Ross, 1990: 100.

[117] Ben Kiernan. 1990. "The Genocide in Cambodia, 1975-1979." *Bulletin of Concerned Asian Scholars,* Vol. 22, No. 2: 35-40: 35.

[118] Ross, 1990: 101.

[119] Census of Cambodia, 1966: 45-58.

[120] Census of Cambodia. 1970. National Institute of Statistics and Economic Research. *Additif Aux Resultats Du Recensement General De La Population 1962 [Supplement to the Results of the General Census of the Population 1962].* Phnom Penh: 1-2, 7-9.

[121] UNICEF, 1990: xiii-xiv.

[122] *Ibid.*: 91.

[123] *Ibid.*

[124] ADB, 1992.

[125] Brian Hunter, ed. 1991. *The Statesman's Yearbook 1991-1992.* London: MacMillan: 265.

[126] Britannica. 1991. *1991 Britannica Book of the Year.* Chicago: Encyclopedia Britannica: 566; Economist Intelligence Unit, 1991: 64.

[127] ADB, 1992: 9.

[128] *Ibid.*

[129] Kawi Chongkitthawon. 1989. "'Khmerization' of Education Reportedly Planned." *The Nation* (Bangkok). *Foreign Broadcast Information Service Daily Report,* No. FBIS-EAS-89-229, Nov. 30, 1989: 38-39: 38.

[130] Phnom Penh SPK. 1991a. "12th National Education Conference Opens." SPK (Phnom Penh). *Foreign Broadcast Information Service Daily Report,* No. FBIS-EAS-91-169, Aug. 30, 1991: 45.

[131] Phnom Penh SPK. 1991b. "176 Students to Study in SRV in 1991-92." SPK (Phnom Penh). *Foreign Broadcast Information Service Daily Report,* No. FBIS-EAS-91-079, Apr. 24, 1991: 33-34: 34; SWB. 1991. *Summary of World Broadcasts.* "Education Conference Told of Increase in Student Numbers." SPK (Phnom Penh). *Summary of World Broadcasts,* No. FE/W0196, Sept. 11, 1991: A6.

[132] Josiane Volkmar-Andre. 1986. "Medical Care Inside Kampuchea." In *Years of Horror, Days of Hope.* Barry S. Levy and Daniel C. Susott, eds. Millwood, New York: Associated Faculty Press: 273-285: 274.

[133] UNICEF, 1990: 44.

[134] UNDP. 1990. United Nations Development Programme. "Cambodia Infrastructure Survey Mission, 18 June-15 July 1990." In *Report of the Cambodia Infrastructure Survey Missions.* New York: September 1990: II-151; Coyaume, 1992: 1.

[135] Coyaume, 1992: 1.

[136] *Ibid.*

[137] UNICEF, 1990: 61-75; Coyaume, 1992: 1.

[138] Coyaume, 1992: 2.

[139] *Ibid.*: 4.

[140] UNICEF, 1990: 45.

[141] Phnom Penh SPK. 1991c. "SPK Quotes AFP on UNICEF Seminar." SPK (Phnom Penh). *Foreign Broadcast Information Service Daily Report,* No. FBIS-EAS-91-132, July 10, 1991: 53.

[142] UNDP, 1990:49-53; UNHCR. 1992a. "Going Home." *Refugees,* No. 88, Jan. 1992: 6-11: 9.

[143] UNICEF, 1990: 49-53; Coyaume, 1992: 2; UNDP, 1990: II-162, II-168.

[144] Possible avenues for the introduction or spread of AIDS in Cambodia include: enhanced transport and communication links with Thailand and returning refugees from Thailand, where the disease is spreading at an alarming rate; the large influx of foreigners in conjunction with the United Nations peace-keeping operation as well as international and non-governmental development projects; and the increased number of tourists which the regime hopes to attract for the perceived economic benefits.

[145] Agence France Presse. 1990. "Official on Risk of AIDS from Transfusions." Agence France Presse (Hong Kong). *Foreign Broadcast Information Service,* No. FBIS-EAS-90-243, Dec. 18, 1990: 33-34.. Khmer Rouge army radio claimed in 1990 that in Phnom Penh city and Kaoh Kong province there were already 35 AIDS patients, 45 AIDS carriers (HIV-positive individuals who have not yet developed full-blown AIDS) and 20 dead from the disease (VNADK. 1990. Voice of the National Army of Democratic Kampuchea. "AIDS Cases in Phnom Penh, Koh Kong Cited." Voice of the National Army of Democratic Kampuchea (in Cambodian). *Foreign Broadcast Information Service Daily Report,* No. FBIS-EAS-90-134, July 12, 1990: 41). The Khmer Rouge insist the disease was spread by Vietnamese prostitutes, and used this accusation to attack the "Vietnamese aggressors and the traitorous Hun Sen/Heng Samrin regime" (VNADK, 1992: 41). No evidence in support of these claims was presented.

[146] William Branigin. 1992a. "Key Phases of U.N. Peace Operation in Cambodia Seen Breaking Down." *The Washington Post,* Oct. 4, 1992: A33, A34.

[147] UNICEF, 1990: 46-49.

[148] *Ibid.*: 20-35.

[149] UNHCR. 1992b. "De-Mining." *Refugees,* No. 88, Jan. 1992: 12-15: 14.

[150] Hong Kong AFP. 1992a. "Factions Refuse to be First to Mark Minefields." *Foreign Broadcast Information Service Daily Report,* No. FBIS-EAS-92-082, Apr. 28, 1992: 34.

[151] Susan Walker. 1992. Speech to the U.S. NGO Forum on Viet Nam, Cambodia and Laos, Stony Brook, New York, June 13, 1992.

[152] Jon Liden. 1991. "A Coward's War." *Far Eastern Economic Review,* Nov. 21, 1991: 58.

[153] UNHCR, 1992b: 13; Rodney Mearns, 1992, personal communication.

[154] UNHCR, 1992b: 13.

[155] "If Only." 1991. *The Economist,* May 18, 1991: 42-44: 42.

[156] Rodney Mearns, 1992, personal communication.

[157] UNHCR, 1992b: 13.

[158] Coyaume, 1992: 3-4.

[159] *Ibid.*

[160] In 1990 it was estimated that the government allotted only US$0.20 per person per year for medical care.

[161] However, there are no reliable figures on the actual size of the economically active population or on what proportion of the approximately 5.14 million people ages 15-64 are economically active.

[162] Economist Intelligence Unit, 1991: 66; Britannica, 1991: 566.

[163] UNICEF, 1990: 26.

[164] UNDP, 1989: 32.

[165] Ross, 1990: 145.

[166] UNICEF, 1990: 111, 115. According to the 1962 Census, 46 percent of all agricultural workers were women (Census of Cambodia, 1966: 53).

[167] Vickery, 1984: 24.

[168] Martin Stuart-Fox. 1985. *The Murderous Revolution: Life and Death in Pol Pot's Kampuchea.* Chippendale, Australia: Alternative Publishing Cooperative Ltd.: 19.

[169] Phnom Penh Domestic Service. 1990. "Project to Expand Phnom Penh Housing Reported." Phnom Penh Domestic Service (in Cambodian). *Foreign Broadcast Information Service Daily Report,* No. FBIS-EAS-90-158, Aug. 15, 1990: 50-51: 51; Ponchaud, 1977: 40; UNICEF, 1990: 9-11.

[170] UNICEF, 1990: 10-11; Hun Sen. 1991. ""Hun Sen Addresses Party Congress 17 Oct." Kampuchea Radio Network, in Cambodian (Phnom Penh). *Foreign Broadcast Information Service Daily Report,* No. FBIS-EAS-91-203, Oct. 21, 1991: 40-47: 41.

[171] Hou Taing Eng, 1992.

[172] UNFPA. 1989. United Nations Population Fund. *Inventory of Population Projects in Developing Countries Around the World 1988/1989.* New York: 89.

[173] Economist Intelligence Unit, 1991: 63.

[174] It is not unusual in Communist countries for officials to ignore anything after a decimal place, rather than rounding numbers up to the next whole number when the decimal is above .5.

[175] Huguet, 1991: 84; Hou Taing Eng, 1992.

[176] Hou Taing Eng, 1992.

[177] Huguet, 1991: 84.

[178] Phnom Penh Domestic Service, 1990: 50-51.

[179] UNDP, 1989: xix.

[180] Walter Grazer and Shep Lowman. 1992. "The Cambodian Repatriation: A Special Trip Report with Recommendations January 12-20, 1992." United States Catholic Conference, Migration and Refugee Services. April 1992: 3.

[181] James F. Lynch. 1989. *Border Khmer: A Demographic Study of the Residents of Site 2, Site B, and Site 8.* Bangkok: Nov. 1989: 32.

[182] Huguet, 1991: 87.

[183] *Ibid.*: 84-87.

[184] The figures for nine provinces are given in Table 3. When taken with those provided in the text for Prey Veng, Takev, and Phnom Penh provinces, there are recent available data for 12 of Cambodia's 21 provinces. For the remaining nine provinces, no recent data are available, except those extrapolated directly from the 1980 survey.

[185] Huguet, 1991: 85-88.

[186] Lynch surveyed KPNLF-controlled Site 2, FUNCINPEC's Site B and the Khmer Rouge's Site 8 camp.

[187] *Ibid.*: 15, 21.

[188] *Ibid.*: 21. The sex ratio is the number of males per hundred females. This table is modified from Lynch.

[189] *Ibid.*: 23.

[190] *Ibid.*: 25.

[191] *Ibid.*: 24.

[192] A recent Cambodia trip report by Walter Grazer and Shep Lowman lists the total camp populations in Thailand as 367,842 (Grazer and Lowman, 1992: 3).

[193] Lynch, 1989: 21.

[194] FBIS. 1992e. "Government Seeks UN Assurance on Refugees." *Bangkok Post* (Bangkok). *Foreign Broadcast Information Service Daily Report,* No. FBIS-EAS-92-050, Mar. 13, 1992. pp. 52-53: 52.

[195] The western provinces selected by most of the returning refugees are heavily mined. A three-month survey by Britain's HALO Trust estimated that in the four provinces, Siemreab, Batdambang, Banteay Meanchey, and Pouthisat, there were at least 400,000 mines (UNHCR, 1992b:14).

[196] Grazer and Lowman, 1992: 1.

[197] Graeme Hugo. 1987. "Postwar Refugee Migration in Southeast Asia: Patterns, Problems, and Policies." in *Refugees, a Third World Dilemma.* John

R. Rogge, ed. Totowa, New Jersey: Rowman & Littlefield: 237-252: Table 24.4; Court Robinson, 1992, personal communication.

[198] Hugo, 1987: 244.

[199] Vietnam 1989 Sample Census. 1990. *Vietnam Population Census - 1989: Sample Results.* Hanoi: Central Census Steering Committee: Table 2.1.

[200] Agence France Presse. 1991. "New Political Party Announces Formation." Agence France Presse (Hong Kong). *Foreign Broadcast Information Service Daily Report,* No. FBIS-EAS-91-214, Nov. 5, 1991: 23.

[201] Thida Khus. 1992. Speech to the U.S. NGO Forum on Viet Nam, Cambodia and Laos, Stony Brook, New York, June 15, 1992.

[202] Nessim Shallon. 1992. Speech to the U.S. NGO Forum on Viet Nam, Cambodia and Laos, Stony Brook, New York, June 15, 1992; Frances Sullivan. 1992. Speech to the U.S. NGO Forum on Viet Nam, Cambodia and Laos, Stony Brook, New York, June 15, 1992.

[203] Sheri Prasso. 1991. "Banker Warns Foreign Investors About Problems." Agence France Presse (Hong Kong). *Foreign Broadcast Information Service Daily Report,* No. FBIS-EAS-91-225, Nov. 21, 1991: 31-33: 32.

[204] Khus, 1992; Susumu Awanohara. 1991. "Rouge, White and Blue." *Far Eastern Economic Review,* Nov. 21, 1991: 55-56. It is estimated that in the first three months of 1992 US$50-US$60 million had been received in remittances from abroad (*The Nation.* 1992. "Bank Governor Discusses Business Activity." *The Nation* [Bangkok]. *Foreign Broadcast Information Service Daily Report,* No. FBIS-EAS-92-072, Apr. 14, 1992. pp. 30-32: 31).

[205] Even our wide range of population estimates for 1992 does not encompass all possibilities. In a recent speech in Indonesia, Prince Norodom Rannariddh, Sihanouk's son and head of the FUNCINPEC faction, stated Cambodia's population as "about 12 million" (Antara. 1992. "Cambodia's Rannariddh Arrives." Antara (Jakarta). *Foreign Broadcast Information Service Daily Report,* No. FBIS-EAS-92-092, May 12, 1992: 1.).

[206] Huguet, 1991: 79.

[207] Ea Meng-Try, 1987: 7.

[208] Nayan Chanda. 1981. "The Survivors' Party." *Far Eastern Economic Review,* June 22, 1981: 22.

[209] Mysliwiec, 1988: 95.

[210] *Ibid.*; UNHCR mimeograph on Indochinese refugees, 1992.

[211] United Nations. 1990. *World Population Monitoring 1989: Special Report, The Population Situation in the Least Developed Countries.* New York: 225; Hugo, 1987: 244.

[212] United Nations, 1990: 225.

[213] Ea Meng-Try, 1987: 7.

[214] John R. Rogge. 1990. *Return To Cambodia.* Dallas: Intertect Institute, Mar. 1990: 31.

[215] Richard Nations. 1979. "Chinese Fleeing Cambodia Pour Over Thai Border." *The Washington Post,* May 18, 1979: A32.

[216] Ea Meng-Try, 1987: 10.

[217] *The Nation*, 1991: 33; Economist Intelligence Unit, 1991: 62; Branigin, 1992c: A14.

[218] Rogge, 1990: 31.

[219] Derived from *Ibid.*; USCR, 1984: 39.

[220] Rodney Tasker. 1989. "Khmer Rouge Role." *Far Eastern Economic Review,* June 29, 1989: 19-20: 20; "The Refugees." 1991. *Indochina Chronology,* Vol. X, No. 1, Jan. - Mar. 1991: 25.

[221] Lynch, 1989: 26.

[222] UNHCR mimeograph on Indochinese refugees, 1992.

[223] *Ibid.*

[224] FBIS. 1992b. "Date for Refugee Repatriation May Be Imposed." Agence France Presse (Hong Kong). *Foreign Broadcast Information Service Daily Report,* No. FBIS-EAS-92-033, Feb. 19, 1992: 51; FBIS. 1992j. "UN Peacekeeping Operation Leaders Arrive." Agence France Presse (Hong Kong). *Foreign Broadcast Information Service Daily Report,* No. FBIS-EAS-92-051, Mar. 16, 1992: 42-43.

[225] FBIS. 1991a. "Khmer Rouge to Forcibly Repatriate 'Thousands'." Agence France Presse (Hong Kong). *Foreign Broadcast Information Service Daily Report,* No. FBIS-EAS-91-196, Oct. 9, 1991: 25-26; FBIS. 1991b. "Refugees to Move to Khmer Rouge Areas." *The Nation* (Bangkok). *Foreign Broadcast Information Service Daily Report,* No. FBIS-EAS-91-208, Oct. 28, 1991: 42-43.

[226] Charles-Antoine de Nerciat. 1992. "Refugee Repatriation Process Reviewed, Detailed." *Foreign Broadcast Information Service Daily Report,* No. FBIS-EAS-92-116, June 16, 1992: 28-29; derived from an assumed Cambodian population in Thailand of 370,000 at year-end 1991; UNHCR, 1991: 10; Mysliwiec, 1988: 99; Briefing. 1992. "More Money for Cambodian Refugees." *Far Eastern Economic Review,* Apr. 2, 1992: 14; FBIS, 1992f: 25; FBIS, 1992g: 23; UNDP. 1992. United Nations Development Programme. *Update,* Vol. 5, No. 9, May 4, 1992: 1.

[227] Lynch, 1989: 21.

[228] de Nerciat, 1992: 29.

The Cambodian Genocide and International Law

Gregory H. Stanton

Cambodia has been a party to the Genocide Convention since 1950. The mass killings committed in Democratic Kampuchea were in clear violation of all the major provisions of that Convention. Political killings are not covered by the Convention unless their intent is to destroy in whole or in part a national, ethnic, racial, or religious group, as such. The evidence has now been gathered that establishes beyond a reasonable doubt the Khmer Rouge intent to destroy Cham Muslims, Christians, Buddhist monks, and the Vietnamese and Chinese minorities.

The Khmer Rouge singled out certain religious and ethnic groups for elimination. A Khmer Rouge order reportedly stated that henceforth "The Cham nation no longer exists on Kampuchean soil belonging to the Khmers."[1] Whole Cham villages were destroyed and their inhabitants murdered. The half of the Cham who survived were forced to speak only Khmer, and their children were taken away to be raised collectively as Khmers (defined as genocide by the Convention's Article 2e). Buddhist monks were disrobed and subjected to especially harsh forced labor, killing over half of them. Christianity was abolished, and only one Christian pastor survived. Dr. Ben Kiernan has uncovered and translated a copy of the CPK Central Committee's order to demolish the Phnom Penh cathedral, part of the Khmer Rouge plan to eradicate all religion.[2] His research demonstrates that the Vietnamese and Chinese minorities were especially hard hit.[3] A crucial intent in the Eastern Zone massacres of 1978 was to eliminate all Eastern Zone people, because they had "Vietnamese minds."[4] All Cambodian ethnic Vietnamese who did not flee into Vietnam were exterminated.

To be punishable under the Genocide Convention, the destruction of a group must be intentional. Intent can be established by a systematic pattern that could only be the result of orders from the top of a pyramid of command. But intent can be proven more definitely through written orders or through testimony by witnesses to oral orders. Such direct evidence has now been collected.

The most dramatic evidence of central government intent in the genocide was collected on my trip to Kampuchea in December 1986. I interviewed numerous eye witnesses with Ben Kiernan. (The interviews were recorded on videotape.) The witnesses told us that when the Eastern Zone was evacuated in 1978, every person was given a blue and white checked scarf by Khmer Rouge cadres from Phnom Penh. Every man, woman, and child from the Eastern Zone thenceforth was required to wear the blue scarf. As numerous witnesses told me, it was "the killing sign." The Eastern Zone people were worked to death or slaughtered. Those who survived were only saved by the Vietnamese invasion. The blue scarves were given out as the evacuees passed through *Phnom Penh* (at Chbar Ampoeu), and were distributed by Khmer Rouge cadres acting on direct orders from the Communist Party Central Committee. The blue scarf in Kampuchea was the equivalent of the Nazi yellow star. It is the most dramatic proof that the genocide was ordered from the top by government leaders of Democratic Kampuchea.

The Genocide Convention sets forth three legal options for prosecution of those who commit genocide. Article 6 provides that 'persons charged with genocide... shall be tried by a competent tribunal of the State in the territory of which the act was committed, or by such international penal tribunal as may have jurisdiction with respect to those Contracting Parties which shall have accepted its jurisdiction.'[5]

The first legal option under the Genocide Convention, therefore, is trial in Cambodia.

In 1979, two of the architects of the genocide, Pol Pot and Ieng Sary, were tried *in absentia* in Phnom Penh. The evidence against them was massive. But the trial was a show trial. The pathetic "defense" offered by Hope Stevens, an aged communist from the New York branch of the Association of Democratic Lawyers, was actually a confession and a lame attempt to shift blame to Vietnam's current enemies, China and the U.S. The hearings departed far from standards of due process and objectivity. Although the verdict (guilty) was surely justified, it was pre-determined, as anyone who knows communist legal systems could have predicted.

This first option still remains open. Mok, Pauk, Deuch, Khieu Samphan, and Son Sen have never been tried. Pol Pot and Ieng Sary could be retried. Currently there are no plans to hold such a trial. When Prince Sihanouk spoke in favor of a trial in December 1991, he quickly added that it would not include the two Khmer Rouge on the Supreme National Council, Khieu Samphan and Son Sen.

If such a trial is held, and I hope it will be, it will only be after the Khmer Rouge have been politically defeated and removed from their seats on the Supreme National Council or a successor repository of Cambodian sovereignty. (That is unlikely before elections are held in 1993.)

A major defect of this option is that in the common law world, trials *in absentia* are not generally considered to fulfill the requirements of due process. Although one of the Nazis convicted at Nuremberg was tried *in absentia*, that trial was conducted under special rules. If objections of many common law lawyers to trials *in absentia* are to be met, the Khmer Rouge leaders must be captured. That task will not be easy, though it could be accomplished after the Khmer Rouge are defeated militarily. Even without full defeat of the Khmer Rouge, capture of their leaders might be achieved through use of sophisticated intelligence and surprise attack, but it would certainly require the use of armed force.

The second option is trial by an international tribunal. No permanent international criminal court has ever been established, as the drafters of the Genocide Convention originally had hoped. But a special tribunal could be established by treaty between Cambodia and other nations. The treaty would have to include Cambodia, or the tribunal would lack jurisdiction under current international law. Many law professors have advocated making genocide a crime of universal jurisdiction, but the Genocide Convention itself does not do so. For the tribunal to have jurisdiction, therefore, Cambodia would have to be a party to such a tribunal-creating treaty. This option, too, awaits a Cambodian government that excludes the Khmer Rouge; it could be convened only after the 1993 elections.

Trial by international tribunal would require capture of the Khmer Rouge leaders if the trial is to accord with due process requirements. So this option also demands the military defeat of the Khmer Rouge, or at least armed capture of their leaders.

The third option is for a party to the Genocide Convention to submit a dispute with Cambodia to the International Court of Justice.

Article 9 of the Convention states:

"Disputes between the Contracting Parties relating to the interpretation, application, or fulfillment of the present Convention, including those relating to the responsibilities of a State for genocide or any of the other acts enumerated in Article 3 [which include conspiracy, incitement, attempt, or complicity to commit genocide] shall be submitted to the International Court of Justice at the request of any of the parties to the dispute."

Any state that is a party without reservation to the Convention (including the Article 9 jurisdiction of the ICJ) could submit the case to the World Court. The complaint would contend that Cambodia has violated the Convention by failing to punish those responsible for committing genocide. It could currently charge that two members of the Supreme National Council, the entity recognized by the United Nations as representative of Cambodia, are themselves responsible for genocide; and that they remain unpunished.

Under Article 36 of the Statute of the International Court of Justice, the Court would have jurisdiction to hear the case. Article 36(1) gives the Court jurisdiction over all matters specially provided for in treaties and conventions in force. Article 9 of the Genocide Convention specially provides for World Court jurisdiction. Cambodia is a party to the jurisdiction conferred by Article 9 of the Genocide Convention.

Article 36(2) also gives the Court jurisdiction over all legal disputes in which the parties have recognized the compulsory jurisdiction of the Court concerning the existence of any fact which, if established, would constitute a breach of an international obligation as well as the nature or extent of the reparation to be made for the breach of an international obligation. Cambodia has accepted the compulsory jurisdiction of the Court. The World Court thus has clear jurisdiction to hear the case.

Any state that is a party to the Genocide Convention has standing to bring a case against Cambodia under the Genocide Convention. The legal requirement of standing is essentially that a state have a particular stake in bringing a case, through injuries to it or through treaty obligations owed to it.

The Genocide Convention itself is the basis for standing to bring a case. Under the Convention, any contracting party that has a dispute with another contracting party relating to the application or fulfillment of the Convention has standing to submit the case to the ICJ. This standing is based on the mutual obligations of the parties to fulfill the Convention.

Australia, Canada, Norway, and the U.K. have had a "dispute" with Cambodia as required by Article 9 since 1978. In 1978 those nations submitted statements to the U.N. Commission on Human

Rights that violations of human rights in Democratic Kampuchea were continuing, including voluminous evidence submitted by the U.S.A., Canada, Norway, and the U.K.[6] This evidence contained the factual basis for a charge of genocide. Democratic Kampuchea rejected the sub-commission's decision to appoint a member to analyze the materials submitted,[7] and it denied all allegations made in the years since. The dispute is ongoing. The Commission on Human Rights has voted each year to keep the situation in Cambodia on its agenda and has received evidence each year, including specific evidence of genocide.

The dispute is not moot, as it was in the *Nuclear Tests* case, because those persons guilty of genocide have never been punished by Cambodian authorities. In the *Nuclear Tests* case the problem was that the court held the dispute moot because France had ceased atmospheric nuclear tests. But in this case, the dispute over the responsibility of Cambodia for genocide continues. It will not be resolved without adjudication by an international court. The Khmer Rouge leadership remains free. They remain part of the Supreme National Council, which holds Cambodia's U.N. seat. And they still order mass murders. Their troops stop trains and machine gun passengers, including children. Their troops carry out genocidal massacres of ethnic Vietnamese in Cambodia. Reports by human rights groups recount continuing abuses and murders in Khmer Rouge controlled camps and areas.

Determination of responsibility for genocide—including past genocide—is specifically within the jurisdiction of the World Court under Convention Article 9.

The World Court would be able to hear the evidence in this case and render its judgment even if Cambodia does not answer the charges or appear before the Court. Because of its acceptance of the jurisdiction of the World Court, Cambodia has a self-imposed obligation to appear. But if it does not, the Court is nevertheless authorized by Article 53 of its Statute to hear the evidence and render its judgment. The Court has exercised this authority numerous times, e.g., in the *Corfu Channel* and *Iranian Hostages* cases.

An advantage of taking the Cambodian genocide case to the World Court instead of to an *ad hoc* tribunal is that Cambodia has already accepted the World Court's jurisdiction. Failure to appear by Cambodia thus would have greater significance, amounting to a confirmation of its disrespect for its obligations under international law.

A World Court case has the major advantage that it would not require capture of the Khmer Rouge leaders. The World Court is not a criminal court, and has no jurisdiction over individuals. The trial would not be of individuals, but rather of the Cambodian state, which in 1980 was still represented in the U.N. by the Khmer Rouge, in 1986 was represented by the Coalition Government of Democratic Kampuchea, which included the Khmer Rouge, and today is represented by the Supreme National Council, which includes two Khmer Rouge leaders, notably Son Sen, who was commander of the entire Khmer Rouge prison/extermination system.

What would a World Court judgment accomplish?

The World Court's judgment would be significant historically, but in addition it would have a direct legal impact on the people who ordered the genocide.

As part of its determination of state responsibility for genocide, it is possible for the court to declare who committed the genocide. Such a finding would call into effect the duty of all parties of the Genocide Convention to "provide effective penalties for persons guilty of genocide" and to grant extradition in accordance with their laws and treaties. It would thereby make the Khmer Rouge leaders into international outlaws, no longer able to roam much of the world from Bangkok and Beijing.

It would quite possibly reduce the support of the Khmer Rouge from other nations and thereby hasten their elimination as an obstacle to peace in Cambodia.

It would establish for all time what happened in Cambodia through a finding by an objective international court. By such a finding and through better understanding of the causes and process of genocide, perhaps future genocides might be prevented. For the people of Cambodia, the criminals who slaughtered their relatives, their religious leaders, and their children would be judged; not individually brought to justice, perhaps, but judged nevertheless.

I first proposed that a case be brought to the World Court in 1980, when I founded the Cambodian Genocide Project. Then the government that would have been served with the charges was the Khmer Rouge's Democratic Kampuchea itself, which still represented Cambodia in the U.N. I proposed that the evidence be gathered in a systematic way and the legal work be done to prepare the way for the case.

The Cambodian Genocide Project has since gathered evidence of the genocide committed in Democratic Kampuchea. That evidence and legal analysis and a draft complaint and memorial were made available to potential parties to a suit. But no government has ever been willing to take the case. It is doubtful that one will now, since a case might "upset the peace process." After elections in 1993, a new Cambodian government will be installed, probably without any Khmer Rouge, so that bringing a case to the World Court would be charging a successor regime, not the perpetrators. The time for a case in the World Court was in the 1980s, when the Khmer Rouge still represented Cambodia in the United Nations.

From the outset, I realized that submitting a case to the ICJ would take a resolute act of political will by a government. The legal issues would have to be resolved before any government would be likely to put its prestige and its money on the line as a plaintiff.

I proposed as a preliminary step that a distinguished group of jurists go to Cambodia to hold hearings, consider the evidence, apply international law, and issue an authoritative report on the Cambodian genocide. The commission would be composed of jurists who carry such personal authority that their conclusions would be accorded great weight by governments and legal experts around the world. They would serve the function of a grand jury, or—in the civil law system—of a *juge d'instruction*, who would take a preliminary look at the facts and the law and would issue the indictment on which the accused would be tried.

The main reason why that step is necessary is that it would provide the authority for a government to confidently undertake the case. Without such legal pathbreaking, I thought it unlikely that a government would summon the political will to take action. The project would be sandbagged by legal Pharisees and political cowards. (That judgment proved to be all too accurate.)

So I set about trying to find a legal group to sponsor such a commission. I realized that any commission sent in by the Cambodian Genocide Project would not have the authority of a commission sent by a large, established human rights organization. In May 1981, I approached the International Commission of Jurists, through the Chairman of its Board of Directors, Mr. William J. Butler, Esq. of New York. To my amazement, Mr. Butler consulted the United States State Department to ask what it thought about sending an International Commission of Jurists delegation to Cambodia. (I had naively thought the International Commission of Jurists an independent, non-governmental organization. See Appendix.)

The issue became whether the ICJ would send in a delegation to investigate only the Khmer Rouge genocide, or whether it would send a delegation only if it could also investigate current human rights in Cambodia. As I said in subsequent letters, the Heng Samrin government refused to permit investigation of its current human rights practices. The result was that the International Commission of Jurists refused to carry out an investigation of the Khmer Rouge genocide.

Sponsorship of a commission of inquiry by the American Bar Association was blocked in 1986 by opposition from Mr. David Hawk, who had meanwhile set up his own group, the Cambodia Documentation Commission. But the Cambodian Documentation Commission never did send in a commission of jurists to lend authoritative weight to the legal case. Instead it directly approached governments to take the case to the ICJ, without success. Michael Posner of the Lawyers' Committee for Human Rights used his influence as chairman of the ABA's Section on Individual Rights and Responsibilities Human Rights Committee to block any attempt to get the ABA to sponsor the delegation of jurists. LAWASIA also refused to sponsor the effort, despite a long courtship.

The position that an organization will not investigate the Khmer Rouge genocide until it can also investigate current human rights violations in Cambodia is the all-or-none approach to human rights. It is similar to arguing that the Nuremberg tribunal shouldn't have been held because one of its sponsors was Stalin's Soviet Union; that the Nazi genocide shouldn't have been investigated because Soviet East Germany wouldn't permit investigation of its current violations of human rights. For human rights groups, it is a self-defeating position.

It was also a position that happened to fit neatly into the *realpolitik* of the Reagan administration's covert support for the formation and arming of the Coalition Government of Democratic Kampuchea, which included the Khmer Rouge.

We are still looking for a recognized human rights or legal group to sponsor a systematic investigation and report on the Khmer Rouge genocide.

Why not just *do* it? Why worry about what organization sponsors the commission of inquiry?

Because without sponsorship by an already recognized human rights or legal organization (or by a government or the U.N.), the report will lack the authority it would have if it came from the International Commission of Jurists or a similarly respected source. That would vitiate its purpose—which is to convince governments to act, to engage their political will to prosecute the Khmer Rouge mass murderers and to block them from ever gaining power again.

The second reason for sponsorship is money. It costs money to send a delegation to Cambodia, pay their hotel bills, and pay for the time they will devote. And you can't raise money from the foundations that support human rights work without established organizational sponsorship. Human rights funding is controlled by an interlocking directorate in which directors of the major human rights organizations also sit on the advisory boards of the foundations that fund them. In some spheres, it would be called conflict of interest. In human rights, it's just good contacts.

In 1986, I approached the government of Australia to sponsor the inquiry and take the case to the ICJ. Australia decided not to take the case to the World Court in 1986, because lawyers for the Australian Department of Foreign Affairs said it would require that Australia grant *de facto* recognition to the Coalition Government of Democratic Kampuchea, which included the Khmer Rouge. That argument was not legally correct, as I pointed out in a memorandum to the Australian Department of Foreign Affairs in July, 1986. It included the following points:

> Cases brought to the World Court are brought against states, not against governments. The state bringing the case would not have to recognize the Coalition Government of Democratic Kampuchea or any other government in order to file a case against Cambodia in the World Court. Article 34 of the Statute for the Court says, "Only States may be parties in cases before the Court." The parties to the Genocide Convention are States. The submission to the World Court would be as a state, though submitted by an agent of the state's government. The Registrar of the Court would then refer the application and memorial to the government or legal entity recognized by the United Nations as representing the state of Cambodia. If the complaining state does not bilaterally recognize a particular Cambodian government, that fact is immaterial, because the World Court exercises jurisdiction over states, not governments.

The domestic law rule that unrecognized states may not use or be sued in domestic courts is irrelevant here. The United Nations has never ceased to recognize Cambodia as a state. The domestic law rule as stated in *Gur Corp. v. Trust Bank of Africa Ltd., Carl Zeiss Stiftung v. Rayner & Keeler Ltd.* ((No. 2) (1967) 1 AC 853, 954), and *Hesperides Hotels Ltd. v. Aegean Turkish Holidays, Ltd.* ((1978) QB 207, 218) follows from the deference of domestic courts to the recognition power of their own domestic governments. (Even that deference, incidentally, is not absolute. In *Hesperides Hotels*, Lord Denning declared that "the courts may, in the interests of justice,... give recognition to the actual facts or realities." American courts have carved out a similar policy exception to the no recognition-no effects rule, e.g., in *Salimoff v. Standard Oil Co.*, 262 N.Y. 220.)

In this case, the United Nations is the executive entity whose recognition will determine what government would represent the state of Cambodia in the International Court of Justice, the United Nations' judicial organ (U.N. Charter, Article 92). Australia's non-recognition of the Coalition Government of Democratic Kampuchea would therefore have had no effect on the acceptance of jurisdiction by the World Court, because the *states* of Cambodia and Australia are both recognized parties to the Genocide Convention, which confers jurisdiction on the Court. The Court has never refused jurisdiction over a case where the *government* of a state does not recognize the *government* of the respondent state. The situation is analogous to the U.N. General Assembly, where member states are all parties to the same multilateral treaty (U.N. Charter) and therefore may participate in all proceedings, even though many of the governments of the member states do not recognize each other.

Submission of the case would not constitute recognition by Australia of the Coalition Government of Democratic Kampuchea (CGDK). Recognition in modern international law is entirely declaratory and must be intentional. The nineteenth century constitutive rather than declaratory theory and the doctrines of *de facto* recognition are no longer law. Modern practice includes many kinds of relations between governments short of recognition. Recognition today can only be made by the intentional declaration of a government. The distinction between recognition of a state and of a government is important. (See Crawford, *The Criteria for Statehood in International Law* (1976-77) 48 Brit. Y.B. Int. L. 308.) As the Canadian government has put it, "Once granted, state recognition survives changes in governments, unless it is explicitly withdrawn" (10 Can. Y.B. Int. L. 308).

If the CGDK answers Australia's memorial with a counter-memorial, it would do so on behalf of the state of Cambodia. When the Registrar conveys documents to Australia, by accepting them, Australia would not be recognizing the CGDK; Australia would only be continuing its recognition of the state of Cambodia. Recognition of the Coalition Government of Democratic Kampuchea could only occur by intentional declaration of recognition by the government of Australia.

Would there be a political as opposed to a legal problem caused by receiving documents produced by the CGDK? In the case of an accusation of genocide, I doubt it. Receiving the response in court hardly implies recognition of the legitimacy of the respondent.

In fact, this case presents a unique opportunity, because the very persons who committed the crimes remain part of the government that will have to answer the charges. Yet they no longer control the territory of Cambodia, so it has been possible to gather the evidence against them. Few cases of genocide provide such an ideal opportunity to confront those who committed the crimes with the charges. I seriously doubt that public opinion will characterize the bringing of charges of genocide in the World Court as some kind of approval or re-recognition of the Coalition Government of Democratic Kampuchea, which is widely known to include the Khmer Rouge. Legally it would not constitute that, and politically it would not either.

Australia has standing to bring the case because Australia has been injured by the effects of the Cambodian genocide through the influx of refugees it caused and the relief programs it made necessary. Australia has accepted more Cambodian refugees per capita than any other country except Thailand. Australia also was directly injured by the Khmer Rouge mass murder of foreign groups. At least two Australian citizens were among the 20,000 murdered at Tuol Sleng prison.

Standing in this case is therefore firm. This case is not like the *Southwest Africa* case, where Ethiopia and Liberia were held to lack standing because they were not parties to the treaty granting the South African mandate and because they had suffered no injury. Here standing is grounded on clear treaty obligations.

The real problem, though, was absence of the political will to prosecute the case. Mr. William Hayden, then Foreign Minister of Australia, took the initiative with his call in Manila on June 26, 1986 for an international tribunal to try the Khmer Rouge leaders.[8] But the Australian government was never willing to go forward with a case in the World Court, and it has never taken any steps to establish the international tribunal called for by Mr. Hayden.

A Commission of Inquiry should still be sent to Cambodia to investigate the genocide committed by the Khmer Rouge. In 1989 and in 1992, I again contacted the International Commission of Jurists and asked them to appoint an international commission of highly eminent jurists to go to Cambodia to look at and hear the evidence, and upon the evidence to issue an indictment. Although the Cambodian government now permits investigations of current human rights practices as well as the Khmer Rouge genocide, the International Commission of Jurists has not taken up the task. I still hope it will. Leading jurists could be chosen from nations in the region (e.g., Australia, the Philippines, India) and around the world.

Among those whom I have contacted and who have agreed to serve are the Hon. Judge Roma Mitchell, former Chief Human Rights Commissioner of Australia, Justice Florentino Feliciano of the Supreme Court of the Philippines, His Excellency Justice Bhagwati, former Chief Justice of the Supreme Court of India, and the Hon. Thomas Buergenthal, former Chief Judge of the Inter-American Court of Human Rights.

A commission of inquiry sent by a respected human rights organization could still have an impact. Its findings could form the basis of criminal indictments inside Cambodia to try the Khmer Rouge leaders after the 1993 elections.

Its hearings, if conducted publicly, as they should be, could have a political impact inside Cambodia, especially if conducted before the 1993 elections. They could become a forum in which the truth about the Khmer Rouge genocide is publicized both inside Cambodia and to the world, through press coverage. They could thus have a healthy impact on the elections and on naiveté about the nature of the Khmer Rouge.

The Khmer Rouge are not just another Cambodian faction. The SNC is a council of a poodle (Sihanouk), a terrier (the KPLNF), a bulldog (the State of Cambodia), and a wolf (the Khmer Rouge). It remains to be seen whether the proposed U.N. peacekeeping force can cage the wolf. I doubt it.

The Khmer Rouge have not changed and they cannot be trusted. They will not honor the Paris Accords except when they can gain legitimacy or power by doing so. The Khmer Rouge refuse to disarm, refuse to participate in elections, and refuse to give up control of the areas they now dominate. The result, after elections in 1993, will be the partition of Cambodia and ongoing civil war. The Khmer Rouge will return to their genocidal ways, first in mass murder of ethnic Vietnamese settlers in Cambodia, then in assassinations of rural government officials. The hope that they can be brought "inside the tent" by the UN peace plan is naive.

The U.N. peace plan is worth implementing because if elections can be held, they will result in a government recognized widely and able to enlist international assistance to defeat the Khmer Rouge. But we should have no illusions about Khmer Rouge willingness to disarm and become law-abiding members of a new coalition government. Eventually, the Khmer Rouge must be militarily defeated and brought to trial.

There are other legal options for action against the Khmer Rouge.

The first is to submit the case to a less authoritative body than the International Court of Justice or a human rights organization like the International Commission of Jurists.

The obvious candidate is the Permanent Peoples' Tribunal, the successor to the Russell Tribunal of the Vietnam War era. This was the approach taken by the Armenians in 1984. Hearings were held during four days in Paris in April 1984, and a tribunal made up of world renowned human rights leaders Sean McBride and Adolfo Perez Esquivel, professors, and other experts on international affairs found the Young Turk regime guilty of committing genocide in Armenia from 1915 through 1917.

A similar hearing could be held on the Khmer Rouge genocide. It *should* be held. All venues for exposing the Khmer Rouge should be used. But there are several drawbacks to the Permanent Peoples' Tribunal:

Its trials are generally considered to be show trials like the original Russell Tribunal's and their verdicts are heavily discounted because of the perceived ideological biases of the judges. The Tribunal's verdicts have no *legal* effect. They create no law. And that is one purpose of trying the Khmer Rouge—to convert the Genocide Convention from a piece of paper into real international law. That takes authoritative decision. The Permanent Peoples' Tribunal isn't considered authoritative by most policy makers or jurists. Its judgments may have historical utility; historians may value them. But the Permanent Peoples' Tribunal will have no effect in making international law.

Nevertheless, the publicity and political influence of a Peoples' Tribunal hearing would be useful. If the hearings are to have their maximum impact, however, the members of the tribunal should be chosen to include only the finest international jurists. The evidence against the Khmer Rouge must stand on its own and not be helped along by biased judges.

Finally, domestic courts in countries besides Cambodia could be used to unleash a barrage of civil lawsuits against individual Khmer Rouge leaders and against the Party of Democratic Kampuchea.

Many countries, including the U.S., permit tort suits by families of victims of crimes, including violations of international criminal law. In the U.S., the Alien Tort statute was used in this way to grant damages to the family of Joselito Filartiga against his torturer and murderer Pena-Irala. That case was possible because the U.S. court could assert personal jurisdiction due to the physical presence of both the plaintiff (Dr. Filartiga) and the defendant (Pena-Irala) in the U.S.

A similar suit in Washington, D.C., the *Tel-Oren* case, failed because former Judge Bork held that the Alien Tort statute only covered crimes against the law of nations as of 1793. That would rule out an action based on genocide in the District of Columbia. The conflict between the *Tel-Oren* decision and the *Filartiga* opinion of Judge Kaufman has never been resolved by the Supreme Court, and human rights groups (with good reason) have been reluctant to take the conflict between the circuits to the Supreme Court for resolution.

But meanwhile, a tort suit remains possible in the Second Circuit. The problem would be that such a suit would require the plaintiffs to serve process on an individual member of the Khmer Rouge leadership (like Khieu Samphan, Ieng Sary, or Son Sen) when he comes to New York. There are numerous potential plaintiffs—families of Khmer Rouge victims who now reside in the U.S. The *pro bono* assistance of U.S. law firms in New York (or perhaps here at Yale) could be sought to prepare such a case. It must be ready to go the next time a Khmer Rouge leader sets foot in New York.

Mr. Alan Keesee has suggested that similar tort suits could be brought in Thailand, where there are also many families of Khmer Rouge victims. The Khmer Rouge leaders have visited Thailand frequently for the past fifteen years. It might be possible to track them down and file suit against them for wrongful death and other torts in Thai courts. The Thai government might try to put political obstacles in the way of such lawsuits, but it is worth exploring this option. The trials would be public and would attract considerable press coverage. Serving process on the Khmer Rouge leaders might be difficult and dangerous, especially because they mostly live inside Cambodia and only visit Thailand under armed guard. In addition, the Thai government is not a party to the Genocide Convention and has not made genocide a crime in Thailand. Khieu Samphan and Son Sen could, as members of the S.N.C., claim diplomatic immunity in Thailand for ordinary torts, including wrongful death. But others, like Deuch or Mok could not.

How can future genocide in Cambodia be prevented?

First we should analyze why the world's nations took no action to stop the Khmer Rouge genocide from 1975 through 1978. Why did the great military powers of the world and the United Nations do nothing to stop the Khmer Rouge genocide?

The reason is that the forces that could have acted were paralyzed:

1) **The United Nations was paralyzed by the likelihood of Security Council vetoes by the Communist powers; at first by the Soviet Union and then by China.**
   In 1978, the best of the human rights organizations (Amnesty International and the International Commission of Jurists) and five governments did bring charges of massive human rights violations (but not explicitly genocide) to the U.N. Commission on Human Rights. A report by the Chairman of the Subcommission, Bouhdiba of Algeria, was then buried. The cynical claims by Cambodia that its sovereignty allowed it to carry out whatever domestic policies it found necessary fell on sympathetic ears among the third world states in the U.N. The U.N. did nothing.

2) **The United States and the Western powers stood back, paralyzed by their defeat in Vietnam from involvement in another ground war in Southeast Asia.** Humanitarian intervention did not occur until Vietnam, under attack by Democratic Kampuchea, finally intervened and overthrew the Khmer Rouge in early 1979. The West's response was to condemn the Vietnamese invasion in U.N. resolutions and through an embargo on Vietnam. Indeed the West continued to vote to seat the Khmer Rouge in the Cambodian seat at the U.N. for years after they were out of power.

3) **Much of the old anti-war movement suffered from liberal paralysis.** During the genocide, deniers like Chomsky questioned the validity of refugee accounts, nit-picking at the massive evidence compiled by Ponchaud and Barron and Paul,[9] casting just enough doubt to cloud the truth—that the Khmer Rouge were committing a massive genocide—so that those who had opposed the Vietnam War and the bombing of Cambodia and Laos did not mobilize. (To his great credit, Senator George McGovern called for humanitarian intervention in Cambodia in early 1978. But he was ignored by the Carter administration, whose National Security Adviser encouraged China to help the Khmer Rouge in 1979 after they were overthrown.) Besides, the anti-war movement was *anti*-interventionist, unlikely to support another armed intervention into Cambodia.

Much of the paralysis was the result of uncertainty about what was happening in Cambodia. The Khmer Rouge sealed off Cambodia and admitted no Western reporters until late 1978, when they let in three, one of whom (Malcolm Caldwell) they murdered the night after he had interviewed Pol Pot. (Perhaps he had learned too much.) But the paralysis was also caused by unwillingness to believe the cognitively dissonant news that the revolutionaries whose victory many anti-war activists had cheered were now committing mass murder on a scale unmatched since Hitler and Stalin.

The Cambodian Peace Plan has shown that the Security Council is no longer paralyzed. As the intervention to repel Iraqi aggression against Kuwait demonstrates, the United Nations can now be mobilized to defeat flagrant aggression by a tyrant who had already committed genocide against his own Kurdish population and who had declared his intention to destroy Israel, undoubtedly including genocide of Israel's Jewish population.

The processes of world order have moved beyond the paralysis caused by a paralyzed U.N. The U.N.'s involvement in Cambodia is one of the most powerful deterrents to future genocide in Cambodia.

But it can only work if the Security Council is willing to use force to block Khmer Rouge attempts to subvert it.

It must never be forgotten that as my teacher W. Michael Reisman has recently written: "Law is not the antithesis of force. Legal systems and the political systems of which they are a part and which they seek to regulate are based upon the authoritative use of force. The question for jurists, then, is not 'the non-use of force,' but the assignment of the competence to use force to appropriate agencies in the community and the determination of the contingencies, purposes, and procedures for use of authoritative force."[10]

Within Cambodia, a U.N. force must be put in place to prevent the Khmer Rouge from filling a power vacuum and seizing power by force. The State of Cambodia's army must not be disarmed until the Khmer Rouge have disarmed. They will not do so, and elections will have to be held without the disarmament called for by the Paris Accords. Elections will not be able to be held in Khmer Rouge-controlled areas. And the State of Cambodia will probably use its police and armed forces to intimidate other parties.

In the future Cambodian government, the best way to prevent future genocide is to install the rule of law and to enforce it by effective government, including an armed security force that can defend Cambodians from the return of the Khmer Rouge. That will require immediate military assistance to the new government, as well as massive aid to rebuild the shattered infrastructure (particularly road-building and de-mining).

Cambodia should also have strong, independent human rights organizations that can monitor the Cambodian government and protest human rights violations. Such organizations could also put pressure on the new Cambodian government to try the Khmer Rouge leaders for genocide.

In the end, the true significance of the case against the Khmer Rouge will be its impact on the future of the people of Cambodia, on efforts to prevent future genocides, and on the advancement of international law. The Genocide Convention can hardly be said to be law if it is never applied. Law is made through authoritative decision. A decision in this case may give pause to future leaders who are contemplating genocide. A failure to act will surely result in future cynics like Adolf Hitler who when asked if the Final Solution would violate international law replied, "Who ever heard of the Armenians."

Appendix. Correspondence with the International Commission of Jurists.

Following my approach by letter in May 1981, Mr. Butler replied:

June 10, 1981

Dear Gregory:

I have just had a reaction to our meeting of May 5th concerning Cambodia. Although the reaction from the State Department was not too enthusiastic, we think that we should take the matter a step further.

Accordingly, I wonder if it would be possible to contact the present Cambodian government in order to see if it would be willing to receive an ICJ fact-finding team for the purpose of inquiring into the present and past Human Rights conditions existing in Cambodia.

I plan to be here until July 31st should you think it possible to establish such a contact here in the United States either through direct contact with representatives of the Revolutionary Council or perhaps with representatives of the present Vietnamese government.

Let me hear from you soon.

Yours cordially,

William J. Butler

I then contacted the government in Phnom Penh and replied to Mr. Butler as follows:

Sept. 13, 1981

Dear Bill:

I just received a reply to the letter I sent into Kampuchea with David French, the current Church World Service representative there. As with all things connected with Kampuchea, it has taken some time. I enclose a copy.

It appears to me that we may get a favorable reply to our request to send a delegation in to investigate the human rights situation under Pol Pot and presently under the current regime.

What I suggested to the foreign ministry there was that a small preliminary delegation be granted visas to come into Kampuchea to speak to the responsible officials there. I think that we can now make plans to send an exploratory group in. I'd suggest just a few persons of your choosing, or even just yourself and one or two others. I'd be happy to go along. How much time we would spend depends on your schedule or the schedules of the people you designate. It is often difficult to see government officials in Kampuchea and I would recommend planning on a week. That will also allow the group to fly in by commercial airline (Air France) from Paris to Ho Chi Minh City (Saigon) and thence into Phnom Penh by Air Vietnam. The Air France flight is just once a week via Bangkok. The only other routes in are through Hanoi and by World Vision flights from Singapore. The latter are rather undependable planes that sometimes break down for weeks at a time.

If you would designate a few persons who would be willing to go into Kampuchea for a week, I will write another letter to the Kampuchean foreign ministry requesting visas for them. If you can get passport numbers, dates of issue, birthdates, birthplaces, and dates of expiry of passport that would be helpful, but names alone would be good enough for the first letter. Some information about the people you choose would also help.

I will contact Paul McCleary of Church World Service about possible funding for this trip.

Sincerely,

Gregory Stanton

I contacted Paul McCleary about funding as promised, and in March, 1982 traveled to Phnom Penh with Mr. David Hawk, for whom I obtained a visa after the initial refusal of the Phnom Penh government to allow Hawk entry. I reported the results of the trip to Butler:

May 4, 1982

Dear Bill:

I vividly remember the meeting we had in your office one year ago—I have just been reviewing the notes I took then. At that time we discussed my idea to systematically document the genocide under Pol Pot in Cambodia. I pointed out the urgency of the need for a "grand jury" to investigate the crimes of 1975-1978 and sought the sponsorship of the International Commission of Jurists for that effort.

Last year you said that the ICJ does not generally take on investigations of past violations without also reviewing current human rights in a country. You suggested that the ICJ might undertake the work as a "country report." Although I expressed skepticism that the Heng Samrin government would accept investigation of the current human rights situation in Kampuchea, I agreed to contact the foreign ministry in Kampuchea to see if they would be open to an inquiry into both the Pol Pot era and the present situation. As you know I wrote a letter July 11, 1981 to ask if they would receive a delegation from the ICJ.

I have returned from another trip to Kampuchea in March in order to set up the investigation of the Pol Pot genocide by human rights groups and legal experts. I went in with David Hawk, former executive director for Amnesty International, U.S.A.

In my talks with representatives of the Foreign Ministry, it became clear to me that investigation of the current human rights situation in Kampuchea is unacceptable to the present government, as I had suspected. But if the inquiry is limited to the genocide committed from 1975 through 1978, the government will give us full cooperation.

Do you think the International Commission of Jurists would be willing to co-sponsor the Kampuchean Genocide Project or to send its own delegation to Kampuchea to investigate some aspect of the genocide committed there? I think it is quite possible that if a delegation from the International Commission of Jurists went to Kampuchea, they would be able to talk to people about the current situation on an informal basis once they got there. And in any case, the investigation of the 1975-1978 genocide has quite current relevance because of the clear and present danger that it will happen again.

In addition to the I.C.J.'s participation, I would very much like your personal assistance. Would you be willing to serve as a member of the board of advisors for the Kampuchean Genocide Project? It would be a great contribution to give us your time and advice.

I look forward to hearing from you.

Faithfully,

Gregory H. Stanton

Mr. Butler replied:

May 6, 1982

Dear Greg,

I am sorry to say that the ICJ still would insist, if it were to undertake such a mission, not only to review the current human rights situation in Kampuchea, but also to seek the explanations and/or positions of the Pol Pot people.

Incidentally, there is some reservation among international people as to whether the word, "genocide" should be employed at all regarding Kampuchea. Genocide has been defined as the systematic extinction of a particular race. The Pol Pot atrocities do not quite fit in to this definition.

In any event, I would love to see you if you could drop by some time when you are in New York.

Warmest personal regards,

William J. Butler

---

[1]   U.N. Doc. A/34/569 at 9. See also Ben Kiernan, 'Orphans of Genocide: The Cham Muslims of Kampuchea under Pol Pot,' *Bulletin of Concerned Asian Scholars*, 20, 4, 1988: 2-33.

[2]   David P. Chandler, Ben Kiernan, and Chanthou Boua, eds., *Pol Pot Plans the Future: Confidential Leadership Documents from Democratic Kampuchea, 1976-77*, Monograph Series No. 33, Yale University Southeast Asia Studies, Yale Center for International and Area Studies, 1988: 4.

[3]   Ben Kiernan, 'Kampuchea's Ethnic Chinese Under Pol Pot: A Case of Systematic Social Discrimination,' *Journal of Contemporary Asia*, Vol. 16, No. 1, 1986: 18.

[4]   Ben Kiernan, 'Wild Chickens, Farm Chickens and Cormorants: Kampuchea's Eastern Zone Under Pol Pot,' in Chandler and Kiernan, eds., *Revolution and Its Aftermath in Kampuchea: Eight Essays*, Yale University, Southeast Asia Studies Monograph No. 25, 1983; and Ben Kiernan, *Cambodia: Eastern Zone Massacres*, Columbia University, Center for the Study of Human Rights, Documentation Series No. 1, 1986.

[5]   78 U.N.T.S. 277, Jan. 12, 1951.

[6]   U.N. Doc. E/CN.4/Sub. 2/414/Add. 8.

[7]   U.N. Doc. E/CN.4/Sub. 2/414/Add. 9.

[8]   *Sydney Morning Herald*, June 27, 1986.

[9]   'Distortions at Fourth Hand,' *Nation*, 27 June 1977.

[10]   W. Michael Reisman, 'Allocating Competences to Use Coercion in the Post-Cold War World - Practices, Conditions, and Prospects,' in Lori F. Damrosch and David Scheffer, eds., *Law and Force in the New International Order.* 26.

Genocide as a Political Commodity

Serge Thion*

Just after the signing of the so-called Peace Agreements on Cambodia in Paris, on the avenue Kléber where the 1973 agreements on Vietnam were also signed, Roland Dumas, the French foreign minister, held a press conference along with Prince Sihanouk and Perez de Cuellar. A nasty journalist, quoting directly from the UN Convention to prevent genocide—a treaty to which France, like a majority of other states, is a party—reminded the audience that, in the absence of an established ad hoc international court, each state was duty-bound to act against the perpetrators of such a heinous crime. It was clear from the text that the French government was bound to place Khieu Samphan and Son Sen, the Khmer Rouge signatories, under arrest and to charge them with the crime of genocide under international law.

The reply was what could be expected from a true statesman: Dumas shrugged and laughed. "Do not worry," he said to the pesky journalist. "We have very good lawyers." (He is a famous lawyer himself.) "It does not matter what documents we give them, they'll always come up with the solution [we want]." He was expressing the absolute cynicism of power. Treaties are worth no more than the paper they are written on when they contradict the policy of the day. Referring to the law is just idle talk.

As I write this, sitting in a garden facing the Royal Palace in Phnom Penh, the second Supreme National Council meeting is taking place inside. Seated there is the same Khieu Samphan, representative of what is left of the Pol Pot regime, which was overthrown in early 1979 by Vietnamese troops. He rode into the palace protected by a strong military escort. There is not much love for him in town. In the plane bringing him from Bangkok, he complained to an American correspondent, Nate Thayer, that some governments in the West are attempting to derail the "peace process" by their reluctance to allow the Khmers Rouges to play their full role in it. There is a grain of truth in what he said.

---

* In memoriam, Allard K. Lowenstein, of early Namibian commitment. [This chapter has been lightly edited.—Ed.]

As James A. Baker III was delivering his speech at the Paris conference, he remarked casually that his government had no objection to a trial of those responsible for past horrors in Cambodia, with whom he was about to sign the agreements giving them a legal share of future power in Cambodia. It was the first time a high-ranking US official had publicly considered such an idea.[1]

Monsieur Dumas escaped this contradiction through laughter. But Mr. Baker does not even seem to know how to smile. He wants to have it both ways: to sign an agreement that jacks up the Khmers Rouges into a legitimate position and also to distance himself from them on moral and legal grounds; his right hand ignores what his left hand is doing. While Monsieur Dumas scoffed at the notion of international law binding sovereign states, Mr. Baker was more subtle. He implied that, although denying it now, his government could, in the future, give its approval to an application of the law if others—Cambodians for instance—choose to take such action. From Pol Pot's point of view, this could be seen as obvious duplicity.

In subsequent weeks, there was a lot of speculation in the Western press, feeding on comments it extracted from Cambodian leaders, on the circumstances that could lead to a trial of the Khmers Rouges for genocide. But nobody so far has considered taking action, and Prince Sihanouk, speaking in the Royal Palace on November 16, aptly pointed out that, before being brought to the dock, Pol Pot must first be found. He suggested that one might ask "the prestigious general Suchinda Kaprayoon, chief of the Royal Thai Army, who told me recently he just had a most agreeable conversation with Pol Pot." In addition, an obviously embarrassed Sihanouk said that he would not visit the Tuol Sleng "Genocide Museum."

Everyone knows that for the last twelve years Pol Pot has been quietly sitting in his compound near the Thai town of Trat, enjoying Chinese money, Royal Thai army protection, and inconspicuous support from what could be called the CIA border network. There he is able to direct the Khmer Rouge political and military campaign in Cambodia and hold long seminars to train his local commanders and apprise them of the new line.[2] Although he has dropped out of public life on the advice of the Chinese, who found that his name was embarrassing in the West, he obviously does not feel at risk. If a move is later undertaken to bring him to court, it will mean the Khmers Rouges' usefulness as a weapon against Communist Vietnam has dwindled into insignificance. By then, of course, the moral strength of the case against them will have diminished accordingly.

These considerations remain valid whichever words—with their varying legal implications—we use to describe the huge human losses that occurred in Cambodia under Communist party rule, with Pol Pot as the highest authority. I shall discuss the use of the word *genocide* later; but first let us look at the facts.

Ben Kiernan has provided information on those limited surveys, conducted in the years immediately following the demise of Democratic Kampuchea (DK), which are available to us.[3] They were carried out by individuals mostly doing research on the border. No institution attempted to do a global survey; only the CIA provided an estimate based on several explicit hypotheses, which raised a number of questions.[4] It should be very clear that we do not know the real figures, and it is also probable we shall never have them, because the "killing fields" were operated with very few written documents. Of those which have been found, many are still inaccessible. Moreover, the killers are still at large in the jungle. Documents are lacking to establish precise figures for the population when the war started in 1970, when it stopped in 1975, when Pol Pot fled in 1979, and even now. They have not been destroyed: they never existed. Moreover, Khmers are not always registered and change their names at will.

On the basis of these few surveys and my own interviews, I fully accept an estimate between 1 and 1.5 million deaths. We must keep in mind that these figures have been constructed by asking individuals to count the number of family members thought to be dead or missing. Some of the missing persons may, of course, be alive somewhere else. The Red Cross tracing system and Khmer newspapers and television still carry requests for information on missing or lost persons, obviously with some results. But the number of people thus accounted for is probably not very high.

On the other hand, Khmers would include in their "family" count a sizable number of non–kin people—sworn friends, adopted children and neighbors—who, for all practical purposes, are family members. But these people would also be claimed by other families as their kin relatives, leading to double accounting. I consider that the proportion of double counts is probably high in the early border surveys and would fully account for the figure of three million produced by the PRK, if this is based on any serious work, which I doubt.

There were three main causes of violent deaths.

1) **The killing of identified Lon Nol regime personnel, heavy at the beginning, following the April 17, 1975, collapse.** There was obviously a central decision to eliminate these people as an extension of the death promised to the seven "supertraitors" leading the ousted regime. Possibly, between 100,000 and 200,000, including relatives, were executed under this blanket order, which was not applied everywhere in the same way. The intention was probably to eliminate all those who had been invested with some form of power in the old society and might therefore be a seed for growing another power hostile to the revolution.

2) **The intra–party purges.** The need for the Party Center to establish itself as the sole source of authority led to the destruction of individuals, and group or zone commands, including relatives, former subordinates, and associated nonparty populations, that were deemed by the Pol Pot group as having either intellectual origins or political affiliations that were not one hundred percent inspired by the Center. They called it the "purification" of the party, and each new wave of purges increased the "level of purity." Several tens of thousands of people were thus disposed of, a lot of them after "confessing" invented treason. The figure may be as high as 200,000 people if we include the destruction of nonparty civilians in the eastern zone in 1978.

3) **Assertive killings.** Local cadres, mostly uneducated peasants or half-educated teachers, had risen to power because they had been good petty military leaders in the war. They compensated for their lack of legitimacy, their incompetence, and their lack of grasp of social mechanisms in an extremely authoritarian way, even to the extent of killing anyone not showing the mask of passive acceptance. It is impossible to estimate the number of those killings not derived from central orders but from the psychological drives of youngsters who needed to assert undue authority; but, on any account, it was massive. Attention should be paid to this phenomenon as its dynamic is still active in today's

society and is even more threatening with the planned demobilization of seventy percent of the troops. The weakness, or the outright lack of institutional links among individuals may lead someone in authority, when facing any form of challenge, to resort to immediate and violent retaliation. This is probably a result of the traditional basic education, handed down from the ancient times when a majority of the people were slaves of the rulers, which insists that authority should never and cannot, for any reason whatsoever, be challenged.[5]

One way or another, these three categories of mass killings had the same purpose: to establish an entirely new type of power, based on an entirely new type of people drawn from social strata in which no one had ever dreamed of climbing to the top. It was, in a nutshell, a revolution, although it was produced by not much more than the power of the gun. We know of violent political changes that are not revolutions, and of revolutions that are not bloody. I shall leave that to the philosophers but it could be useful to remember that the old regime, until 1970, treated its opponents in a very rough way, including the use of systematic violence, which it claimed to be a legitimate response to opponents of bad faith. Sihanouk's regime pushed the future revolutionaries into the forested wilderness, whence they emerged in 1975 to pluck power like a ripe fruit.

This may lead to a more thorough examination of the problems presented to us for comment.

What were the social, political and economic preconditions for genocide in Cambodia?

The most obvious answer is the war, which produced a political vacuum in Phnom Penh in 1975. In the wake of the March 18, 1970, coup, the war apparently started as a continuation of the American war against the Vietnamese Communists. But it immediately cracked Khmer society wide open, with, very broadly speaking, on one hand, the urban bourgeoisie thirsty for dollars and Western consumer goods, and on the other, the more traditionalist peasantry almost untouched by the modern economy. The republican regime quickly dissipated any hope of reform and immediately lost the war. Then the war went on as a massive destruction of the countryside by airpower. The most important political change to come about was the provision inserted by the United States into the Paris Agreements of 1973 obliging the VC/NVA to evacuate Cambodia, in a naive attempt to revive the Lon Nol regime. As a result, the Vietnamese handed over the administration of the countryside to Pol Pot, who immediately began to eliminate, one by one, his allies in the "Front" and the "impure" elements—that is, those who had not been directly forged by him—inside the Communist party. Under the heaviest bombings ever launched up to that time on a country, radicalization was accelerated and in some areas an authoritarian policy was implemented that was to become standard after April 1975. Without the war, which, in a bitter paradox, was needed by the Americans in preparing their orderly withdrawal from Vietnam, Pol Pot's tiny Communist party would certainly have met the same fate as its equivalents in Malaysia, Thailand, and Burma, as a marginal insurrection partly fed by China and doomed to slow extinction.

The conditions of this war permitted the progressive elimination of all moderates or less–than–extremists, with the exception of the person of Sihanouk, carefully preserved in Peking as a symbol. A small secretive clique arose, entirely devoid of experience in organizing economics or maneuvering social forces. Their narrow nationalism led them to believe that Cambodia on its own was now able to solve problems that were lying unresolved elsewhere. If efforts failed, if the Cambodian revolution quickly turned into a bloody mess, it was mainly for intellectual and cultural reasons. These "thinkers" never suspected the complexity and contradictory nature of social evolution. They did not master the meaning of the ideas they were using and, unable to convince, they either hid their views or resorted to terrorism and passive acceptance.[6] Stalin, at least, was a realist. Pol Pot, a much-watered-down imitation of a faded Chinese copy of Uncle Joe, was and still is, an unimaginative idealist, a forest monk, lost in dreams. The tragedy came when an imported war offered him hosts of uneducated wild youngsters toting guns to translate his dreams into a deadly reality. As this war drags into its twenty–second year, the man is still there, still preaching the same bad news.

What were the aims and methods of the Khmer Rouge movement?

The Khmer Rouge aim was to establish, for the first time since the mythological period of Angkor, an independent state, without any foreign interference or influence (that of the Chinese went unacknowledged), more or less autarchic. Destroying the towns, the bourgeois class, and even religion (also seen as foreign) was deemed necessary in order to retrieve the "Original Khmer," which happens to be the name Pol Pot used in his first known article, written in Paris in 1952.[7] These ideas of a pre–Hindu, pre–urban, pre–state, "original" Khmer society, ideally organized in a kind of basic village democracy, that was later adulterated by all successive forms of state power establishing oppressive authority on the basis of doctrinal ideas borrowed from outside (India, China, Europe), had been elaborated by a brilliant young Khmer intellectual, Keng Vannsak, probably the most influential figure in the Khmer intelligentsia in the middle of this century. Although not a Marxist himself, he blended a Marxist view of history with a Rousseauist concept of a primitive form of democracy based on a "contract," adapted to the tentative reconstruction of Khmer history by French orientalist historians. Although far from being supported by hard facts, this interpretation had the advantage of placing the blame for all evils on the kingship and of channeling energies to fight the puppet king and the French colonial authorities who were using him in such a blatant way.

This struck at the very heart of a controversy raging among colonial historians at the beginning of this century concerning the nature of those Southeast Asian societies which during the last two thousand years had developed statecraft along the lines of successive Indian patterns, sometimes called "Hindu–ized kingdoms." George Coedès, who coined this expression, used to write: "The Cambodian is a hinduized Phnong,"[8] referring to the Khmer word for the "savages" living a tribal life in the mountains, outside the royal realm, and speaking dialects different from but related to the Khmer lowland language. Military expeditions sometimes brought Phnongs back as slaves, who then became Khmer through integration into a state and culture imported from India. This is the process alluded to by Coedès in a sentence that raised the question about the real depth of this acculturation and about what remained of the non–Indian origins in the true culture of Cambodia.

In Paris, Saloth Sar (the future Pol Pot) and Keng Vannsak became close friends, and though Vannsak did not join the French Communist party, they worked together, agitating against Sihanouk and his rotten alliance with the French. That was student politics at the time, but when he came back to Phnom Penh and chose to fight in the ranks of the Democrat party, trying to renovate its leadership and radicalize its opposition to Sihanouk who was tied by his subservience to the colonial masters, Vannsak enlisted the aid of Pol Pot, by then a full-time member of the Communist party's Phnom Penh leadership, to reorganize the party and prepare for the elections. Sihanouk, using the most undemocratic means, forced an electoral rout on both the Democrat party and the Pracheachon (legal arm of the Communists), and Pol Pot, promoted to secretary-general after the killing of the previous one, Tou Samouth, by the secret police, decided to go hide in the forest. When he left Phnom Penh in 1963, the man who took him on the ship upstream to Krauchmar, where he was to fade from public life, was none other than Keng Vannsak.

After some time spent in Base 100, a Vietcong logistical area in the northeastern province of Rattanakiri, Pol Pot moved to live among the Phnongs (the "savages"), away from the Vietnamese. There he discovered the tribal life of these "original" Khmers and learned to deeply appreciate these people, later holding them up as examples of "purity," meaning that they had not been spoiled by royalty, Buddhism, money, or any other imported foreign ideas and instruments of domination. He used them as bodyguards and encouraged cadres to marry tribal women. He transferred the "primitive democracy" that Vannsak had put in a time framework (the "origin") into a space category according to which purity, now on the periphery, would come to encircle the soiled heartland of the country and, in a graphic Maoist way, conquer it. This highly debatable view of the Khmer past thus left a recognizable imprint on Pol Pot's mind and limited historical knowledge; and this utopian vision of a "democratic village state" buried in the past led to the curious and unorthodox appellation of the new state—literally, "Kampuchea Democracy," more usually translated as "Democratic Kampuchea" (DK).[9]

The methods used to achieve this desperate nationalistic vision of a country returning to its buried roots were classically Asian Communist, learned from the Vietnamese and Chinese professional organizers, but learned as Cambodians do learn—by rote, being more accustomed to reproducing the form than to capturing the spirit.

These methods included the indoctrination of the young (considered as naturally "pure") with a crypto–Buddhist morality emphasizing modesty and obedience, and the use of terror instead of political persuasion, a sophisticated technique to which, unlike other Asian Communists, Cambodians had rarely resorted.

Terror spread gradually, giving birth to specialized organs, which, as in other Communist revolutions, outgrew their objectives and set about to destroy the very cradle from which they had sprung. If we compare the short Pol Pot era with the beginnings of Communist state power in the Soviet Union, Mongolia, China, Albania, Yugoslavia, to take examples of indigenous movements taking over, and even Korea, the Cambodian case is comparable in the scope of the destruction brought about by the requirements of establishing a completely new social order. The difference lies in the direct American involvement in the chaos leading to this great destruction and the presence of television crews at the border in the heat of events. Also, the sudden fall deprived Pol Pot of the time to "normalize." There were indications that he was moving in that direction. Who remembers clearly the early purges led by Choibalsan or Kim Il Sung or Enver Hoxha?

What were the results? Who were the victims? How many were they?

I have already addressed these questions in part. I should add, concerning the case of the minority Chams, that I believe there is no evidence at all for a persecution based on "race" or ethnicity, but that they were victims of an attempt to eradicate religion as a matter of general policy, exemplified by the razing of the Catholic cathedral in Phnom Penh, undertaken early after the victory, and by the general suppression of Buddhism. Chams were (and still are) the core and the majority of the Muslim community in Cambodia. If there was more resistance among the Muslims, and then more repression, it is because Islam as a cement was stronger than other religious beliefs. Anyway, the use of terms like "national minorities," introduced into the political language of Cambodia by the Vietnamese after the Soviet and Chinese models, are entirely misleading and do not at all describe the traditional status of small religious or linguistic groups in the country. This complicated issue would require a lengthy development I shall avoid here. But, generally speaking, people were persecuted under DK because of what they believed, or were supposed by security organs to believe, and because of family links with those suspected of harboring wrong beliefs or thoughts detrimental to the state. Killings based on racist hatred involved only the small number of Vietnamese residents left after the May 1975 evacuation and the wanton murdering of Vietnamese farmers in the raids across the border in 1977–1978. The practice of systematically killing Vietnamese civilians is still the policy of the Khmers Rouges. Chinese and Sino–Khmers were not murdered as such, but as traders and capitalists in the greatest need of "reformation," killed mostly by hard labor. From the point of view of the Genocide Convention, destroying an ethnic or a religious group is the same crime. But the search for a "racist" motive in the persecution of the Chams seems to stem from an unconscious desire to equate the Chams and Pol Pot with the Jews and Hitler (the same phenomenon as the Kurds and Saddam Hussein). This might be good propaganda but it is poor history.

Besides the killings motivated by politics, the large majority of those who perished during the DK era died of hunger, deprivation, and diseases related to malnourishment and exhaustion. The greatest part of the human losses must be ascribed to the *economic* policy of the Communist Party of Kampuchea. The whole population sent back to the rice-fields were organized into large units called cooperatives, although these were nothing more than state farms with slave manpower. The Center decreed quotas of rice to be delivered to the state and, emulating the Chinese communes, set up very unrealistic quotas for a country with one of the lowest levels of rice productivity in the world. Very soon, although this varied according to local conditions,[10] the cooperatives could not deliver the required quantities in any other way than by taking it from the food reserves set aside for the workers. The leaders of the cooperatives understood that failure to meet the quotas was tantamount to treason, a crime they would pay for with their lives. Although they obviously also used food to discriminate between friends and foes, thus placing most of the burden due to the lack of food on the shoulders of the former urban population, they could not dispute the targets imposed on them from above. In fact, many of them were later killed when the Southwest Zone cadres, more trusted by the Center, came and took over, after information about the disastrous situation had started to filter up and reach Pol Pot's offices. The bad news was ascribed to treason anyway, and purges were launched on a wide scale. But in general the Southwest cadres, under Ta Mok, were even more ruthless than their predecessors, because they had very good reasons to see that the failure to meet these unrevised quotas was an urgent matter of life and death. Everyone had to suffer in order to ensure the survival of the tormentors. But if the leadership had not been so unrealistic, the system could have worked without starving the workers, as some improvements in productivity were introduced in some places, at least for a while.

What were the effects on the survivors? —on neighboring countries?

Survivors in early 1979 were left with a totally disrupted social and economic life. Families were scattered and everyone was scavenging for food. It was worse than any war, because the tragedy affected everyone, everywhere in the country. The word *rebuilding* never had such a full meaning. Whereas people slowly started to settle down and reunite whichever members of the family had survived, a considerable number of the surviving elite decided that Cambodia was to be written off, that it was not worth rebuilding under the Vietnamese saviors, and then made the individual choice of rushing to the border to escape to the "dreamland" of abundance, a third country in the West. Enacted by people who professed nationalist fervor both before the catastrophe and after it, from the safety of exile, this exodus shows how conventional and superficial the attachment to the idea of nation had been among the educated elite. They abandoned the sinking ship at a time when their lives were no longer being threatened and their flight heavily handicapped the redevelopment of the country for at least one or two generations. The flight of the trained teachers or their refusal to return to the schools, in particular, produced the nightmarish plight of education in today's Cambodia.

The psychological effects of these years of terror and suffering are certainly very deep, but have not been studied at all. The resumption of medical services was entirely on the side of physical health and, up to this day, there is no psychological therapy available other than the rather efficient one provided by traditional healers. Some limited clinical observations suggest that damage has been widespread,

particularly among women, and that a great many people are still
suffering from the effects of traumatic experiences. This field is still
wide open for analysis and action.

Another set of consequences has been a kind of political freeze
due to the Vietnamese military and political presence for ten years.
The threat of a return of the Khmers Rouges cooled the people into
a passive acceptance of a regime in which there was much to criticize,
although it had been quite efficient in the use of the small resources
it could muster. Even the Paris Agreements provided a system ensuring
the military factions—ghosts from the past—a political role that
Cambodians would probably not choose if they had a chance freely
to express their will.[11]

Among the consequences of the terror, we should include the
systematic elimination of critical minds. Cambodian culture certainly
emphasizes submission, but though most people would keep their
inner thoughts to themselves, a small number do develop highly
organized critical views and provide the only channel through which
those in power learn anything about public opinion. The absence of
most of these people in Cambodia after DK made the redirection of
the political course set by the new regime very difficult. Moreover,
many survivors hide their shame in having been silent slaves. Very
often, they had not been able to maintain their moral standards, and
this in itself, may be the cause of recurrent depressions.

The effect of the rise and demise of the DK on neighboring
countries was to lure them into a new cycle of conflicts. Thailand, after
swallowing some bloody Khmer Rouge incursions in border villages,
quickly reached an agreement with the new masters in Phnom Penh
through which a small-barter border trade was resumed and rather
friendly relations were established. The Thai military, closing its eyes
to Pol Pot's dealings with the Thai Communists, saw the new regime
as escaping from Hanoi influence and, as such, reopening this buffer
area to possible later Thai influence. This was a calculated strategic
advance after the disastrous end of the Vietnam war. It paved the way
for the January 1979 decision to accept the Chinese proposal of a
tripartite alliance among the Thai military, the battered Khmer Rouge,
and Chinese logistics providing Pol Pot with military equipment and
money, under the cloak of silent US approval. The Khmers Rouges
were to act as a battering ram in the ongoing Western war with
Vietnam, in the best interest of a China bent on pressuring the
Vietnamese into "normal" tributary submission.

The only country deeply affected was Vietnam. The Communists had withdrawn their forces from Cambodia in early 1973, leaving behind only storage facilities in the remote northeastern border area. But within days of the fall of Phnom Penh, the Khmers Rouges attacked the large island of Phu Quoc and several incidents occurred at sea. Then, in the process of the evacuation of towns, all remaining ethnic Vietnamese, many of them born in Cambodia, were expelled. Uneasy peaceful relations were restored and lasted until about the end of 1976. The death of Mao and the subsequent crisis in Peking somehow created waves in Phnom Penh and triggered the beginning of the high-level purges. It was probably at this time that preparations for the first cross-border raids were made. The year 1977 saw several dozen incidents, typically involving two or three hundred Khmer soldiers attacking a Vietnamese village, slaughtering the peasants—including women and children—stealing the cattle, and burning the place to the ground. Local militias could not stop this well-armed infiltration. Vietnamese provincial authorities evacuated between one and two million persons away from the border. The losses were kept secret while Hanoi still hoped for a diplomatic solution to this undeclared border war. This later proved to be a costly mistake, because it prevented Hanoi from showing that it was acting in self-defense when its armies struck at the center of Pol Pot's military defense.

The motivations of Pol Pot behind this policy to attack Vietnam are not very clear to this day. We may rule out local initiatives and must ascribe this decision to the Party Center, which later claimed it had determined much earlier, in secrecy, that the Vietnamese were the "acute enemy." Although this policy of aggression may seem to us silly and self–defeating, we must remember that most certainly the Party Center considered the Vietnamese weak, even cowardly, as shown by the fact that they had consented to negotiate with the U.S. and sign the 1973 Paris Agreements. Most probably, Pol Pot believed that he had single-handedly defeated U.S. imperialism; the proof of it was that Saigon fell *after* the fall of Phnom Penh.

Although the DK never officially claimed it, there are indications that local commanders told their troops that they were going to reconquer Kampuchea Krom, the lost provinces absorbed by Vietnam two centuries before. Successive royal Khmer governments, including Sihanouk's, always maintained that, though they did not ask to alter the maps, they had never fully recognized the successive transfers of sovereignty accomplished by the Annamese emperors or the French colonial government. In a rather atypical way, Ieng Sary's foreign ministry gave a slightly privileged status to Cambodia's only legal expert on the border question, Sarin Chhak, who, though not a Communist, was left quietly to work on historical documents and provide the CPK leadership with information, notes, and explanations on these complicated issues.[12] Though Sarin Chhak disappeared at the hands of Vietnamese troops on January 7, 1979, his papers have survived and are now in private hands in Phnom Penh, a testimony to the deep attention Pol Pot paid to the question of the lost provinces and the claims the Cambodian state could still eventually lay to them.

The consequences are well known. Hanoi reacted to the threat against its southern provinces with a mixture of diplomatic, political and military moves that have been well described by Nayan Chanda, and my own research fully concurs with his findings.[13] Pol Pot paid for his miscalculation with the destruction of his regime. Had he refrained from going over the border, he most probably would still be in power, the killings would have subsided, and we would have another North Korea, another "hermit kingdom" of silent slaves, about which our information—and our indignation—would be very sketchy.

What problems arise in defining *genocide*? Does the Cambodian case fit the requirements of the Genocide Convention?

It is certainly appropriate to sit here, in the Yale Law School, in a Raphael Lemkin symposium, and discuss the problem of defining *genocide*, because the very word was coined exactly fifty years ago by a Polish-Jewish jurist named Raphael Lemkin. A zealous Zionist, he warned of the impending destruction of the European Jewry at the hands of the Nazis and drew argument from the persecution—in the process inventing a word to name the killing of a race—to reassert the necessity to create a Jewish state where all the Jews of the world could migrate and thus eliminate the necessity for any "Jewish question."[14] He wanted to impress upon his readers the idea that the forcible eradication of the Jews from the face of the earth would be, among nations, comparable to suppressing a person among fellow humans. He spent three years lobbying in the newly established United Nations before he succeeded in getting his draft Convention voted by the General Assembly in December 1948. Then followed a long fight for ratification. Successive American administrations tried to get a ratification because they saw in it a potential anti-Soviet weapon, but they had to face very determined opposition from the American Bar Association, which saw in the text contradictions with U.S. constitutional principles. We must remind ourselves that, up to now, nobody, certainly not the Nazis, has ever been brought to court to face the charge of genocide, with the ridiculous exception of Ceaucescu in the mock trial before his summary execution.[15] Does the fact that this crime has never been tested in court mean that it has never been committed since it has been registered in international law? Or does it mean that it is an unusable category, legally flawed, that prosecutors discard because they would rather rely on more solidly established criminal charges?

Lemkin's neologism lingered for a long time. The notion was a curiosity and was not much seized upon. After World War II, the standard word for what had happened to the Jews in the Eastern territories was *extermination*. Technically, there was no need for a new word. The UN vote in 1948 was a mere diplomatic battlefield for East/West ideological fights, with Lemkin himself in the unexpected role of Cold Warrior. Mass murders, massacres, and suppression of aborigines or minorities fill the pages of history books, and there was, unfortunately, "nothing new under the sun." George Orwell was writing books to show what kind of consequences were implied by the change of words. By the end of the war, Allied powers had decided to try the Axis leaders in an attempt to use guilt to destroy in advance any attempt toward the revival of a national spirit, both in Germany and Japan. In order to achieve this, the Allies created a special military court, with special rules, and invented a new category of crime, "crime against humanity." It was to be applied retro—actively, which, we should remind ourselves, is prohibited by the Declaration of Human Rights. Any lawyer knows that if they had been submitted to any appellate court, the Nuremberg trials would be have been annulled, in normal times. But these times were not quite normal. There was, of course, no legal need for this. The simple application of German law would have provided straightforward condemnations; but there was the political need for a device to destroy an already vanquished nation, morally to go beyond a mere military defeat. The device failed in Japan but succeeded well in Germany, where Christianity provided a ready ground for the acceptance of guilt. But nobody picked up the invention of Lemkin, and it seems that the word *genocide*, as a legal tool, cannot be found in the forty-two volumes of the proceedings of the International Military Tribunal.

Perhaps the word, and the idea behind it, have a built-in weakness. The idea was to describe the killing (*-cide*) of a people. But instead of using the Greek roots for people (*demos*) or nation (*ethnos*), or more simply the Latin root for people (*populus*), Lemkin had chosen the word for "race," or "group related by blood and kin," including the notion of shared heredity that is inherent in the word *genetics*. Like most people in the first half of this century, including scientists, Lemkin, educated in Lvov and Heidelberg, thought that mankind was divided into "races." Classifications varied according to authors (Caucasian, Nordic, Black, Mongoloid, Semitic and so on). Many Jewish authors were also writing of a "Jewish race." It was only later, when the advance of biological sciences showed that although individuals may vary genetically, these variations have little significance and that there is no such a thing as "race" inside the global human population, that the concept of biological racism began to disintegrate.

The notion of "killing a race" (the original meaning of the word *genocide*) might have been embarrassing for the big powers, considering the dismal record shown in the recent past by the United States and its treatment of the native Amerindians; by the USSR and its deportation of populations collectively accused of "collaboration" with the Germans; by the Allied colonial powers, such as France and Great Britain, which were still using race as a political basis for their supremacy, and so on. To explain further why genocide was never an influential concept, we may refer to a French lawyer, Maître Bernard Jouanneau, who wrote for the Socialist party the bill that became a law in France, in July 1990, making it a crime to dissent publicly from the verdict of the Nuremberg trial.[16] In a radio program (Saturdays, 9AM, with *Finkelkraut on France–Culture*), he explained that they had wanted to find a way to punish those who deny that the Nazis perpetrated genocide against the Jews. But when we tried to define what genocide was, Jouanneau said in essence, we found the past was full of events that could be so described—like the slave trade, wars of destruction, the Spanish conquest of America, and even some ugly episodes in the French Revolution—and that controversies existed about the nature of these events. As it seemed impossible to rule by law what historians could or could not say about all past events but one, the lawyer-turned-legislator resorted to a legal enforcement of respect of the Nuremberg verdict—which, however, does not speak of genocide. So, if jurists, politicians, and historians (with the exception of Cold War diplomats) found this notion too vague to handle with any amount of practical usefulness, a reality demonstrated by the fact that in fifty years no one has ever been indicted on this count in a fair trial, why has it now crept into such a general use?

For a long time, the word was used in only one connection, the one for which Lemkin had coined it. The trial of Adolf Eichmann in 1960 triggered a slow evolution of the Western understanding of World War II: as the real causes of the war receded into the past, obscured by a new world order born with the victory, the relative importance of the Nazi persecution of the Jews was given growing prominence, until, a generation later, many people believe that the fate of the Jews lay at the core of the war. It is a little bit as though, in one or two generations from now, writers and historians would try to have people believe that the whole Pol Pot enterprise centered around the desire to exterminate the Chams. In an Islamic view of things (already more or less prevalent, for instance, in the Malaysian perception of Pol Pot), this could be perfectly understandable, and indeed supported by a carefully selected portion of the facts.

From the 1960s onward, the growing needs of Israel for Western support, money, weapons, and general protection shifted the moral grounds of its requests more and more onto what the Nazis had done. No more massive Jewish immigration was anticipated, and the enormous military requirements, at one point increasing the Israeli share to almost half of the aid given by the United States to the rest of the world, led to a considerable effort to spread the Israeli point of view across Western public opinion. The vocabulary itself testifies to the spread of the word *genocide*, the explosion of the word *holocaust* (with a completely distorted meaning), the appearance of the word *shoah* and the near disappearance of words like *destruction*, *extermination*, etc. A check on book titles together with their date of first printing would tell us a lot about our changing ideological view of things past and present.

If, for a long time, the notion of genocide was restricted to one event, having happened once in history to one people, the political benefit it provided to the State of Israel could only attract attention and give rise to emulation. The next ones to adopt it as a political instrument were the Armenian nationalists. The Israeli example of the "rebirth" of a state that had disappeared in antiquity could not but appeal to radical Armenian nationalists who were eager, not to revive a state—they had one under Communist rule in the Soviet Union— but to claim its former political space, now the northeastern corner of Turkey, where "historical Armenia" was once to be found, and whence all Armenians had been forcibly expelled in 1915. By all sorts of means, including terror, Armenian nationalists tried to obtain from Western governments the official pronouncement that what had been known all along as the 1915 "Armenian massacres" and deportation had really been a "genocide," possibly the first in our time. This word, internationally recognized, would have paved the way to a process of dismantling Turkish territory. It was precisely for this reason that Western governments, put under pressure, nevertheless refused to include it in official statements, not out of lack of sympathy for the Armenian cause, but from fear of creating an unmanageable conflict with a valuable ally.[17] A wise decision, when one observes the war that has been going on for two or three years between the former Soviet republics of Armenia and Azerbaijan for the control of Upper Karabagh, a small district inhabited mostly by Armenians. The most violent Armenian militants, requesting recognition of genocide, belonged to the ASALA movement, born in Beirut among youngsters who had been under strong Palestinian influence. Those Palestinians were under the spell of the Israeli success in attracting international support and were prone to imitate Israeli moves, including use of the notion of genocide (victims of which, in this case, would be the Palestinian people).

Recently, Serbia justified its attacks on Croatia by calling the mass murders which occurred in the region during the last war genocide. Every mass killing is becoming a genocide when the memory of it is used as ground for national expansion, war against neighbors, or any form of violence that is difficult to legitimize. The usual inflation of political vocabulary also led to a growing misappropriation of the word. We currently hear that weekend road accidents are causing a genocide, that a mad killer shot eleven people in a genocide, that AIDS is a potential genocide, and so on. Examples may be culled from any of the media.

The concept of "ethnocide," launched in 1968 to describe the cultural destruction of native tribes in places like Brazil or Guatemala, never really got off the ground and instead "cultural genocide" (implying the death of a culture, not the physical destruction of the people) has been widely used to describe, for instance, the near-total annihilation of cultural sites and goods in Tibet during China's so-called Cultural Revolution.[18]

Does the Cambodian case fit the requirements of the Genocide Convention?

If we, as most people do, understand genocide as the killing of people on purely ethnic grounds, or the attempt at it, then Cambodia does not fit in. Even cases of indiscriminate killings based on purely ethnic or tribal discrimination—as we have seen taking place, for instance, in Burundi or elsewhere in Africa, Sabra and Shatila, the Sumgait pogrom against Armenians, the killings of Tibetans in Eastern Tibet, the destruction of a third of the population of East Timor by the Indonesian army, the destruction of Brazilian or other Amerindian tribes, and many other similar massacres have taken place since the Genocide Convention has been "active" (1951)—show that the international community cannot handle this idea because too many of its members are or have been guilty of barbaric acts of this kind. Big powers not only close their eyes when it is committed by one of their allies, but they usually help them to commit and cover up the crime.[19] The press and the judicial powers are usually accomplices, either by silently approving or by assigning selective blame to the enemy's misdeeds.

When speculating about these questions concerning Cambodia, few writers in the West address the Cambodian reaction to them. The concept of genocide is, of course, a complete novelty in that country. But in general Khmer ideas about law may look rather confused. It would take a long time to try to show that two entirely different modes of thought—the first inherited from Theravada Buddhism mixed with traditional wisdom, the second painstakingly brought into the country by the colonial administration—have coexisted without really blending together. The Cambodian codes were mostly a matter of oral tradition, and justice was administered by political authorities and based on wise judgment rather than any fixed set of abstract principles, even though some crimes entailed established penalties.[20] Colonial administration needed a body of logically related concepts as a framework upon which its power and activities, entirely new in the country, could be established. The Cambodians could not care less, and the new legal system remained largely restricted to the French sphere of action. For instance, there were repeated attempts from the start to involve the Cambodians in establishing a land-ownership system entirely alien to them.[21] Later, concepts of Roman law were incorporated into state laws. There were written laws, voted by an elected assembly, a system of courts and even a faculty of law. But this alien system affected the population only slightly and never put down intellectual roots there. The arbitrary behavior of a mostly corrupt administration, the violence of state power and the unlimited greed of the commercial class in any case made a mockery of any pretense of a rule of law.

In this *ancien régime* mentality, no justice can be expected from a system entirely devoted to the interests of the mighty and the wealthy. This does not mean that Cambodia is a lawless society. On the contrary, a complicated set of implicit moral rules regulates everyday life, and very clear standards of good conduct are taught to the youth. If circumstances of war, famine, and political crises have created massive ruptures and if the necessity to survive has forced individuals outside the normal rules, these rules later reassert themselves. But they are not, in themselves, strong enough to impose an order on what we might be tempted to call the "natural anarchy" of the Khmers. So far, only some form of terror has succeeded because the law is not deeply rooted in the peoples' consciences.

The idea of a particularly defined concept of *genocide* and the trial of a political chief would seem rather ludicrous to most Cambodians. Revenge is understandable, but retribution belongs to future lives. The trust in an independent judiciary just does not exist, and for good reasons. A trial held by foreigners would be just another kind of foreign business. With the exception of a tiny number of intellectuals and politicians acquainted with Western mores, everyone would see in the complicated procedures of a court the useless prelude to a retaliatory killing. And, anyway, it did take place. In the summer of 1979, an international tribunal was convened in Phnom Penh to try Pol Pot and Ieng Sary in absentia. Documents, testimonies, and witnesses were produced. I believe that around a thousand pages of documentation were presented. A summary was later published.[22] As it had obviously been organized by the Vietnamese, the Western press ignored it. Ten years passed before this same press started toying with the idea of a genocide trial, while Cambodia had all along been subjected to an economic embargo the criminal nature of which could also be tested in court. May I submit this idea to our interested lawyers?

Pol Pot is not even really considered a person in Cambodia. His name has become a common word: "Twelve pol pots entered village so and so." It certainly expresses feelings of hatred and resentment. (The name Pol Pot is never used in Khmer Rouge speech, where the man is usually referred to as *number 87*). Any form of violence would seem to be legitimate. When the crowd surrounded the house of Khieu Samphan in Phnom Penh, in November 1991, the rumor was that "Pol Pot" was there. And even more than blood, what the people wanted to see was the *face* of the man—a face they have never seen, a face they probably thought of as inhuman. The man never really exposed himself and his name is nothing more than a symbol.

We must start from the fact that Cambodians were never in a position to know the reasons for this bloody mess. In these ill-clad wild boys, they could only recognize the naked figure of power doing what power has always done in this country: humiliate or eliminate. (This goes far towards explaining what some would describe as suicidal tendencies, in individuals as in society.) Renunciation is the only narrow escape from these cruel alternatives but this time even monks and hermits were trapped. Would then, a trial be a great educational move, at last providing for the new generation an opportunity to reconcile remembrance and understanding? It probably would. Although historians usually pass severe judgments on this kind of great political trial, such staged dramas may have a cathartic effect, reorder collective thought, and provide new bridges for the legitimization of emerging powers. But we should remain lucid: the law is built upon concepts, and politics upon symbols. A political trial is a hybrid exercise where lawyers perform their intellectual tricks while the audience at large watches a symbolic play.[23]

Today, Cambodians both remember and forget. The pains they suffered, as individuals, as members of crushed families, are deeply ingrained, and the wounds will probably never heal. But the catastrophe seems to remain circumscribed in personal history. Paradoxically, this period of totally collective life gave rise to an individualistic struggle for life, aimed at surviving and, later, at reestablishing some form of normalcy. The global dimension was just an added burden and, for many, the sense of a collective drama seems to be waning.

In the West, the paradigm of genocide is still very much centered on Auschwitz. This is so true that, in an effort to evoke part of the sinister charisma of Auschwitz, the masters of the new Cambodian regime, in early 1979, commissioned some Vietnamese experts trained in Poland to refurbish the interrogation center called Tuol Sleng.[24] Very few people have seen it in its original state. But this paradigm also plays in another field called, in a vague manner, *memory*. As opposed to *history* (reconstruction of the past based on documents and material evidence), *memory* would be a tale of the past based on personal remembrance, subjective feelings, nostalgic attachment to *roots*. Some even think that *memory* has more truth in it than the cold reasoning of *history*. Genocide and the *memory* of it (basically, a reconstruction made by the *descendants* of the survivors) are linked with a refusal to mourn (and accept the passing away) of those who died an unnatural death. Psychoanalysis has a lot to say about this.[25] Jews and Khmers do not mourn and bury the dead in the same way, and there is the risk that our Western concept of *memory* could be entirely irrelevant to the Khmers who obviously have their own. I wish we would not succumb to the temptation to force our views upon them here, as we have already done in so many other areas.

When we compare the Cambodian terror with the legacy of fascism—and we have no doubt of the legitimacy of this comparison—we should note that, in the case of Europe, there was a struggle against fascism. Later, people could identify with that struggle, whatever had been the reality of their own commitment, and build a memory, somewhat selective, around these feelings of refusal, the struggle of good against evil, and eventual victory. But in Cambodia, there was no struggle; the level of terror was too high. There was not even a victory, as Pol Pot is still alive and kicking. Foreigners were engaged in the struggle and, with them, a handful of Khmers who were later largely rewarded with the gift of exclusive state power. So Cambodians have nothing positive to rely on, except an association with a foreign power that most of them would prefer not to have. If there is a political memory, it is a rather shameful one of abject submission, fear, passivity, inability to protect one's own family, of helpless dying children, stealing bits of revolting food. It is difficult to build even hatred on these bases. And when the government, in the 1980s, organized a yearly Day of Hatred, which would have delighted Orwell's sarcastic mind, people observed it casually.

When the crowd rioted in front of Khieu Samphan's house, an old lady came with her kitchen knife in order to chop him into pieces. The striking fact is that she was alone of her kind. When the people watched the event on TV and saw a white-haired man with blood dripping down his face, there was a general reaction of disapproval— a fear, stronger than anger that to bring back this memory would endanger the present. In Cambodia there is a will to forget. The idea that the Khmers Rouges have changed, which they try so hard to disseminate, could come as an anxiety-killing pill for many people.

Because the government established by the Vietnamese made large use of a rather simplified view of the recent past to justify its policies and its temporary dependence on foreign troops, it was perceived as government propaganda and, as such, obliterated the survivors' ability to build up their own retrospective understanding. On the coalition side, it was worse: the victims were coerced into working closely with the killers. Following Father Ponchaud, they had to fabricate the myth that the Vietnamese were even more "genocidal" than the DK. Even now Pol Pot refers constantly to the "genocidal and aggressive Yuon enemy." Sihanouk went to great lengths, on American television, to explain that the Khmers Rouges were "no longer criminals."

If we understand genocide in a broad sense as meaning unjustified mass murder, then Cambodia, as well as many other states, is a case of it, and its leaders should be brought to an international court— which, by the way, does not currently exist. If, on the other hand, we consider genocide as something specific, then we have to expand its meaning considerably to include Cambodia. This is what I tried to convey, many years ago, when I wrote that "if words have a meaning, there was certainly no genocide in Cambodia."[26] I understand that some Cambodians took exception to this statement, but then, is not their use of the word a kind of substitute for a victory over Pol Pot they could not win on the battlefield, and even less by being his political ally?

If we could catch Pol Pot and give him a fair trial, he would certainly claim that he was not the worst killer in Cambodia.[27] He would point out that many victims of starvation suffered the consequences of the aerial destruction wrought on the Cambodian countryside. He would remind us that Richard Nixon and Henry Kissinger concentrated US airpower on his country and destroyed around 600,000 lives in the process. Would they sit in the same dock?

Would they also face the charge of genocide in Cambodia for having killed Khmer peasants "as such"?

Who was it who fought for months and months to include in the future Peace Agreement on Cambodia a reference to the "genocidal practices of the past," in order to provide a ground for the political elimination of the Pol Pot group, at the risk of jeopardizing the whole diplomatic process? It was the Phnom Penh government, led by people who had been very junior leaders in the Khmer Rouge movement and who knew, better than most, its true nature. And what happened? The American government gave its full support to the Chinese scrapping of this infamous label. The final version of the agreements does not mention genocide at all, in order to make it possible to reincorporate the Khmers Rouges into Cambodian public life, very much against the will of the huge majority of the people there. The hypocrisy of American officials who claim they did everything possible to prevent the return of Pol Pot to Phnom Penh is revolting, particularly when one remembers that at the UN Geneva Conference in 1981 they voted down the ASEAN proposal to look for a political solution based on a disarmament of the Khmers Rouges.

In fact, there are two entirely different concepts of genocide: the one we all know and use on occasions, as a kind of historical category; and the one used by the lawyers, based on the widely unread UN Convention, which could technically allow the murder of two people to fall into the *genocide* category, according to the motive given to this crime. The discrepancy between the two definitions is so wide that confusion is inevitable.

The reality is that *genocide*—massacres, wiping out entire peoples or cultures, and other inhuman atrocities, such as torture, massive corruption, and so on—is part and parcel of government policies and as a charge is leveled at foreign countries. There is no other law than the law of the jungle. If we want to change this situation, we must first reform our own laws, strip the authorities of their political immunity, abolish the reason of state and the system of official secrecy that conceals all these crimes. If we could reach a stage where any official had to be tried according to the same rules that apply to you and me, in other words, to any other ordinary human being, we would not need all these extraordinary concepts, because the common law is quite enough.

Just after the Algerian war, the French government passed a law of amnesty: the thousands of crimes committed by the troops in this seven-year conflict were erased. They reputedly never took place. Nobody was punished and nobody may be publicly named in connection with those crimes. As for the United States, checking the name of the My Lai village in a Vietcong list of villages wiped out by the US ground forces, I found out that it was one among several hundreds, recorded long before My Lai became a public affair. Was any inquiry made into the destruction of those villages? Were those responsible for the slaughter in My Lai ever really punished? Who are we to give moral lessons to others?

I of course fully agree that Pol Pot should be prevented by any means from returning to power. I find it paradoxical that so much blame has been heaped on the Vietnamese, who did just that—prevented him from coming back—by people who did so much to promote the same Pol Pot and insisted that he keep his seat in the United Nations. I am also fully in favor of a trial of Pol Pot, his accomplices, and his foreign associates—including American, Thai and Chinese officials who conspired to support him when he was in power and after his fall. For events which took place in Cambodia, I suggest the application of the ordinary Cambodian law.

Genocide is nothing other than a political label aimed at the excluding a political leader or party from the bonds of mankind. Accusing others of genocide leads us to believe we are good, that we have nothing to do with these monsters. This is entirely misleading. Pol Pot was produced by our political world, is part of it, is using it, and is growing strong from it. Before saying he is dirty—which, without a doubt, he is—we should first clean our own house.

February 4, 1992, Phnom Penh.[28]

---

[1] "Cambodia and the United States are both signatories to the Genocide Convention, and we will support efforts to bring to justice those responsible for the mass murders of the 1970s if the new Cambodian government chooses to pursue this path." (*New York Times*, 24 October 1991: A16.) The USA ratified the Convention in 1986, long after Cambodia.

[2] See Christophe Peschoux, *Enquête sur les "nouveaux" Khmers rouges, Reconstruction du mouvement et reconquête des villages* (Paris, May 1991), 173 pp.

[3] Ben Kiernan, "The Cambodian Genocide: Issues and Responses," in. G. Andreopoulos, ed., *Genocide: The Conceptual and Historical Dimensions*, (University of Pennsylvania Press) 1994 (forthcoming).

[4] *Cambodia, a Demographic Catastrophe* (GC80-100190), May 1980, which I reviewed in *Libération*, Paris, Sept. 17, 1980. Michael Vickery discussed it in "Democratic Kampuchea: CIA to the Rescue," *Bulletin of Concerned Asian Scholars*, 14:4, 1982.

[5] On traditional wisdom, see the texts edited and translated by Saveros Pou, *Guirlande de Cpap'*, (Paris, Cedoreck), 2 vols., 1988.

[6] Pol Pot would agree. In December 1988, in a speech to his Women's Association cadre, he said: "Our troops previously did not know how to conduct popular work because the concrete fact was that they did not yet have any faith in the people and instead relied exclusively on bullets and other material things," an interesting comment coming from the man who has been in charge of a guerrilla movement for twenty-five years.

[7] Translated in *Khmers rouges!*, Serge Thion and Ben Kiernan (Paris, 1981): 358-661.

[8] Introduction, *Les Etats hindouisés d'Indochine et d'Indonésie*, Paris, De Boccard, 1948: 3.

[9] See Keng Vannsak, "Recherche d'un fonds culturel khmer," unpublished thesis (Paris, Sorbonne), 1971.

[10] A good analysis of regional and local variations is to be found in Michael Vickery, *Cambodia, 1975-1982* (Boston, 1984), chapter 3.

[11] See Serge Thion, "Time for Talk," *Internationales Asienforum* (Cologne), December 1988: 337-348.

[12] See Sarin Chhak, *Les Frontières du Cambodge* (Paris) 1966.

[13] See Nayan Chanda, *Brother Enemy* (New York), 1986.

[14] See Raphael Lemkin, *Axis Rule in Occupied Europe: Laws of Occupation, Analysis of Government, Proposals for Redress* (New York, Columbia University Press), 1944. Lemkin had been a technician of law in the Polish civil service until 1939. He then went to Sweden and in 1941 to the USA. The concept of genocide occupies a rather limited space in the book. It included cultural assimilation: for instance, the Germans were imposing a genocide on the Poles because they were pushing pornography and gambling. Lemkin died in 1959.

[15] Gregory Stanton informs us that the former president of (formerly Spanish) Equatorial Guinea, Francisco Macías Nguema, a very bloody dictator indeed, has been condemned for genocide. I still believe that some more obvious candidates could be found, excluding new regimes putting their predecessors on trial. On the circumstances surrounding Macías 'coming to power, see Donato Ndongo Bidyogo, *Historia y tragedia de Guinea Ecuatorial* (Madrid, Editorial Cambio 16), 1977.

[16] "Will be punished [up to three years in jail] those who have contested [through the press] one or several crimes against humanity as they have been defined by Article 6 of the statute of the international military tribunal annexed to the London Agreement of Aug. 8, 1945..." (Art. 9, Law of 13 July 1990). This law is an obvious violation of basic constitutional rights but, in

France, citizens cannot appeal to the Constitutional Council, which is usually staffed by former politicians.

[17] The very political nature of the wording is fully recognized in the *1991 Annual Report of the Cambodia Documentation Commission,* headed by David Hawk in New York when it says: "At the 1989 Paris Conference on Cambodia, the Khmers Rouges, China and Singapore insisted on the removal of the reference to genocide." (5) Then a footnote adds: "The point is not a legal technicality. The use or non-use of the word 'genocide' (a crime under international law) was *diplomatic code language* for the present and future role of the top Khmers Rouges leaders. The substitution of the more vague formulation 'past policies and practices' for the word 'genocide' was the signal that top Khmers Rouges leaders such as Pol Pot, Ieng Sary, Nuon Chea, Khieu Samphan, Son Sen, Ta Mok *et al.* would not be barred from potential and actual, de jure and de facto, leadership roles in Cambodia's future."

[18] In a list of publications provided by *Cultural Survival Quarterly* (Cambridge, Mass.), 14:3: 55, out of 46, three titles refer to "ethnocide" and three to "genocide" to describe quite similar situations of threatened indigenous peoples. It does not seem that any legal action is implied.

[19] The case of Indonesia, for instance, is heavily loaded, with the massacre of more than 500,000 Communist affiliates in 1965, the violent oppression exercised in Irian Jaya since 1969 when the international community approved the forceful take over of Western New Guinea, and the invasion of Portuguese Timor in 1975, followed by massacres equaling those of Pol Pot. But Indonesia is a trusted ally of the West, which generously provides the armaments to carry on the mass murders. In which press would it be possible to call Suharto a "genocider"?

[20] See Adhémard Leclère, *Recherches sur le droit public des Cambodgiens* (Paris), 1894.

[21] See A. Boudillon, *La Réforme du régime de la propriété foncière en Indochine, Rapport au Gouverneur Général* (Hanoi,) 1927; Roger Kleinpeter, *Le Problème foncier au Cambodge* (Paris), 1937.

[22] *People's Revolutionary Tribunal held in Phnom Penh for the Trial of the Genocide Crime of the Pol Pot -Ieng Sary Clique* (Phnom Penh), 1988, 311 p.

[23] For an Asian context, see Paul Mus, "'Cosmodrame' et politique en Asie du Sud-Est," reprinted in Mus, *L'Angle de l'Asie* (Paris, Hermann), 1977.

[24] The analogy is always tempting. See, for instance, what a distinguished Khmer senior economist with the Asian Development Bank, Someth Suos, said recently in Penang: "The killing field was a world major historical event that surpassed Hitler's killing of the Jews" (Workshop on Reconstruction and Development, [Penang], 1991, p.37). He later adds: "The Khmer rouge cadre should be accorded a role in the society." The parallel with Nazi Germany is nothing but sloppy thinking.

[25] See the numerous references to "mourning" in *The Complete Psychological Works of Sigmund Freud* and, in particular, "Mourning and Melancholia" and

"Thoughts for the Times on War and Death" (written in 1915), in vol. 14, Standard Edition (The Hogarth Press). For Cambodian context, see James K. Boehlein, "Clinical relevance of Grief and Mourning among Cambodian Refugees," *Soc. Sci. Med.*, 25:7: 765-772. I am grateful to Lane Gerber ,who provided me with a copy of this article.

[26] Introduction, Serge Thion and Ben Kiernan, *Khmers rouges!*, (Paris), 1981: 35.

[27] Ieng Sary recently answered this question in a conversation with two journalists (*Le Nouvel Observateur*, 17-23 November 1991): Genocide? 'A lie[...]. I am human. I never thought I committed acts of genocide, I shall never recognize that.' Any regrets? 'Yes, I regret I could not efficiently oppose erroneous points of views which prevailed at certain times, I regret I had not the courage [...] to directly oppose some people.[...] Maybe I could not have stayed alive until now.'

[28] I wish to thank Helen Jarvis and David Chandler for their useful suggestions after reading previous drafts of this paper.

The Inclusion of the Khmer Rouge in the Cambodian Peace Process: Causes and Consequences*

Ben Kiernan

A Vietnamese-backed Cambodian government, headed by Heng Samrin and Hun Sen, replaced Pol Pot's Khmer Rouge regime in 1979. In 1989, Vietnam's troops withdrew from the country, preceded by all but a few Vietnamese military advisers. Now calling itself the State of Cambodia, the regime then offered its noncommunist opponents, Norodom Sihanouk and Son Sann (but not their Khmer Rouge ally), a political role and free elections.[1] Meanwhile, neighboring Thailand's policy shifted toward rapprochement with its Indochinese communist neighbors, best illustrated by the hosting of three visits by Cambodian Prime Minister Hun Sen to Bangkok in 1989. In the same period, regional—particularly Southeast Asian—diplomacy showed promise of an emerging consensus to exclude the Khmer Rouge as well as the Vietnamese.

But the great powers, particularly China and the United States, played a spoiling role, maximizing their influence with and support of their Cambodian protégés to outflank the regional diplomacy.[2] Negotiations at great-power level, in Paris and especially in the UN Security Council, displaced the regional ones, returning the Khmer Rouge to the diplomatic forefront. Such a UN settlement, a recipe for renewed civil war if not genocide, could now be imposed on Cambodia. Meanwhile the country remained diplomatically isolated, economically blockaded, and under military attack by Pol Pot's Chinese-backed Khmer Rouge and their U.S.-funded allies. The international isolation and blockade ended only when the Hun Sen government agreed to readmit the Khmer Rouge to the Cambodian political arena and to risk its power in UN-organized elections amid continuing Khmer Rouge military attacks.

* Parts of this chapter have been published by the Institute of International Studies, University of California, Berkeley, as "Deferring Peace in Cambodia: Regional Rapprochement, Superpower Obstruction," in *Beyond the Cold War: Conflict and Cooperation in the Third World*, edited by George W. Breslauer, Harry Kreisler, and Benjamin Ward (Berkeley, 1991), and in the *Bulletin of Concerned Asian Scholars*, 24, 2, April-June 1992, as "The Cambodian Crisis, 1990-1992: The UN Plan, the Khmer Rouge, and the State of Cambodia."

The War in Cambodia

During the Pol Pot period, from 1975 to 1979, Cambodia was subjected to probably the world's most radical political, social and economic revolution. The country was cut off from the outside world, its cities were emptied, its economy was militarized, and its Buddhist religion and folk culture destroyed, and 1.5 million of its eight million people were starved and massacred, while foreign and minority languages were banned and all neighboring countries were attacked.

Thus an international conflict was intertwined with genocide that provoked a civil war. On 10 May 1978, Phnom Penh radio broadcast a call not only to "exterminate the 50 million Vietnamese" but also to "purify the masses of the people" of Cambodia. When Cambodian communists rebelled in the Eastern Zone, Pol Pot was unable to crush them quickly. Over the next six months, more than a million easterners were branded as "Khmer bodies with Vietnamese minds," and at least 100,000 were exterminated by Pol Pot's forces.[3] In 1979, surviving leaders of the Eastern Zone dissidents (like Hun Sen and Heng Samrin) succeeded Pol Pot, once Hanoi had driven his Khmer Rouge army into Thailand.

The Cambodia-Vietnam conflict had started in 1977, with Pol Pot's regime staging repeated savage raids into Vietnamese territory, massacring thousands of Vietnamese civilians and causing hundreds of thousands to flee from their homes.[4] Hanoi's complaints to this effect were corroborated at the time by both U.S. intelligence reports and the testimony of Vietnamese refugees fleeing abroad from the war zone, and were later extensively documented from both sides of the border.[5]

After Pol Pot's regime refused to negotiate peacefully or accept international supervision of the border,[6] Vietnamese forces intervened and overthrew it in early 1979. Western rhetoric aside, Hanoi's invasion of Cambodia was not "aggression" (unprovoked attack). Vietnam's immediate reason for intervention was self-defense. China joined Cambodia as an aggressor state when Pol Pot's ally Deng Xiaoping retaliated against Hanoi with his own invasion of Vietnam.

Vietnamese troops remained in Cambodia, offering to withdraw only in return for two concessions: the exclusion of Pol Pot's forces from the country and an end to the new Chinese threat to Vietnam itself. China, the Association of Southeast Asian Nations (ASEAN) and the West, on the other hand, demanded an unconditional Vietnamese withdrawal, recognized the ousted Pol Pot regime as the "legitimate" representative of the Cambodian people, and rearmed and supplied its forces. With this aid and in the sanctuary of Thailand,[7] the Khmer Rouge rebuilt an army of about 25,000, and in 1982 were joined in a coalition government-in-exile by two small Western-backed groups nominally loyal to Norodom Sihanouk (the ANS) and Son Sann (the KPNLF).

Nevertheless, from 1980 Hanoi began withdrawing its advisers, and in 1982 began official partial withdrawals of its troops, as the new Cambodian government consolidated its position. As we shall see, Vietnam successively dropped its two conditions for a withdrawal, which it completed *unilaterally* in September 1989. But then the opposition coalition intensified its attacks, although refusing to acknowledge the withdrawal or make reciprocal concessions, and possibly several thousand Vietnamese combat troops briefly returned to Cambodia in November 1989. They reportedly left again in January 1990. A few technical military advisers apparently remained.[8]

Vietnamese Troop Strength in Cambodia, 1979-1989
(U.S. Sources)[9]

Year	Troop Numbers
1979	224,000
1982	180,000
1983	150,000
1987	circa 120,000
1988	100,000
Early 1989	50,000
September 1989	None

The State of Cambodia forces then held the country, belying Western predictions that a collapse would quickly follow any Vietnamese withdrawal. (A mid-1987 Australian intelligence assessment, for instance, had put the chances of a Vietnamese withdrawal by 1990 at "1 in 300," in which case the Phnom Penh regime would last only "seven months.")

During their ten-year occupation, the Vietnamese trained a large Cambodian defense force. The three levels of the army — national, regional, and local — probably mustered over 100,000 regular troops and 200,000 militia. The Vietnamese also helped establish a full-fledged Cambodian government led by Khmer nationalists,[10] but it was the economy that became the most pressing problem for Phnom Penh with the end of Eastern European and much Soviet aid in 1990.[11]

The 1985 fifth congress of the ruling People's Revolutionary Party had formally legalized and endorsed the private sector. More recent economic reforms in Cambodia included the privatization of agricultural land, housing, and the industrial and commercial sectors. Political reforms made Buddhism the state religion, legalized Christianity, officially declared neutrality in foreign policy, and changed (at Sihanouk's request) the official name of the country and the flag. Cambodia remained a one-party state, although Hun Sen favored a multiparty system for a postwar Cambodia.[12]

Any agreement among the Cambodian parties that included the Khmer Rouge clearly risked later breakdown and a new civil war far more destabilizing than the status quo. But there was potential for a settlement between the State of Cambodia and the non-communist opposition groups, should the latter have been able to break their dependence on the Khmer Rouge and take advantage of the rehabilitation of their country by the Cambodian government the Vietnamese had established there. Whether Sihanouk and Son Sann would have accepted this is unclear. As heads of the two smallest factions, they were most dependent on their great-power backers, who required a role for the Khmer Rouge. But the Cambodian balance of forces was compatible with the emergence of a regional, Southeast Asian consensus to exclude the Khmer Rouge.

The Regional Diplomacy

In March 1980, the Malaysian prime minister Datuk Hussein Onn and Indonesia's President Suharto met in the Malaysian coastal town of Kuantan. The meeting produced the "Kuantan principle." The two Southeast Asian leaders released a statement noting their concern over the Soviet role in the Cambodia conflict, through Vietnam, but also over China's role in Indochina. As the *Far Eastern Economic Review* put it: "Hanoi's reaction was cool. But elsewhere, the principle was widely seen as a step in the right direction. Vietnam, it was generally thought, would withdraw only if there was no more Soviet aid to make the occupation viable, and if there was some guarantee that China would not leap into the breach after the withdrawal."[13]   In other words, Hanoi had some legitimate concerns, that were shared in Southeast Asia.   Indonesia, for instance, was not to establish diplomatic relations with China for another decade.   These concerns had to be addressed in negotiations.   According to Nayan Chanda, Indonesian Armed Forces chief Benny Murdani made two secret trips to Hanoi in 1980 and 1982 to attempt to mediate in the dispute.[14]

In 1983 Bill Hayden, Australia's new foreign minister, identified the two key issues dominating the Cambodian conflict.   These were the problem of a threatened Khmer Rouge return to power, and the need for a Vietnamese withdrawal.   Hayden launched an effort to "facilitate dialogue" on the Cambodian question. Indonesia encouraged this effort, even expressing the vain hope that Australia would restore its aid program in Vietnam.   In February 1984, Benny Murdani concluded a third visit to Vietnam with the statement that Hanoi posed no threat to Southeast Asia.   He also recognized that Hanoi's invasion of Cambodia had been undertaken in self-defense, "to maintain Vietnam's own existence" against Pol Pot's attacks.[15]   Soon after, Hanoi made a new diplomatic proposal, which Indonesia's foreign minister, Mochtar Kusumaatmadja, called "a significant step forward." The Thai foreign minister, Siddhi Savetsila, also welcomed unspecified "new elements" in Hanoi's position.[16]

These new elements became clear in 1985.   Hanoi, after capturing all twenty of the Khmer Rouge and allied camps along the Thai-Cambodian border, dropped its demand that the Chinese threat would have to end before any full Vietnamese troop withdrawal from Cambodia.[17]   In early March 1985, Hayden visited Hanoi, and heard further Vietnamese proposals from Foreign Minister Nguyen Co Thach, which Hayden claimed were "a considerable advance."   He asserted that his trip had "been quite successful and that will be proved."[18]   Indonesia's Mochtar concurred that there had been another "advance in substance" in the Vietnamese position.[19]

While in Vietnam, Hayden had a meeting with Hun Sen, becoming the first of many regional leaders to meet the Cambodian premier. Hun Sen told him: "We are ready to make concessions to Prince Sihanouk and other people if they agree to join with us to eliminate Pol Pot." Hun Sen later announced that the Vietnamese troops would all leave Cambodia by 1990, or earlier if there was a settlement. (The previous date set by Hanoi had been 1995.)

Vietnam now insisted only that the Khmer Rouge be prevented from returning to power. This meant that the Cambodian problem could from that point be resolved within Southeast Asia, principally by Thailand, which could cut off sanctuary and supplies to the Khmer Rouge, and by Vietnam, which could withdraw the rest of its own troops. China's cooperation in a settlement was no longer necessary.

However, China (and, as we shall see, the United States) disagreed. On 10 April 1986, the *Far Eastern Economic Review* reported that in June, ASEAN ministers would finalize "a detailed blueprint for a settlement of the Cambodia question":

> The confidential outline attempts to satisfy Hanoi's demand that the withdrawal of its troops from Cambodia be coupled with cessation of Chinese arms supplies to the Khmer resistance by proposing to station an international peace-keeping force along Cambodia's land and sea borders. The sea border is being specified to assure Vietnam China would not be able to continue the supplies once the land routes from Thailand have been closed in the wake of a successful settlement.

However, within two weeks, China and the Democratic Kampuchea factions over-ruled this initiative. The June ASEAN foreign ministers' meeting in Manila, it appears, did not discuss it.

But Hayden did address the question of the Khmer Rouge. At the Manila ASEAN meeting, he proposed the establishment of a tribunal to try the Pol Pot leadership for its crimes. Although U.S. Secretary of State George Shultz declined to support the idea, it was immediately endorsed in principle by the Malaysian foreign minister,[20] and a few weeks later the Indonesian foreign minister added his own agreement.[21] Chinese and U.S. opposition to the idea was accompanied by that of Australia's prime minister.[22]

It was another year before Prince Sihanouk withdrew, even temporarily, from the Khmer Rouge coalition. He met Hun Sen for the first time in December 1987 and carried to Beijing Hun Sen's proposal to disarm the Khmer Rouge. As Kelvin Rowley points out, China rejected the idea, and Sihanouk canceled his next round of talks with Hun Sen.

But in July 1988 the first round of the Jakarta Informal Meetings (JIMs) took place, attended by all ASEAN and Indochinese countries, and all Cambodian factions. This meeting leapt a major hurdle, the refusal of the Cambodian sides to meet face-to-face, each having long insisted it would negotiate only with the foreign backers of the other. In Jakarta the ice was broken by having the Cambodian parties meet first, with the Southeast Asian supporters of each then joining the conference.

The "consensus statement" from the meeting, released by the new Indonesian foreign minister Ali Alatas, stressed the two problems Hayden had identified: a Vietnamese withdrawal (promised for 1990), and prevention of "a recurrence of the genocidal policies and practices of the Pol Pot regime."[23] In April 1989 the Vietnamese undertook to withdraw their forces by September 1989. Sihanouk and Hun Sen met again in Jakarta the following month. They reached general agreement, and Sihanouk said he was prepared to go it alone without the Khmer Rouge should they prove recalcitrant.[24] However, he reneged on this undertaking immediately after leaving Jakarta. The prince had lost his nerve, becoming a genuine puppet of the Chinese and the Khmer Rouge. As the last Vietnamese troops were pulling out, Sihanouk called for a civil war in Cambodia to overthrow the Hun Sen government, threatening Cambodia's people with "danger to yourself" unless they rallied to his coalition to "avoid the charge of treason" after its victory.[25]

The third Jakarta Informal Meeting, in February 1990, broke down over the Khmer Rouge objection to use of the word "genocide" in the final communiqué. Although it had appeared in previous statements, the Khmer Rouge now opposed its inclusion, insisting instead on mention of "Vietnamese settlers," to which Hun Sen and Vietnamese Foreign Minister Thach objected. The Australian foreign minister, Gareth Evans, then proposed placing an asterisk next to each disputed phrase, with a note that these had not been agreed upon unanimously. Hun Sen and Thach agreed to this compromise. But the Khmer Rouge refused, and the talks broke up.[26] Again, Sihanouk and Son Sann had declined to break with the Khmer Rouge.

In Tokyo in June 1990, Sihanouk did go ahead in cease-fire talks with Hun Sen, despite a Khmer Rouge boycott. He signed an agreement on "voluntary self-restraint," and subsequently named six members of the noncommunist forces to an agreed twelve-member Supreme National Council, with Hun Sen naming the other six. But again, Sihanouk tore up this agreement after the Khmer Rouge expressed opposition.[27] Hun Sen later commented: "It is regrettable that Prince Sihanouk rejects all our accords as often as I enter into agreement with him."[28] The Pol Pot-Sihanouk-Son Sann coalition

long held firm. It seems unwise to rely on any future commitment
from Sihanouk, who revealed in September 1990 that he "would
agree to anything the Khmer Rouge wanted."[29]

But meanwhile the policy of Thailand, the "front-line state" most
threatened by Hanoi's 1979 removal of the Pol Pot regime, shifted.
Thailand's first elected prime minister since 1976, Chatichai
Choonhavon, held office from 1988 until he was ousted in a military
coup in 1991. During this period, sensing advantage in the accelerating
Vietnamese withdrawal, Bangkok moved closer to both Hanoi and
Phnom Penh, hoping to turn Indochina from "a battleground into a
trading ground." In Southeast Asia, the Cambodian issue was the
major one dividing the region, and the momentum developed for a
settlement.[30]

The Southeast Asian consensus, at the JIM meetings and elsewhere,
usually favored a settlement that would exclude both Vietnamese
troops and the Khmer Rouge—potential common ground with Hanoi.
And the Tokyo meeting of Cambodian parties went ahead without the
Khmer Rouge. Any likely regional settlement would have excluded
them as well.

These advances were possible because the great powers,
particularly China and the United States, were not involved. But there
was no settlement precisely because of Chinese and U.S. rejection of
any such move to exclude the Khmer Rouge. The great powers
continued to offer the Khmer Rouge a veto, which was regularly
exercised.

A major role in this process was played by Australia. In late 1989,
Foreign Minister Gareth Evans came under intense domestic pressure
from opponents of the Western/Chinese proposal, which Evans had
publicly backed, to return the Khmer Rouge to positions of power as
full partners in a new "quadripartite" Cambodian government. On 24
November 1989, the day after the John Pilger-David Munro film
Cambodia Year Ten was shown on national television, Evans
announced a new Australian plan. This called for the United Nations
temporarily to administer Cambodia and hold elections. He said its
aim was to exclude the Khmer Rouge, with Cambodia's UN seat
declared vacant. Subsequent international "support for the Australian
plan" ignored the crucial latter point, which was not implemented.

But the proposal never involved any concrete action by Australia.
It quickly degenerated into a refusal to take any action without Khmer
Rouge "acceptance" — not at all a means to exclude them. Evans

stated: "The simple fact is that, in the absence of a comprehensive settlement supported by China and accepted by the Khmer Rouge, the Cambodian tragedy will continue."[31] Thus the Evans Plan to end the threat of the Khmer Rouge instead offered them veto power to paralyze the peace process and two years' valuable time to advance their war aims.

The Region and the Great Powers

"I do not understand why some people want to remove Pol Pot," Deng Xiaoping said in 1984.[32] "It is true that he made some mistakes in the past but now he is leading the fight against the Vietnamese aggressors." In May 1989, Prince Sihanouk revealed to foreign diplomats that Deng had threatened to "fight" him should he abandon his alliance with the Khmer Rouge.[33] Chinese support for the Khmer Rouge, including a large delivery of weapons in mid-1990[34] despite a previous undertaking to cut arms supplies in return for Vietnam's withdrawal,[35] remained strongest. China provided the Khmer Rouge forces with US $100 million per annum, according to U.S. intelligence.[36] (Beijing possibly saw the Khmer Rouge and their two anti-Vietnamese allies replaying China's wartime anti-Japanese struggle, when the Chinese Communist Party's united front tactics also gave its bourgeois allies two of the "three-thirds" of coalition posts.[37])

Meanwhile the USSR, while continuing to supply Vietnam and Cambodia at reduced levels (aid to Vietnam fell by sixty-three percent in 1990),[38] rapidly lost interest in the region, owing to Vietnam's mismanagement of its aid and Soviet domestic problems. The Soviet Union, as Steven Erlanger of the *New York Times* reported in mid-1990, "no longer has the money or, seemingly, the will to project an ideology onto developing countries anywhere."[39] The Soviet military withdrawal from Cam Ranh Bay in Vietnam underscored that lack of interest.[40]

On the other hand, the three major planks of U.S. policy towards Cambodia remained unchanged. These were: the U.S. veto of aid to Cambodia, including UN, World Bank, and International Monetary Fund aid;[41] U.S. support for a Khmer Rouge role; and U.S. military support for the Khmer Rouge's allies ($17-32 million per annum).[42] All three policies continued despite the Beijing massacre of June 1989 and the Vietnamese withdrawal from Cambodia in September 1989.

They even continued after Washington's proclaimed policy "shift" on Cambodia in July 1990.[43]

Unlike the affected regional countries, great powers can afford to ignore for years the damage their policies inflict on small nations. A British diplomat expressed this distance when he remarked on Cambodia in 1986, "We're only talking about six million people."[44] France, too, like the United States, was unenthusiastic about any settlement arrived at independently in Southeast Asia.[45] And given the choice, China naturally blocked isolation of its Khmer Rouge client, as well as resisting moves toward regional concord, demonstrating its preference for a Balkanized Southeast Asia with many roads to Beijing. Yet any agreement to isolate the Khmer Rouge between Vietnam and Thailand, if backed by ASEAN and the West, would have been very hard for Beijing to subvert. China must live with Southeast Asia and would have accepted a bipartisan Southeast Asian settlement.

The withdrawal of the Vietnamese army from Cambodia in 1989 belied the myth that Chinese and Western backing for Pol Pot's forces (and his allies) since 1978 was primarily aimed at forcing a Vietnamese withdrawal. As Deng Xiaoping had stated in December 1979: "It is wise for China *to force the Vietnamese to stay in Cambodia*, because that way they will suffer more and more."[46]

The real question, then, was who ruled Cambodia. The Vietnamese presence was a pretext not just for China, but also for the United States, to oppose their Cambodian enemy candidate: the pro-Vietnamese, anti-Pol Pot, Hun Sen regime. Despite obvious difficulty in justifying it, the West maintained an embargo on Cambodia (renewed by Washington in September 1990 for its twelfth year), yet still supported Pol Pot's allies and opposed his Cambodian opponents, and continued to offer the Pol Pot forces a veto over any proposed settlement.

For over a decade, official Western support for Deng Xiaoping's China spilled over into Western support for his protégé Pol Pot. Former U.S. National Security Advisor Zbigniew Brzezinski says that in 1979: "I encouraged the Chinese to support Pol Pot....Pol Pot was an abomination. We could never support him but China could."[47]

They both did. The United States, Brzezinski says, "winked, semi-publicly" at Chinese and Thai aid for the Khmer Rouge after their defeat by Hanoi. Washington also pressured UN agencies to supply the Khmer Rouge. In *Rice, Rivalry and Politics*, the major study of the relief effort for Cambodian refugees in Thailand, Linda Mason and Roger Brown, graduates of the Yale School of Management, revealed: "The U.S. Government, which funded the bulk of the relief operation on the border, insisted that the Khmer Rouge be fed." They add: "When World Relief started to push its proposal for aid to the Khmer Rouge, the US was supportive, though behind the scenes... the US preferred that the Khmer Rouge operation benefit from the credibility of an internationally-known relief organization." Congressional sources also cited a figure of $85 million for U.S. aid to Pol Pot's Khmer Rouge from 1979 to 1986.[48] This may explain why, under U.S. influence, the World Food Program alone handed over $12 million worth of food to the Thai army to pass on to the Khmer Rouge. "20-40,000 Pol Pot guerrillas benefited," according to former Assistant Secretary of State Richard Holbrooke.[49] Mason and Brown note that the health of the Khmer Rouge army "rapidly improved" throughout 1980. "The Khmer Rouge had a history of unimaginable brutality, and having regained their strength, they had begun fighting the Vietnamese."[50]

In May 1980 the U.S. Central Intelligence Agency produced a "demographic report" on Cambodia which denied that there had been *any* executions in the last two years of the Pol Pot regime.[51] (The toll from executions in 1977-1978 had in fact been around half a million people.[52]) In November 1980, former deputy director of the CIA, Ray Cline, made a secret visit to a Khmer Rouge camp inside Cambodia.[53]

In the diplomatic arena, the United States led most of the Western world to line up behind China in support of the Khmer Rouge. The Carter and Reagan Administrations both voted for Pol Pot's representative, Thiounn Prasith, to occupy Cambodia's seat in the United Nations. He did so until late 1990, and in 1992 continued to run Cambodia's UN mission in New York. As of 1993, no Western country had voted against the Khmer Rouge in the thirteen years that their tenure has been challenged.

In 1981, at an international conference on Cambodia, then U.S. Secretary of State Al Haig dismayed the Southeast Asian countries by backing China's firm support for the Khmer Rouge. Some of Haig's subordinates soon regretted this "shameful episode."[54] The United States and China cooperated to force the exiled Cambodian leaders Prince Sihanouk and Son Sann to join, in June 1982, a coalition with Pol Pot;[55] after they had done so, they received U.S. aid.[56] The Reagan administration then justified the Khmer Rouge flag flying over New York by reference to its "continuity" with the Pol Pot regime.[57]

In 1983, U.S. Secretary of State Shultz described as "stupid" the efforts of Australian Foreign Minister Hayden to encourage dialogue over Cambodia.[58] In 1985, Shultz visited Thailand and again warned against peace talks with Vietnam. According to the *Bangkok Post* of 13 July 1985, "A senior US official said Shultz cautioned ASEAN to be extremely careful in formulating peace proposals for Kampuchea because Vietnam might one day accept them."

Washington's fears were realized. Rapprochement in Southeast Asia, particularly between Thailand and Vietnam, facilitated the Vietnamese withdrawal and allowed the prospect of a settlement of the Cambodia question. The key remaining issue was the future of the Khmer Rouge, armed by Deng's China, whom Washington gives "most favored nation" status.

By contrast, the Bush administration threatened to punish Thailand for *its* defection from the aggressive U.S.-Chinese position. As the *Far Eastern Economic Review* put it in 1989: "Officials privately warned that if Thailand abandoned the Cambodian resistance and its leader Prince Norodom Sihanouk for the sake of doing business with Phnom Penh, it would have to pay a price. Thailand should consider whether the total value of any new Indochinese trade would even cover the US trade access privileges it still gets under the Generalized Special Preferences, one administration official said."[59] Soon afterwards, the U.S. ambassador in Thailand stated that the Khmer Rouge could not be excluded from the future government of Cambodia, while U.S. Secretary of State James A. Baker proposed their inclusion.[60]

The removal of the negotiations from the regional forum in Jakarta to the great power forum in Paris, with the introduction of a unanimity requirement, gave the Khmer Rouge both direct superpower backing and a veto over resolution of the conflict. At the International Conference on Cambodia in Paris in August 1989, Baker restated his proposal to return the Khmer Rouge to positions of power. The conference failed to foster a Sihanouk-Hun Sen alliance against the Khmer Rouge. As the *Economist* put it on 30 September 1989: "The talk among the delegates is that the American State Department torpedoed the deal."[61]

Washington sought not merely an independent Cambodian government, but an *anti-Vietnamese* one. According to the *Far Eastern Economic Review*, "Thai officials believe that, despite its publicly expressed revulsion towards the Khmer Rouge, the US has been quietly aiding the Khmer Rouge war effort for several years." One senior Thai official said: "We would like to see a lead against the Khmer Rouge taken by the U.S...."[62]

After ten years of U.S. opposition to its role in Cambodia, Vietnam withdrew. The Hun Sen government did not collapse. Then Washington moved the goal posts. "Hanoi has an obligation to do more than just walk away," Assistant Secretary of State Richard Solomon now said. Now began the search for a "comprehensive settlement." The United States called on Hanoi to force another change of government on the Cambodians, one that would appease Pol Pot's Khmer Rouge. Washington's policy demonstrated that it would not reduce its support for the genocidists, or take any action against them, before their only Cambodian opponents, the Hun Sen regime, were first displaced from power.

In November 1989, Australia's foreign minister Gareth Evans launched his proposal for a UN administration to run Cambodia and hold elections, with the UN seat being vacated by the Khmer Rouge and their allies. Although the Hun Sen government in principle accepted the idea,[63] the Khmer Rouge on many occasions refused it, preferring to step up attacks on the country while keeping their enemies talking.

Roger Normand, fieldwork editor of the *Harvard Human Rights Journal*, obtained the contents of some of Pol Pot's confidential speeches, recorded in briefing notes taken by Khmer Rouge commanders who defected in 1989.[64] They show Pol Pot's conscious use of the veto the West had given him over the negotiation process through its push for a unanimous "comprehensive settlement." In 1988, Pol Pot secretly revealed plans to "delay the elections" until his forces "control all the country," when his officials "will lead the balloting work." In this secret briefing to Pol Pot's commanders, Khieu Samphan, his delegate to the negotiations, added: "The outside world keeps demanding a political end to the war in Kampuchea. I could end the war now if I wanted, because the outside world is waiting for me, but I am buying time to give you comrades the opportunity to carry out all the tasks... If it doesn't end politically, and ends militarily, that's good for us." Here Pol Pot interrupted, saying that "to end the war politically" would make his movement "fade away": "We must prevent this from happening." Since then Pol Pot has been playing the international community on a break.

Yet the struggle for peace continued. After the breakdown of the Paris talks, *Asiaweek* reported: "The only sign of settlement is a conference of the four factions along with ASEAN and Vietnam, suggested by Thailand's fence-mending Prime Minister Chatichai Choonhavan. ...Washington, whose say-so is important, has indicated that it disapproves. That has put a damper on the plan."[65] The United States then also opposed Thailand's proposals for a cease-fire and establishment of neutral camps to protect Cambodian refugees from the depredations of the Khmer Rouge and their allies.[66] According to diplomatic correspondent Nayan Chanda, Washington "politely dismissed" even Japan's peace plan, which called for "elections in Cambodia with a limited UN participation."[67] Before the 5 June 1990 cease-fire talks in Tokyo, Chanda reported, Richard Solomon made a secret trip to deliver a warning to the Thais.[68] The talks went ahead and did produce a shaky cease-fire agreement. But like the Khmer Rouge who boycotted them, Solomon publicized U.S. opposition, and the U.S.-backed KPNLF, ally of Pol Pot's forces, foreshadowed that it would not respect what it called "only a document... a play on words."[69]

On 14 June 1990 Thailand's Prime Minister Chatichai visited Washington and met with U.S. President George Bush. They disagreed on Cambodia. Chatichai called for U.S. pressure on China to reduce its support for Pol Pot's forces. Bush favored a "comprehensive solution" that included them. As Richard Solomon remarked, "We're at a fork in the road."[70] On 18 July 1990, Washington announced a "policy shift." This amounted to readiness for talks with Hanoi over Cambodia, a modicum of humanitarian aid for children there, and a vote against the Khmer Rouge coalition for Cambodia's United Nations seat. Although Washington later began direct talks with Phnom Penh, U.S. leaders were aware that they could rely on the forthcoming UN Plan (agreed among the five permanent members of the UN Security Council, the "Perm-5," on 17 July) to absolve them from casting the promised vote against the Khmer Rouge. U.S. goals had not changed: displacing the Hun Sen regime and returning the remnants of Cambodia's pre-1975 regimes to power. These non-communist factions had been unable to translate twelve years of covert and overt U.S. and allied military aid into significant military power. So, in the absence of a settlement with Phnom Penh, their ambitions remained dependent on their Khmer Rouge partners' inflicting critical damage upon the State of Cambodia. This looked an easy road to follow, but it was blocked farther ahead. Any Khmer Rouge defeat of Phnom Penh would likely turn Khmer Rouge aggression against their coalition allies, whom they privately regarded as enemies.

The American search for leverage over Cambodia's future demanded two things. First, increased power for its noncommunist protégés. U.S. policy remained wedded to the hope of Sihanouk and Son Sann riding to power on the back of the Khmer Rouge. Washington continued to aid them despite the explicit contrary undertaking of Under-Secretary of State for Political Affairs Robert Kimmitt, when he explained the policy shift on July 18. When asked: "Are you telling the noncommunist resistance to pull away from Pol Pot, or the United States will desert them?" Kimmitt replied quite clearly: "Any time they are in any form of association with the Khmer Rouge, that makes U.S. support no longer possible."[71] Nevertheless, Washington extended overt and covert aid to Sihanouk and Son Sann's forces despite their unabated cooperation with the Khmer Rouge. Sihanoukist commander Kien Van boasted in early October 1990 that the Khmer Rouge would provide him with 2,000 troops for an attack on Siemreap, as well as twelve tanks plus jeeps, trucks, and heavy weapons provided by China to the Khmer Rouge in the previous two months. Sihanouk's son Norodom Rannariddh added, as if he had been warned to keep Washington's secret: "I have to say very frankly, and Washington will criticise me again—that against Siemreap the Khmer Rouge will be the major attacking forces..."[72] U.S. policymakers pursued a calculated risk of assisting an eventual Khmer Rouge takeover—and prospects for another genocide.

Second, the United States naturally had more leverage over Cambodian discussions held in a great-power forum, than in the more finely balanced regional environment. If necessary to maintain U.S. leverage, Washington favored a great-power forum, allowing the Chinese their say as well. That, too, entailed a continuing Khmer Rouge role.

These two factors prompted the search for a "comprehensive solution," as designed by the U.S.A. with the other "Perm-5" members of the United Nations Security Council. Because American hopes for influence remained wedded to Khmer Rouge ambitions, Washington's policy refused any reduction in its continuing support for the Khmer Rouge until the only Cambodian opponents of these genocidists were first displaced from power.

Risks and Solutions

The Perm-5 proposal of August 1990 called for the United Nations to introduce civilian personnel to "supervise or control" five key sectors of Cambodia, and hold elections under the scrutiny of UN troops who were supposed to disarm and cantonize all four Cambodian armies. Reflecting U.S. and Chinese interests, this proposal entailed risks for Cambodia. Not least was its refusal to address the issue of the Khmer Rouge genocide. The Perm-5 Plan read blandly: "Necessary measures should be taken in order to observe human rights and ensure the non-return to the policies and practices of the past."

Within days, the UN's Human Rights Subcommission decided to *drop from its agenda* a draft resolution on Cambodia. This resolution had referred to "the atrocities reaching the level of genocide committed in particular during the period of Khmer Rouge rule," and called on all states "to detect, arrest, extradite or bring to trial those who have been responsible for crimes against humanity committed in Cambodia," and "prevent the return to government positions of those who were responsible for genocidal actions during the period 1975 to 1978." "The sub-commission's chairman, Danilo Turk of Yugoslavia, decided to drop the text from the agenda after several speakers said it would render a disservice to the United Nations after the five permanent members of the UN Security Council issued a joint plan this week aimed at ending the fighting..."[73]

The 1991 version of the UN plan gave Pol Pot's Khmer Rouge "the same rights, freedoms and opportunities to take part in the electoral process" as any other Cambodian, and aimed to "prohibit the retroactive application of criminal law."[74] Here the Perm-5 signaled to future genocidists that the worst they can expect is to have their opponents disarmed and removed from office, and to face them in unarmed combat with immunity from prosecution.

Yet there was no serious UN attempt to spell out how the Khmer Rouge forces were to be located, supervised, disarmed or "cantonized." This clearly would be much more difficult to do to the Khmer Rouge, who were located in remote, jungle areas, than to the Hun Sen army defending fixed bases, cities and populated areas. During the 1989 Paris Conference, the Khmer Rouge successfully kept the UN military investigation mission away from their secret military camps.[75] The likelihood now was that any effective disarming would be lopsided and would favor the Khmer Rouge. Even if all the Cambodian armies were in fact disarmed, the process would most disadvantage the Hun Sen army, easily the largest (over 200,000, compared to its opponents' combined 50,000). Thus genocidists, who threaten to repeat their crimes against humanity,[76] would undergo less UN control than those who had opposed them. This may have been why China agreed to the proposal.

The Khmer Rouge were not willing to hand over their arms, only to hide their troops if necessary.[77] A settlement that would not effectively disarm them was illusory. Popular support does not exist to offer the Khmer Rouge hope of power by peaceful means, and they could merely bide their time before attempting a coup, a return to insurgency, or "death squad" activity.

The concept of a UN government supported by an International Peacekeeping Force was also misleading. The only army that could stop a Khmer Rouge offensive was the Cambodian one, and the only peaceful way to ward off the Khmer Rouge was to stop their supply of bullets before they were fired. This meant cutting their supply lines in Thailand, and denying them sanctuary and international recognition as a "legitimate" government. Normal diplomatic recognition was instead denied to the long-established government of the country, the State of Cambodia. This was no act of neutrality: it assisted the Khmer Rouge greatly, as any insurgency benefits from an embargo on its enemy. Normal international and bilateral aid was denied the long-suffering Cambodian people, though with such aid the threat of another Khmer Rouge genocide would recede.

As part of a fresh effort to break the Cambodian deadlock, Japan made three new proposals in early 1991: UN monitoring from the start of a cease-fire, expulsion from the settlement process of any group that violates the ceasefire, and establishment of a special commission to investigate the Khmer Rouge. In Bangkok on 18 March 1991, U.S. Assistant Secretary of State Richard Solomon criticized Tokyo's proposals, as "likely to introduce confusion in international peace efforts."[78] This was a critical U.S. decision: not only would it free the Khmer Rouge to violate the cease-fire with impunity, but unlike in El Salvador, no Truth Commission would investigate their gross abuses of human rights.

In June 1991, the four Cambodian parties assembled in Jakarta once more. Sihanouk and Hun Sen agreed for the second time that the former would head the Supreme National Council, and the latter would be deputy chairman. The next day, once again, Sihanouk announced that his Khmer Rouge allies had rejected the agreement.[79] This scenario was likely to recur.

The Cambodia conflict was played out on three levels: the national, regional, and great power levels. Within Cambodia, the balance of forces favored the incumbent State of Cambodia. In the UN Security Council, its opponents had hegemony. But at the intervening regional level, the forces were fairly evenly divided. Southeast Asia's ten nations are politically diverse, none has overall preponderance, and few could be ignored. Those who sought a solution to the conflict could be found on both sides of the ASEAN-Indochina divide, and, unlike in the UN Security Council, none of the Southeast Asian countries readily identified with the remaining obstacle, the Khmer Rouge. The only lasting solution to the Cambodia conflict was to be found in Southeast Asia. But that avenue was blocked by the great powers. Another stage of the drama was about to begin.

Progress in the Cambodian peace negotiations dramatically accelerated from June to October 1991. A long-term factor, as we have seen, was the world's continuing isolation of the Phnom Penh regime. Since the Vietnamese overthrow of the genocidal Khmer Rouge in 1979, the United Nations had embargoed Cambodia, threatening it with economic collapse. All Western governments refused trade, aid and diplomatic relations to the only anti-genocidal Cambodian faction, while aiding its enemies. This policy, it was made clear, would continue until the Khmer Rouge were readmitted to the Cambodian political arena.[80]

But a second, more immediate factor was an unexpected realization that the State of Cambodia had the upper hand on the battlefield. It was unlikely to be overthrown in the foreseeable future. The Chinese-backed Khmer Rouge were not making headway, nor were their noncommunist allies.

A third factor was China's achievement of its major strategic goals in countries neighboring Cambodia, which allowed Beijing to capitalize on its predominance in mainland Southeast Asia and broker a settlement that would ensure the Khmer Rouge and their allies a share in Cambodia's political future despite their comparative military weakness.

The Military Stalemate

Vietnam's withdrawal from Cambodia in September 1989 brought no significant change in the military balance. In late 1989 the Khmer Rouge captured Pailin, a district town on the Thai border, and their noncommunist allies captured two district towns, Svay Chek and Thmar Puok, but soon lost Svay Chek to a Phnom Penh counterattack. In the interior of the country, a combined force of Khmer Rouge and noncommunists captured Staung district town in Kompong Thom province, but quickly lost it again to government forces.

Over two years after the Vietnamese withdrawal, all twenty provincial capitals, and all but two of 172 district towns, remained in Phnom Penh's hands, as did all the lowland, rice-growing, populated areas. This amounted to over ninety percent of Cambodia's territory and population. The failure of the opposition offensive revealed the extent of the Vietnamese achievement in Cambodia. Starting from scratch in 1979, and despite an international embargo of both countries, Hanoi had not only helped to establish a Cambodian government capable of returning the nation to near normalcy after the Pol Pot holocaust, but it had also successfully trained and armed a Cambodian army to take the place of its own expeditionary force, which had numbered 200,000 in 1979.

After a visit to recently besieged Kompong Thom city in July 1990, former British diplomat John Pedler concluded that the military situation was "fundamentally sound." On 19 July the *Far Eastern Economic Review* reported: "Government forces may be poorly paid and badly trained, but they have shown a marked willingness to fight in recent engagements." Three days later the *New York Times* quoted Khmer Rouge ally Norodom Ranariddh as saying that "it seems we may have lost on the battlefield." The following month Steven Erlanger reported from Phnom Penh in the *New York Times*, "No credible analyst or official here sees any imminent political or military collapse."[81]

Between June and October 1990, the Chinese and Thai armies delivered at least twenty-four Chinese T-59 tanks to the Khmer Rouge,[82] the first tanks available to them since 1978. *Jane's Defence Weekly* described the new Khmer Rouge tanks as "the most significant increase in firepower the resistance to the Vietnamese-installed government has ever received."[83] Even this upgrading of the opposition's military hardware does not seem to have altered the balance of forces.   In April 1991, according to the *Bangkok Post*, "military sources said the Khmer Rouge seem to be suffering far more than the Heng Samrin side since the dry season offensive began" in January.[84]   Jacques Bekaert, also writing in the *Bangkok Post*, noted that Phnom Penh's army, the Cambodian People's Armed Forces (CPAF), was equipped to resist the Khmer Rouge tank attacks. "The growing role played by tank units," he said, "did serve Phnom Penh well."[85]   On 20 May 1991, Bekaert elaborated on "the resistance's present weakness": "During the dry season, the resistance lost some ground... It is not that the CPAF is such a great army, but plenty of artillery and tanks are beginning to make a difference.... Prime Minister Hun Sen was probably right when he told us... that it is impossible for the resistance to conduct large-scale operations in the country, much less to launch vast offensives." The Khmer Rouge, he wrote, "still cannot occupy and maintain large tracts of territory."[86]

Their allies fared little better. Bekaert wrote in late August 1991 that the KPNLF's military wing, the Khmer People's National Liberation Armed Forces, "are fast collapsing": "Military experts say that maybe no more than a few hundred men still obey orders. The Sihanoukists of the National Army for Independent Cambodia have their own trouble and probably no more than a few thousand men—at best— still under control."[87] In late October an ASEAN diplomat involved in the peace process reported that the KPNLF "is on the point of being wiped out."[88]

A major by-product of this military frustration of the Khmer Rouge and their allies was a continuing series of massacres of Cambodian civilians. On 1 July 1990, Khmer Rouge forces stopped a passenger train in the countryside south of Phnom Penh. They fired directly into the carriages. One witness, Svay Pech, "saw eight people killed in her carriage alone," reporting that "the shooting went on a long time." The Khmer Rouge shot the two soldiers guarding the train, and then separated the state employees from the rest. Svay Pech saw five more people, several working for the railway company, shot dead. Those still alive were forced to carry the booty for the Khmer Rouge into the hills. Some too weak to march were left for dead along the way. According to Phnom Penh, at least twenty-four passengers and other civilians were murdered, and fifty-two wounded. Svay Pech suggests the toll was higher. Ten were still missing two weeks later.[89] In a second train attack two weeks later in Kompong Chhnang province, the Khmer Rouge killed another thirty people.[90]

In another Khmer Rouge massacre, on 27 July 1990, the victims were thirty members of their own armed forces, accused of being "ringleaders" of a movement demanding greater freedom. Six were allegedly shot dead in their beds, and another twenty-four are believed to have been executed in a nearby forest. On similar charges, another seventy people are alleged to have been detained and "repeatedly and severely beaten by military police interrogators," eliciting forced confessions that implicated those executed.[91] None of this behavior was new to students of the Khmer Rouge.[92]

Nor was this: "They beat me and shoved my head in a plastic bag so I couldn't breathe," a nineteen-year-old Khmer farmer in Kompong Speu province told UPI's Paul Wedel in August 1990. A local woman added: "They tied up my cousin and took him away. We never saw him again." In Kompong Cham province, another farmer told Wedel: "They say they are looking for Vietnamese soldiers, but they take our rice. We have to give, because they kill anyone who objects."[93]

In a third train massacre, south of Phnom Penh in mid-October 1990, the Khmer Rouge murdered another fifty civilians.[94] A Khmer Rouge source unconvincingly explained that "its soldiers had probably confused a civilian carriage with an armoured one."[95] In fact, they targeted Cambodian civilians and soldiers indiscriminately. Three days earlier, Khmer Rouge soldiers had ambushed a passenger bus on the highway south of the capital, killing one person and injuring two. On 24 October 1990, a Khmer Rouge land mine detonated under a military truck carrying civilian passengers north of Phnom Penh. Seven civilians were killed and twenty-four wounded.[96]

In late January 1991, Khmer Rouge artillery shelling near Battambang, in northwest Cambodia, killed at least three civilians and wounded twelve, including "an eight year-old girl ripped by shrapnel," according to an official of *Médecins sans Frontières* there. After warning the civilians of Battambang, Cambodia's second largest city, to flee their homes, the Khmer Rouge bombarded it on 10 February, and "killed at least 16 civilians and wounded dozens of others."[97] Khmer Rouge radio proclaimed two days later that after heavy attacks, "Battambang town was set ablaze nearly the whole night."[98] This was an exaggeration, like the claim of January 1990, when Battambang was proclaimed to be "burning brightly" under a Khmer Rouge barrage.[99] Neither boast, however, suggested that the Khmer Rouge intentions had changed since they had forcibly emptied the town the first time, in April 1975. On 21 April 1991, Khmer Rouge forces shelled

Poipet market near the Thai border, killing three traders, two of whom were women.[100]

Media speculation had it that the Khmer Rouge had "changed."[101] It stemmed not from their current activities but from Western governments' legitimization of the Khmer Rouge return to Cambodia. This has taken unusual forms. As one reporter recorded: "Western intelligence sources along the Thai-Cambodian border say that Pol Pot recently issued a directive calling on Cambodians not to poach birds and animals, and to refrain from killing them for any reason." The Khmer Rouge were building up a healthy body of environmental case law, with conservationist courts "normally" sentencing offenders to "four days' labor on constructing fencing for animal sanctuaries." Pol Pot's military commander, Mok, whom Cambodian villagers called "the chief of the butchers," was characterized by the same Western intelligence sources as "hot on ecology issues and protection of endangered species."[102] This is nonsense,[103] but no flash in the pan. An "analyst at a Western embassy in Bangkok" described the Khmer Rouge as "much more respectful of civilians than the other three factions,"[104] while the *Far Eastern Economic Review* reported that "diplomats say that the Khmer Rouge would not have signed an agreement it did not intend to follow."[105] (Re-read that sentence!)

But in January 1992, Khmer Rouge troops made a concerted attack on twenty-five villages in Kompong Thom province. They mortared and burned "whole villages," killed thirteen people, wounded eighteen, and drove ten thousand from their homes. While some diplomats called this "the worst violation so far," other officials of unnamed governments preferred to add a new twist: "The Khmer Rouge apparently mounted the attacks to hasten deployment of UN peace-keepers to the area, diplomats said."[106] (Read *that* again, too!)

But the journalist Jacques Bekaert best epitomized the revisionism: "In the past, most incidents and armed attacks on civilians were routinely blamed on the Khmer Rouge. It seems that such attacks *never* really occurred."[107] The Khmer Rouge might have been surprised to hear this. In 1987 their officers were told by Pol Pot himself that Mok "is the best battlefield commander. Despite his brutality, the good outweighs the bad." Mok added: "I know that people inside Cambodia fear me." His junior commanders regard him as "cruel but reasonable," two of them told Harvard *Human Rights Journal* editor Roger Normand in 1990.[108]

While the Khmer Rouge continued to distinguish themselves with by far the most appalling human rights record, their allies were not innocent of atrocities. In February 1991, KPNLF troops attacked a refugee camp inside Cambodia, "torching houses and killing at least nine civilians," according to a Western aid worker who described it as "a direct and deliberate attack on a civilian population." The nine civilians killed included a pregnant woman, two children, and a seventy-four- year-old man. Some of the bodies had been "terribly mutilated," the aid worker reported from the scene. Fifteen other refugees were wounded in the KPNLF attack. An official of the International Committee of the Red Cross said: "It's clearly a civilian camp that could not be mistaken for a military target."[109]   It was a camp for refugees who had fled the fighting in a KPNLF attack on Svay Chek farther north. Many more refugees had fled areas attacked or occupied by the Khmer Rouge. In 1991, the number of civilians displaced in post-1989 fighting and living in camps set up in territory held by the State of Cambodia reached nearly 200,000.[110]

Meanwhile the Khmer Rouge emphasized their continuing hard-line stance. At a border press conference in May 1991, one Khmer Rouge official tried to present a moderate face, but suddenly "beat a retreat with his aides" when a second cadre arrived, "dressed in Chinese khaki army fatigues." This cadre, a "hardliner," "spoke forcefully and with obvious authority," predicting: "When there are no more Vietnamese in Cambodia, we will take the rich people to work in the fields." He added: "Mr. Pol Pot did not have bad ideas and wanted equality for everyone. There was no poverty and all were equal until the Vietnamese came and tried to grab our land."[111]

On 12 September 1991, as the peace process reached its final stages, a Spanish aid worker was shot and wounded in the leg and chest, three miles from the UN refugee camp in northeast Thailand known as O'Trao, controlled by Mok's Khmer Rouge guerrillas. The "bandits" who carried out the attack "spoke Cambodian and wore Khmer Rouge uniforms," and used AK-47 assault rifles. Reuters called this "the most serious attack on a Western aid worker in 12 years of international relief work on the border."[112]

On 30 September, the "moderate" Khmer Rouge leaders of Site 8, the showcase Khmer Rouge camp in Thailand for contact with outsiders, were suddenly replaced in what was described as a minor "coup d'état." The twenty camp leaders were called to a meeting with Khmer Rouge leaders, and disappeared, reportedly into a prison at

Khmer Rouge Main Areas of Operation
October 1991

Khmer Rouge Main Areas of Operation
March 1993

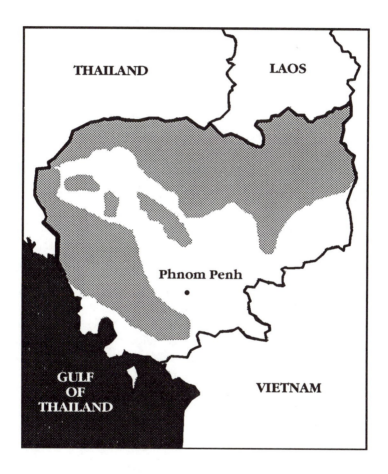

Source for both maps: Craig Etcheson, "The Calm Before the Storm," CORKR Situation Report, March 1993; March 1993 map is based on UNTAC military situation maps photographed in numerous provincial batallion headquarters.

Khao Din, a Khmer Rouge zone inside Cambodia. Their place was taken by five hard-line Khmer Rouge military officers, who instructed the families of the disappeared to cross the border into Cambodia. They refused to go, but the changeover spread "panic" among the 44,000 refugees in the camp, who feared a forcible repatriation to Khmer Rouge zones where they faced the danger of land-mines, malaria, and lack of rice and medicine. The Khmer Rouge designated forty community leaders to lead the way. "This has struck the fear of God into them, like it's back to the old days," said a UN official. The UN-trained civilian police force in Site 8 was also replaced by armed Khmer Rouge soldiers. According to the UN, "there are also similar reports that pressure is being exerted on the population of the O'Trao camp." On 11 October the Khmer Rouge announced that it would not allow people to leave its control, and a senior Thai official told Reuters that Thailand "will not intervene in Khmer Rouge plans to resettle its people."[113] At the UN on October 17, after a Chinese veto, the Security Council's Perm-5 members (the USA, the USSR, China, Britain, and France) backed down from a commitment to warn the Khmer Rouge against forcibly moving refugees.[114]

Private warnings delivered by UN officials obliged the Khmer Rouge to shift their focus to the less accessible O'Trao camp. There, 275 refugees "were ordered over the border in November" by Mok. A Thai officer told Reuters in January 1992 that Thailand had allowed this, but had then changed its policy to prevent Mok's continuing "attempts to take people back." "Mention of Ta Mok scares people to death," he added. A Thai ranger at O'Trao reported: "The refugees here are still in a state of fear because a group of about five to ten armed men are still sneaking into the camp at night and forcing people to go back." Cheun Sopeak, a mother of four, said: "I am so scared that in the night we do not light lamps. We hide in the dark when they come to take us."[115]

The Chinese Role in Southeast Asia

Nothing suggested that China had "abandoned" the Khmer Rouge.[116] Rather, Chinese support for them now focused on the political arena.[117] According to Nayan Chanda, "Beijing seems to have become disillusioned with the Khmer Rouge's *military* capability. Despite massive Chinese military assistance and Khmer Rouge claims to have liberated vast parts of Cambodia, the guerrilla group has been unable to shake the control of the Phnom Penh regime over the country."[118] This naturally brought a degree of Chinese impatience to the negotiating process. Another important factor was the substantial achievement in recent years of China's strategic goals in Southeast Asia, which centered on its rivalry with Vietnam.[119] Shunned by the United States and abandoned by the USSR, Hanoi was forced to turn to China for aid.

The most visible symbol of this was the Vietnamese accession, at the Seventh Congress of the Vietnamese Communist Party in June 1991, to the Chinese demand for the head of reformist Foreign Minister Nguyen Co Thach.[120] Beijing considered Thach an opponent of its interests, and those of its Khmer Rouge protégés. For its part, Hanoi was finally prepared to remove him because of his inability to deliver the needed diplomatic reconciliation with the U.S.A. Fortunately for China, the U.S. had continually spurned Vietnamese overtures and concessions such as the withdrawal from Cambodia, and Beijing was able to reap the reward.[121]   As Michael Oksenberg put it: "The United States... should seek to draw Vietnam out of its isolation through diplomatic recognition, dropping trade embargoes and offering economic assistance. Tying these moves to a resolution of the Cambodian conflict—the current American policy—places the cart before the horse and enables China, through its support of the Khmer Rouge, to exercise veto power over American policy in Indochina."[122] Because Washington policy-makers long ignored such advice, for the time being at least, China had its way with Vietnam.[123]

High-level talks between China and Vietnam were soon arranged by General Le Duc Anh, who had been named Number Two in the Vietnamese Politburo at the June Congress, with responsibility for military, security and foreign affairs matters. Deputy foreign ministers of the two countries met in Beijing on 7-10 August, and agreed on "quickly restoring their relations in economy, trade, communications, postal services and other fields."[124]   On 5 November, the leaders of Vietnam's party and government arrived in Beijing to "conclude the past and open up the future," as New China News Agency put it.[125]

As noted, Soviet aid to Vietnam had been drastically reduced, and the Soviet withdrawal from Cam Ranh Bay ended any leverage Hanoi possessed in Moscow. The 19 August 1991 coup attempt there, weakening the position of the reform communists led by Gorbachev, was also a blow to their counterparts in Vietnam, now overruled by hardliners who saw China's communists as a necessary ally.

The achievement of other Chinese goals in Southeast Asia further reduced Cambodia's significance to Beijing. As with Vietnam, China's relations with Laos were patched up by the military. From 23 to 28 June 1991, a high-level Lao military delegation visited China at the invitation of its national defense ministry, and China's defense minister accepted an invitation to visit Laos. An editorial on Lao radio commented: "Amid confusing world developments, mutual relations, cooperation, and assistance on national security are more necessary than before."[126] On 12 September Lao and Chinese officials agreed on a border treaty between their two countries.[127]

The February 1991 military coup in Thailand against the democratically elected Chatichai government was welcomed by China as a "correct and just" action.[128] China had developed a close relationship with the Thai armed forces over a decade of international aid to the Khmer Rouge via Thailand. In April 1991 the new strongman in Bangkok, Army Commander Suchinda Krapayoon, told a visiting U.S. senator that he considered Pol Pot a "nice guy."[129] (In 1985 Marshal Siddhi Savetsila, foreign minister of the former military regime, had described Pol Pot's deputy, Son Sen, as "a very good man.")[130] In May 1991 the new prime minister of Thailand, Anand Panyarachun, pointedly told Khmer Rouge leader Khieu Samphan: "Sixteen years ago, I was also accused of being a communist and now they have picked me as Prime Minister. In any society there are always hard-liners and soft-liners, and society changes its attitude to them as time passes by."[131] Pol Pot himself met with Suchinda personally just before the June 1991 Cambodian negotiating session in Thailand, where Pol Pot played a back-room role.[132] As a settlement approached in September, Suchinda pleaded that Pol Pot had no intention of regaining power, and that it was time to treat him "fairly."[133]

Chinese arms transfers to Thailand had reached very high levels. With purchases of US$283 million in 1985-1989, Bangkok ranked sixth among China's clients for major weapons, including purchases of three submarines in 1986 and six guided-missile Jianghsu-class frigates in 1988-1989. The latter sale, according to R. Bates Gill, "is unprecedented; Bangladesh and Egypt have received only one and two such vessels, respectively." With its 1988 purchase of eighteen Chinese copies of the Stinger surface-to-air missile, Thailand joined

Pakistan, Iran, the Khmer Rouge and the Afghan *mujaheddin* as the only known recipients of these weapons. Only Thailand and Iran had received "a recent Chinese weapons development, the C-801 antiship missile," of which Thailand obtained fifty in 1990. Bangkok's anticipated receipt of 1,000 armored personnel carriers will make it the site of "the largest assemblage of Chinese-made APC's outside of the PRC."[134]

Burma, the other state quick to recognize the overthrow of Thai democracy, is also high on the list of China's arms customers. In 1991, Burmese dictator General Saw Maung made his first visit abroad since his 1989 seizure of power. He visited Beijing on 20-25 August. China has become "Burma's most important trade partner," while Burma is "China's chief foreign market for cheap consumer goods." An estimated US$1.5 billion-worth of goods are exchanged annually along the Burma-China frontier, since the 1988 opening of border trade. With an arms trade worth an additional US$1.4 billion, Rangoon is "one of China's important customers for military aid." One Asian diplomat has even claimed: "The Burmese also depend on the Chinese for advice on diplomacy and propaganda. We have reports about regular meetings between SLORC officials and Chinese Embassy staff in Rangoon when they discuss these matters."[135]

China had abandoned its 1960s "party-to-party" relations with Southeast Asian insurgents, for army-to-army relations with governments. New alliances with Vietnam, Laos, Thailand, and Burma meant that its southern border was strategically sealed. Beijing was now in a better position than ever before to project its influence, from a tier of mainland Southeast Asian states into the archipelago. The withdrawal of U.S. bases from the Philippines augured well for China's role as the superpower of Southeast Asia.[136] Its main rival is Japan. Tokyo's emerging role in the Cambodian peace process in 1990-1991 at times threatened to sideline the Khmer Rouge.[137] China's new, flexible posture was designed to prevent that, and if possible to broker the negotiations itself. As Kelvin Rowley put it two weeks before Hun Sen's first visit to China, on 16-17 July: "When they go to Beijing, the representatives of the Phnom Penh government will be expected to pay fulsome homage to Beijing's regional hegemony. In return, they will seek to get Beijing to accept that Cambodia's internal affairs should be settled by the Cambodians themselves."[138]

The Peace Process Begins: Cease-fire

In May 1990 the U.S.A. had opposed Thai prime minister Chatichai's suggestion of a cease-fire as a first step.[139] On 5 June 1990, with Thai backing, the non-Khmer Rouge Cambodian parties met for talks in Tokyo. They agreed to form a Supreme National Council (SNC), and to a shaky, "voluntary" cease-fire.

In April 1991, the cochairs of the Paris International Conference on Cambodia, France and Indonesia, proposed a meeting of Cambodia's Supreme National Council in Jakarta on 2-4 June. In the meantime they called on the factions to observe a cease-fire from 1 May.[140]

On 1 May 1991 a cease-fire was duly proclaimed by all sides in Cambodia. The first independent confirmation of its violation came on 19 May, when Khmer Rouge artillery attacked a distribution site where four western Red Cross officials were helping deliver supplies to Battambang civilians. "It is outrageous that they should be shelling a civilian site," an aid worker told UPI.[141]

At the Jakarta SNC meeting in early June, Hun Sen and Sihanouk agreed to prolong the cease-fire indefinitely (and to no longer accept foreign military aid)—while for their part, the Khmer Rouge declared the cease-fire over.[142] This SNC meeting was quickly followed by another, at Pattaya on 24-26 June. There all Cambodian parties (including Pol Pot, who secretly directed the Khmer Rouge negotiators from his room in the hotel where the meeting took place)[143] agreed to a new cease-fire. But over the next two weeks, sources from four different provinces of Cambodia all reported new Khmer Rouge military attacks, including two on refugee camps in central Cambodia.[144] On July 9, UPI quoted "a Thai military officer who said he had talked with Khmer Rouge commanders" on the Cambodian border: "The Khmer Rouge are planning big attacks on Battambang and Banteay Meanchey provinces," he said.[145] In the south of Cambodia, the train linking Phnom Penh with Kampot province was hit by rocket fire on 30 July, and Khmer Rouge forces in the province launched a series of attacks on 6 August.[146]

The other three factions had nevertheless broadly observed the cease-fire from 1 May. This was the first sign of a concerted Cambodian departure from the Perm-5 Plan, which called for a "comprehensive settlement," not a step-by-step one.[147] This progress was made outside the Perm-5's framework, and not through the efforts of the Perm-5 but of other countries, such as Indonesia, Thailand, and Japan.

The Breakthroughs

Considering himself above the political process, Norodom Sihanouk had declined to attend the September 1990 meeting in Jakarta, and had thus been left out of the Supreme National Council. The next six months saw his repeated attempts to become its chairman, and a compromise was reached whereby he would do so as an additional representative of his own party, FUNCINPEC. In return, he agreed to the State of Cambodia (SOC) nominating a seventh representative, and to Hun Sen becoming vice-chairman of the SNC and chairman of Cambodia's UN delegation. However, this arrangement was opposed by the Khmer Rouge, given veto power by the Perm-5's insistence on consensus. At the SNC meeting in Jakarta in early June, the Khmer Rouge again vetoed the proposal. Sihanouk then announced that he would join the SNC as an ordinary member, replacing an elderly associate. On 6 June, after his successful Jakarta meeting with Hun Sen, Sihanouk announced his intention to return to Phnom Penh for the first time since 1979, for a two-month visit beginning in November 1991. He began to speak of common ground between "the non-Khmer Rouge Cambodians."[148] As Hun Sen later pointed out, all this added a sense of urgency to the negotiations: those opposed to Phnom Penh did not want Sihanouk to go there without a settlement.[149]

Nor did they want Japan to broker one with Phnom Penh. On 13 June, Hun Sen met with the Japanese foreign minister Taro Nakayama in Ho Chi Minh City. Afterward, Hun Sen referred to Nakayama's view that "the Cambodia question has reached its final stage" and "will be settled by the Cambodians themselves, not by imposition from outside." Sen quoted Nakayama, who was to meet China's foreign minister Qian Qichen on 26 June, as saying that Tokyo would ask China to persuade the Khmer Rouge to be more flexible.[150]

At the next SNC meeting in Pattaya from 24-26 June, the body announced its intention to establish itself in Phnom Penh. This meant it would become operational, and that embassies could be established in the Cambodian capital without express recognition of the SOC. At Sihanouk's request Australia, Japan and France immediately announced their intention to open embassies there, and they were soon followed by Thailand, Indonesia, and Canada[151] and later by the other ASEAN countries, China, the USSR, and North Korea.[152] A hallmark of the process was the theme taken up on 13 June by Japan's foreign minister Nakayama with Hun Sen, that it was time to end international imposition upon the Cambodians. At his meeting with Nakayama in Japan on 26 June, China's Qian Qichen echoed that it was time for "Khmer chefs to make Khmer food." Two months later Sihanouk revealed that France, China and Thailand had all informed him: "You Cambodians find out solutions by yourselves and we will back you."[153]

Again, France excepted, the Perm-5 were by no means in the forefront of this move, which a U.S. analyst protested in July was "outside the context of the Perm-5 process."[154]   Several days later another U.S. official said: "We simply have to lean on the prince to stick to the UN plan."[155] A month later in Bangkok, Assistant Secretary of State Richard Solomon restated the U.S. commitment to an unchanged Perm-5 Plan. Sihanouk responded: "I am aware of the U.S. position, but we have to be realistic."[156] He even warned "that the United States may try to scuttle agreements because they differ from terms of the UN Security Council framework."[157] But a settlement was emerging, almost despite the "Perm-5 process" and the strong U.S. opposition to any changes to its blueprint for Cambodia. A Bangkok-based diplomat quoted in the Thai press on 26 August described the SNC as the "nucleus" of diplomatic progress, with China, Vietnam and Thailand making the inside running in the "first circle" around it. The "outer circle," the diplomat added, "is the Permanent Five countries, some members of which have either been caught off guard by the pace of recent meetings, or moving more slowly." He stated that reluctance, especially on the part of the United States, to allow any deviation from the Perm-5 blueprint "has unexpectedly delayed and could impede the peace process."   A "Cambodian resistance source" went further, suggesting that the Americans "are digging their own grave": "If [the USA] remains the only one of the Permanent Five to oppose the Cambodian approach to find their own solutions, it could be viewed as trying to infringe upon a small nation's sovereignty."[158] Sihanouk pointed out that the Khmer Rouge were being more flexible than the U.S.A. in their attitude to the UN plan.[159]

The June SNC meeting in Pattaya had reached agreement on a modest UN peacekeeping force of seven hundred people, but the UN Special Representative, Ahmed Rafeeuddin, noted that such a force would not achieve its goals.[160] After the July SNC meeting in Beijing, the Perm-5 also met there and again declined to authorize a UN monitoring force for lack of a "comprehensive" settlement.[161] But it was at the Beijing SNC meeting that Sihanouk resigned from the Khmer Rouge-dominated resistance and even from his own party, agreeing to become a neutral, non-voting chairman of the SNC. This left the Phnom Penh delegation with a notional majority on that body of six to five, as the peace process edged away from the Perm-5 Plan.

1. "Dismantling" the SOC

The least tangible change made to the Perm-5 Plan for Cambodia concerned its proposed UN administrative role in Cambodia. As we have seen, the Perm-5 Plan had developed from a 1989 proposal by Australian foreign minister Gareth Evans, who called upon the Hun Sen government to "step back from its present role as the de facto government of the country" so that Cambodia could be run by an interim UN administration.[162]

This idea was adopted in principle by the Perm-5 in its "Framework Document" of August 1990, which called for "direct UN supervision or control" of the five key sectors of foreign affairs, information, finance, interior and defense (with the additional requirement that all Cambodian forces be disarmed).[163] The proposed implementation of this approached virtual displacement of the Hun Sen government, as spelled out in considerable detail by the Perm-5's "Implementation Plan" of November 1990. To the chagrin of Australian and Indonesian officials, this document went much further than its predecessor. For instance:

> (1) "all administrative agencies, bodies and offices" in the five key areas "will be placed under the direct control" [not "supervision or control"] of the UN Transitional Authority on Cambodia (UNTAC), which "will determine what is necessary and may issue directives" to them, which "will bind all Cambodian Parties";

> (2) the UN in consultation with the SNC "will determine which other administrative agencies, bodies and offices ... will be placed under direct supervision or control of UNTAC and will comply with any guidance provided by it;" and

> (3) the UN will also "identify which administrative agencies, bodies and offices could continue to operate... if necessary, under such supervision by UNTAC as it considers necessary."

Thus, the UN could "supervise" all Cambodian organizations, and three of four categories (the five key areas *and* two further categories) were subject to either its "direct control" or "direct supervision or control," which included the power "to require the reassignment or removal of any personnel," even in Cambodian organizations which "could continue to operate" allegedly without having to "comply with any guidance provided" by the UN. [164]

The year 1991 saw a move away from this, allowing the Cambodian government (and its opponents in the much smaller areas they control) to remain in place, apparently limiting UN involvement to organizing elections and ensuring that they were free and fair. An Explanatory Note, delivered to Phnom Penh in January 1991 by the UN Secretary-General's Special Representative Rafeeuddin Ahmed, specified that UN "interaction" with the "existing administrative structures" will be "limited to those functions and activities... which could directly influence the holding of free and fair elections in a neutral political environment. Other functions and activities will remain unaffected."[165] However, this specification does not appear in the final agreement, whose language is that of the "Implementation Plan," strongly interventionist. The agreement specifies that: "In all cases, the Secretary-General's special representative will determine whether advice or action of the SNC is consistent with the present agreement." (This contradicts the previous paragraph which calls the SNC "the legitimate representative of Cambodian sovereignty."[166]) Yet there was no sign of any UN intention to so intervene in Khmer Rouge organizations.[167]

2. Demobilization of troops

A more significant breakthrough was to allow each army to maintain its relative strength. The Perm-5 Plan had proposed total disarmament and demobilization, which would most benefit the militarily weakest parties, backed by the U.S.A. But it would also substantially benefit the next weakest party, the Khmer Rouge. As we have seen, the Perm-5 made no serious attempt to spell out how all Khmer Rouge forces were to be "disarmed" and "cantonized." The likelihood was that any effective disarming would be largely lopsided, to the advantage of the Khmer Rouge.[168] In 1988 Pol Pot predicted to his followers that in the event of a settlement, "Our troops will remain in the jungle for self-defense."[169] The risk of them hiding forces (possibly up to five thousand in number but not many more, should the UN perform its task even minimally), and thus emerging with the only remaining Cambodian army, proved difficult to ignore.

Phnom Penh continued to demand "concrete measures" to prevent the return of the Khmer Rouge genocidal regime. Along these lines, at the opening of the SNC meeting in Pattaya on 26 August, the SOC offered to demobilize only forty percent of its forces, with the remaining sixty percent placed in cantonment under UN supervision. The Khmer Rouge, on the other hand, proposed "a reduction to 6,000 men on each side," knowing that additional Khmer Rouge forces hidden from UN view would give them the advantage.[170] By the end of the meeting, a compromise had been reached on the basis of a French proposal. Seventy percent of all forces would be demobilized.[171] This proportional arrangement would allow the largest army, that of Phnom Penh, continuing numerical superiority. This was strongly opposed by the U.S.A., but supported by Australia in a "political confrontation between Canberra and Washington." While the U.S. wanted total demobilization along the lines of the Perm-5 Plan, "Australia argued strongly that the Cambodian troops needed to keep at least 30 percent of the army intact as a safeguard against the Khmer Rouge." The U.S.A. backed down.[172]

Hun Sen was counting on the UN to do its utmost to demobilize seventy percent of all Khmer Rouge forces, not just those presented for inspection. He estimated the Khmer Rouge strength at 12-15,000. Should five thousand manage to escape the UN's view, the Khmer Rouge could still muster eight thousand troops after the demobilization. To pressure for maximum Khmer Rouge demobilization, Hun Sen agreed to total demobilization of the SOC militia (or *senachon*, part-time village and subdistrict forces), which he claimed to number 220,000. He saw no justification for excluding any Khmer Rouge "militia" or "police" from the UN's muster.[173] As for the SOC's regular forces, Hun Sen informed the UN that they totaled 140,000 troops (regular, provincial, and district forces, all full-time).[174] He presumably expected to present these for seventy percent demobilization, leaving the SOC with 42,000 troops. He insisted that the SOC's 47,000 police not be demobilized, but placed under UN control.[175]

This scenario would have left the military balance as follows: Khmer Rouge forces of 5-10,000, and their noncommunist allies, at most 3,000;[176] State of Cambodia forces, 42,000. While this would not preserve the ten-to-one predominance usually considered necessary for a government to defeat an insurgency, it maintained the overall balance of forces instead of reshaping it in favor of the Khmer Rouge, as the Perm-5 Plan for total demobilization would have done.

However, two caveats should be noted here. There were varying estimates of Khmer Rouge strength. Some sources, notably Australian and Thai, put it at over 40,000.[177] This would have put the Khmer Rouge in a much better position, especially if they were able to hide a large proportion of such a force from UN detection. But "Western intelligence sources" had recently given a figure only one-third as high.[178] Second, there was no reason to be confident that the UN would effectively monitor Khmer Rouge areas to minimize dissimulation of forces.   Apart from cost factors, it was clear that political pressure from the Perm-5, from journalists, and from other observers mainly based in Phnom Penh, would all focus attention on the issue of SOC compliance with the Agreement. Few UN or other monitors would risk mines and malaria to comb the Cardamom mountains, or the jungles of northern Cambodia, to uncover hidden Khmer Rouge camps and caches.

Further, the UN Plan itself was ominously weak on procedures for locating hidden arms depots. Annex 2 stipulated that upon signing the Agreement, the Cambodian parties will provide the UN with total lists of their forces (paragraph 3a) and "comprehensive lists of arms, ammunition held by their forces, and the exact locations" (3b). However, in neither case was it specified that these lists provided by each party (about itself) were to be supplemented by lists provided by the parties about one another. Such was specified only in paragraph 3c, which discusses "detailed record of their mine-fields," adding "together with any information available to them about mine-fields laid or booby-traps used by the other parties." No *cross-checking* of information was provided for in paragraphs 3a or 3b, which related to troops and arms caches.   And so in the next stage, UNTAC "will check the arms, ammunition and equipment handed over to it against the lists referred to in paragraph 3b... in order to verify that all the arms, ammunition and equipment in the possession of the Parties have been placed under its custody."   Thus, the weapons handed over by the Khmer Rouge were to be checked against lists of their weapons previously supplied by the Khmer Rouge.   It was disingenuous to describe this as "verification."[179] Only at an unspecified later date were more serious procedures envisaged; these did not include systematic searching or satellite surveillance.[180]

The day after the Agreement was signed, the *Bangkok Post* revealed the existence of a secret Khmer Rouge army of "several thousand" troops, which had long been camped in isolated jungles in southwest Cambodia, shunning outside contact. They were described by an informed source in Thailand as "pure and hard like the original Khmer Rouge," a kind of "Praetorian guard" to Pol Pot. "They have no experience with the more relaxed ambiance and the trading along the border. They are the least changed and their leaders want to keep it that way," the source added. A second, Cambodian source said there are several "completely inaccessible" Khmer Rouge base camps in the mountains, which the UN would find it "very difficult" to inspect.[181] Three days later Khieu Samphan was asked to comment on these reports, and declined to do so.[182] The *New York Times* later confirmed from Phnom Penh that according to diplomats and relief workers, the Khmer Rouge were already "hiding troops and a huge cache of weapons in preparation for the possible resumption of the Cambodian civil war." A Western diplomat who had helped draw up the Paris agreement confessed, "There's no way to detect a lot of it."[183]

Thus the Perm-5 Plan gave the Pol Pot forces the chance actually to improve their relative military capacity: many more anti-Khmer Rouge soldiers than Khmer Rouge ones were to be disarmed and demobilized. With careful monitoring of the Thai-Cambodian border, the Plan would ensure an end to most outside military supplies to the Khmer Rouge. But analysts agreed that the Pol Pot forces already had "years" of supplies stocked up,[184] and the immediate military and political benefits to the Khmer Rouge of the Perm-5 Plan might outweigh a future military liability.

On 28 February 1992, the UN Security Council voted to "strongly urge" the Cambodian parties to ignore their agreement on demobilizing seventy percent of their armed forces. The UN now proposed a return to the one hundred percent demobilization formula, depriving the Khmer Rouge of any Cambodian military opposition. When questioned how the Cambodians might react to such a change to the Agreement, a UN official replied: "What choice do they have?....it will be very hard for anyone to contradict the wishes of the Security Council."[185]

3. Elections

The Australian Plan for Cambodia had suggested a system of proportional representation for the election process.[186] The reasons were largely financial and administrative. However, there was no stipulation of a threshhold percentage, so that in a National Assembly of 120 seats, such a proportional system would allow representation for any party that achieved even 0.83 percent of the vote. This would guarantee some representation in the Assembly for the Khmer Rouge, who revealed that winning even a single seat would lead them to demand representation in the new government, and thus a share in power.[187]

Phnom Penh objected to this. It proposed instead a system of single-member constituencies, as had been used for every election in Cambodian history. The belief was that the Khmer Rouge would be unlikely to garner a majority or plurality of the vote in any consituency, and thus would be much less likely to win seats. Sihanouk and Hun Sen agreed to this structure, but with some extra seats to be allocated on a proportional basis.[188] This would most probably have excluded the Khmer Rouge also; if there were, say, ten proportional seats, 10 percent of the national vote would be required to win a single seat. However, the Khmer Rouge and Son Sann opposed this agreement, as did the UN Secretary-General's Special Representative, for cost reasons. The result was that elections would be held on a proportional basis, with each province a multimember constituency. Battambang province, for instance, currently had eleven seats in the National Assembly, so a party winning nine percent of the provincial vote would gain a seat. According to SOC foreign minister Hor Namhong, the Khmer Rouge would "definitely" win representation under this arrangement.[189]

One reason was that UN control of the election process would not prevent the intimidation of voters in Khmer Rouge-dominated areas, such as kidnapping villagers' children and promising to return them after the village votes correctly in the elections.[190] This is what Pol Pot meant when he predicted in 1988 that "our cadres will lead the balloting work."[191]

The UN had no intention of monitoring each remote locality during the campaign, nor even each polling booth on election day. The 1990 Australian Plan assumed that 5,600 polling places would be required, noting that it was "wholly unlikely" that the necessary "22,400 staff, or 5,600 presiding officers, could be provided from the resources of the UN." The only feasible procedure "in remote areas," then, was "a spot-checking system." By contrast, the areas under SOC control would be effectively monitored: "certainly the major urban and heavily populated centres (perhaps involving some 1,000 polling booths in all) would require a UN presiding officer to be there full time." But the remaining 4,500 polling places would merely be spot-checked, by another one thousand city-based UN officials,[192] which would have little effect against Khmer Rouge intimidation of voters and stuffing of ballot boxes. So, half the UN officials would monitor one thousand polling booths, in urban areas where the Khmer Rouge are not active, and the other half would be stretched out over 4,500 polling booths. Here we see the potential bias of UN intervention, surpassing the Perm-5's mandate to treat genocidists and their opponents as equals (and even "build confidence" between them).[193]

In its February 1992 plan of action, the UN proposed to station two international officials in each of Cambodia's 172 districts, with some additional reserves making up a rural electoral administration of around 400, for a campaign period of perhaps "six to eight weeks." Greater numbers would be involved at either end: "800 five-man registration teams" comprising mostly locals, to register voters; and "8,000 polling teams" each of seven local people, and an additional "1,000 international personnel" to staff the 1,400 polling stations and verify the balloting.[194] This could ensure a fair ballot count, but would be inadequate to prevent Khmer Rouge intimidation of rural voters during the campaign. The UN would have no effective presence at the subdistrict or village levels except for very brief periods.

But before the Paris Agreement, Sihanouk and Hun Sen had come up with a plan to reduce the potential danger of the Khmer Rouge. The prince agreed to be neutral in the Assembly elections; he had resigned from FUNCINPEC, leaving it to his son Rannariddh, and now predicted a Hun Sen victory.[195] In return, Hun Sen agreed that there would be no SOC candidate standing against Sihanouk in the presidential election to follow.

4. Genocide

The years 1988-1991 saw the progressive elimination of diplomatic criticism of the 1975-1979 Cambodian genocide. At the first Jakarta Informal Meeting on 28 July 1988, as we have seen, the Indonesian chairman's final communique had noted a Southeast Asian consensus on preventing a return to "the genocidal policies and practices of the Pol Pot regime."[196] But the 3 November 1989 UN General Assembly resolution watered this down to "the universally condemned policies and practices of the recent past." Then the February 1990 Australian proposal, on which the Perm-5 Plan was based, referred only to "the human rights abuses of a recent past." And the Perm-5 emasculated this in August 1990, vaguely nodding at "the policies and practices of the past."

Following the SNC meeting in Jakarta in early June 1991, the two cochairs of the Paris International Conference on Cambodia, Indonesia and France, accepted Phnom Penh's proposal that the final Agreement stipulate that the new Cambodian constitution should be "consistent with the provisions of ... the UN Convention on the Prevention and Punishment of Crimes of Genocide."[197] This too was a departure from the Perm-5 process. But it was short-lived, a further example of a regional initiative being overruled by great power interest. The Perm-5 rejected it, and reference to the Genocide Convention disappeared from the draft of the Agreement.

However, in Western countries public pressure on governments mounted. One result was the British government's disclosure on 27 June 1991 that, despite repeated denials, its elite SAS military teams had indeed trained forces allied to the Khmer Rouge, from 1983 to at least 1989.[198] The UN Sub-commission on Human Rights, which the previous year had quietly dropped from its agenda a draft resolution condemning the Pol Pot genocide, now changed its mind and passed a resolution noting "the duty of the international community to prevent the recurrence of genocide in Cambodia" and "to take all necessary preventive measures to avoid conditions that could create for the Cambodian people the risk of new crimes against humanity." As an initiator of the resolution, Raoul Jennar, put it, this was the first time that the genocide was acknowledged "in an official international arena."[199] The *New York Times* then called on Washington to publish its "list of Khmer Rouge war criminals and insist on their exclusion from Cambodian political life," and for their trial before "an international tribunal for crimes against humanity."[200] In an attempt to draw some of the fire, Pol Pot, Ieng Sary and Mok announced that they would not stand for election, but insisted on their right to campaign for the Khmer Rouge candidates.[201] It was nevertheless clear that they would continue to lead the organization from the shadows.

Washington eventually decided to address the issue, but to leave the task to others. In September, unnamed diplomats revealed that "Western nations want the former head of the notorious Khmer Rouge to leave his nation, quickly and quietly," and that the US had approached China for help in ensuring this "or at a minimum, making sure he remains in a remote part of Cambodia." However, Khieu Samphan retorted that Pol Pot had no plans to leave Cambodia,[202] and this appeared to be the case. U.S. pressure on China or the Khmer Rouge remained verbal; Washington's material policy involved pressure on Hanoi, "to see that Vietnam holds Hun Sen's feet to the fire."[203]

On 17 October, Assistant Secretary of State Richard Solomon said the U.S. "would be absolutely delighted to see Pol Pot and the others brought to justice for the unspeakable violence of the 1970s." However, he then blamed Hun Sen for the Agreement's failure to include provision for a trial. "Mr. Hun Sen had promoted the idea over the summer months of a tribunal to deal with this issue. For reasons that he would have to explain he dropped that idea at the end of the negotiations."[204] In Paris on 23 October, the day the final Agreement was signed, Secretary of State James Baker stated: "Cambodia and the US are both signatories to the Genocide Convention and we will support efforts to bring to justice those responsible for the mass murders of the 1970s if the new Cambodian government chooses to pursue this path."[205] Australia's Foreign Minister Gareth Evans, who had also previously balked at taking legal action against the Khmer Rouge, now said: "We would give strong support to an incoming Cambodian government to set in train such a war crimes process."[206] If the noncommunist allies of the Khmer Rouge were to win the election, they could decline to establish a tribunal. The charges of genocide, crimes against humanity, and war crimes remained hostage to political convenience.

The Khmer Rouge Strategy: Exploiting and Subverting the Paris Agreement

Although it was marketed to the concerned international public as a means to dispatch them, the Khmer Rouge gained the most from the October 1991 Paris Agreement on Cambodia. It allowed them to move into the political arena without abandoning their military options.

An Asian diplomat had predicted this in August 1991: "I hope it is remembered that we are also one step closer to a return of the Khmer Rouge to legitimacy in Phnom Penh. There may be peace, but how long will it last?"[207] The *Economist* also warned: "The Khmer Rouge are not short of money. Gem mining and logging are reckoned to bring them at least $100 million a year."[208]

As of April 1993, UNTAC had achieved some successes: 350,000 Cambodian refugees had nearly all been returned home (a few against their will),[209] a score of new political parties had been established in Phnom Penh and many provinces, and 4.6 million Cambodians had registered to vote in the May 23-27 elections.[210] But war and genocide both threatened Cambodia more than they had in 1991. The "comprehensive settlement" had failed.

Through their peace plan, the Permanent Five members of the U.N. Security Council (the U.S., Britain, France, Russia and China, known as the "Perm-5") allowed the Khmer Rouge to establish a presence in Phnom Penh for the first time since 1979. The faction built a new headquarters in the capital, behind the royal palace. Even Pol Pot, the Agreement made clear, enjoyed "the same rights, freedoms, and opportunities to take part in the electoral process" as all other Cambodians.[211] Khieu Samphan and Son Sen, president and deputy prime minister in an ousted genocidal regime, were twelve years later re-appointed under UN auspices to a body that enshrined "Cambodian sovereignty," the SNC. And in this forum they could not be outvoted, for the Perm-5 Plan stipulated that the SNC should proceed not by majority vote but by "consensus."[212]   One result of this paralysis fostered by the Perm-5 Plan was that in April 1993 Cambodia's UN Mission was being run by Pol Pot's chosen ambassador, Thiounn Prasith, as it had since 1979. Even had the paralysis within the SNC been resolved, or over-ridden by the UN, the Khmer Rouge would still have benefited as they did from the turmoil engendered by the Peace

Plan's attempt simultaneously to freeze hostilities and open up political competition.

The Khmer Rouge had gained a solid base from which to attempt a return to power if their long-time allies won a plurality or majority of seats in the election. They would also benefit from continuing political paralysis. In such an atmosphere, they could continue their military offensives and civilian massacres, or bide their time until UN forces (originally scheduled to be reduced to 5,430 by October 1992)[213] were reduced to minimal numbers, or launch their death squads to discipline their enemies and enforce popular acquiescence. Quite apart from their genocidal record and known future intentions,[214] the Khmer Rouge were also in a better position than the other parties to subvert the Agreement.

Phase One: The Cease-fire Violated

The Khmer Rouge breached the ceasefire many times in the first months after signing the Agreement in October 1991, even as the UN's Advance Mission in Cambodia (UNAMIC) was establishing itself in the country. The ceasefire was the first of many UN deadlines that the Khmer Rouge spurned.

In November 1991, Khmer Rouge forces in Pursat province attacked a Cambodian village and massacred 60 men, women and children there. In Kampot province, the Khmer Rouge also stepped up their raids after the Agreement. Reuters reported: "The Khmer Rouge occupied Dang Tung district and raided Kompong Trach in November, aid workers said. They hit Chum Kiri in December, killing a teacher and torching government buildings. In other attacks they were said to have burned houses of people trading with Vietnamese. They are blamed for a run of kidnaps..." In Kon Sat village, they killed two people in November. A villager told a journalist: "I would like to believe in peace, but every day the Khmer Rouge comes down to our village and steals everything and sometimes kills people. Right now it's impossible to live here."[215]

In January 1992, the Khmer Rouge forcibly drove ten thousand people from their homes in Kompong Thom province.[216] In a secret draft document dated February 6, Khmer Rouge leader Ieng Sary outlined a confidential plan to continue the Khmer Rouge's "strategic offensive in the countryside," attacking villages to "throw the situation into confusion," and to "open up a battlefield in Phnom Penh." The document, later captured and authenticated, went on: "If we attack the enemy, everybody will be confused and concerned. We want the enemy to be confused. If the situation is not in chaos, then Thailand and China will think it is too easy."[217]

The Khmer Rouge began another wave of attacks in mid-February.[218] The French commander of UNAMIC, Brigadier-General Michel Loridon, said that the Khmer Rouge had "refused UN liaison officers access to areas under their control and stalled on marking minefields," and that "the UN unit assigned to Khmer Rouge headquarters in Pailin is barred from moving more than 400 yards from their quarters." The International Committee of the Red Cross added that the Khmer Rouge were the only faction preventing its delegates from visiting their zones to supervise releases of prisoners of war.[219]

According to a European diplomat in Bangkok: "It's quite clear the Khmer Rouge have no goodwill toward implementing the agreement." "I am very angry about that," said Loridon. "It is no problem for the other three (factions) but the (Khmer Rouge) are not fully cooperative... I was very strong with them... but they were delaying, saying, 'yes possibly, not now, maybe next week.'"[220] Khmer Rouge troops then fired on a UN helicopter in Kompong Thom, wounding the Australian force commander.[221] Barring UN observers from areas of Kompong Thom they now controlled, the Khmer Rouge launched another offensive there, while the commander of the Sihanoukist forces in neighboring Siemreap province reported Khmer Rouge attacks on both government troops and his own forces "every day now."[222] At the same time there began "large-scale movements of Khmer Rouge forces and equipment... from two of their strongholds in the north and northwest towards the government-controlled Route 68." [223]

On 7 March, 1992, Sihanouk accused the Khmer Rouge of creating "artificial difficulties" to deliberately stall the peace process. "All the problems are created by them. If there were no Khmer Rouge there would be no problems. You wouldn't even need UNTAC," he added (ignoring the UN Perm-5's role in including the Khmer Rouge in the process).[224] Four days later, U.S. Assistant Secretary of State Richard Solomon, on a visit to Phnom Penh, also bewailed "the lack of cooperation for the UN settlement process by the Khmer Rouge."[225]

Loridon again accused the Khmer Rouge of violating the accord by denying access to the UN and also "refusing to provide information to the UN for the disarmament and demobilization of soldiers."[226] The reason is clear. The Khmer Rouge had brought in "at least 3,500" troop reinforcements, and immediately launched yet another series of attacks to expand their zones of control. The Bangkok *Nation* reported on 14 March: "UN officials said Khmer Rouge soldiers this week attacked more than a dozen strategic areas in northern Cambodia in an unusually well-coordinated offensive." Ten Cambodian soldiers were killed and forty wounded, according to a UN official. Around March 10, Khmer Rouge forces began seizing control of stretches of Highway 12, Preah Vihear province's only link to the rest of Cambodia. "There is no question that [the Khmer Rouge] are violating the peace agreement," said the UN commander in Kompong Thom.[227] Two days later the Khmer Rouge refused a UN request for a cease-fire around the province capital, and Sihanouk described their commander Mok as "a warmonger."[228] They again refused a cease-fire on 22 March, and now SOC threatened to counterattack.[229] A new Khmer Rouge offensive began on 23 March, and government forces responded the following day, recapturing Highway 12. Only now did the Khmer Rouge agree to send military representatives to negotiate in Kompong Thom.[230]

But a week later UNTAC's newly arrived director, Special Representative Yasushi Akashi, accused the Khmer Rouge of denying his officials access to a major road. Fighting continued as Khmer Rouge forces remained in government areas. Akashi said on April 9: "Our people are very frustrated. Time is running out... I have not excluded reporting them to the Security Council on this matter." On 21 April, Akashi announced that Khieu Samphan had agreed to allow UN forces into five Khmer Rouge-held areas. Akashi said: "We welcome it... but we have to see if it is total uninhibited access and whether more sites than these five will be opened up in the future." UN surveys of the sites were completed on April 29.[231] On 1 May, Akashi reported that "the ceasefire has been restored in Kompong Thom."[232]

But on May 4, according to a UN official, the Khmer Rouge launched "coordinated attacks" against six government-held villages in Kompong Thom. After moving four hundred trucks loaded with supplies into the province, they softened up the villages with heavy artillery bombardments, then attacked in battalion strength. UN military sources described these attacks as "the worst violation yet seen." Reuters reported: "A UN officer who asked to remain anonymous called for satellite surveillance of Khmer Rouge positions, claiming the guerrillas were sending large reinforcements into Kompong Thom province." "They've got a freeway up in that jungle," he said. Government forces counterattacked and held the villages.[233]

On 14 May, Khmer Rouge forces shelled an aid distribution site in Battambang province, killing eight civilians.[234] On 26 May, Akashi again accused the Khmer Rouge of hindering the implementation of the Agreement, and again threatened to report them to the UN Security Council.[235]

In the six months after the signing of the Paris Agreement, the Khmer Rouge consistently and seriously violated the ceasefire and many other provisions, even kidnapping refugee camp leaders.[236] They expanded their territorial control and caused massive refugee displacement, loss of life, and material destruction.[237] The Khmer Rouge were stopped not by the UN, but only by SOC forces. This was despite the fact that, as UNTAC military commander Lieutenant-General John Sanderson confirmed, "the UN forces had prevented the Phnom Penh army from significantly building up for the counter-offensive."[238]

Nevertheless, on May 29, Khmer Rouge forces mined a position which they had previously demanded be the site of a UN border inspection station. The next day, Akashi and Sanderson were stopped at a Khmer Rouge roadblock in Battambang province, preventing them from linking up with UNTAC forces that had been blocked on the other side of the Khmer Rouge zone. Sanderson called this "outrageous." The day after that, Khmer Rouge in Preah Vihear province "attacked a UN cantonment site where government troops had gathered to surrender their weapons to UN officials. The UN troops immediately fled..." SOC troops held the Khmer Rouge at bay, while shelling continued. On 1 June, Khmer Rouge forces held a UN officer, Captain David Wilkenson, "at gunpoint" for nearly two hours.[239]

UNTAC has also complained about less than full cooperation from the State of Cambodia government. A plague of corruption discredited many SOC members and led to student and worker demonstrations in December 1991. Police and troops fired on the crowds, killing perhaps a dozen people. 1992 saw up to fifty political killings. As many as ten of the murders were conclusively attributed to SOC police,[240] and a small number to members of opposition parties.[241] These attacks damaged the atmosphere of political pluralism and the neutral electoral environment that UNTAC has gone some way to create.

On the other hand, SOC also cooperated with UNTAC on a greater scale than any of the other Cambodian parties. SOC handed over its air force, tanks, armoured personnel carriers, and most of its navy patrol boats to UNTAC control,[242] and disbanded most of its 200,000-strong village militias. Since no Khmer Rouge forces were disarmed or disbanded, cooperation with UNTAC put the SOC (and Khmer villagers) at a military disadvantage.

SOC also provided UNTAC with a radio station for its own use. It allowed UNTAC free movement within its territory, and varying degrees of monitoring (not "control") of the five specified areas of administration mentioned in the Agreement, though the Khmer Rouge allowed no UNTAC activity in its zones at all. Enforcing its powers against only one side in the conflict, during 1992 UNTAC also removed from office several SOC province governors and city mayors. UN Secretary-General Boutros-Ghali reported to the Security Council on 15 February 1993 that "the Party of the State of Cambodia has offered substantial cooperation to UNTAC since the operation began."[243]

Phase Two: The Disarmament Disregarded

Phase Two of the Paris Agreement, the UN's cantonment and disarming of all forces, and the demobilization of seventy percent of them, was to begin on 13 June 1992. On 10 June Akashi announced that he had received a letter from Khmer Rouge General Nuon Bunno stating that his army "was not in a position to allow UNTAC forces to proceed with their deployments" in Khmer Rouge-held areas. The Khmer Rouge would not be disarmed, nor allow any other parties into their newly conquered zones. Akashi described this as "a clear breach of the Paris agreement," and therefore "unacceptable."[244] The Khmer Rouge had violated a second UN deadline.

The UN Security Council noted lamely on 12 June that "one party was not able to allow the necessary deployment of UNTAC in areas under its control." It did not discuss sanctions against the Khmer Rouge. Marrack Goulding, UN undersecretary general of peacekeeping operations, said: "I don't think we should be talking about sanctions."[245]

In mid-June, Akashi charged that the Khmer Rouge "seems to have returned to the offensive in the northern part of Cambodia," committed "pretty serious violations," and "gravely compromised" the settlement.[246] In early July a UN helicopter flying near the Khmer Rouge base of Pailin was hit by ground fire. UNTAC responded with more restraint.[247]

US Deputy Secretary of State Lawrence Eagleburger talked tougher: "We do not believe that efforts to halt the [peace] process should be cost-free to those involved... We must resolve to ensure that the saboteurs of peace would be the ones to suffer the most."[248] French Deputy Foreign Minister Georges Kiejman even proposed a plan "to prevent the Khmer Rouge from getting resources as they do right now through the more or less illicit trading of gems" from Pailin, and timber.[249] But these policies were not implemented.

The Khmer Rouge's intransigence soon provoked a split in UNTAC ranks. Loridon, who favored a tough approach, resigned in mid-July 1992 after being over-ruled on the issue. "I am leaving Cambodia frustrated by my inability to implement the UN mandate," he told journalist Nayan Chanda. "Here was our chance to deal with the Khmer Rouge, push them to implement the accords they have signed. But I haven't succeeded in getting my superiors to agree with me." UNTAC, he said, was "just sitting and waiting for the Khmer Rouge leaders to agree to disarm their troops." Loridon believed that firm action would have brought results: "it is possible... at some point they will try to block the UN move by force. If it comes to that one may lose 200 men—and that could include myself—but the Khmer Rouge problem would be solved for good." The UN Security Council, Akashi and Sanderson rejected this approach.[250]

The Khmer Rouge not only refused to cease their attacks, disarm their soldiers, or otherwise participate in this second phase of the implementation of the Paris Agreement. They also, according to an Australian UN military officer, "moved into areas of Battambang and Siemreap provinces to fill the vacuum created by the cantonment" of their opponents,[251] particularly the SOC. And in mid-July, the Khmer Rouge again escalated their violence. Eight civilians were killed and eleven injured in fighting in central, northern, and southern Cambodia. Akashi blamed the Khmer Rouge, saying: "Unfortunately the present cease-fire violations continue to increase in number and seriousness. The nature of these actions points to a deliberate policy of terror against ordinary Cambodians."[252]

This terror included mass murder. On 28 April Khmer Rouge troops, armed with B-40 rocket launchers and AK-47 rifles, stormed a village in Kompong Chhnang province, and killed seven ethnic Vietnamese civilians. Four days later, UNTAC sent a representative to the village, and locals appealed to it to station ten troops there for their protection. But this was not done, and on 14 May the Khmer Rouge struck again. "The people have lost hope and left," a local official said. 1,500 people fled the area.[253]

On 21 July in a small village near the Vietnamese border, an ethnic Vietnamese couple and their seven-day old son, four other children aged seven to sixteen—Cambodians whose grandmother was Vietnamese—and their uncle, were all massacred and mutilated by Khmer Rouge gunmen.   But no suspects were apprehended, and much damage was done by an UNTAC predilection to take seriously the propaganda of the Khmer Rouge,[254] despite their recent similar attacks, history of genocide, and record of deception.

The Khmer Rouge threatened yet another racial pogrom after the U.S. Chief of Mission in Phnom Penh, Charles Twining, stated his fear that history might repeat itself, with bodies of ethnic Vietnamese seen floating down the Mekong as in 1970. Khmer Rouge leader Khieu Samphan said: "If the Cambodian people cannot see a peaceful resolution to the problem, they will seek other means. So Twining's nightmare might become a reality."[255]

Most of the country's 450,000 ethnic Vietnamese community had been expelled by the US-backed Lon Nol regime in 1970, when eight hundred bodies floated downstream. More were driven out by Pol Pot in 1975, the rest systematically murdered. Only after Pol Pot's overthrow by Hanoi's army in 1979 did some of the refugees return from Vietnam, along with some newcomers. Independent estimates of the total ethnic Vietnamese population in Cambodia in 1992-1993 vary from 150,000 to 200,000-500,000.[256] The community is smaller than it was in the 1960s.

Khmer Rouge targets were not restricted to Vietnamese residents. The 1991 UN Peace Agreement by no means ended the terrorism against civilian targets by Pol Pot's forces.[257]   Three days before the July massacre, Khmer Rouge guerrillas mortared a Cambodian Buddhist monastery in Siemreap province, killing one monk and injuring three others. The temple was destroyed in the attack.[258] In July, defectors reported to UNTAC that "a Khmer Rouge general executed their company commander" for his willingness to respect the Agreement on cantonment of troops under UN supervision.[259]

The UN Security Council voted on 21 July "to ensure that international assistance to the rehabilitation and reconstruction of Cambodia from now on only benefits the parties that are fulfilling their obligations."[260] But virtually no aid reached those who were fulfilling their obligations, and no effective measures were taken against those who were not.[261]

On 26 July the Thai foreign minister, Arsa Sarasin, gave the Khmer Rouge yet another deadline. He announced after an ASEAN ministerial meeting that the Khmer Rouge had until the end of August to comply with the Paris Agreement.[262] This date, too, passed by unnoticed. On 24 September the UN again lamely expressed "serious concern."[263]

The Western policy towards the Khmer Rouge amounted to appeasement,[264] and it elicited similar results. Australian foreign minister Gareth Evans had asserted in February that the "genocide issue and all the emotion that's associated with that" had now been "resolved."[265] He stated in July that the Khmer Rouge's complaints have "some reasonable foundation," and he "agreed with the idea of holding meetings with the Khmer Rouge, and that things should not be as before."[266]

On 20 August, the U.S. State Department warned that "if the Khmer Rouge continue to obstruct the peace process, we expect that the Security Council may have to [consider] further measures against the Khmer Rouge."[267] But no action was taken, and wishful thinking prevailed. Sanderson expressed optimism that UNTAC would be able to "bring the Khmer Rouge back to the peace process," saying he was "certain he can persuade local Khmer Rouge leaders to disarm."[268] UNTAC officials even claimed that "Khmer Rouge officers in several provinces have said they are making active preparations to cooperate in the cantonment process in the weeks ahead."[269] Nothing came of this, either.

While Thailand appeared amenable to sanctions against the Khmer Rouge,[270] Lawrence Eagleburger, now U.S. Acting Secretary of State, moved away from advocating them. Now, he said, "the fundamental point" was that the Khmer Rouge "are not going to benefit from the agreements if they are not going to play by the rules."[271] But the Khmer Rouge had already benefited enormously from the implementation of the Agreement. Denying them further benefits would not punish them for failure to respect an agreement they had signed, which other parties were implementing to their cost.

In late August, the former director of the US State Department's Office for Vietnam, Laos and Cambodia, Shep Lowman, urged action. He acknowledged that from 1978 until 1986, "the U.S. countenanced the revival and building up of the Khmer Rouge's political and military capacity as ways to counterbalance Vietnamese might." But from 1986 on, Lowman asserted, the U.S.A. had to "find a way to control the monster that we had allowed to be created."[272] Few people were more associated with the creation of the monster than Jeane Kirkpatrick, who as U.S. ambassador to the UN had voted for the Khmer Rouge to represent their Cambodian victims in international forums.[273] But ten years later Kirkpatrick underwent a change of heart. In August 1992, she wrote that "the Khmer Rouge refuses to turn in its weapons or permit U.N. access to areas under its control." Because the "aggressor... has refused to carry out an agreement to which it had acquiesced," the Cambodian peace plan "is on the verge of collapsing." "The Khmer Rouge," Kirkpatrick continued, "has used a painstakingly negotiated international agreement for disarmament, resettlement and elections as an opportunity for its troops to re-enter Phnom Penh and other areas of Cambodia from which they had been driven." However, UN officials speak as if Pol Pot "rather suddenly developed a will to peace and could be counted on" to honor his commitments—next time. "They talk as if they did not know the consequences of such delays are irreversible."[274] Likewise, Lowman argued that now the Khmer Rouge "must be made to comply with the terms of their agreement or be cut out of participation."[275]

On 2 September Prince Sihanouk announced that the elections should go ahead without the Khmer Rouge, who should be "set aside."[276] On 12 September, Sihanouk, Akashi, and representatives of the five permanent members of the UN Security Council made a pilgrimage to Pailin. They attempted to persuade the Khmer Rouge to rejoin the peace process, but failed.[277]

The Khmer Rouge called the world's bluff. The international community gave them valuable time to expand their military control, move into the political arena, store weapons, and make vast sums of money, all without the UN control which the Agreement stipulates and to which the other Cambodian parties were subjected. As the Cambodian economy collapsed amid continuing denial of aid, the Khmer Rouge still threatened the people of Cambodia. Without resolute international action, they would become an integral part of the country's political future, despite their genocidal past.

On 25 September 1992, the UN Security Council warned the Khmer Rouge that it could push ahead without their participation in elections, and would decide whether to do so at a meeting the following week. It would also decide "whether to close Thailand's border with Cambodia to cut off the Khmer Rouge's export trade in tropical lumber and precious stones, the group's main source of income."[278] The Security Council's October decision, however, was to hold elections on schedule in May with no attempt to prevent the Khmer Rouge denying a vote to the people in its zones, a weak response to repeated violations of the cease-fire and the other provisions of the Agreement. The Khmer Rouge responded by blowing up two bridges, "the closest yet the Khmer Rouge have attacked to Phnom Penh," according to a UNTAC official.[279]

Again the UN failed to apply sanctions. In mid-November, Secretary-General Boutros-Ghali disregarded another UN deadline and said he favored "patient diplomacy."[280] Over the next six weeks the Khmer Rouge tested Boutros-Ghali's patience. In late November and December 1992, they abducted eighty seven UN officials and peacekeeping troops in half a dozen separate incidents, even threatening to kill some of them if their demands were not met.[281]

Then, in their "15th dry season offensive," Khmer Rouge forces renewed their attacks, including what a UN spokesperson described as a "a deliberate shelling of military and electoral people" at an UNTAC post in Siem Reap province, forcing its evacuation by helicopter on 31 December.[282] In another four incidents in January 1993, the Khmer Rouge temporarily seized 20 more UN peacekeepers.[283]

The most effective sanctions against the Khmer Rouge were promulgated not by the UN Security Council but by the Cambodian SNC, with Akashi's support. From 31 December 1992, it became illegal for Cambodians to export logs from the country. Unfortunately, the Khmer Rouge, major exporter and target of the sanctions, refused as before to allow UN personnel in their zones to monitor compliance, and the Thai government, citing its national sovereignty, barred UN monitors from its side of the border.[284] Thus, the parties to suffer from the SNC's sanctions were those complying with the Agreement.[285]

The Result of Appeasement: The Aggression Escalates

Meanwhile, the Khmer Rouge accelerated their campaign of ethnic cleansing. A senior Khmer Rouge commander admitted in October 1992 that his guerrillas had kidnapped eight ethnic Vietnamese, and the bodies of another ten were found near the Cambodian coast.[286] In December, the bodies of three more Vietnamese fishermen were found floating in the Mekong River in northeast Cambodia.[287] Soon after, in what was then "the deadliest violation of the Cambodian peace accord," two boatloads of Khmer Rouge troops entered a fishing village in central Cambodia and murdered thirteen ethnic Vietnamese, including six females and five children, and two Cambodians.[2888] Khieu Samphan kept his word.

The Khmer Rouge's longtime allies, the U.S.-backed parties led by Son Sann and Norodom Ranariddh, had also called for virtual "ethnic cleansing" of Vietnamese from Cambodia.[289] According to Prince Sihanouk, his son Ranariddh's party was infiltrated by "a large number of Khmer Rouge," and by 1993 its armed forces had rejoined the Khmer Rouge in attacks against the government army.[290] Ranariddh proposed to include unelected Khmer Rouge representatives in his government should he win the election.[291] He had forgotten, as Chanthou Boua points out, "that the Khmer Rouge, when in power between 1975 and 1978, killed their own people for having 'Vietnamese heads on Khmer bodies.'"[292]

Indeed, in 1993 the Khmer Rouge continued murdering Cambodians. Two Khmer women working for UNTAC's electoral component, and a girl of seven died in a Khmer Rouge attack on an UNTAC post in Siemreap province. Two weeks later another Khmer Rouge attack in that province killed eight people, including three policemen and a thirteen-year-old girl.[293]

Then, in a raid on the floating village of Chong Kneas on 10 March, Khmer Rouge forces murdered thirty-four ethnic Vietnamese civilians, including fourteen women and eight children, and four Cambodians. "There were babies with their hands shot off. [Attackers] got into one houseboat and shot the kids in the head. It's that savage," said a UN investigator. More than forty civilians were wounded. "The object had to be terror and genocide," said a UN official. "It was done with military precision." The Khmer wife of one of the Vietnamese managed to shoot two attackers dead, enabling the UN to identify them as members of the 92nd Regiment of the Khmer Rouge 980th Division.[294]

Khmer Rouge radio approved the slaughter as "correct." Another Khmer Rouge massacre of eight ethnic Vietnamese fisherfolk in Kompong Chhnang province, including a boy of twelve and a girl of fourteen, followed on 24 March. Two days later a Khmer Rouge spokesman in Phnom Penh boasted that Vietnamese "cannot hide, even if they are children."[295]

More importantly, they could not defend themselves. The *Phnom Penh Post* reported that the victims had "had their own guns confiscated by State of Cambodia (SOC) officials when UNTAC arrived promising peace." According to a Cambodian witness: "UNTAC told us not to be worried, but we are still afraid... Before UNTAC arrived each family in the village had a gun and we guarded our village every night. Now UNTAC has collected them from us." The *Post* added: "Local Cambodians say the Vietnamese of Chong Kneas were heavily armed before UNTAC came..., as were the Cambodian fishermen. But since the Khmer Rouge took advantage of the cantonment of Phnom Penh government troops to increase their territory, they now have access to areas previously inaccessible before the signing of the peace agreement and the people in these areas are now under threat."[296]

Twenty thousand Vietnamese civilians began fleeing the area in boats.[297] But the week beginning 25 March saw "a new wave of violence throughout Cambodia," with a variety of victims. The first UNTAC soldier to be killed by hostile fire in Cambodia was a Bangladeshi, who died in a "deliberate" attack by the Khmer Rouge. In early April, Khmer Rouge squads murdered three Bulgarian UNTAC troops in what Akashi called "a cold-blooded execution," then killed another Bulgarian in a separate attack. In a series of widespread attacks in early May, Khmer Rouge forces killed a Japanese soldier, wounded a dozen Indian and Dutch peacekeepers, attacked Chinese and Polish troops, and ambushed a civilian train, killing thirteen Cambodian passengers and wounding seventy.[298] In the worst incident, twenty-nine Khmers were killed and thirty-one injured on 1 April when Khmer Rouge forces attacked a video hall in Kompong Thom. A UN spokesman said: "The group did not show any mercy. They appear to have shot even those who were pleading for their lives."[299]

A few days after this atrocity, UN Secretary-General Boutros-Ghali visited the Cambodian capital. His policy was: "Even if people disagree, even if certain parties don't participate, it is important to maintain a dialogue."[300] Within a week, Khmer Rouge representatives abandoned their UN-protected compound in Phnom Penh for the movement's clandestine headquarters in the countryside.

By the end of 1992, the *Far Eastern Economic Review* had already concluded, "the chief result of the "peace process" appeared to have been to legitimise the murderous Khmer Rouge."[301] The process of appeasement comprised a total of eleven deadlines, each ignored by both the Khmer Rouge and then by the international community. Throughout, the Khmer Rouge continued to violate the Agreement with virtual impunity. On 31 January 1993 the Khmer Rouge maintained not only their refusal to participate in the elections, but also their determination to deny the people they control the right to vote. A Khmer Rouge official had already announced that the election would not bring "the right government" to power, threatening a new war after the election.[302]

In January 1993, the head of UNTAC's civil administration component, Gerard Porcell complained that "we don't have the will to apply the peace accords." Porcell went on: "This absence of firmness with the Khmer Rouge was a sort of signal for the other parties who saw there the proof of UNTAC's weakness towards the group that from the start eschewed all cooperation." In February, UN Secretary-General Boutros-Ghali singled out problems with the SOC in "recent months,"[303] apparently including more assassinations of oppositionists. Another UN official revealed that within UNTAC, agreement with Porcell's criticisms was "widespread but... for the sake of the mission people don't want to talk about it."[304] Akashi also stated his own view: "The main problem has been the failure of the [Khmer Rouge] to stick to the peace agreement... As a direct consequence of this, the other three Cambodian factions, especially the State of Cambodia party, have also been less than consistent in their adherence to Paris agreements."[305]

All this was only partly the fault of UNTAC itself. In his first speech after his triumphant return to Cambodia in November 1991, Sihanouk pointed out that "the Cambodians were forced by the five permanent members of the UN Security Council, the United States, the Soviet Union, China, Britain and France, to accept the return of the Khmer Rouge."[306] In February 1992 UN diplomat Hedi Annabi, who for many years dealt with Cambodian matters for the Secretary-General's Special Representative in Southeast Asia, warned with acumen that "the operation can only succeed if all the parties abide by the commitments that they freely entered into when they signed the agreements."[307] Despite the myopia of Western diplomats whose governments drew up such a plan, there was never any likelihood that the Khmer Rouge would meet their commitments.[308]

The UN failed to achieve the "comprehensive settlement" for which it conceded so much to the Khmer Rouge. The killing in Cambodia increased, and shows no sign of abating. The Khmer Rouge now control perhaps half a million Cambodians,[309] four times as many as they did in 1991, and their threat to other Cambodians is much greater than before the Peace Plan went into effect.[310]

However, the situation is not hopeless. Reliable estimates put current Khmer Rouge strength at around fifteen thousand.[311] The Vietnamese-trained SOC army of 60,000-100,000 will be needed to defend Cambodians against the Khmer Rouge for the foreseeable future. Cambodia's predicament of continuing war remains a threat to stability in Southeast Asia.

Nevertheless, the international community maintains an "open door" to Pol Pot. Partly because of Thailand's violations of the Agreement, the limited economic sanctions imposed on the Khmer Rouge are relatively ineffective.[312] Their opponents underwent far more UN scrutiny and control.

Legal action against the Khmer Rouge for their 1975-1979 crimes has long faced Chinese and US opposition. In 1991, the US and Australia both said they would help a newly-elected government of Cambodia bring the Khmer Rouge to justice. But in 1992 the US State Department prevailed upon Senator Charles Robb to drop his Khmer Rouge Prosecution and Exclusion Act from Senate consideration.[313] The US and Australian commitment needs to be strengthened now. The record of the genocidists should be studied by an international Truth Commission.

The new Cambodian government emerging from the 1993 elections must be encouraged to refrain from racial discrimination, but also given all necessary international aid to resist Khmer Rouge offensives.[314]

[1] See Elizabeth Becker, "Vote the Communists Out of Cambodia," *Washington Post*, 20 May 1990.

[2] For parallel United States tactics against regional rapprochement in Central America, see Terry Lynn Karl, "Central America at the End of the Cold War," in Breslauer, *et al.*, eds., *Beyond the Cold War: Conflict and Cooperation in the Third World*: 222-251, esp. pp. 237-8: "The Reagan administration scuttled Contadora at the very moment when successful peace negotiations seemed imminent..."

[3] Ben Kiernan, "Genocidal Targeting: Two Groups of Victims in Pol Pot's Cambodia," and Chanthou Boua, "Genocide of a Religious Group: Pol Pot and Cambodia's Buddhist Monks," in P. Timothy Bushnell, *et al.*, eds., *State-Organized Terror*, Westview, Boulder, 1991: 207-40.

[4] See, for instance, Bernard Edinger, "Cambodians Behead Vietnam Villagers," AAP-Reuters, *The Asian* (Melbourne), November 1977: 11. Edinger noted that "reliable sources said there was no doubt that the fighting was started by Cambodian central authorities." Earlier, "during the summer... hundreds of people were killed when Cambodian troops stormed close to 40 villages set up within Vietnam's "new economic areas' programme."

[5] According to *Asiaweek*, "Most intelligence analysts in Bangkok agree that Cambodian raids and land grabs escalated the ill-will ... until peace was irretrievable" (22 September 1978). See also Ben Kiernan, "New Light on the Origins of the Vietnam-Kampuchea Conflict," *Bulletin of Concerned Asian Scholars* 12, 4 (1980): 61-65, esp. p. 64, and *How Pol Pot Came to Power* (London, 1985): 413-21; Michael Vickery, *Cambodia 1975-82* (Boston, 1984): 189-96; and Gary Klintworth, *Vietnam's Intervention in Cambodia in International Law* (Canberra, Australian Government Publishing Service Press, 1989).

[6] Hanoi's proposal of 5 February 1978 offered a mutual pullback 5 kilometers each side of the border, negotiations, and consultation as to an appropriate form of international supervision. Democratic Kampuchea rejected this.

[7] See Ben Kiernan, "Kampuchea: Thai Neutrality a Farce," *Nation Review* (Melbourne), 24 May 1979.

[8] However, according to a *Bangkok Post* report by Richard Ehrlich from Phnom Penh on 8 July 1990, "several senior Western and Eastern diplomats in Cambodia and Vietnam agreed there is 'no evidence' to support reports that Vietnamese troops have been secretly fighting against the resistance in Cambodia."

[9] See for instance the references in John McAuliff and Mary Byrne McDonnell, 'Ending the Cambodian Stalemate,' *World Policy Journal*, Winter 1989-90: 71-105: 104 n. 10.

[10] For more recent information on this, see Steven Erlanger, "Political Rivals Jockey in Phnom Penh," *New York Times*, 11 August 1990.

[11] Steven Erlanger reported from Phnom Penh in the *New York Times*, 6 August 1990: "No credible analyst or official here sees any imminent political

or military collapse. The main concern, they say, is the economy, which the Khmer Rouge is trying to disrupt. Economic collapse could lead to the kind of panic that would quickly undermine an army that is *still holding its own.*" [Emphasis added.]

[12] In an interview with U.S. National Public Radio on 27 July 1990, Hun Sen said: "Once we reach a political solution, a multiparty system will be automatically adopted...to allow all political parties to participate in an election. I know we can be asked why we do not allow a multiparty system at this time. I'd like to argue that we do not want to fight simultaneously on two fronts, for the danger facing the Cambodian people is not the question of a multiparty system or a one-party system, but the return of the Pol Pot genocidal regime."

[13] Far Eastern Economic Review, *Asia 1981 Yearbook* (Hong Kong, 1981): 191.

[14] *Brother Enemy* (New York, Harcourt Brace Jovanovich, 1986): 393.

[15] *Age* (Melbourne), 16 March 1984.

[16] *Ibid.*, 16, 19 and 27 March 1984.

[17] That the Hanoi position had been poised to change since the previous year is evident from a *Nhan Dan* article of November 1984, which began by proclaiming that Vietnamese forces would withdraw from Cambodia "when the Chinese threat and the danger of Pol Pot's return have been removed and when the security of Kampuchea is fully ensured," but then revealed the coming offer of a new deal: "To discard the Pol Pot remnants, rather than calling for Vietnam to unilaterally withdraw troops from Kampuchea, is a crucial and imperative demand of peace in the region." Report by Michael Richardson in the *Age* (Melbourne), 29 December 1984.

[18] Ben Kiernan, "Kampuchea: Hayden is Vindicated," *Australian Society*, 4, 8, August 1985: 20-23.

[19] *Age*, 21 March 1985.

[20] *Sydney Morning Herald*, 27 June 1986.

[21] This was at a press conference in Jakarta on 8 August 1986, reported in *Indonesia Times*, which claimed that his support was merely "tongue-in-cheek." However a year later, Mochtar again publicly endorsed the proposal to try the Pol Pot regime before the World Court for genocide (*Christian Science Monitor*, 17 June 1987.) Hayden's successor as Foreign Minister, Gareth Evans, ignored this record, merely stating that Hayden's proposal had not been greeted "with equal enthusiasm by ASEAN" (Evans, Beanland Lecture, Melbourne, 24 August 1989).

[22] In the meantime, two thousand Cambodians living abroad had signed a petition to Australian Prime Minister Bob Hawke (and leaders of other governments) asking for action against the Pol Pot regime in the World Court (see, for instance, *Far Eastern Economic Review*, 14 July 1988). Hawke refused. Opposition Leader Andrew Peacock supported the idea, as did the Australian section of the International Commission of Jurists. The case is

outlined in Ben Kiernan, "Cambodian Genocide," *Far Eastern Economic Review*, 1 March 1990, and 'The Genocide in Cambodia, 1975-1979,' *Bulletin of Concerned Asian Scholars*, 22, 2, 1990: 35-40.

[23] *Far Eastern Economic Review*, 11 August 1988: 29.

[24] "Sihanouk to Return as Cambodia's Head of State," and "Move to Dump Khmer Rouge," *Sydney Morning Herald*, 3 and 4 May 1989.

[25] Kelvin Rowley quotes Sihanouk's speech on 24 September 1989, broadcast on the Voice of the National Army of Democratic Kampuchea: "You must get rid of the regime immediately.... Rally to the tripartite forces of our resistance movement before it is too late, so that the real patriots... can undoubtedly see that you are also patriotic. By so doing, you in Cambodia can avoid the imminent danger to yourself....It is impossible this time for me to defend you." I am grateful to Rowley for this reference.

[26] Roy Eccleston, "Evans Plan Stumbles over an Ugly Word," *The Australian*, 2 March 1990.

[27] *Far Eastern Economic Review*, 19 July 1990: 14. Only a few weeks earlier, on June 29, Congressman Stephen J. Solarz, a leading supporter of Pol Pot's allies and opponent of Pol Pot's opponents, had made the unfortunate claim that the Tokyo meeting proved Sihanouk was not a "front man for the Khmer Rouge." Solarz had said: "This is hogwash. The best evidence that it is hogwash is the fact that one month ago the Japanese convened a conference in Tokyo to move the peace process on Cambodia forward... If Sihanouk is a front man to the Khmer Rouge, why would he be signing agreements opposed by the Khmer Rouge and which exclude the Khmer Rouge from power?" After the House of Representatives had accepted Solarz's amendment to aid Sihanouk's forces, Sihanouk accepted the Khmer Rouge amendment of the Tokyo agreement.

[28] Interview on U.S. National Public Radio, 27 July 1990. See also note 63, below.

[29] *Indochina Digest*, No. 90-37, 15-21 September 1990.

[30] For the background to this regional feeling in the common postwar anti-colonial struggles, see Ben Kiernan, "ASEAN and Indochina: Asian Drama Unfolds," *Inside Asia* 5 (Sept.-Oct. 1985): 17-19.

[31] See Ben Kiernan, "Time is Ripe for Evans to Dump Khmer Rouge," *Sydney Morning Herald*, 12 January 1990, and Nick Cumming-Bruce, "US Tries to Allay Fears on Cambodia," London *Guardian*, 28 July 1990, quoting Evans.

[32] Nayan Chanda, "Sihanouk Stonewalled," *Far Eastern Economic Review*, 1 November 1984: 30.

[33] Gareth Porter, "Cambodia: The American Betrayal," unpublished paper, 1989.

[34] *New York Times*, 1 May 1990.

[35] This undertaking was given by Chinese premier Li Peng on a visit to New Zealand in January 1989.

[36] "Sihanouk: No Council without K. Rouge," *Bangkok Post*, 23 July 1990. *New York Times*, 19 July 1990.

[37] Kyoko Tanaka, "The Civil War and the Radicalization of Chinese Communist Agrarian Policy," *Papers on Far Eastern History*, vol. 8, September 1973: 49-114, at p. 54 note 13.

[38] *Far Eastern Economic Review*, 30 August 1990: 65. See also *New York Times*, 16 April 1990.

[39] Steven Erlanger, "Cambodians Face Loss of Eastern Aid and Trade," *New York Times*, 12 August 1990.

[40] Nayan Chanda, "For Reasons of State," *Far Eastern Economic Review*, 2 August 1990.

[41] See Steven Erlanger, "Cambodians Face Loss of Eastern Aid and Trade," *New York Times*, 12 August 1990. The similar U.S. blockade of international aid funds to Vietnam, including from the International Monetary Fund, was also said to be punishment for Hanoi's overthrow of Pol Pot's regime in 1979. But it actually began before that, when Vietnam had become the first communist country to join the IMF. And after the Vietnamese withdrawal from Cambodia, as the *Far Eastern Economic Review* (28 September 1989) reported: "To the profound disappointment of many officials at the IMF and the World Bank, the US and Japan—countries with major voting rights in the two institutions—have blocked Vietnam's re-entry into the international economic community, despite what is considered an exemplary Vietnamese effort at economic stabilisation and structural adjustment." British, West German and French executive board members of the IMF, on the other hand, had "endorsed Vietnam's stabilisation programme and implied the country was ready for a formal IMF programme." Only in mid-1993 did the US relent.

[42] *Far Eastern Economic Review*, 12 July 1990: 14. $7 million of this is overt "non-lethal" military aid. Another $10 million is said to have been provided by Singapore in "military hardware and other supplies." *New York Times*, 19 July 1990, and also 8 July 1990.

[43] See Ben Kiernan, "Pol Pot Stomps in Deng's Footsteps, and with US Support," *Sydney Morning Herald*, 13 July 1989, and "US Policy Turn on Cambodia is Incomplete," London *Guardian*, 23 July 1990.

[44] Eva Mysliwiec, personal communication, 1987. See her book, *Punishing the Poor: The International Isolation of Kampuchea*, Oxford, Oxfam, 1988.

[45] See, for instance, "France in Bid to Gag Report on Cambodia," *The Australian*, 26 February 1990.

[46] Nayan Chanda, *Far Eastern Economic Review*, 18 December 1979.

[47] Elizabeth Becker, *When the War Was Over* (New York, 1986): 440.

[48] Letter from Jonathan Winer, counsel to Senator John Kerry, Member of the U.S. Senate Foreign Relations Committee, to Larry Chartienes of Vietnam Veterans of America, 22 October 1986, citing "information from the Congressional Research Service." The details cited included the following annual amounts of U.S. aid to the "Khmer Rouge" for "development assistance, food assistance, economic support, and in smaller amounts for the Peace Corps, narcotics enforcement and military assistance": (in FY 87 dollars) 1980

$54.55 million, 1981 $18.29 million, 1982 $4.57 million, 1983 $2.46 million, 1984 $3.70 million, 1985 $0.84 million, 1986 $0.06 million. This has since been denied by the US State Department, while the Congressional Research Service has reportedly transferred its employee who provided the statistics. If their initial provision was a mistake, a convincing explanation for it does not appear to exist. In a letter to Noam Chomsky dated 16 June 1987, Jonathan Winer reported: "It is my understanding that US funding to Cambodia has been restricted to non-Khmer Rouge recipients since 1985 (FY 86). An earlier such restriction on direct aid put into place in 1979 was repealed in part on December 16, 1980, when humanitarian assistance to the Cambodian people was permitted, and repealed entirely on December 29, 1981....On August 8, 1985, aid to the Khmer Rouge was again banned, although small amounts have been since made available to non-Communist Cambodian resistance forces," who had allied themselves with the Khmer Rouge in 1982. This is corroborated by Sec. 906 of the 1985 US International Security and Development Cooperation Act (Public Law 99-83) which stipulates: "All funds... which were obligated but not expended for activities having the purpose or effect of... promoting, sustaining, or augmenting, directly or indirectly, the capacity of the Khmer Rouge or any of its members to conduct military or paramilitary operations in Cambodia... shall be deobligated and shall be deposited in the Treasury of the United States as miscellaneous receipts" (464-465); C. Etcheson, personal communication.

Additional evidence of U.S. military support for the Khmer Rouge remains to be either corroborated or pursued. On 27 August 1981, syndicated columnist Jack Anderson reported that "through China, the CIA is even supporting the jungle forces of the murderous Pol Pot in Cambodia." On 10 October 1983, *Newsweek* reported that the American CIA "is working with the Chinese to supply arms to the forces of former Cambodian ruler Pol Pot." On 4 June 1987, the *Far Eastern Economic Review* published a letter alleging that a U.S. consular official in Thailand had attempted to recruit a former British soldier "to a job smuggling guns to Pol Pot for payment in gold." "The American identified himself with a card issued by the US Government," claimed the "witness." In the same year an Australian veteran told friends of his own claimed involvement in secret American supply operations on behalf of the Khmer Rouge. In late 1989, Sihanouk said he had "received intelligence informing me that there were US advisers in the Khmer Rouge camps in Thailand, notably in Site 8 camp.... The CIA men are teaching the Khmer Rouge human rights!" (*Le Figaro* [Paris], 30 December 1989. I am grateful to Jack Colhoun for this last reference.) On 14 August 1990, United Press International quoted a former U.S. Green Beret sergeant in Thailand, Bob Finley, as claiming that he had been ordered to destroy incriminating documents that "would have linked the US Joint Military Assistance Group ... with the security council and the Thai government" in the 1988 sale of U.S. ammunition and explosives on the Thai black market, where they may have fallen into the hands of the Khmer Rouge. The *San Francisco Examiner* on 12 August 1990 offered corroboration from the Pentagon Inspector General's Office.   Another ex-Green Beret sergeant, Mike Bracy, who had been assigned as part of an internal military investigation into the matter, stated, "US Army Special Operations lost control of millions of dollars of American arms and ammunition over five years... $1 million worth dropped off the books in a two-month period, including Russian ammunition, anti-tank rounds, chemical agents, dynamite and C-4." According to *Indochina Digest*, "Sources in Bangkok say munitions sold on the black market make their way to the Cambodian resistance, including the Khmer Rouge." Another U.S. sergeant who reportedly "knew the details" of the illicit sales and "the most about the scandal" was killed in his office in Okinawa by a bomb (*Indochina Digest* Nos. 90-32 and 90-33, 11 and 17 August 1990).

[49] William Shawcross, *The Quality of Mercy: Cambodia, Holocaust and Modern Conscience* (New York, 1984): 289, 395, 345. Omang and Ottoway, writing in the Washington *Post* on 27 May 1985, also report that the US government provided food-aid to the Khmer Rouge in 1979, but they say this was stopped by Congress in 1980. See note 49, above.

[50] Linda Mason and Roger Brown, *Rice, Rivalry and Politics: Managing Cambodian Relief* (University of Notre Dame Press, 1983): 136, 159, 135.

[51] *Kampuchea: A Demographic Catastrophe*, National Foreign Assessment Center, Central Intelligence Agency, May 1980. For critiques of this document, see Michael Vickery, "Democratic Kampuchea: CIA to the Rescue," *Bulletin of Concerned Asian Scholars* (BCAS) 14, 4 (1982): 45-54; and Ben Kiernan, "The Genocide in Cambodia, 1975-1979," BCAS 22, 2 (1990): 35-40, and references cited.

[52] On statistical issues, see Ben Kiernan, "The Genocide in Cambodia, 1975-1979," *Bulletin of Concerned Asian Scholars*, 22, 2, 1990: 35-40.

[53] "Thais Furious at Cambodians for Disclosing Visit by Reagan Aide," *Los Angeles Times*, 5 December 1980. I am grateful to Jack Colhoun for this reference.

[54] Nayan Chanda, *Brother Enemy*: 388-89, 457.

[55] Both Sihanouk and Son Sann reported being pressured by the United States to join the coalition with Pol Pot. [See Ben Kiernan, "Kampuchea 1979-1981: National Rehabilitation in the Eye of an International Storm," *Southeast Asian Affairs 1982*, Institute of Southeast Asian Studies, Singapore (Heinemann, 1982): 167-95, at p. 187 (citing the Melbourne *Age*, 29 April 1981), on Sihanouk; and David J. Scheffer, "Arming Cambodian Rebels: The Washington Debate," *Indochina Issues*, no. 58, June 1985: 4, on Son Sann.] In a statement released to the *New Yorker* on 13 February 1992, US Ambassador to China Stapleton Roy denied this, but conceded that in a meeting with Sihanouk on 25 April 1981, Roy, then U.S. chargé in Beijing, had told Sihanouk "that achievement of a broad-based coalition/front would enhance considerably [Sihanouk's] chances of receiving outside assistance." (I am grateful to Stan

Sesser of the *New Yorker* for making Roy's statement available.) This confirms Sihanouk's account in the *Age* of 29 April 1981: "After that," he quoted Roy as saying, "it will be easier for friendly countries to help you." They did: see note 56 below.

[56] "Washington has been providing the coalition's non-communist members with covert financial aid for several years, using the CIA as a conduit... Sources [in Bangkok] say the aid has probably run to "well over" US$2 million annually for the past two years." Paul Quinn-Judge, "The Tactics of Delay," *Far Eastern Economic Review*, 25 October 1984: 52.

[57] See Ben Kiernan, "Kampuchea 1979-1981," *Southeast Asian Affairs 1982*, and John Holdridge (U.S. Department of State), Hearing before the Subcommittee on Asian and Pacific Affairs of the Committee on Foreign Affairs, House of Representatives, 97th Cong., 2nd sess., 14 September 1982: 71.

[58] "Peace Plan 'Stupid'—U.S. Rap," *Herald* (Melbourne), 28 June 1983. This report from Bangkok by Nikki Savva and Australian Associated Press added: "Mr. Shultz criticised and severely questioned Australia's motive and made it plain the US was not expecting much success from Mr. Hayden's Hanoi visit... Australian officials said Mr. Shultz had given Mr. Hayden "an extremely tough time.". "a hell of a hammering.".. in the first closed session of the ASEAN five-minister summit. They claimed the US had coordinated a strong anti-Australian stand before Mr. Hayden went into the closed meeting... [But] By the afternoon session, when Mr. Hayden met the five ASEAN Foreign Ministers alone, the mood had changed. Mr. Hayden was able to gain strong support for the Australian initiatives...Mr. Hayden was given ASEAN's approval for any progress Australia could make and will take a verbal message of goodwill to Hanoi tomorrow." However, through Australian Prime Minister Bob Hawke, Shultz managed to force Hayden to abandon the Labor Party's 1983 election pledge to restore bilateral aid to Vietnam, despite Indonesian support for such aid.

[59] *Far Eastern Economic Review*, 2 March 1989.

[60] Mary Kay Magistad, "Khmer Rouge are Closer to New Chance at Power," Boston *Globe*, 17 April 1989.

[61] When the Paris Conference on Cambodia foundered in August 1989, Washington "reiterated its support for a Khmer Rouge role in a transitional government" (Associated Press, *Bangkok Post*, 1 September 1989). As a result of U.S. support, the Khmer Rouge emerged strengthened from the failed conference. As one diplomat put it, the Khmer Rouge "got the US and Western countries to block a Vietnamese attempt to isolate and contain them." (Joseph de Rienzo of Reuters, Bangkok *Nation*, 31 August 1989).

[62] *Far Eastern Economic Review*, 7 September 1989. See also the five "Cambodia" films by John Pilger and David Munro, and the 1990 American Broadcasting Company documentary, "From the Killing Fields," for further evidence on these lines, as well as the report by Raoul Jennar, for ten years

a foreign affairs adviser to the Belgian Senate, "How the West is Helping the Return of Pol Pot," Brussels, May 1990, in *Cambodia: And Still They Hope*, compiled by John Nichols (Australian Council for Overseas Aid [Box 1562, Canberra ACT 2601 Australia], July 1990): 21-31.

[63] See for instance, "New Hope for Cambodia Peace," *Australian Financial Review*, 14 December 1989: "According to news reports out of Cambodia, Mr. Hun Sen has agreed to the proposal, overcoming one of the first hurdles. However, Prince Sihanouk, who initially supported it, reversed his stand once Mr. Hun Sen came on board." See also "Evans Plan Finds Support in Hanoi," *Sydney Morning Herald*, 13 December 1989; "Cambodia Agrees to UN role in Peace Process," *The Australian*, 2 February 1990; and "Cambodian Prime Minister Announces Support for Sweeping UN Role," by Ruth Youngblood, United Press International, 28 February 1990. Nayan Chanda reports further that in May 1990 the Australian negotiator Michael Costello visited Phnom Penh and put to Hun Sen the version of the Australian plan known as Option II (b), which Hun Sen accepted. Subsequently, however, Costello was unable to get the agreement of the opposition coalition (Nayan Chanda, personal communication.)

[64] For some of the contents of these speeches, see Roger Normand, "The Teachings of Chairman Pot," U.S. *Nation*, 27 August 1990; also Roger Normand and Ben Kiernan, "Khmer Rouge Poised to Gain from US policy," letter to the *New York Times*, 6 August 1990; and Ben Kiernan, "US Policy Turn on Cambodia Is Incomplete," and "Medieval Master of the Killing Fields," London *Guardian*, 23 and 30 July 1990. I am grateful to Normand for making this information available.

[65] *Asiaweek*, 13 October 1989.

[66] Paul Wedel, United Press International (UPI), "US Opposes Proposed Ceasefire in Cambodia," 14 May 1990.

[67] Nayan Chanda, "Japan's Quiet Entrance on the Diplomatic Stage," *Christian Science Monitor*, 13 June 1990.

[68] *Christian Science Monitor*, 13 June 1990.

[69] *Indochina Digest*, no. 90-20, 25 May-1 June, 1990, citing UPI, 31 May 1990.

[70] *Indochina Digest*, no. 90-23, 18 June-22 June 1990.

[71] MacNeil-Lehrer News Program, PBS-TV, July 18, 1990, interview with Jim Lehrer.

[72] "We will have seized Angkor Wat and Siemreap by January at the latest," Kien Van predicted inaccurately. "Khmer Rouge Receive Chinese Tanks," by Nate Thayer, Associated Press Writer, AP, 7 October 1990. *Indochina Digest*, no. 90-40, 6-12 October 1990.

[73] *Agence France Presse* report from Geneva, 30 August 1990.

[74] UN Security Council statement on Cambodia, released 11 January 1991: 24, 27.

[75] Michael Haas, "The Paris Conference on Cambodia," *Bulletin of Concerned Asian Scholars*, 23, 2, 1991: 4-6.

[76] In a secret 1988 briefing to his commanders, recounted by defectors to Roger Normand, Pol Pot blamed most of his regime's 1975-1979 killings on "Vietnamese agents." But he defended having massacred the defeated Lon Nol regime's officers, soldiers and officials. "This strata of the imperialists had to be totally destroyed," he insisted. In "abandoning communism" now, Pol Pot added, his movement discards its "peel," but not the fruit inside. "The politics has changed, but the spirit remains the same." The Khmer Rouge predict their return with this slogan: "When the water rises, the fish eat the ants, but when the water recedes, the ants eat the fish."

[77] Normand's Khmer Rouge defector informants quote Pol Pot as saying in 1988: "Our troops will remain in the jungle for self-defense," in the event of a settlement.

[78] *Daily Yomiuri*, 5 May 1991.

[79] *Sydney Morning Herald*, June 3 and 4, 1991.

[80] See Ben Kiernan, "Deferring Peace in Cambodia: Regional Rapprochement, Superpower Obstruction," in George W. Breslauer, Harry Kreisler and Benjamin Ward, eds., *Beyond the Cold War: Conflict and Cooperation in the Third World*, International and Area Studies Research Series No. 80, University of California, Berkeley, 1991: 59-82; Eva Mysliwiec, *Punishing the Poor: The International Isolation of Kampuchea*, Oxfam, Oxford, UK, 1988; and Michael Haas, "The Paris Conference on Cambodia, 1989," *Bulletin of Concerned Asian Scholars*, 23, 2, 1991: 42-53.

[81] *New York Times*, 6 August 1990. See also S. Heder, *Reflections on Cambodian Political History*, Strategic and Defence Studies Centre, Australian National University, Canberra, 1991: 18.

[82] "Khmer Rouge Receive Chinese Tanks," by Nate Thayer, Associated Press, Bangkok, 7 October 1990. According to the Chinese ambassador in London, "from the beginning of January" 1990, Beijing had begun sending the tanks to the Khmer Rouge. (Cited in UK House of Commons, Parliamentary Debates, 26 October 1990: 674.) A witness interviewed by journalist David Feingold reported that five Chinese T-59 tanks were handed over to the Khmer Rouge near the Thai province of Trat on 21 June 1990 (Feingold, personal communication). Though questions remain about their vintages, a total of 24 had arrived in Cambodia by October, according to *Jane's Defence Weekly* (Thayer, "Khmer Rouge Receive Chinese Tanks"; *Indochina Digest*, 6-12 October 1990), and the Khmer Rouge possibly received as many as 28 tanks. On 4 February 1991, UPI reported from Phnom Penh that Cambodian government forces said they were now facing these Khmer Rouge tanks in battle. Thai intelligence on the Cambodian border confirmed in March 1991 that in a nearby engagement the Khmer Rouge were "backed by T-62 tanks" (Bangkok *Nation*, 23 March 1991). At least one Khmer Rouge tank (possibly "four or five") was captured by Cambodian government forces and was displayed in Battambang for foreign observers (*Bangkok Post*, 21 April 1991). On 6 December 1990, Australia's Foreign Minister Gareth Evans had falsely

denied this, stating that "there is no evidence available to the Australian government that the Khmer Rouge have recently received tanks from China. Indeed, the consensus among the experts is to the contrary." Perhaps these experts were the same ones who in mid-1987 had put the chances of a Vietnamese withdrawal by 1990 at "1 in 300," in which case the Phnom Penh regime would last only "seven months."

[83] *Indochina Digest*, No. 90-40, 6-12 October 1990.

[84] *Bangkok Post*, 2 April 1991.

[85] *Bangkok Post*, 6 April 1991.

[86] Jacques Bekaert, "Peace, What Peace?," *Bangkok Post*, 20 May 1991.

[87] Jacques Bekaert, "The 'Military Question' and Real Life Tragedy," *Bangkok Post*, 31 August 1991.

[88] "Cambodia Peacebrokers Worry about Future," AFP, Bangkok *Post*, 25 October 1991.

[89] "Khmer Rouge leave trail of blood," London *Independent*, 14 July 1990.

[90] Associated Press, Bangkok, 2 September 1990, quoting Amnesty International. AP added that the Khmer Rouge radio had accepted responsibility for the attack and claimed that its guerrillas killed 15 soldiers and wounded 15 others, mentioning no civilian casualties. (I am grateful to Kelvin Rowley for this reference.) See also UPI, Bangkok, 4 October 1990; and "Khmer Rouge Attack on Trains inside Cambodia on the Rise," Bangkok *Nation*, 28 May 1991.

[91] "Cambodia: New Allegations of Extrajudicial Killings by the *Partie* of Democratic Kampuchea ("Khmer Rouge")," *Amnesty International*, London, April 1991.

[92] See Chanthou Boua, Ben Kiernan, and Anthony Barnett, "Bureaucracy of Death: Documents from inside Pol Pot's Torture Machine," *New Statesman*, 2 May 1980.

[93] Paul Wedel, UPI, report from O-Koki, Cambodia, 19 August 1990.

[94] UPI, Bangkok, 21 October 1990.

[95] "War on a political front," *Jane's Defence Weekly*, 2 March 1991.

[96] *Indochina Digest*, No. 90-42, 26 October 1990, citing AFP, 22 October and UPI, 21 October 1990.

[97] "KR shells kill 16 in Battambang," Bangkok *Nation*, 14 February 1991.

[98] "Khmer Rouge shelling forcing civilians to flee to Battambang," Bangkok *Nation*, 8 February 1991, and "Khmer Rouge 'sets Battambang on fire'," *Bangkok Post*, 13 February 1991.

[99] See Ben Kiernan, "Time is Ripe for Evans to Dump the Khmer Rouge," *Sydney Morning Herald*, 12 January 1990: 9.

[100] "5 Mortar Shells Land on Border Market, Killing 3," *Bangkok Post*, 22 April 1991.

[101] Ben Kiernan, "Green Grow the Killing Fields of Cambodia," *Guardian Weekly* (London), 28 April 1991.

[102] James Pringle, "Pol Pot Calls on Cambodians to Protect Wildlife," *Bangkok Post*, 31 January 1991. "KR Commander 'is Chief of Butchers'," *Bangkok Post*, Sheri Prasso, AFP report from Takeo, 19 March 1992.

[103] See for instance, "The Green Khmer Rouge?," by Charles-Antoine de Nerciat, AFP, *Nation*, 17 February, 1991.

[104] Nate Thayer, "A Khmer Ruse," *Far Eastern Economic Review*, 7 March 1991.

[105] *Far Eastern Economic Review*, 7 November 1991: 28.

[106] *New York Times*, January 21, 1992, and "Peace accord violation leaves 13 dead: Khmer Rouge forces attack villages," *Financial Times*, January 21, 1992. Both Ieng Mouly of the KPNLF and Prince Sihanouk also suggested that they held the Khmer Rouge responsible for the attacks. (See David Brunnstrom, "UN to Send Units to Disputed Cambodia Provinces," Reuters, Phnom Penh, 24 January 1992.) *Far Eastern Economic Review* correspondent Nate Thayer alone ascribed no blame to the Khmer Rouge, alleging that "government forces clashed with Khmer Rouge guerrillas, causing the worst ceasefire violations since the signing of the peace accord in November" (27 February 1992: 26). On 26 February, Khmer Rouge forces fired on a UN helicopter in the area, wounding the commanding officer of the Australian contingent in Cambodia. See "Khmer Rouge Said to Shoot UN Officer," Washington *Post*, 27 February 1992.

[107] Jacques Bekaert, *Bangkok Post*, 31 August 1991. (Emphasis added.) *Far Eastern Economic Review*, 7 November 1991: 28, reports again that "diplomats" say "it now appears that many of them were instigated by renegade troops from the Phnom Penh army and the two non-communist resistance groups."

[108] In 1990 Roger Normand was kind enough to show me the briefing notes recorded by his interviewees.

[109] "Resistance Attacks Cambodian Refugee Camp, Killing Nine," by Sue Downie, *UPI*, 22 February 1991, and "Cambodian Guerrillas Kill at Least Nine at Refugee Camp," Agence France Presse, 22 February 1991. For earlier evidence of the appalling human rights record of the US-funded KPNLF, see Ben Kiernan, "Pol Pot's Allies: The Right in Kampuchea," *Australian Left Review*, no. 99, 1987: 30-34; and pp. 49-68 of *Seeking Shelter: Cambodians in Thailand*, and pp. 24-40 of *Refuge Denied*, both published by the Lawyers Committee for Human Rights, New York, 1987 and 1989. *Indochina Digest* reported on 6 September 1991: "A report issued by the General Accounting Office (GAO) on 28 August indicates the US Agency for International Development (AID) is unable to give a comprehensive accounting for some $20.3 million supplied to Cambodian resistance groups since 1986... AID personnel are not allowed into battle zones to verify the aid reached the intended groups." (No. 91-36.)

[110] "Guerrillas Send 180,000 Fleeing," Associated Press, *Bangkok Post*, 14 June 1991.

[111] James Pringle, "The Khmer Rouge Vision of the Future," *Bangkok Post*, 17 May 1991.

[112] David Brunnstrom, "Spanish Aid Worker Shot in Bandit Attack Near Cambodian Camp," *Reuters*, Bangkok, 13 September 1991.

[113] Angus MacSwan, "Khmer Rouge Stage 'Coup D'État' in Refugee Camp," *Reuters*, 9 October 1991; *Indochina Digest*, No. 91-41, 11 October 1991; and Coalition for Peace and Reconciliation, "Update #1 On the Detention of the Site 8 Civilian Administrators by the Khmer Rouge Military and the Threat of Forced Repatriation of the Site 8 Population," 14 October 1991. See also Press Statement by the Special Representative of the UN Secretary-General, Bangkok, 12 October 1991. Interestingly, the date of the "coup," 30 September 1991, happened to be the fortieth anniversary of the foundation of the Cambodian communist movement.

[114] "UN to Warn Khmer Rouge on Refugee Shift," and "China Bars UN Warning to Khmer Rouge," *New York Times*, 17 and 18 October 1991.

[115] "Thai Army Stops Khmer Rouge Forcing Refugees Back," by Sutin Wannabovorn, *Reuters*, 17 January 1992.

[116] During a visit to Beijing on 5 September 1991, US Congressman Stephen J. Solarz pronounced "the termination of direct Chinese assistance to the Khmer Rouge." He described this as an "extraordinarily significant development." However, the next day Beijing stated that it continued to give aid to the Khmer Rouge, but claimed to have cut off military assistance, a claim widely doubted. See "Chinese End All Aid for Khmer Rouge," *Bangkok Post,* 6 September 1991, and "China Rectifies Stand on Khmer Rouge Aid," Bangkok *Nation*, 7 September 1991.

[117] Apart from other support, China has nominated as its new Ambassador to the Supreme National Council Mr. Fu Xue Zhang, who served in the Chinese embassy in Phnom Penh during the Pol Pot period, when his wife worked as a broadcaster on the Voice of Democratic Kampuchea radio. In 1989, Fu was a counselor at the Chinese embassy in Bangkok.

[118] Nayan Chanda, "China Plays Key Role in Cambodia Settlement," *Asian Wall Street Journal Weekly*, 22 July 1991: 1. Emphasis added.

[119] See Ben Kiernan, "China, Cambodia and the UN Plan," in Dick Clark, ed., *The Challenge of Indochina: An Examination of the US Role*, Aspen Institute, 1991: 13-16.

[120] "According to diplomatic sources, Thach's removal was a Chinese precondition for normalisation." "Comrades Again: Hanoi and Peking Set to Normalise Relations," *Far Eastern Economic Review*, 22 August 1991: 8. A Politburo member, Thach lost all his positions in the Vietnamese Communist Party at the June Congress, and also resigned his Ministerial post on 27 June. Another casualty of the Congress was hardline Interior Minister Mai Chi Tho, who was not politically close to Thach, though both had once been associated with Tho's brother, former Politburo member Le Duc Tho, who incurred Chinese wrath.

[121] For quite different reasons, domestic Vietnamese opposition to Thach dovetailed with China's demands. Jean-Claude Pomonti emphasizes that Vo

Nguyen Giap had campaigned strongly against Thach, so much so that Giap was himself downgraded for sectionalism, though this did not help Thach. Pomonti reports that China's opposition to Thach combined with Vietnamese military rancor over Thach's advancing of the Cambodian withdrawal date from late December 1990, preferred by the army, to September 1989. He believes that Thach's fate was sealed by January 1991. Personal communication, 28 November 1991.

[122] Michael Oksenberg, "The China Problem," *Foreign Affairs*, Summer 1991: 16.

[123] See for instance the interesting analysis by Kelvin Rowley, "China Key to Cambodian Ceasefire Breakthrough," *Canberra Times*, 5 July 1991: 9.

[124] *Far Eastern Economic Review*, 22 August 1991: 8.

[125] *New York Times*, 6 November 1991.

[126] *Indochina Digest*, No. 91-28, 12 July 1991.

[127] *Indochina Digest*, No. 91-38, 20 September 1991.

[128] "China, Burma Recognize Thai Junta," *Indochina Digest*, No. 91-10, 8 March 1991,

[129] Senator Bob Kerrey, testimony before the US Senate Foreign Relations Committee, 11 April 1991.

[130] Reuters, Melbourne *Age*, 3 September 1985.

[131] "Khmer factions pleased with Anand," Bangkok *Nation*, 10 May 1991.

[132] "Pol Pot Secretly Met Suchinda—Paper," Ba*ngkok Post*, 6 September 1991.

[133] "Pol Pot's Plans for Cambodia," *Economist*, 5 October 1991: 25.

[134] R. Bates Gill, "China Looks to Thailand: Exporting Arms, Exporting Influence," *Asian Survey*, 31, 6, June 1991: 526-539, at p. 533-5. More recent reports indicate, however, that Bangkok is becoming disillusioned with Chinese military equipment, and is turning back towards US and French arms suppliers.

[135] "SLORC Salvation: Peking's diplomatic priorities benefit junta," *Far Eastern Economic Review*, 3 October 1991: 24-5.

[136] China will continue to benefit from disputes among Southeast Asian countries over the Spratley islands, which China also claims. See Ben Kiernan, "China, Cambodia and the UN Plan"; and *Indochina Digest*, 7 December 1990, 23 August, 6 and 20 September 1991, and 24 January and 21 February 1992, for reports of competing activities on the islands by the Philippines, Vietnam, Malaysia and Taiwan. Moreover, China seems to have benefited not only from the recent pronounced anti-democratic trend in Southeast Asia, but also from Third World consternation over the 1991 US military destruction of Iraq (see *Far Eastern Economic Review* [FEER], 31 January 1991: 6, and 14 February 1991: 14, for strong condemnations of the US by China, the Philippines and Vietnam), as well as from the collapse of the USSR as a counterweight to the USA, which has delivered China more advantageous relations with India (see FEER, 26 December 1991: 10,11) and Iran, among other powers.

[137] See for instance Hiroshi Yamada, "Japan's Cambodia Peace Plan Proposes to Disarm Factions," *Daily Yomiuri*, 5 May 1991, which details Tokyo's proposal to a "special committee" to "explore concrete measures to ensure the non-return of the policies and practices of the past." See also *Indochina Digest*, No. 91-19, 10 May 1991, on Japanese diplomacy.

[138] Kelvin Rowley, "China Key to Cambodian Ceasefire Breakthrough," *Canberra Times*, 5 July 1991: 9.

[139] Paul Wedel, United Press International (UPI), "US Opposes Proposed Ceasefire in Cambodia," 14 May 1990.

[140] Raoul M. Jennar, *The Cambodian Gamble: Three Months of Negotiations Towards a Peace Fraught with Dangers*, September 1991: 6.

[141] *Indochina Digest*, No. 91-21, 24 May 1991.

[142] *Indochina Digest*, No. 91-23, 7 June 1991.

[143] Nayan Chanda, *Asian Wall Street Journal Weekly*, 5 August 1991. This report was later confirmed (see Raoul Jennar, *The Cambodian Gamble*: 16). Two months later Norodom Rannariddh was still proclaiming: "I think that Pol Pot is today simply a nominal leader of the Khmer Rouge..." *The Dominion*, Wellington, 21 August 1991. For an informed view, see Sutin Wannabovorn, "Elusive Pol Pot No Mystery Man in Border Region," *Bangkok Post*, 13 August 1991: "He is believed still to be paramount leader... Many in eastern Thailand say he is far from retiring."

[144] See the details in, for instance, "Rebel Raid Breaks Cambodia Truce," *Hong Kong Standard*, 2 July 1991, and "Phnom Penh Renews Truce Violation Charges," Bangkok *Nation*, 7 July 1991, which reported: "Western aid workers in Kompong Speu province 80 km. from Phnom Penh and in the central province of Kompong Thom say the Khmer Rouge attacked refugee sites on June 29 and July 3."

[145] "P. Penh: Shelling of Our Forces Continues," UPI, *Bangkok Post*, 9 July 1991. The same Thai officer also predicted on the basis of his conversations with the Khmer Rouge that they would continue "disruptive, small-scale guerrilla attacks... in an effort to harass government supply lines."

[146] Personal communication from Phillip Hazelton, an Australian aid official who visited Kampot at the time.

[147] "Proposed structure for the agreements on a comprehensive political settlement of the Cambodia conflict" (known as the "Perm-5 Implementation Plan"), 26 November 1990, : "The cease-fire shall take effect at the time this Agreement enters into force" (p. 5, Section V, Article 9), and shall only begin to be "supervised, monitored and verified by UNTAC" four weeks after that (p. 21, Annex 2, Article 1).

[148] *Indochina Digest*, 7 and 14 June 1991, Nos. 91-23 and 24.

[149] Hun Sen, address to the Aspen Institute meeting on Indochina, New York, 16 September 1991.

[150] *Indochina Digest*, 14 June 1991, No. 91-24.

[151] *Indochina Digest*, 19 July 1991, No. 91-29.

[152] *Indochina Digest*, 26 July 1991, No. 91-30 and, for North Korea's announcement, Bangkok *Nation*, 17 September 1991, citing SPK of the previous day.

[153] *Indochina Digest*, 23 August 1991, No. 91-34.

[154] Quoted in *Indochina Digest*, 19 July 1991, No, 91-29.

[155] Quoted by Nayan Chanda, "China Plays Key Role in Cambodia Settlement," *Asian Wall Street Journal Weekly*, 22 July 1991: 1.

[156] Quoted in *Indochina Digest*, 23 August 1991, No. 91-34.

[157] Philip Shenon, "Cambodian Talks Stall on Election Question," *New York Times*, 29 August 1991.

[158] Quotations from Kulachada Chaipipat and Yindee Lertcharoenchok, "Pattaya II: Another Try at Peace," Bangkok *Nation*, 26 August 1991.

[159] *Indochina Digest*, 23 August 1991, No. 91-34.

[160] K. Rowley, "China Key to Cambodian Ceasefire Breakthrough," *Canberra Times*, 5 July 1991: 9, and Hedi Annabi, personal communication.

[161] "Perm-5 Insists on Comprehensive Plan," *Indochina Digest*, 19 July 1991, No. 91-29.

[162] Quoted in Milton Cockburn, "No Room for Khmer Rouge: Evans," *Sydney Morning Herald*, 25 November 1989.

[163] "Statement of the Five Permanent Members of the Security Council of the United Nations on Cambodia," 28 August 1990 (known as the "Perm-5 Framework Document"): 9, 11. Of the five key areas, the document says: "To reflect the importance of these subjects, UNTAC needs to exercise such control as is necessary to ensure the strict neutrality of the bodies responsible for them. The UN in consultation with the SNC would identify which agencies, bodies and offices could continue to operate in order to ensure normal day-to-day life in the country." (9)

[164] "Perm-5 Implementation Plan," 26 November 1990: 13-14.

[165] Annex III, "Explanatory Note," UN Security Council, 11 January 1991, A/46/61, S/22059: 35-7. According to the Bangkok *Nation* [quoted in *Indochina Digest*, No. 91-19, 10 May 1991], the Khmer Rouge-dominated resistance refuses to acknowledge this document, and according to informed sources in Washington, the US dissociates itself from it.

[166] Paris Conference on Cambodia, "Agreement on a Comprehensive Political Settlement of the Cambodia Conflict," Text adopted by the Coordination Committee on 21 October 1991, Annex 1, Section A 2 (e) and (d).

[167] "Agreements on a comprehensive political settlement of the Cambodia conflict," 27 September 1991: 12-13.

[168] "Khmer Rouge Insists P. Penh Disband Army," *Bangkok Post*, 13 June 1991.

[169] Roger Normand, personal communication, based on his interviews with Khmer Rouge defectors in 1990. See Normand, "The Teachings of Chairman Pot," U.S. *Nation*, 27 August 1990.

[170] "SNC Talks Fail on Khmer Troop Demobilisation," *Bangkok Post*, 27 August 1991.

[171] *Indochina Digest*, No. 91-35, 30 August 1991.

[172] Lindsay Murdoch, "Cambodia's Peace Deal a Risk to Human Rights," Melbourne *Age*, 24 October 1991.

[173] Likewise SOC Deputy Defense Minister Ke Kim Yan told reporters on 26 October: "If we allow our militia to have arms in their houses it's a pretext for the other side to hide weapons in the forest." *Bangkok Post*, 27 October 1991.

[174] I had earlier arrived at a similar figure based on my own observations and research on the growth of the Phnom Penh army in Cambodia during the 1980s. See Ben Kiernan, "Balance of Forces in Cambodia," *Nation*, Bangkok, 13 October 1989: "The Cambodian army of Prime Minister Hun Sen is now much stronger than most outsiders suspect. It probably has 150,000 troops under arms, plus 200,000 militia... Hun Sen seems confident his government can hold on after its Vietnamese allies departed late last month."

[175] Author's interview with Hun Sen, New York, 23 September 1991.

[176] These figures are based on independent estimates of current strengths at 4,000 troops ("at the most") for the KPNLF and 5,000 for the Sihanoukists, and 13,000-22,000 for the Khmer Rouge. AFP, *Bangkok Post*, 18 September 1991.

[177] According to Thailand's Supreme Command Headquarters, the Khmer Rouge had "48,000" troops, the Sihanoukists 23,000, and the KPNLF 17,000, while the SOC has been badly outnumbered with 60,000. *Bangkok Post*, 27 September 1991.

[178] *Indochina Digest*, No. 91-34, 23 August 1991. See also note 98, above.

[179] "Agreements on a comprehensive political settlement of the Cambodia conflict," 27 September 1991: 17-20.

[180] *Ibid.*: 24, Article 8, paragraph 1: "Each Party agrees to provide to the Commander of the military component of UNTAC, before a date to be determined by him, all information at its disposal, including marked maps, about known or suspected caches of weapons and military supplies throughout Cambodia." "2. On the basis of the information received, the military component of UNTAC shall, after the date referred to in paragraph 1, deploy verification teams to investigate each report and destroy each cache found."

[181] James Pringle, "Pol Pot Has Secret Army Hidden in Mountains," *Bangkok Post*, 24 October 1991.

[182] Supapohn Kanwerayotin, *Bangkok Post*, 28 October 1991.

[183] *New York Times*, 11 November 1991: 1, 7.

[184] "According to intelligence reports and accounts from Cambodian refugees crossing into Thailand, the Khmer Rouge has put aside enough weapons and ammunition in the Cardamom mountains of Western Cambodia to allow it to fight on for years. Khmer Rouge soldiers are also being told to hide in remote base camps to prevent their detection by United Nations inspectors." *New York Times*, 11 November 1991: 7.

[185] "UNTAC Proposal Unveiled," and "Security Council Approves UNTAC Plan, *Indochina Digest*, 21 and 28 February 1992.

[186] *Cambodia: An Australian Peace Proposal: Working Papers Prepared for the Informal Meeting on Cambodia, Jakarta, 26-28 February 1990,* Canberra, Australian Government Publishing Service, 1990: 42.

[187] Raoul M. Jennar, personal communication, after his interview with Khmer Rouge leader in Site 8, Mey Mann, in March 1991.

[188] Hun Sen, address to the Aspen Institute meeting on Indochina, New York, 16 September 1991.

[189] Author's interview with Hor Namhong, New York, 23 September 1991.

[190] See Steven Erlanger, "No Haven from Agony for Cambodians," *New York Times,* 2 May 1991: A18. According to Raoul Jennar, the Khmer Rouge kidnapped ten peasant children in a separate incident in Kampot province in September 1991. According to Reuters, the Khmer Rouge "are blamed for a run of kidnaps" in Kampot. ("Khmer Rouge consolidates presence in southeast," by Angus MacSwan, Reuters, Bangkok *Nation,* 15 January 1992.)

[191] Roger Normand, personal communication, based on his interviews with Khmer Rouge commanders who defected in 1989. See his "The Teachings of Chairman Pot," *Nation,* 27 August 1990: 198-202, at p. 199.

[192] *Cambodia: An Australian Peace Proposal:* 52-3.

[193] "Agreements on a comprehensive political settlement of the Cambodia conflict," 27 September 1991: 24: "All Cambodians, including those who at the time of signature of this Agreement are Cambodian refugees and displaced persons, will have the same rights, freedoms and opportunities to take part in the electoral process." On the UN's mandate to "build confidence among the Parties to the conflict," see pp. 5, 20, 24.

[194] UN Security Council, "Report of the Secretary-General on Cambodia," S/23613, 19 February 1992, 43 pp., at pp. 7-10. The UN plans to station another 72 international staff in Phnom Penh, and 126 in provincial capitals.

[195] "Hun Sen to Win Poll: Sihanouk," by Norman Kempster of the *Los Angeles Times,* Melbourne *Age,* 26 September 1991.

[196] *Far Eastern Economic Review,* 11 August 1988: 29.

[197] *Indochina Digest,* 7 June 1991, No. 91-23.

[198] See John Pilger, "West Conceals Record on Khmer Aid," *Sydney Morning Herald,* 1 August 1991, and "Culpable in Cambodia," *New Statesman and Society,* 27 September 1991. A report by Asia Watch and Physicians for Human Rights notes that "China and the United Kingdom are, or have been, involved in training Cambodian resistance factions in the use of mines and explosives against civilian as well as military targets." *Land Mines in Cambodia: the Coward's War,* New York, September 1991, see pp. 25-27, 59.

[199] Raoul Jennar, *The Cambodian Gamble,* 13 September 1991: 35-6.

[200] *New York Times,* 28 August, 1991, editorial.

[201] *Indochina Digest,* 30 August 1991, No. 91-35.

[202] "Western Nations Want Former Cambodian Leader to Leave Country," by Evelyn Leopold, Reuters, UN, 22 September 1991.

[203] US Deputy Assistant Secretary of State for East Asian Affairs, Kenneth Quinn, address to the Global Business Forum, Georgetown Club, Washington, D.C., 16 September 1991. Quoted in John Pilger, "Organised Forgetting," *New Statesman and Society*, 1 November 1991: 10-11.

[204] *Indochina Digest*, 1 November 1991, No. 91-44. The facts are that the US had never supported the idea of a trial from the time it was first broached by Australian Foreign Minister Bill Hayden in 1986, and that, as we have seen, the US and China had forced Hun Sen to drop the demand.

[205] This statement was reported in the *New York Times*, 24 October 1991: A16.

[206] "Evans Backs Pol Pot Trial," Melbourne *Age*, 24 October 1991: 1.

[207] *New York Times*, 28 August 1991.

[208] "Pol Pot's Plans for Cambodia," *Economist*, 5 October 1991. This report belies the later claim by William Shawcross that "Western diplomats.. failed to predict... the communists' ability to finance their own arms purchases from the sale of timber and gems in areas they control along the border with Thailand" (*Time*, 28 December 1992: 32). The facts were known before the Agreement was signed on 23 October 1991.

[209] In March 1993, 800 Cambodian refugees in Thailand protested to demand they be sent to other countries instead of returning to their homeland. "There will be no peace in Cambodia in the future because the Khmer Rouge will never join the elections," said one of the protesters, Mak Samoeun, 33. "Samoeun said he has relatives in New Zealand and had applied for resettlement there, but was refused by UNHCR." "Last Cambodian Refugee Camp Closed Amid Protests," UPI, Site 2, 30 March 1993.

[210] *Indochina Digest*, 5 February 1993.

[211] Paris Conference on Cambodia, "Agreement on a Comprehensive Political Settlement of the Cambodia Conflict," Text adopted by the Coordination Committee on 21 October 1991, Annex 3, section 3.

[212] Paris Conference on Cambodia, "Agreement," Annex 1, section 2 provides only that in the absence of consensus, decisions could be made by Sihanouk or the UN Secretary-General's Special Representative, not by majority vote. According to a US official, this means the Khmer Rouge do not have a veto. But in December 1991, Sihanouk canceled his planned visits to Vietnam and Laos after "written official objection" from both Son Sann and Khieu Samphan. The Bangkok *Nation* explained that "the Khmer Rouge have veto rights, as the SNC functions by consensus" (6 December 1991).

[213] UN Security Council, "Report of the Secretary-General on Cambodia," 19 February 1992: 20, 43.

[214] In 1988 Pol Pot had predicted to his followers that in the event of a settlement, "Our troops will remain in the jungle for self-defense." Roger Normand, personal communication, based on his interviews with Khmer Rouge defectors in 1990. See Normand, "The Teachings of Chairman Pot," U.S. *Nation*, 27 August 1990. On the Pol Pot regime's record, see Ben Kiernan, "The Genocide in Cambodia, 1975-1979," *Bulletin of Concerned Asian Scholars*, 22, 2, 1990: 35-40.

[215] "Khmer Rouge consolidates presence in southeast," Angus MacSwan, Reuters, Bangkok *Nation*, 15 January 1992.   P. S. Goodman, "Guerrillas Threaten Peace," San Francisco *Chronicle*, 2 December 1991.

[216] See "Peace Accord Violation Leaves 13 Dead: Khmer Rouge Forces Attack Villages," *Financial Times*, January 21, 1992. Ieng Mouly of the KPNLF and Prince Sihanouk also suggested that they held the Khmer Rouge responsible for these attacks. See D. Brunnstrom, "UN to Send Units to Disputed Cambodia Provinces," Reuters, Phnom Penh, 24 January 1992.

[217] Sheri Prasso, AFP, "K. Rouge wants to open battlefield in P. Penh," *Bangkok Post*, 10 December 1992 (using my translation). See also Nayan Chanda, "Strained Ties," *FEER*, 17 December 1992; Chanda's translator rendered the last passage: "If we launch attacks that create panic, then everybody will panic—the whole world will panic. We need there to be panic. What we are worried about is that the situation will just continue to be cozy."

[218] See "Ceasefire Violations Occur in Cambodia," AFP, Bangkok *Post*, 15 February 1992, which quotes "diplomatic and military sources" to the effect that the latest fighting again "appeared to be instigated by the Khmer Rouge."

[219] See A. MacSwan, "Khmer Rouge Commitment to UN Accord Questioned," Reuters, Bangkok, 27 February 1992.

[220] "Khmer Rouge Commitment to UN Accord Questioned," by A. MacSwan, and "UN General Says Khmer Rouge not Cooperating," *Bangkok Post*, 21 February 1992. General Loridon noted that the Khmer Rouge had broken their agreement to allow each faction to station observers in the others' territories, refused to allow access to UN personnel, stalled the marking of their minefields, and refused to allow cartographers to fly over sensitive areas. See also "Khmer Rouge Denies Being Uncooperative," *Nation*, 24 February 1992.

[221] "Khmer Rouge Said to Shoot UN Officer," Washington *Post*, 27 February 1992, and "UN General to Grill Khmer Rouge Chiefs: Guerrillas Suspected of Attack," *Nation*, 28 February 1992, which reported that colleagues of the wounded Australian officer "blamed the Maoist Khmer Rouge."

[222] "UN Gives Priority to Halting Truce Breach," AFP, Nation, 3 March 1992, and "KR Rushes Troops to Northern flashpoint," *Nation*, AP, 1 March 1992.

[223] Thai military sources reported this later. "Factions Refuse to Stop Fighting in Cambodia," *Bangkok Post*, AFP, 28 March 1992.

[224] "Prince Accuses KR of Stalling Peace Process," Bangkok *Nation*, AFP, 8 March 1992.

[225] "US Says KR Attitude Harming UN's Efforts," *Nation*, Reuters, 12 March 1992.

[226] "Khmer Rouge Stages Widespread Attacks," Bangkok *Post*, AP, 14 March 1992.

[227] "Khmer Rouge Stages Widespread Attacks," and Nate Thayer, AP dispatch from Phnom Penh, 13 March 1992; "P. Penh Opens Fresh Offensive in KR-held Area," *Nation*, AP, 30 March 1992; "P. Penh, Khmer Rouge Fight as Generals Discuss Peace," *Bangkok Post*, AFP, 1 April 1992.

[228] "Khmer Rouge Refuses to Order End to Fighting," *Bangkok Post*, AFP, 15 March 1992; "KR Commander is 'Chief of Butchers,'" *Bangkok Post*, AFP, 19 March 1992.

[229] "Khmer Rouge Spurns Ceasefire Call," *Nation*, Reuters, 23 March 1992.

[230] "Fighting Erupts in Cambodia," *Indochina Digest*, 27 March 1992. UNTAC military commander Lieutenant-General John Sanderson also described the government action as "a counter-offensive." "Factions Refuse to Stop Fighting in Cambodia," *Bangkok Post*, AFP, 28 March 1992; "P. Penh, Khmer Rouge Fight as Generals Discuss Peace," *Bangkok Post*, AFP, 1 April 1992.

[231] *Indochina Digest*, 10, 17 and 24 April 1992; *Cambodia Peace Watch*, 4, 1, April 1992, citing Reuters and UPI of 9 and 29 April 1992. For evidence of further Khmer Rouge ceasefire violations in this two-week period, see "UN Moves into Kompong Thom," *Nation*, 27 April 1992.

[232] UN Security Council, *First Progress Report of the Secretary-General on the United Nations Transitional Authority in Cambodia*, S/23870, 1 May 1992: 1.

[233] *Indochina Digest*, 8 May 1992; "Khmer Rouge Launch Fierce Attacks," Reuters, Phnom Penh, *Bangkok Post*, 6 May 1992.

[234] Susan Walker, personal communication, 24 May 1992.

[235] "United Nations Senior Official Accuses Khmer Rouge of Threatening Peace," UPI, Phnom Penh, 26 May 1992. *Indochina Digest*, 29 May 1992.

[236] Following earlier patterns, on 20 March 1992, a force of 10-14 armed Khmer Rouge arrested and detained the civilian leaders of Site K, a refugee camp in Thailand, holding them for five days in a village 20 km. inside Cambodia. ("Detention of Camp Leaders Upsets UN," *Nation*, AFP, 26 March 1992.) The Khmer Rouge also attempted to detain the wife of the camp leader, who "sought shelter with friends."

[237] "Cambodia Clashes Cause New Wave of Displaced," Reuters, *Nation*, 3 April 1992. "About 15,000 Cambodians, many of them farmers with sick and starving children, have been forced to leave their homes... One man said he walked for three days to escape the fighting. "Yes, I saw the Khmer Rouge, and that's why I'm here," he said. "Sometimes the Khmer Rouge set fire to homes and stables."

[238] "Factions Refuse to Stop Fighting in Cambodia," *Bangkok Post*, AFP, 28 March 1992.

[239] *Cambodia Peace Watch*, 5, 1, May 1992, citing UPI, 30 May and 2 June 1992; *Indochina Digest*, 5 and 12 June 1992; and "Khmer Rouge on the Attack," *Australian*, 2 June 1992.

[240] The U.S. Department of State's February 1993 Human Rights Report on Cambodia states: "It is clear that political opponents of the SOC were assassinated, that the SOC did not fully and impartially investigate the killings, and that SOC security officials appear to be involved in some of the assassinations. During 1992 perhaps as many as 50 such political killings occurred, although solid evidence is available on fewer than 10 cases. Given the secrecy of SOC security organs and impediments to effective investigations,

the responsibility of the SOC for these acts of political violence cannot be determined." The State Department's overall view is that in 1992 Cambodia "made notable progress in human rights, although serious problems remain." UNTAC's Human Rights Component, in a "Background Note on UNTAC Human Rights Activities in Cambodia" dated 18 November 1992, noted that by 10 November it had received 298 complaints, including 112 of harassment and intimidation, 63 of wrongful imprisonment, 14 of wrongful death, and 118 concerning land disputes.

[241] In 1992 UNTAC arrested a member of Rannariddh's FUNCINPEC for the public shooting death of an SOC official in Kompong Cham province. The US State Department's February 1993 Human Rights report on Cambodia notes: "In non-Communist controlled areas, KPNLF or FUNCINPEC security forces carried out arrests with no judicial oversight. While there are reports that some detainees were summarily executed, these cannot be confirmed." Sihanouk has claimed that his son's party is infiltrated by "a large number of Khmer Rouge," who are "tasked with eliminating... true royalists" (*Cambodia Peace Watch*, Folio 2, Vol. 2, No. 1, February 1993). In April 1993, General Kann Rath, fourth-ranking commander in the Sihanoukist military hierarchy, defected to the SOC with two sons, claiming that "Violences in Banteay Meanchey province in Battambang were committed by FUNCINPEC itself, but the blame was put on the SOC" (State of Cambodia, Press Release, No. 16, 6 April 1993).

[242] See for instance, "Cambodia Turns over 21 MIGs to UN forces," *Bangkok Post*, 28 June 1992.

[243] Boutros Boutros-Ghali, Report to the UN Security Council, 15 February 1993, excerpted in *Cambodia Peace Watch*, Folio 2, Vol. 2, No. 1, February 1993.

[244] *Indochina Digest*, 12 June 1992. According to the *New York Times* of 15 June 1992: "The Khmer Rouge have long charged that large numbers of Vietnamese troops remain in Cambodia in support of the Phnom Penh government. Foreign diplomats say that there is no evidence to support the allegation." Murray Hiebert of *FEER* (11 June 1992) adds that "UN military observers say they have found no evidence to support this claim." A confidential UNTAC report obtained by *FEER* in November 1992 stated that "there are indeed foreign forces within the meaning of the Paris Agreement operating in Cambodia, but they are from Thailand. Thai army units move freely in the DKZ [Democratic Kampuchea Zone, or Khmer Rouge-controlled territory] and have been accused of aiding the NADK [Khmer Rouge armed forces] militarily." Nayan Chanda, "Strained Ties," *FEER*, 17 December 1992.

[245] Bangkok *Nation*, 21 June 1992.

[246] *Indochina Digest*, 19 June 1992.

[247] UNTAC merely sent a letter "to the senior liaison officer in Pailin, requesting troops in the area... to refrain from such actions." *Indochina Digest*, 10 July 1992.

[248] *Indochina Digest*, 14 August 1992, quoting a speech by Eagleburger in Tokyo on 22 June.

[249] *Indochina Digest*, 26 June 1992.

[250] Nayan Chanda, "UN Divisions," *Far Eastern Economic Review*, 23 July 1992.

[251] Chanda, *Far Eastern Economic Review*, 23 July 1992.

[252] "Top Peacekeeper Lashes KR over Accord Violations," Bangkok *Nation*, 24 July 1992.

[253] Nayan Chanda, "Dark Days at Kok Kandal," *Far Eastern Economic Review*, 30 July 1992.

[254] See Philip Shenon, "Age-old Hatreds Haunt Vietnamese in Cambodia," *New York Times*, 21 August 1992. Villagers told UNTAC that "after the slaughter, the men ran towards a hideout of the Khmer Rouge." However, a UN official in Phnom Penh said "there is no evidence" that the attack was carried out by the Khmer Rouge. (UPI, *Bangkok Post*, 25 July 1992.) A UN officer even claimed that renegade government forces were responsible. (AFP, Bangkok *Nation*, 27 July 1992.) Then the Khmer Rouge blamed the massacre on the SOC. (Bangkok *Nation*, 1 August 1992.) UN officers further claimed that a government military unit stationed nearby had done nothing to stop the hour-long attack. All this proved false. When UNTAC's Civilian Police Component concluded its investigation in August, UNTAC Deputy Representative Behrooz Sadry said that 'witnesses' testimony and other evidence proved the government soldiers did try to catch the assailants and that Khmer Rouge guerrillas were to blame." ("UN Investigation Concludes KR Slayed Vietnamese Families," *Phnom Penh Post*, 27 August 1992. See also Bangkok *Nation*, 20 August 1992.)

[255] *Indochina Digest*, 21 August 1992. The quotation appeared in the *Far Eastern Economic Review*.

[256] Sheila McNulty, AP, Phnom Penh, 26 March 1993, and Mark Dodd, Reuters, Phnom Penh, 26 March 1993, give the different estimates. A 1992 UNTAC estimate had been 100,000. Dodd, Reuters, Phnom Penh, 3 June 1993, said "independent estimates" range "between 200,000 and 300,000."

[257] Four days before the Kompong Chhnang attack, they mortared Chba Ampou village, inhabited by Cambodians. "Khmer Rouge Strike North of Phnom Penh," Bangkok *Nation*, 26 April 1992. For Pol Pot's continuing leadership of the Khmer Rouge, see *Indochina Digest*, 21 August and 18 September 1992.

[258] "Buddhist Monk Killed as Khmer Shell Temple," Bangkok *Nation*, 20 July 1992.

[259] *Indochina Digest*, 26 June 1992.

[260] *Indochina Digest*, 24 July 1992.

[261] Philip Shenon, "Most Cambodians See Nothing of Aid," *New York Times*, 21 February 1993.

[262] "August-end Deadline for KR to Honour Pact," Bangkok *Nation*, 27 July 1992.

[263] *Indochina Digest*, 25 September 1992.

[264] See for instance Kavi Chongkittavon, "Khmer Peace Brokers Move to Appease KR," Bangkok *Nation*, 23 June 1992.

[265] Gareth Evans of the Australian TV program *Sunday*, 17 February 1992, cited by Dennis Shoesmith in *Cambodia After the Paris Agreements*.

[266] Bangkok *Nation*, 25 July 1992, and *Bangkok Post*, 26 July 1992.

[267] *Indochina Digest*, 21 August 1992.

[268] "UNTAC is 'likely to bring back K. Rouge,'" *Bangkok Post*, 21 August 1992.

[269] *Indochina Digest*, 28 August 1992.

[270] "Prasong: End trade with Khmer Rouge," *Bangkok Post*, 9 August 1992.

[271] "We may have to come to that," Eagleburger said, describing sanctions as "something we may have to look at reasonably soon." Coming eleven weeks after his 22 June warning that violations should not be "cost-free" and "the saboteurs" should "suffer," this softened Eagleburger's stand. *Indochina Digest*, 11 September 1992.

[272] Shep Lowman, *Christian Science Monitor*, 28 August 1992, quoted in *Indochina Digest*, 4 September 1992.

[273] Like the Carter Administration in 1979 and 1980, the Reagan Administration voted in 1981 for the Khmer Rouge government of "Democratic Kampuchea" to represent Cambodia's people in the United Nations. In 1982 Jeane Kirkpatrick reiterated: "We expect to support the coalition Government of Democratic Kampuchea including... the Khmer Rouge" in the U.N. (*Australian*, 25-6 September 1982.) Indeed she did support the Khmer Rouge in the 1982 U.N. vote, and in April 1993 the Khmer Rouge's ambassador heads Cambodia's UN mission.

[274] Jeane Kirkpatrick, "Globally, the Villains Seem to be Winning," *New York Post*, 3 August 1992.

[275] Shep Lowman, *Christian Science Monitor*, 28 August 1992.

[276] "Seek Peace Without Khmer Rouge, Sihanouk Says," *New York Times*, 3 September 1992.

[277] *Indochina Digest*, 18 September 1992. Sihanouk, at the behest of China, then withdrew his statement that the UN peace process should go ahead without the Khmer Rouge.

[278] "Cambodia Guerrillas Told to Stick to Peace Plan," *New York Times*, 26 September 1992.

[279] "UN Accuses Khmer Rouge of Bridge Attack," Reuters, Phnom Penh, 15 October 1992.

[280] "UN chief against KR sanctions," and "KR hails UN chief's stance on sanctions," *Bangkok Post*, 22 and 30 November 1992.

[281] *New York Times*, 20 and 21 December 1992; *Cambodia Peace Watch*, 12, 1, December 1992. Akashi had previously insisted that UNTAC was "entitled to send civilian and military police to zones under [Khmer Rouge] control at a suitable point in the near future." *Indochina Digest*, 7 August 1992.

[282] *Cambodia Peace Watch*, 12, 1, December 1992; *Indochina Digest*, 8 January 1993.

[283] *Cambodia Peace Watch*, Folio 2, Vol. 1, No. 1, January 1993.

[284] See also "A Ruby Rush Gone Bust," *JewelSiam*, Nov.-Dec. 1992: 60-75.

[285] "Logging Lumbers On," *Indochina Digest*, 19 February 1993.

[286] "Khmer Rouge Deny Knowledge of Bridge Demolition," Reuters, Phnom Penh, 15 October 1992.

[287] *Indochina Digest*, 24 December 1992.

[288] "UN Says the Khmer Rouge Killed 12 Ethnic Vietnamese," *New York Times*, 30 December 1992; *Indochina Digest*, 8 January 1993.

[289] Asia Watch, *Political Control, Human Rights, and the UN Mission in Cambodia*, New York, September 1992: 58-9.

[290] *Cambodia Peace Watch*, Folio 2, Vol. 2, No. 1, citing FEER, 4 February 1993, New York Times, 12 February 1993, and Reuters, 18 February 1993; and Folio 2, Vol. 3, No. 1, March 1993, citing UPI, FBIS and Reuters reports, confirming a report in *Indochina Digest*, 5 March 1993. General Kann Rath, fourth-ranking commander of the Sihanoukist forces, claimed after defecting to the SOC in April 1993: "The FUNCINPEC leaders have been allied with the Khmer Rouge... Prince Rannariddh declared on August 29, 1992 to his army in Romchang base that FUNCINPEC had made an alliance with the Khmer Rouge." (State of Cambodia, Press Release, No. 16, 6 April 1993).

[291] "Cambodian Election Campaign Begins Despite Attacks," UPI, Phnom Penh, 6 April 1993.

[292] Chanthou Boua, "Cotton Wool and Diamonds," *New Internationalist*, Special Issue *Cambodia: Return to Year Zero*, April 1993: 20-21.

[293] Reuters, 13 January 1993, and *Indochina Digest*, 15 and 29 January 1993. On 9 February, gangsters apparently linked to Khmer Rouge forces staged another attack in Siemreap. They wounded two foreigners, killed three Cambodians, and stole eleven historic statues from the Angkor conservatory. Charles Keyes, personal communication.

[294] The attackers were led by Loeung Dara, a Khmer Rouge officer under Mok's command. *Indochina Digest*, 12, 19 and 26 March 1993; *Cambodia Peace Watch*, Folio 2, Vol. 3, No. 1, March 1993; Mark Dodd, "Cambodian Security Deteriorates near Angkor Wat," Reuters, 14 March 1993; "Terrified Vietnamese Fleeing Cambodia," UPI, 23 March 1993; and Craig Etcheson, "The Calm Before the Storm: Cambodia, March 1993," report on a trip to Cambodia by the Executive Director of the Campaign to Oppose the Return of the Khmer Rouge, 318 Fourth Street N.E., Washington, D.C. 20002: 15-16.

[295] *Cambodia Peace Watch*, Folio 2, Vol. 3, No. 1, March 1993, quoting Khmer Rouge radio of 15 March 1993; *Indochina Digest*, 26 March 1993. "Khmer Rouge blamed for latest Vietnamese massacre," UPI, Phnom Penh, 26 March 1993.

[296] Katrina Peach, "UNMOs Powerless to Protect Ethnic Vietnamese," *Phnom Penh Post*, March 26-April 8, 1993: 4, and Peach's reconstruction of the massacre from accounts of participants and witnesses, "Chong Kneas: From Both Sides of the Gun": 5.

[297] Washington *Post*, 8 April 1993, citing UN naval observers.

[298] "UNTAC Personnel Killed," *Indochina Digest*, 9 April 1993, quoting Akashi, and accounts in *New York Times*, 4, 5, 6 and 7 May 1993.

[299] *Indochina Digest*, 2 April 1993.

[300] Washington *Post*, 7 April 1993.

[301] "Year in Review '92", *Far Eastern Economic Review*, 24-31 December 1992: 34.

[302] "KR: 'Right' govt will not be elected," Bangkok *Nation*, 29 January 1993.

[303] Boutros Boutros-Ghali, Report to the UN Security Council, 15 February 1993, excerpted in *Cambodia Peace Watch*, Folio 2, Vol. 2, No. 1, February 1993.

[304] Quoted in *Indochina Digest*, 26 February 1993.

[305] Quoted in *Indochina Digest*, 19 March 1993. FUNCINPEC's violation of the ceasefire has been noted. KPNLF troops, too, laid booby-traps in northwest Cambodia, damaging a Thai truck. Reuters, Bangkok, 15 March 1993.

[306] "Sihanouk Tells Cambodians They Must Deal with Khmer Rouge," by Kevin Cooney, Reuters, Phnom Penh, 16 November 1991. See also: *Time*, 6 September 1993: 12.

[307] Remarks at a February 1992 conference at Yale University, in Ben Kiernan, ed., *Genocide and Democracy in Cambodia: The Khmer Rouge, the United Nations, and the International Community*, Yale Southeast Asia Studies Council, page 290, below. For prescient critical views of the U.N. Plan, see Michael J. Horowitz, "The 'China Hand' in the Cambodia Plan," *New York Times*, 12 September 1990, and Chet Atkins, "Cambodia's 'Peace:' Genocide, Justice, and Silence," *Washington Post*, 26 January 1992. Elizabeth Becker called the UN plan "a fine compromise" (*New Republic*, 17 February 1992), but later argued against sanctions on the Khmer Rouge for violating it ("Cambodia Comes Back to Life," *New York Times*, 25 August 1992). More recent analyses include Ben Kiernan, "Rouge Awakening," *ALR* (Sydney) No. 148, March 1993: 10-11; Nayan Chanda, "The U.N.'s Failure in Cambodia," *Wall Street Journal*, 11 March 1993; and Henry Kamm, "Cambodia Election Snared as Peace Pact Unravels," *New York Times*, 18 March 1993.

[308] Former director of the US State Department's Office for Vietnam, Laos and Cambodia, Shep Lowman, writing in the *Christian Science Monitor*, 28 August 1992, observed that "Khmer Rouge obstructionism was fully expectable." Quoted in *Indochina Digest*, 4 September 1992.

[309] Australian Foreign Minister Senator Gareth Evans, quoted in *Indochina Digest*, 22 January 1993.

[310] For the evidence of this, see Ben Kiernan, "The Cambodian Crisis, 1990-1992: The UN Plan, the Khmer Rouge, and the State of Cambodia," *Bulletin of Concerned Asian Scholars*, 24, 2, April-June 1992: 3-23, and "The Return of Pol Pot," *New Statesman*, 9 July 1993: 14-15.

[311] Others vary from 5,000-10,000 to as many as 27,000. (Elizabeth Becker, *International Herald Tribune*, 10 November 1992; William Shawcross, *Time*, 28 December 1992.) But UNTAC director Yasushi Akashi states that Khmer

Rouge forces increased from 10,000 to 15,000 in 1992-3. Quoted in *Indochina Digest*, 21 May 1993, and *Cambodia Peace Watch*, Folio 2, Vol. 5, No. 1, May 1993.

[312] See for instance Ken Stier, "Log Rolling: Thai forestry contracts help to fund the Khmer Rouge," *FEER*, 21 January 1993: 15-16. For further Thai violations of the Agreement, see *FEER*, 17 December 1992, and *Indochina Digest*, 6 November 1992 and 19 February 1993.

[313] Statement of Sen. Charles Robb (D-VA), during testimony of Mr. Winston Lord, Senate Foreign Relations Committee, Asia Sub-committee hearing, 16 June 1993.

[314] No encouragement should be given to Rannariddh's and other proposals to include unelected Khmer Rouge in the post-election government (see *New York Times*, 28 February 1983, and UPI, Phnom Penh, 6 April 1993). For a different view, see *New York Times* editorial, 17 July 1993, stating that "it ill behooves Washington to get suddenly sanctimonious over the prospect of Cambodian leaders now making a pragmatic deal of their own with the Khmer Rouge."

Development Aid and Democracy in Cambodia

Chanthou Boua

In 1988 I was asked by the umbrella group for nongovernmental organizations (NGOs) in Australia to launch a new book called *Punishing the Poor*, by Eva Mysliwiec. It was about the international NGOs' efforts in Cambodia since 1979, and Mysliwiec was just the right person to write such a book. She had been sent to Cambodia by the American Friends Service Committee (AFSC) as their first director in Phnom Penh, in 1979. A very experienced and dedicated person, who since then has worked for many other NGOs in Cambodia, she is still there today, directing the Cambodian Development Resource Institute.

In her book, which she wrote in 1986, Mysliwiec said that "Cambodia is the only Third World country that is denied United Nations development aid."[1]   For thirteen years, from 1979 to 1992, Cambodia did not receive UN development aid. The reason is that the government of the State of Cambodia was not recognized by the UN or Western countries, the donors of UN funds, despite the fact that it was this government which ended the suffering and genocide perpetrated by the Khmer Rouge (KR) regime. Until 1991, the UN seat was occupied by a coalition "government" of the Khmer Rouge and two noncommunist opposition factions. It is well known that the KR is by far the strongest element in this coalition. So, like the poor in the title of Mysliwiec's book, 8.5 million Cambodians living under the Hun Sen regime continued to be punished by the world community. It is interesting to investigate who those 8.5 million people are.

Cambodians After Pol Pot's Rule

When I returned to Phnom Penh in 1980 for the first time since leaving it in 1972, I saw a country in ruins: schools, hospitals, government buildings, roads, and private homes were largely destroyed, and the people psychologically shattered by their experiences during the previous four years under Khmer Rouge leadership.

The people I met were mostly women, who comprise sixty to sixty-five percent of Cambodians. Their fathers, husbands, sons, and brothers had been killed by Khmer Rouge forces or had died of starvation and disease. Women, too, died and were killed; but men suffered in larger numbers, because they represented more of a threat to the KR regime than the women. As a result of the war over the last fifteen years and its increasing death toll among men, we now find a situation in Cambodia where thirty to forty percent of families are headed by women raising young children and sometimes the orphans of friends or relatives, as well as the corollary fact that fifty percent of the people are now under the age of seventeen. Therefore it is these women and children whom the world community and the UN are punishing. And their livelihoods and lives have been jeopardized by the UN-sponsored "peace" agreement.[2]

After the Pol Pot period, these women went back to their villages to find their family homes destroyed, their pots and pans and household goods gone, farming equipment and draft animals in short supply, and rice-fields ravaged.

The last fifteen years have been tough for Cambodian women. The vast majority (ninety percent) of the population live in rural areas, therefore the bulk of the womenfolk earn a living through farming. The isolation of Cambodia, exacerbated by the denial of UN development aid and the U.S.-led economic and trade embargo, has hurt Cambodia in every area. Agriculturally, it has meant that U.S. equipment ranging from tractors to shovels could not be purchased by or given to Cambodia; tools, irrigation pumps, draft animals, vaccines for animals, and fertilizers are very difficult to come by. So, year after year, women have faced the ongoing problems of not having enough fertilizer, insecticide, seed, and so on to boost their production. As a result, agricultural production has been low despite their heroic efforts. Still, they fight on, doing whatever they can to make their livelihood, while the world watches, almost unmoved at the sight of Cambodia taking its place as one of the poorest counties in the world.

In other fields similar determination existed. Throughout the country, teachers and nurses went through training and retraining to fill the positions as educators and care-givers. They had been decimated during the Pol Pot era. Schools were reopened in great numbers, and by 1984 there were more children attending school even than during the Sihanouk time.[3] People were enthusiastic: they considered themselves so lucky to have survived the KR period that they worked tirelessly and were determined to rebuild their country. And they worked for very little. The sacrifice was enormous: civil servants, teachers, and nurses were paid enough rice for their families plus a monthly salary equivalent to something like two kilograms of sugar or pork. Like their peasant counterparts, life was tough. And during that time, the early 1980s, many people left Cambodia. The desire to leave was quite understandable, because Cambodia was very poor: one could easily die of diarrhea or fever, as there was no adequate medicine supply; and of course the threat of the KR was real and reinforced by the fact that they were recognized by the UN, and the Phnom Penh government was not. I myself helped to sponsor a few refugees to Australia, where I lived at the time.

The Response of the International Community Since Pol Pot

Not everybody, of course, failed to hear the cries of the Cambodian people. A dozen or so international NGOs responded to their needs. One of them was the AFSC, which first sent Eva Mysliwiec to direct its program in Cambodia. Others from America included Church World Service, Oxfam America, and the Mennonite Central Committee. Against the policy of their government, they battled on with their small budgets, characteristic of all NGOs. Their task of aiding Cambodia was made extremely difficult because of the U.S. embargo against Cambodia and the Trading with the Enemy Act.

Many were more interested in discrediting their activities, claiming that their aid was 'going to the Vietnamese' or was not reaching the people for whom it was intended.[4] I have been involved in evaluating some of the NGO programs. An evaluation I made for Oxfam America found that their irrigation pumps, rice seed, and fertilizer were put to use effectively and were much appreciated by the villagers. Of course, there was nowhere near enough aid. Oxfam had only a limited budget, and at that time only fifteen irrigation pumps were given to a village of 344 families. But still, to a certain extent, it improved the livelihood of that village.

So the new Heng Samrin government was not a failure. The help of NGOs and other friends from India and the Socialist bloc, and the dedication of the Cambodians themselves, managed to revive

Cambodia from 'Year Zero,' as John Pilger called it in his film, to a respectable state, however poor. They went through many stages of reform: economic, agricultural, state controlled, semi-state controlled, joint ventures of state and private agencies, and so on. With their meager resources Cambodians tried to survive, through all sorts of reforms, against the embargo.

Their success was not accidental; it was largely due to the sensible economic policy of the government. It was inspired by Marxist ideology, but it was what Cambodia needed at the time. I remember writing a report for Oxfam U.K. about a desperate family I met in 1986. This young family with no parents, under the Sihanouk or Lon Nol regimes, would have fallen destitute, or its women become prostitutes in urban slums, but instead, the agrarian policy existing at the time enabled them to remain in the village, living, not prosperously, but with access to land, and with dignity and a future to look forward to.

The dedication of the Cambodians impressed many NGO workers and visitors alike. I remember interviewing a Church World Service director, an experienced aid worker, who said Cambodia was the easiest country he had worked in, that he received full cooperation from the government, and how pleased he was that all the aid reached the people, which was not always the case in other countries in which he had worked.

The early 1980s was an exciting time for Cambodia watchers. I feel privileged to have witnessed such a rebirth of a nation. I went there quite often during that period, and every time the progress made never failed to surprise me: a new shop here, a restaurant there, a new set of pots and pans for this family, a new cut of cloth for that woman. These were small things, but those who emerged from the Pol Pot regime with nothing appreciated them more, and took pride in that first step toward the accumulation of wealth. Nonetheless, progress was slow; there were simply no resources. So, while it was an exciting time, the process was painful to watch.

In the second half of the 1980s many Western NGOs working in Cambodia and scholars of Cambodia argued in favor of international recognition of the de facto government and restoration of the long overdue international aid. But to no avail.

The argument for denying aid to Cambodia at the time was that the Vietnamese were occupying the country. There were Vietnamese advisers and troops in Cambodia then. The fact is, though, that the

Vietnamese army was very much welcomed by the people of Cambodia, at least for the first few years. There is no shortage of Cambodians at home, or even here in the United States who say that the Vietnamese liberated them from the KR. However, not all of them were appreciated by the Cambodians, and some, especially Vietnamese advisers, outstayed their welcome. The advisers started leaving in 1981 and were gone by 1988. The troops followed them a year later; the last were gone by 1990.

Still the externally-imposed isolation continued. There was no development aid from the UN or the West. The latter said that they wanted a 'comprehensive' settlement before aid could be given to Cambodia. This meant including the Khmer Rouge in Cambodia's future. Desperately needing foreign assistance after the Vietnamese and the Eastern bloc had left the scene, the Phnom Penh government entered into UN peace negotiations with the other three factions, including the KR, in 1989. At no stage during these negotiations did the UN's Permanent Five powers try to exclude the KR.

The UN Peace Plan

The UN-sponsored peace negotiations took place at the time when the Cambodian people had just started to reconsolidate their lives. In the rural areas as well as the cities, they had just started to enjoy the fruits of their hard work. While Prime Minister Hun Sen was traveling the world negotiating, back in Cambodia people grew nervous. The rural people were anxious about the prospect of the return of the KR, and what would happen to their newly distributed land and animals, and the civil servants feared that they would have to share power with the other three factions. There has never been a peaceful relinquishment of power in modern Cambodian history, but the Permanent Five members of the UN Security Council insisted that the Phnom Penh government must go through it. The same for a democratic election: there has never been one in Cambodia (or the rest of Indochina), and even in modern Southeast Asia democracy is a rarity, where it even exists. Yet Cambodia was forced to have elections, despite the presence of an army that committed genocide in close living memory. Those responsible for that genocide were allowed to move into politics too. Sometimes I wondered why the world was doing this to Cambodians, people who had already suffered unbearably.

There were other demands being made on the Hun Sen government. The KR, for example, successfully demanded that the word *genocide* be omitted from the UN Peace Plan. Sihanouk, on the other hand, had long demanded a complete liberalization of the economy, which Hun Sen delivered. A quick liberalization saw Cambodia moving toward a pseudo-capitalist regime, where the gap between rich and poor widens. In the absence of any bilateral aid from the West or multilateral development aid through the UN, along with the insecurity of civil servants about their future careers in an ambiguous political transition, levels of corruption like those elsewhere in Southeast Asia predictably emerged. From that point I sadly watched Cambodia deteriorate into a state of instability. This benefited the Khmer Rouge enormously.

The success of the UN agreement in finding peace for the Cambodian people depended totally upon the goodwill and the willingness of the four main political factions to play by the rules. As we have seen the Khmer Rouge has never played by the rules. They refused to be disarmed and persistently violated the ceasefire, and the UN had no mandate to force them to comply. This imposed on the Cambodians an enormous risk and long range uncertainties. This behavior of the Khmer Rouge is not out of step with their past. The world's leaders had been warned by scholars and NGO workers about the possibility of this happening.

Development Aid

Development aid is a crucial factor to the success of democracy in a developing country such as Cambodia, where many people are still concerned about where their next meal is coming from. Democracy cannot take root among people with empty stomachs. Most of Cambodia's 8.5 million people live below the poverty line, with an estimated per capita GNP of less than US$110. It is a country which is perennially short of food. I have heard an opinion, expressed by KPNLF leader Son Sann among others, that economic or development aid should not be sent to Cambodia until after the election, that is, extending the international embargo to a later date. This seemed to be the policy of the international community. Until now little aid money has been spent and the people's living conditions remain poor.[5]

I think this view was wrong. First, there was no excuse for continuing to punish the people of Cambodia by denying them their entitlements to international aid as citizens of a member country of the world community. Second, the election simply could not be successfully held in an unstable political and military environment such as that fostered by the world's continuing enforcement of Cambodian poverty. Unless the country's economic and communications infrastructure is maintained and developed, and other sectors (like education, health) allowed to function with appropriate assistance as in any other Third World country, the UN presence in Cambodia will be ineffective. Third, if the country is economically impoverished and the people's lives are insecure or threatened, the election will have little meaning for the population, even if its administration goes ahead effectively as planned.

Over the years, the UN Development Program (UNDP) has accumulated US$80 million of unspent money earmarked for Cambodia. With others I have been urging UNDP not to sit on this fund any longer, but until now only a small fraction of this fund has been disbursed. There are lots and lots of things to be done. To take just one example: most of Cambodia's 9,000 miles of highways and provincial roads are in ruins. You cannot have an effective communications system, and thus a democratic election, without being able to move around quickly and freely.

It is obvious for visitors to Cambodia that the people's living standard must improve especially in the rural areas and especially among women, before a democracy can take root. Women are an important factor in this new democracy, by definition, as they are the majority, and it is important that their livelihood be beyond intimidation by political factions. My own studies over the last fourteen years have shown that women, or families headed by women, have remained persistently poor and are among the poorest in every village.[6] To improve their living standard, the UN aid should concentrate specially on women. So far, not enough work has been done for them. The SOC government, too, has not treated their womenfolk favorably enough. It is time they improved their record.

I remember reading an AFSC report about its income-generating project for women. Each family headed by a woman was given vegetable seeds, baby chickens, or ducks worth US$30. With vegetables growing in their gardens and chickens laying eggs under their houses, the women felt more secure about their family's livelihood than ever before. AFSC has a limited budget, and at the time only about two hundred families were being assisted in this way. I could not help calculating that to carry out this project for all the families headed by women throughout Cambodia would cost a mere US$10 million. That's really infinitesimal, compared with the billions of dollars the UN is planning to spend on other things.

To achieve true democracy the UN must ensure that the people are physically as well as economically secure so that they can choose their leaders without intimidation. This is a big job, but this is the only way to achieve the UN mandate, which is to find democracy for Cambodia. We must all bear in mind the appalling record of the UN towards the Cambodian people since 1979. The result is that an accomplice in mass murder like Thiounn Prasith for example, is still even today taking his turn to run Cambodia's UN Mission—as he has done for the last fifteen years.

Multi-party Democracy

In January 1993, at the Cambodiana, the country's only five-star hotel, the U.S. International Republican Institute and the National Democratic Institute carried out a workshop to train Cambodians about how democracy is built around the world. Democracy is a beautiful word for every Cambodian, but they did not know that one can be taught how to build it. The room was packed with over two hundred participants. Most of them had never imagined such a luxurious wall-to-wall-carpeted room overlooking the muddy Mekong River. They came from the twenty or so political parties mushrooming in Phnom Penh. At the time of the signing of the peace agreement in Paris in October 1991 there had been only four. "Ten from each political party," I was told by a participant I recognized from Long Beach, California. The atmosphere was quite tense and full of mistrust. On the platform were six foreign men with short haircuts, conservatively dressed. One of them spoke in English, which was simultaneously translated into Khmer. He spoke about how conflict can be resolved and how democracy can be established. At the end of his speech, he introduced to the audience a colleague from El Salvador, who he said would tell the workshop about the practical experience of how democracy was built in his country. I found out later that he was from Arena—the most murderous political party in El Salvador. He spoke about the problems his country had faced in the early 1980s from 'Marxist-Leninist' groups. He did not elaborate on how the problems were solved, but did imply that some sort of democratic means were used, and that his country is now free of the problem. The saddest thing is that most of the participants did not know where El Salvador was and had no idea of its recent history. They took notes seriously and innocently.

The workshop organizers urged the participants to make use of their expert resources, which include an office in Phnom Penh staffed by eight people. Having listened to the El Salvadoran, I thought back to the dozen or so political parties whose offices I had visited in the previous two days. The top leadership of these parties were exclusively from overseas, mostly the U.S., a few from Europe. Most of them had returned to Cambodia recently, for the first time since the 1960s or 1970s. They recruited local people who became party members, guards and hangers-on. The leadership ranges from gas station or Dunkin Donut owners to MBA holders to lawyers, all with their self-proclaimed expertise to solve ailing Cambodia's problems. In the course of my interviews, many of them resorted to French or English to express their views. One of them went through the whole interview in English despite my frequent interjections in Khmer. Two party presidents vowed to stand for the presidency against Prince Sihanouk. Funnily enough, one of them showed me his flag of Cambodia, which consisted of five stars, a map of Cambodia and a small Angkor temple in the middle, all on a light blue base. The five stars, he assured me, represented the five superpowers who oversee Cambodia. This, he said, would ensure peace and prosperity for Cambodia. As I left his office he bade good-bye to me, in Thai ! He was poised to abolish corruption. On my way out, his party's notice-board displayed a picture of him with Mrs. Imelda Marcos.

Judging by the notice-board of another party, one could easily conclude that an American presidential election campaign was in progress. There was a photo of Richard Nixon standing between the party's president and his wife. Plus many more photos of George Bush and Dan Quayle posing or shaking hands with the president. Obviously he had lent a hand to the Republican cause in the recent U.S. election. (In fact it was for California congressman Dana Rohrabacher.) That the Republicans lost the Presidential election did not deter him from using the publicity. The point is that average Cambodians do not necessarily know about this.

Another party has a banner proclaiming "Communism Is Evil" in front of its headquarters, next to the New Market in the middle of Phnom Penh. When a journalist suggested to this party's leader that he must have been to other provinces to open offices, he was startled and denied any such action, and insisted that he was not going to do any of that himself, as, he claimed, Americans promised to do it all for him.[7]

An official of another party mistook an American woman I know for his financier. He insisted that she hand over money that he said the CIA had promised him. I was surprised to find out that American church money had also found its way to a political party in Phnom Penh.

I asked each party leadership to name their party's three priorities in the event that they win office. National reconstruction was obviously their first priority and was invariably followed by national reconciliation. This, of course, raised the question of the Khmer Rouge. How reconciliation is to be attempted with the Khmer Rouge varies from party to party, ranging from 'forgetting the past,' to 'forgiveness,' to 'non-violence and peaceful negotiation,' to 'winning over the Khmer Rouge supporters through land reform, social justice or economic alleviation.' What struck me was their optimism in achieving this goal. Having watched the Khmer Rouge ignore one UN deadline after another and refuse to comply with the UN peace plan, determined to win power by force, I feel sorry for the Cambodian people, as we know well that party leaders can leave Cambodia for the U.S. or France again, whenever the Khmer Rouge approach Phnom Penh. The Cambodian people who have nowhere to go, however, are the ones who will be left to endure the Khmer Rouge.[8]

The English version of the book *Punishing the Poor* recently lost the support of its publisher and distributor. From its first edition in 1988, Oxfam had published and distributed it in the United Kingdom. But in 1991, the official United Kingdom Charity Commission criticized Oxfam for having 'persecuted with too much vigour' its public education campaign on the nature of the Pol Pot regime and the threat of its return. I can assure you that few Cambodian people share this view. But, because of pressure from the U.K. Charity Commission, Oxfam ceased its distribution of this book, which has now become unavailable.[9] The U.K. is a member of the UN's Permanent Five. With friends like this in high places, one could hardly feel optimistic about the prospects for the poor under the UN Peace Plan. Can states that enforce the withdrawal from circulation of 'politically unacceptable' books demand the right even to teach democracy to Cambodia, let alone to impose on it the return of the Khmer Rouge?

----

[1] Eva Mysliwiec, *Punishing the Poor: The International Isolation of Kampuchea*, Oxford: Oxfam, 1988: 73. This remains true today: only a small amount of aid has arrived in Cambodia. See 'Most Cambodians See Nothing of Aid,' *New York Times*, 21 February 1993.

[2] My view of the UN Plan at its signing is in *Vietnam Generation*, 4, 1-2, Spring 1992: 48-51.

[3] For early descriptions of post-Pol Pot Cambodia, see Ben Kiernan, 'Kampuchea 1979-1981: National Rehabilitation in the Eye of an International Storm,' in Huynh Kim Khanh, ed., *Southeast Asian Affairs 1982*, Singapore: Heinemann, 1982: 167-195; and Chanthou Boua, 'Observations of the Heng Samrin Government, 1980-1982,' in David P. Chandler and Ben Kiernan, eds., *Revolution and Its Aftermath in Kampuchea*, New Haven: Yale Southeast Asia Council Monograph No. 25, 1983: 259-290.

[4] See for instance G. Henderson, 'Aid to Kampuchea Must be Questioned,' Melbourne *Age*, 2 April 1983.

[5] By February 1993 only $95 million of the $880 million pledged for Cambodia at the June 1992 Tokyo conference had been disbursed (i.e. collected). Most of this was spent on repatriation of the 350,000 refugees and on the newly-established zones of the factions opposing the Phnom Penh government. See the report of Secretary General Boutros Boutros-Ghali to the UN Security Council, 15 February 1993, excerpted in *Cambodia Peace Watch*, Folio 2, Vol. 2, No. 1, February 1993.

[6] See for instance Chanthou Boua, 'Women in Cambodia Today,' *New Left Review*, January-February 1982: 45-61.

[7] See also Philip Shenon, 'For the Cambodian Vote, a Fourth of July Flavor,' *New York Times*, 17 February 1993.

[8] For more details, see Chanthou Boua, 'In the Killing Fields, A Crying Game,' U.S. *National Catholic Reporter*, 14 May 1993: 14, and Amitav Ghosh, 'Holiday in Cambodia,' *New Republic*, 28 June 1993: 21-25.

[9] Nick Cohen, 'Oxfam activities censured as too political,' *Independent*, 10 May 1991, and John Pilger, 'In Defence of Oxfam,' *New Statesman and Society*, 17 May 1991: 8. Following the Charity Commission Inquirer's 'unacceptable' finding on 'the tone and content of some parts and particularly the prescriptive sections' of *Punishing the Poor*, Oxfam 'decided that we should not reprint it or further distribute it ourselves.' *Oxfam Team Briefing*, no. 13, November 14, 1991.

Appendix 1

The United Nations Plan for Cambodia*

Hédi Annabi

Much of this conference has discussed the tragic past of Cambodia and the intense suffering imposed on its people by the genocidal policies and practices of the Khmer Rouge regime. Now we turn to the present and to the future, to the United Nations Plan, and the prospects for democracy in Cambodia. What I would like to do, is address two questions. One is the United Nations Plan as it is commonly called. The other is the work undertaken by the United Nations to implement the plan.

The so-called UN Plan is contained in the Agreements on the Comprehensive Political Settlement of the Cambodia Conflict, that were signed in Paris on October 23, 1991. These agreements foresee a major role for the United Nations in their implementation. They are based on a framework document developed by the five permanent members of the Security Council in the course of high-level negotiations that took place between January and August, 1990. Let us look briefly at the content of the Paris Agreements. I would like first to recall the main institutional provisions of the agreements and then to discuss the mandate foreseen for the United Nations in these agreements.

The Paris Agreements foresaw a transitional period beginning with the signature of the agreements and running until the holding of free and fair elections in Cambodia, in order to designate a constituent assembly, which would draft and adopt a constitution and then transform itself into a legislative assembly to produce the new government. The agreements provided for the establishment of a national reconciliation body called the Supreme National Council (SNC) that would bring together the four Cambodian parties under the chairmanship of Prince Norodom Sihanouk. The basic assumption

*Remarks to the Schell Center conference, *Genocide and Democracy in Cambodia*, Yale University Law School, 22 February 1992.

made by the five permanent members of the Security Council was that in order to reach an enduring peace in Cambodia, it was necessary to bring all the Cambodian factions under one tent, so to speak. So the agreements assumed that the SNC would be the unique, legitimate body and source of authority during the transitional period, that it would embody the sovereignty of Cambodia, and that it would represent the country externally during the transitional period, including at the United Nations. The SNC is frequently misrepresented as a kind of government. The SNC is not a government. The existing administrative structures in Cambodia will continue to exist and each of the Cambodian parties will continue to administer the area under its control during the transitional period.

The agreements also conceived the establishment of a United Nations Transitional Authority in Cambodia or UNTAC, to which, at the time of the signing of the agreements, the SNC delegated all powers necessary to ensure the implementation of those agreements. UNTAC will be placed under the authority of the Special Representative of the Secretary General, Mr. Yasushi Akashi, who was designated by the new Secretary General in early January.

What mandate did the agreements prescribe for the United Nations? The agreements foresee responsibilities for the United Nations in seven major areas, extending well beyond the concept of peacekeeping as it has traditionally been understood. For lack of a better term, we may call it peace building.

The first set of functions lies in the military field. In this area the UN is expected to supervise the cease-fire; verify the withdrawal of foreign troops and ensure that they do not return to Cambodia; monitor the cessation of external arms supplies; and put in place a mine awareness program, training in mine clearance and actual assistance in mine clearance. It is also expected to regroup, canton, and disarm all forces of all factions, demobilize at least seventy percent of them, and—hopefully, with their agreement—to go beyond that and achieve full demobilization.

The second set of responsibilities is in the field of civil administration. In this area there is much confusion about what the UN is expected to do. We read frequently in the press that the UN has been mandated to practically take over the administration of Cambodia. This is not the case: it has never been considered and is obviously not possible. What is being contemplated are three different levels of scrutiny over the activities of the existing administrative structures to make sure they do not do anything that would prejudice the holding of free and fair elections. The entire rationale for the presence of the UN is precisely to enable these elections to take place and create a neutral political environment for them. Everything will be done from that point of view. In this area of civil administration, it is foreseen that five areas, considered as sensitive in the agreements, will be placed under direct control of the UN, which will exercise that control as necessary, again in order to create a neutral political environment. These areas are foreign affairs, defense, finance, information and public security. It is also anticipated that the UN would also supervise the other administrative agencies and bodies which could prejudice the holding of free and fair elections. And, finally, the third level is what is left.

The third area of responsibility is law and order. Again, the UN will not be taking over the maintenance of law and order in the country. That remains the responsibility of the existing police in the country. What the UN is expected to do is supervise or control the activities of the existing police to insure that law and order are maintained and human rights protected. It is foreseen, therefore, that there will be a substantial UNTAC civil police component in the operation. And the UN is expected to supervise other law enforcement and judicial processes as necessary.

The fourth area of responsibility concerns the elections themselves, which the UN is expected to organize and conduct. This is an unprecedented responsibility. In other countries, you may recall, the UN merely supervised elections organized by the local administrations. In this case, we are being asked actually to organize and conduct the elections, which means taking responsibility for the whole process right from the beginning and from the writing of the electoral law.

The fifth area of responsibility is in the field of human rights. Here, in view of Cambodia's past, the agreements have entrusted a special mandate to the UN and we are expected to do three things in this area. First, to develop and implement a human rights education program in the country. Second, to exercise a general human rights oversight during the transition period. And third, to investigate allegations of human rights violations that may be brought to UNTAC's attention or that UNTAC may decide to investigate on its own initiative.

The sixth area of responsibility is repatriation. The UN will have to repatriate some 360,000 refugees who are presently in camps along the Thai border and this will be done by the United Nations High Commission on Refugees which will take the lead role in this area.

Finally, the UN is expected to put into place a rehabilitation and reconstruction program during the transition period, with the first phase of rehabilitation to coincide more or less with the transition period, and reconstruction being more of a long term goal.

What has been done since the signing of the agreements to prepare for their implementation? The agreements foresee that the cease-fire, which came into being with their signing, would be implemented in two phases. During the first phase the Secretary General is expected to extend his good offices to the Cambodian parties, in order to help them to maintain their own cease-fire. During the second phase the UN would assume the responsibility of supervising the cease-fire, but this phase obviously can only begin when UNTAC is fully deployed. In anticipation of the signing of the Paris Agreements, in September 1991 the Secretary General had proposed to the Security Council the establishment of a United Nations Advance Mission in Cambodia, or UNAMIC. The creation of UNAMIC was approved by the Council in mid-October and became operational on the ninth of November. Initially, UNAMIC had three main functions. First, as I mentioned, was to help the Cambodian parties maintain their own cease-fire until the larger operation is in place. This is being done by the stationing of small teams of military liaison officers in the military headquarters of each of the Cambodian factions to help them communicate, to avoid incidents and where incidents occur, to try to bring them together to analyze what happened and learn how we can avoid further incidents.

The second responsibility of UNAMIC is to establish a mine awareness program; and the third is to ensure a liaison function with the SNC to prepare for the deployment of UNTAC and handle other matters related to the role of the UN in the implementation of the agreements. The mandate of UNAMIC was expanded in early January 1992, again on the basis of a proposal made by the Secretary General, presented to the Security Council in December. The mandate of UNAMIC was expanded to include training of Cambodians in mine clearance, and the actual initiation of a de-mining program. The hope was that as much work as possible should be done before the onset of the rainy season when things would be more difficult. This expansion of UNAMIC added about a thousand people to the 380 already deployed to perform the initial functions. Once UNTAC is established, it will absorb UNAMIC.

What are the preparations for UNTAC and how far have they proceeded? The Paris Agreements were endorsed by the Security Council on October 31, 1991, when it adopted a resolution calling on the Secretary General to prepare a detailed plan for the implementation of the mandate foreseen in the agreements for the UN. To that end, the Secretary General sent a number of survey missions to Cambodia between October and December to collect the information that was still missing or that the parties were not really prepared to give until the agreements had been signed, at which point it became an obligation. On the basis of the information gathered by these missions, a comprehensive plan of implementation of the agreements was formulated and submitted to the Security Council on 19 February 1992.

A quick word about the main features of the implementation plan presented to the Council. As noted, UNTAC will have seven components: human rights, elections, the military, civil administration, police, repatriation, and rehabilitation. The election component's staff will arrive in three waves over the next few months. The first wave of two hundred people will be based in Phnom Penh and at the provincial level in every province. The second wave of four hundred people would be deployed in every district in Cambodia. And a third wave of over a thousand people would come only for a short period of two weeks during the actual polling.

The police component will comprise 3,600 UN police monitors who would cover every police station in Cambodia and would be as mobile as possible to be able to supervise and control the activities of the existing police and make sure that nothing is done to jeopardize the holding of free and fair elections.

The largest component would be the military component which will reach a maximum strength of 15,800 people, including twelve infantry battalions and over five hundred military observers, as well as signals, engineer, logistics, and other support units. It will reach this peak for about four months during the regrouping, cantonment, disarming and demobilization phase. The numbers will be reduced after demobilization and then again after the elections.

In conclusion, UNTAC will undoubtedly be one of the most difficult, complex and challenging operations ever undertaken by the United Nations. Will this operation work? There are, of course, doubts. But we believe that it can work if two basic conditions are met. It is always useful to remember them, as they are not always well understood and it is important to know that this is the way the UN works. The first condition is that the UN must be provided, in a timely and assured manner, with the substantial monetary resources necessary to carry out this operation. On the basis of preliminary estimates, it is expected that UNTAC will cost about 1.7 billion dollars. Obviously, unless these resources are forthcoming, there is no way that this operation can be carried out, or even set up in an effective manner.

The second, even more important condition is that the operation can only succeed if all the parties abide by the commitments that they freely entered into when they signed the agreements. This applies, first and foremost, to the Cambodian parties but it also applies to those who have assumed a special role in the negotiating process. The Cambodian parties must feel, throughout the process, that the permanent members of the Security Council and the international community as a whole, are fully committed to the implementation of the Paris Agreements and stand fully behind the UN. Only under these conditions will there be a fair chance of restoring peace in Cambodia and of building democracy and a better future for the Cambodian people.

22 February 1992

Appendix 2

The Cambodian Factions in the Democratic Process

Khieu Kanharith

Asked about democracy in the 1950s, Cambodians from that generation would call to mind the assassination of the leading figure of the opposition groups and the chairman of the most influential party of that time, Mr. Ieu Koeus, in 1950; the shooting to death of Mr. Nop Bophann, director of the leftist newspaper, the *Pracheachon* ('People'), in 1959; and also the more or less perfidious maneuvers to monopolize power and to sideline the faction considered by the regime as the most threatening. For the generation of the 1960s, it was the moral and physical violence against those journalists and politicians who were opposing the regime, the vote-buying and the internal splits encouraged by different political options. And all these deviations from the democratic process led to the most horrible tragedy in contemporary Cambodian history: two decades of fratricidal war grafted onto a genocide of unprecedented scale since the end of World War Two.

The year 1987 saw the first breakthrough in the Cambodian conflict with the appeal made by the Phnom Penh government for a national reconciliation "except the principal leaders responsible for the genocide." This opening would bring about a series of diplomatic shuttles: the Sihanouk-Hun Sen meeting, the four warring factions meeting with various concerned countries, the sessions of the permanent members of the UN Security Council and the international conferences to try to settle the Cambodian conflict in Paris and Jakarta.

Finally, on 23 October 1991, in Paris, the four Cambodian factions and eighteen foreign ministers signed four documents:

♦ An accord for a global political settlement of the Cambodian conflict;

♦ An accord concerning the sovereignty, independence, integrity and inviolability of the territory, the neutrality and national unity of Cambodia;

♦ A declaration on the rebuilding and reconstruction of Cambodia; and

♦ A final act on the Paris Conference on Cambodia.

These Paris agreements are being implemented by two main mechanisms:

1. The Supreme National Council (SNC) composed of six representatives of the government of the State of Cambodia (SOC) and six others representing the three opposition factions: the Khmers Rouges (KR) of Mr. Pol Pot, the monarchist FUNCINPEC of Prince Sihanouk, and the republican KPNLF of Mr. Son Sann;

2. During the transitional period, the UN will be in charge of monitoring the cease-fire and the dismantling of 70% of the various military forces, the creation of a neutral environment for a fair and free election by taking under its control certain administrative bodies that might influence the electoral process.

The UN was to be deployed in two stages:

2.1 After the signing of the peace agreement, a UN Advanced Mission in Cambodia (UNAMIC) of 268 persons was to be dispatched to Cambodia to facilitate the commitment to the cease-fire of the four factions and to collect data concerning the strength and the equipment of different troops, to launch the de-mining and mines awareness programs and to provide all the necessary information to the deployment of the UN Transitional Authority in Cambodia (UNTAC).

2.2 Once having defined and funded the necessary and sufficient human and financial needs, UNTAC will begin its activities to assure a full implementation of these peace agreements.

Can all these projects be implemented? If so, can they assure a stable and lasting peace in Cambodia? Can the long-martyred Cambodian people finally enjoy true democracy or not?

I think the answer to these questions depends, for the time being, on the attitude of the four existing Cambodian factions now composing the SNC. This does not mean that the other factions are to be neglected or that they have no role or influence in the society. But the fact is that these four factions possess all the means - political, financial, organizational and military - that could decisively influence the peace process in Cambodia. Moreover, we must also mention the role of Prince Sihanouk that might contribute to the success or the failure of the Cambodian peace plan.

Now, let's try to analyze one by one these various actors of the Cambodian political show.

Prince Sihanouk: Dancing on the Tightrope

At the beginning the Prince had the strategy to rely on the KR's might to weaken the Phnom Penh government in order to impose his conditions and become the sole architect of a Cambodian peace. But after his return to Phnom Penh and his understanding of the reality on the ground, the continuation of this strategy appeared to be doing him more harm than good. Feeling he was solicited by all the rival factions, his decision to stay neutral and be above all the political confrontations will reinforce him in the new role as a main guarantor of peace. Enjoying support from many foreign governments and benefiting from the respect accorded to his age, a very important thing in Cambodia, the Prince, if he can maintain his neutrality, could play a crucial stabilizing role in this first stage of the peace.

But the Prince has to overcome three main obstacles to succeed in dancing on this very tight rope: his myth, the republicans, and his entourage.

In fact, if we take a look at the reality of things, what gives the Prince his strength is his myth. He is supposed to be a symbol of independence and unity of the Nation, the benefactor King and the Messiah bringing peace, stability and even prosperity to the country. But in confrontation with reality, myths fade away. And adding to this is that today everybody has placed so much hope in him without noticing that he is also trapped in global geopolitical torments.

Furthermore, the age that gives him a certain respectability on the political scene becomes his handicap in the preparation of his successor. Combining together these two factors, at the point when the Prince feels his power fading away or when he cannot realize the hopes placed in him, he might be tempted to concentrate power in his hands or in his group's and that, in the long run, would once again tip the country back into chaos.

The Republicans will also give him a hard time. Whether Sihanouk becomes a king or President of a Republic, the republicans will always put obstacles in his way. Although right now, every faction is trying to please him, the conflicts arising from time to time with the republicans of the old generation are a good illustration of this hidden animosity.

Most of all, the entourage who were the cause of his fall in 1970, are the main danger to the Prince today as well. This phenomenon is not typical only in Cambodia nor does it have implications for Sihanouk alone, but due to his current role and the need of his moral authority in this every fragile situation, the Prince has the very best interest in avoiding as much as possible his name being used for narrow or Byzantine interests of a clan or group in such a way that, like a boomerang, it could affect his whole credibility.

Currently, it seems that the Prince is adopting a "wait and see" policy and so is tiptoeing in the political maze. At the same time he is showing a certain preference for cooperation between FUNCINPEC and the CPP (the ruling Cambodian People's Party), because the Prince knows well that the CPP is an unavoidable factor in the process and, what is more, he has more trust in Hun Sen's government than in any other faction.

FUNCINPEC: What Degree of Cooperation?

Since Prince Sihanouk decided to quit this faction and become neutral, FUNCINPEC has run into a leadership crisis. Formed mostly by Cambodian expatriates, this faction lacks popular local figures and has no strong popular base inside the country. Adding to this, the internecine conflict has considerably reduced FUNCINPEC's capacity for action to gain strong support for its cause.

It's clear for FUNCINPEC that the threat to it does not come from the Phnom Penh group but rather from the KPNLF and the KR. But the difference lies in the evaluation of this threat and the degree of cooperation with the CPP during the transitional period and the coming electoral campaign.

For the FUNCINPEC group that supports the idea of a coalition with Phnom Penh, they think that it will bring more advantage that harm. The reason is that because of the proportional voting system in the UN-sponsored agreement, there will be a possibility that no faction may get a majority in the new Assembly to enable it to form a government alone. And the cooperation of these two factions (CPP and FUNCINPEC) will boost the group's chances to get a majority to form a relatively stable government and not depend too much on a hung Parliament subject to changing moods. Secondly, because of the many uncertainties that could hinder an effective implementation of the peace agreement, Phnom Penh will be the best life insurance should something go wrong in the future.

For the non-cooperating FUNCINPEC group, their first concern is the risk of FUNCINPEC being swallowed by the CPP and then losing its identity. Secondly, there is a risk of its losing the support of its rank-and-file members by making an alliance with the government the latter considered as a Vietnamese creation and also corrupt. But it is probable that this last point is only a justification of a position rather than a political and philosophical concept. For the deep reason behind this group's attitude is rather a conflict of personalities existing within this faction itself. Nonetheless, this conflict in the long-run could be settled by mutual consensus and sacrifice for the long-term interest of all sides.

The KPNLF: The Republican Alternative

At the beginning, the Khmer People's National Liberation Front enjoyed a lot of support from many Cambodian expatriates and also some people inside Cambodia, because it represented an alternative between the monarchy, viewed as obsolete, and the despotic KR-style communism. This illusion is fading and will continue to fade very quickly, because of the intra-factional power struggle plaguing the KPNLF and the widespread corruption in its camps and its army. Despite this situation, this faction could maintain its existence due to the support of the USA and Thailand, who wish to counterbalance the power of the KR and to keep a margin of maneuver against the regional strategy of China and Vietnam.

With the split within the KPNLF between Mr. Son Sann and General Sak Sutsakhan, it is premature to accurately assess the balance of forces between these two groups. But General Sak's strategy now is to establish and consolidate his popular base by renewing contact with former republican officers and soldiers and also those intellectuals who are displeased with the Phnom Penh government. These groups, in the near future, could become efficient propagandists among the local masses in the elections.

For Mr. Son Sann, his strategy aims at both short-term and long-term targets. In the short-term, knowing he has little chance of winning the election—the emergence of new political groups supporting democratic institutions will seriously undermine his republican alternative—he will try to present himself as the leader of the republican and democratic groups in order to form a strong opposition that any government will have to deal with in the future National Assembly. This position would secure him a chance, if the President and Vice-President of a republic are to be elected by the National Assembly, to gain the post of Vice-President under Sihanouk and to give him more room to maneuver against both the President and the Government. His long-term strategy aims to reduce the influence of Hun Sen, who might be appointed as Prime Minister if the cooperation between CPP and FUNCINPEC proves successful, as wished by Prince Sihanouk.

The Khmer Rouge: The Two-Track Policy

Pol Pot has been well prepared for many years for the event that the Cambodian conflict should be resolved—for good or bad—through a political solution which would inevitably end up in some form of an electoral contest. But at the same time he insists that the situation is temporary and sooner or later the civil war will break out again. From this analysis, the KR have changed their purely military strategy to a strategy which has electoral as well as military goals.

For their electoral strategy, the KR have adopted three priorities: consolidate the area under their control, exploit the dissension among the different factions and their weak points, and lead a campaign of education, both political and economic, among their cadres.

For their military strategy, they aim at two essential goals; keep secretly hidden part of their elite troops, with two distinct tasks. In the case of a general election supervised by the UN, these forces along with their political propagandists will exert pressure in the areas controlled by the other factions in order to influence the vote in their favor, and at the same time eliminate their most dangerous rivals and also their own cadres who do not totally follow their policies. The second task is a sort of emergency exit. In case things get out of control, these hidden forces will go into battle immediately, first of all to destroy the elite forces of the other factions.

But the KR also have three uncertainties concerning the degree of efficiency of their strategy. The first is that, although the other factions will see a dispersion of their vote as an unfailing result of the emergence of new political parties, their political monolith which is a crucial advantage to the KR, could be seriously threatened by the free communication of ideas and by opening to the outside world. Their second uncertainty is, if the international community determines to give the aid necessary for the reconstruction of Cambodia, the living conditions of the people would be noticeably improved, which could attract many KR soldiers to a return to a normal life, thus weakening the fighting capacity of this faction. The third uncertainty is the degree of efficiency of the UN's control and also the length of the presence of UN forces on the ground.

The Cambodian People's Party: In Search of Coalitions

For more than ten years, the CPP is the only faction which has fought against the return of the Khmer Rouge. It is also the faction which controls the most territory and population in Cambodia, and at the same time it is the most structured of the factions. Although it previously had a structure and ideology which closely resembled those of most communist parties, the CPP is seeking a future that is appropriate to Cambodian society. Further, it was the first ruling Marxist party to recognize individual private property in agricultural and urban land. The recent changes in the CPP's political platform, dropping references to communist ideology demonstrate this continuing effort towards a broader accommodation to the social and political reality of the country.

But this faction is facing many problems, especially the erosion of authority after a decade in power, but secondly, the image of a government installed by Vietnam, and thirdly, the economic difficulties caused by the Western trade embargo and the ending of aid from the former communist countries of Eastern Europe and the USSR.

In this context, the CPP is trying to establish an alliance with other groups politically closer to its ideas, to face its most dangerous adversary.   The success of this or these coalitions will considerably influence the political process of the country.   There are two reasons for this:

1. The first is that without a genuine coalition the government could find itself in an unstable situation. And without stability one cannot ensure a sound environment for guaranteeing a democratic election in the country.

2. The second reason is that no matter which other faction wins the election, the CPP is an unavoidable element, if one wants relatively stable government to tackle effectively the task of reconstruction and creation of lasting peace.

In short, despite some reluctance on all sides, and some accidental eventualities such as we have seen in the past two months, the four factions which compose the SNC know well that an election is inevitable and they are preparing, each in their own way, to face a political confrontation.

Certainly, there will be new factions appearing, but they will encounter three serious handicaps. They will lack an organizational structure, funds, and candidates who know the country well. It is too soon yet to assess the potential of such groups, because in the course of the electoral process, alliances between parties will inevitably come into play. This multi-party image does not necessarily signify democracy, but at least it constitutes the first step towards the democratization of Cambodian society. Democracy is a process and is not achieved in one or two elections. Other factors will also influence this process: the place of the army on the future political scene, the effectiveness of various pillars of democracy such as the press, the degree of respect for human rights, the degree of popular participation in political life, the equitable distribution of national wealth, and especially the determination of the international community to encourage a real and genuine democracy appropriate for Cambodia.

Problems Ahead, and Some Proposed Solutions

Four months after the Paris Agreement, some positive steps have been undertaken toward its effective implementation. They are:

♦ The deployment of the UN Advance Mission In Cambodia (UNAMIC)
♦ The return of Prince Sihanouk to Phnom Penh and his restoration as Head of State;
♦ The meetings of the SNC held on Cambodian territory;
♦ The accreditation of various embassies and missions to the SNC; and
♦ The preparation of the refugee repatriation program along with the mine-clearing process.

But all of these are just small steps on the long and rocky road to a lasting peace. The problems that still remain are the questions of shifting from a battlefield to political confrontation, and of how to make national rehabilitation succeed and prevent Cambodia from collapsing into chaos again.

The remainder of my paper will be divided into three parts. The first will deal with the problem of peace in Cambodia, the second with the social rehabilitation, and in the third, I would like to propose some solutions to successfully implement the UN peace plan.

1. From Battlefield to Political Confrontation

The basis of the success of the UN peace plan is merely the concept that everybody will sincerely commit themselves to the process and that UNTAC will effectively control the strict application of the agreement by all the rival factions.

Nonetheless, despite lots of promises from the KR faction, many Cambodians living inside the country, and also foreigners who closely follow the Cambodian situation, remain skeptical. Pol Pot is still masterminding the political, economic and military strategy of the KR and adopting the same practices as in the past. The fact that the UNAMIC mission which was recently dispatched to inspect the KR-controlled area was not allowed to perform freely its tasks nor to have direct contact with the people there does not help to increase confidence in their promises of change. And the recent attacks on government positions to expand the KR-controlled area in order to influence the vote in the coming election show that the KR are still playing by their own rules and raise the question of their sincerity in the implementation of the peace plan.

On the other hand, if it is easy to control and to disarm the government forces, it is proven that things will not so easy with the guerrilla troops. Even if all the KR soldiers accept to be disarmed and return to live as ordinary people in the villages, their numerous arms caches and their organization would give them the possibility to immediately become an effective combat force, once their leaders decide to take up arms again.

And this brings into question the effectiveness of the UNTAC, and its room to maneuver to impose strict application of the Accord. This effectiveness and this readiness must apply throughout the whole process: during the transitional period, in the electoral process, and after. And this is unlikely to happen. We must remember that UNTAC would withdraw its forces if its good offices can no longer maintain the rival factions in a peaceful settlement. And the possible result is the destruction of the democratic forces that UNTAC is supposed to encourage.

Another problem of the peaceful transition is the lack of democratic traditions in Cambodia. After all these years of fighting and distrust and the absence of a civic political culture, the electoral process might turn out to be a factor of social division and a vote-buying opportunity that will pervert totally the idea of democracy. Along with these possibilities, the unscrupulous politicians or political groups could also exploit the situation to jeopardize the whole process if these politicians or political groups feel they might be under threat of political extinction.

To create a neutral environment means also the need to ensure political and social stability. Without it, a fair and free election would be impossible. Up to now, the government of the SOC, despite some shortcomings, is the only one which has the capacity and potential to block any attempt made by the KR to seize power by force, and it is also the only one effectively controlling the majority of the people and territory, and carrying out the task of economic recovery of the nation. The thirteen years of the Western economic embargo imposed a lot of constraints on it and this is also one of many factors leading to the re-emergence of corruption in Cambodian society. The question of whether the SOC might win or lose the election is a matter for the people's decision, but if this government collapses before the election, it would be a challenge to the hope of a lasting peace in Cambodia.

2. From Fighting to Social Rehabilitation

Three other areas are the remaining pillars supporting the political and social stability of Cambodia: (1) the reintegration of the nearly four hundred thousand displaced people, living in camps both inside the State of Cambodia and in Thailand, (2) the future of more than two hundred thousand demobilized soldiers, and (3) the potential of the country to absorb foreign aid.

The repatriation and resettlement of displaced people are the preconditions of the UN-supervised general election. The speed of resettlement will determine the length of the transitional period. The longer the latter lasts, the higher is the risk of any violation of the Accord. There were a lot of promises on this point before the signing of the Paris Agreement. But later on, once the paper was signed, many governments showed more reluctance to provide the nearly US$109 million package of aid needed to implement this long and detailed program. When the resettlement program is implemented two problems must be resolved: how to avoid the conflict between the residents and the newcomers, and how to soften the culture shock of the youth who have grown up outside their society for nearly a decade.

The demobilization of troops must be undertaken alongside the program of social rehabilitation. Without any plan for their re-insertion into normal life, these people might turn out to be a threat to society. A striking example is what happened after independence from France in 1953. Banditry spread, and some soldiers became a tool in the hands of the warlords and some commanders made attempts to transform the army into a powerful political group, challenging even the authority of the central government. Recent developments have shown to the army the role it could play in the Cambodian political scene, if it succeeds in institutionalizing itself as a guarantor of social order.

The capacity of absorption of the country will be crucial to enhance a steady growth in national wealth. Up to now, Cambodia can absorb only two to three hundred million US dollars per year. This figure is too low and this pace too slow to rebuild the country rapidly and to carry out successfully an equitable distribution of national wealth that will be vital to pave the way to economic development. The priority in this area is the problem in all fields of training the trainers and constituting a future intellectual nursery of the nation.

3. On Some Proposed Solutions

Once having spotlighted the most urgent problems of Cambodia today, what are the most suitable solutions to be adopted?

The solutions must aim at two targets: the prevention of the return of the past tragedy, and a harmonious economic development taking into account the inherent value of human beings.

First of all, the Cambodian people should enjoy the benefits of international solidarity which will help them to have a decent life within the international community. In particular, development aid must be granted without delay, to stabilize the current situation and the living conditions of the people. There are many positive reasons for this. With stability, there is a fair chance for every faction and good insurance for a democratic confrontation. Economic development can give the people more freedom from any manipulation, pressure or vote-buying and also will encourage the rank-and-file fighters to put down their guns and to return to normal life. This special level of aid must be continued for a period of time after the election, to guarantee the success of national rehabilitation.

Secondly, despite the policy of "forgive and forget," a tribunal to punish the act of genocide and prosecute the people responsible for it must be held, to remind the young generation that it can not be used by any leader, nor can anyone take up any ideological reason to massacre any others. It would be immoral to pretend to condemn the genocide without bringing the people guilty of this crime to justice. This does not mean that the whole KR must be condemned and become outlaws. These ordinary KR people must have their role in the future Cambodian society. But to allow the people responsible for planning and ordering the genocide to come back again and enjoy the same rights as their victims is really an obscenity. Human tragedy is the same everywhere and at every time so is justice. National reconciliation is needed, but justice is imperative too.

New Haven, 22 February 1992.

Appendix 3

Cambodia's Legal Tradition and the Democratic Process*

Douc Rasy

A Brief Overview of the Legal Tradition

In talking about law in traditional Cambodia, we are bound to stress the distinction between form and substance—or to put it in more technical terms, between *instrumentum* and *negotium*. Although both can be changed by the sovereign (whether king or not) at his discretion, *negotium* generally prevails over *instrumentum*. This is so true that basic laws, such as devolution of the crown, are left to the uncertainty of events: should the eldest son inherit the throne from the king, his father, or should it be somebody else? This question of substance is not yet settled. However, we do know how the coronation ceremony has to proceed. The king, on the podium, is surrounded by eight Brahmins, one at each of the main points of the compass. The king faces each of them in turn, and each of them repeats: "My Lord, this country, land, water, trees, men, women, animals, belong to you. Command and you shall be obeyed." In that doctrine, the law is determined by, indeed equated with the will of the sovereign. As this particular sovereign has no wish to institutionalize the regime, the rule of law in Cambodia remains in a state of permanent uncertainty.

In civil life, Cambodians know a certain form of custom that was codified by the French Protectorate. For instance, a husband has the right to keep three wives: a first one named "great wife," a second one named "middle wife," and a third, "small wife." On the face of it, primacy is given to the first: to marry the other two, a man has to obtain the agreement of the great wife. However, if she maintains her veto, the man is allowed to divorce her.

---

* Remarks at the Schell Center conference on 'Genocide and Democracy in Cambodia,' 22 February 1992. Translated from the French by Phillippe Hunt.

The regime of goods (ownership) provides another telling example. Under monarchist doctrine, God has entitled the king, as his representative, to distribute land to the people but also to take it away from them for whatever purpose. This entails that there is no definite ownership, no property. People cannot be certain of keeping anything. No *res publica* is recognized, and the people have no motivation to defend the kingdom in case of invasion. The French Protectorate tried to interest people by introducing full property, and this was a success.

The French also tried to introduce decentralization, which should teach people about self-administration and later lead them to self-determination. But centralization was too strong to allow this achievement, which was felt to involve a reduction of the king's power. Also, no means were given to the mayor: he had no municipal staff and no town hall, and had to work at home, with his wife and sons as his only staff. You can easily imagine the consequences.

Now, fundamentally, this age-old situation has not changed. Pol Pot's Khmer Rouge introduced the law of the jungle. The present regime [February 1992], which denies any links with the Khmer Rouge, is still dominated by absolutism, be it monarchist or communist. It is of no small interest to note that the communist government and the monarchist government proceed in the same way: without any freedom for the people, without any recognized opposition. That is why, now, Norodom Sihanouk and Hun Sen can unite their destinies. They have accepted human rights under pressure from Western powers, but are trying to avoid their application.

Cambodia Today: Between Despair and Hope

As Cambodia looks like a ship in the middle of a hurricane, its problems have to be considered as a whole, not in a piecemeal manner. The conventional method of splitting an issue into discrete parts in order to better understand each separate part has little chance of coping with such a reality, as some of the main factors will from time to time alter or distort the side issues.

For the time being, the main factor dominating the whole situation is the enslavement of Cambodia to what remains a despotic power. The UN plan tries to introduce democracy into the country, but the parties to the war are skillful enough to *seem* to accept its provisions without in fact implementing their substance. The UN project itself has been distorted by the belligerents in their effort to maintain their exclusive influence over the people. As a consequence of that distortion, the prospects for democracy in Cambodia are dim. The only hope comes from the facts.

The Australian peace proposal, the document that served as a basis for the elaboration of the Paris agreements, had intended to implement democracy without favoring any individual or party. It required that the belligerents should disarm completely before the elections. This would ensure the right conditions for people freely to choose their representatives. The factions realized how dangerous this might be, since without their arms they will have no prospects ("the kings are naked," as the saying goes); the people of Cambodia remember only too well what these people were like when they were in power. At that point, the negotiations nearly got bogged down. A French diplomat suggested that one should allow them to keep thirty percent of their weapons, thinking probably that with this level of armament they could not fight for long. But as they could not put themselves in the Cambodians' place, foreign negotiators were unable to imagine that the remaining forces would be turned against the Cambodian people. Now public feelings about the UN plan tend to vary widely, yet for the sake of democracy public guarantees are essential to ensure that people will dare to unite their efforts and build a civil society free from oppression.

Moreover, according to the Paris agreements, to stand for election, party affiliation will be required (Annex 3, section 6); to form a party, it is necessary to gather five thousand registered voters (Annex 3, section 5); to know who is a registered voter, it is necessary to wait until the voter registration period opens. At this stage, no party outside the belligerents can be formed. The Phnom Penh authorities feel entitled to repress any group suspected of being hostile to them. So far, the UN plan has not acted as a factor for political liberation: it has only maintained the privileges of the belligerents.

What is the actual status of public liberties going to be during or after the registration period? As the belligerents will be keeping thirty percent of their forces, they can easily use intimidation and threats to prevent people from adhering to parties unfriendly to them. The UN cannot prevent this intimidation, as UNTAC has to withdraw after the elections and leave the field open for the victors. Suppose that, despite these difficulties, a party independent from any belligerent faction can gather five thousand adherents and manages to present a list of candidates. If even one of its members leaves or dies, it will only have 4,999 adherents left, and it will lose its legal qualification and, therefore, its ability to stand for election. As the belligerents will be keeping their weapons, they can easily cause such defections.

Prospects for Democracy under the Paris Agreements

As I have stated, the people of Cambodia have little hope of being free from the belligerent factions. Recent developments confirm this feeling.

When N. Sihanouk reached Phnom Penh on November 14, 1991, Prime Minister Hun Sen said first that he was welcoming him as chairman of the Supreme National Council (SNC). However, on the twentieth, he recognized him as head of state over all Cambodia, *Chef de l'état de tout le Cambodge*. Sihanouk invited the UN to collaborate fully with the Hun Sen government which, he said, was "doing a good job."

In that situation, the SNC becomes devoid of all meaning, as UNTAC has nothing to do with a sovereign state—foreign affairs, national defense, finance, public security and information (as stipulated in the Agreements) are the responsibility of the government. This is a case of *fraud* against an international convention. The good faith which is tacitly involved in any international instrument is being flouted.

As the international community is keeping silent, Sihanouk and Hun Sen are able to ignore the SNC outright and simply to share the benefits of their position. As Hun Sen gave Sihanouk's son and daughter access to public affairs (N. Chakrapong becoming Deputy Prime Minister and Bopha Devi Vice-Minister of Culture and Information), Sihanouk for his part raised Hun Sen and Chea Sim to the peerage: they have now become Their Royal Highnesses.

These two clans have so combined their interests that no one dares to stop any violation of human rights. When, on 21-22 December 1991, the police killed demonstrators who were protesting against huge sales of goods in public ownership, Sihanouk tried secretly to denounce Hun Sen's team, but the latter warned that any weakening of the Phnom Penh authorities would also weaken the Sihanouk clan. Sihanouk therefore kept quiet.

At this point in time in Cambodia, nobody can defend human rights. Even the staffs of non-governmental agencies fear for their safety.

On 22 January 1992, Tea Bun Long, a civil servant of the Phnom Penh regime, was assassinated because he had criticized government corruption, and in particular the diversion of funds that were intended for the victims of floods. On 28 January, 1992, Ung Phan was wounded in an assassination attempt. He was a former minister in the Hun Sen government but was jailed for seventeen months for trying to form another political party. Liberated in October 1991, he said last month to a journalist: "I am afraid of being jailed again or of being assassinated by them. The communists in this government have only changed their color" (by which he meant, not their policies).

Recent news from Phnom Penh has emphasized the reinforcement of control over telephone and fax links with the outside world. This shows how strong the leaders' concern about their own power is. Administrative dysfunction, the poverty of civil servants, a general loss of confidence, corruption, anarchy—these foster a sense that one is at the end of a reign.

The Only Hope: Disarmament

Perhaps in an anarchic situation, the facts are stronger than any convention. General Loridon, commander-in-chief of UNAMIC, recently expressed a "reasonable optimism" about his mission. The Cambodian people he met praised the UN's actions (except in Pailin, under Khmer Rouge rule, where people are not allowed to meet him). "They are very cooperative, they provide important information about the location of arms caches. Given this, Cambodia could be rid of armaments within a reasonable time limit." The UN aim (according to Loridon) will be to fight banditry and to enact social measures in order to give a fair chance of living to displaced people and former fighting men. To fulfill this aim, UNTAC needs 9,000 military, 6,000 policemen, 6,000 civil servants, and one billion US dollars.

Asked about whether the factions might be able to oppose this plan, Loridon said that the UN can hire any competent men and women who wish to be paid a decent salary for their job. These will come from all sides, and the belligerent factions will thereby be deprived of their executive arms.[1] This confirms what we have noted:

the Khmer people are fed up with hopeless fighting and empty cooking pots and wish to return home to civil life. The only obstacles in the way of this desire are the armed factions and the difficulties of their reconversion. People of goodwill, I suggest, should encourage the fulfillment of these people's needs.

To this end, UNTAC when it becomes operational, can apply forcefully section 4a of Article V, Annex 2, regardless of all other provisions on merely partial disarmament. That provision allows UNTAC to "control and keep under guard all arms, ammunition and equipment of the parties throughout the transitional period." It is fair enough to act in this way, given the lack of good faith of the belligerents, as we have mentioned above. Without arms these factions will have to be friendly with people whose votes they are seeking. Then there will be a fair chance that democracy can be implemented in Cambodia.

However, though total disarmament is a necessary precondition for the implementation of democracy in that country, it is not a sufficient condition, since democracy has to be learned and defended. I think that the program my organization drew up last month will be able to cope with that aim.[2]

This is my modest contribution to an understanding of Cambodia's problems and later, I hope, to the happiness of our homeland.

New Haven, 22 February 1992.

---

[1] As I wrote this, two groups within Sihanouk's faction were fighting each other in northwestern Cambodia: Norodom Rannariddh's men tried to oppose the move by Chakrapong's troops intending to join Hun Sen's army (Reuters News Agency, 17 February 1992). Rannariddh and Chakrapong are both sons of Sihanouk. This kind of fighting could happen from time to time as long as supplies last, but it will not change the trend of history.

[2] 'Proclamation of the Khmer Revival Movement.' Available from *Le Salut Khmer, 5 place Gabriel Fauré, 94510 La Queue-en-Brie, France.*

Convention on the Prevention and Punishment of the Crime of Genocide. Adopted by the U.N. General Assembly (9 December 1948)

Article I. The Contracting Parties confirm that genocide, whether committed in time of peace or in time of war, is a crime under international law which they undertake to prevent and to punish.

Article II. In the present Convention, genocide means any of the following acts committed with intent to destroy, in whole or in part, a national, ethnical, racial or religious group, as such:

a) Killing members of the group;
b) Causing serious bodily or mental harm to members of the group;
c) Deliberately inflicting on the group conditions of life calculated to bring about its physical destruction in whole or in part;
d) Imposing measures intended to prevent births within the group;
e) Forcibly transferring children of the group to another group.

Article III. The following acts shall be punishable:

a) Genocide;
b) Conspiracy to commit genocide;
c) Direct and public incitement to commit genocide;
d) Attempt to commit genocide;
e) Complicity in genocide.

Article IV. Persons committing genocide or any of the other acts enumerated in Article III shall be punished, whether they are constitutionally responsible rulers, public officials or private individuals.

Article V. The Contracting Parties undertake to enact, in accordance with their respective Constitutions, the necessary legislation to give effect to the provisions of the present Convention and, in particular, to provide effective penalties for persons guilty of genocide or of any of the other acts enumerated in Article III.

Article VI. Persons charged with genocide or any of the other acts enumerated in Article III shall be tried by a competent tribunal of the State in the territory of which the act was committed, or by such international penal tribunal as may have jurisdiction with respect to those Contracting Parties which shall have accepted its jurisdiction.

Article VII. Genocide and the other acts enumerated in Article III shall not be considered as political crimes for the purpose of extradition. The Contracting Parties pledge themselves in such cases to grant extradition in accordance with their laws and treaties in force.

Article VIII. Any Contracting Party may call upon the competent organs of the United Nations to take such action under the Charter of the United Nations as they consider appropriate for the prevention and suppression of acts of genocide or any of the other acts enumerated in Article III.

Article IX. Disputes between the Contracting Parties relating to the interpretation, application or fulfillment of the present Convention, including those relating to the responsibility of a State for genocide or for any of the other acts enumerated in Article III, shall be submitted to the International Court of Justice at the request of any of the parties to the dispute.

Bibliography

Ablin, David A. and Marlowe Hood, eds. 1987. *The Cambodian Agony.* Armonk: M.E. Sharpe.

ADB. 1992. Asian Development Bank. *Cambodia: Socio-Economic Needs and Immediate Needs.* Produced jointly with the International Monetary Fund, United Nations Development Programme and the World Bank. May 1992.

Agence France Presse. 1990. "Official on Risk of AIDS from Transfusions." Agence France Presse (Hong Kong). *Foreign Broadcast Information Service,* No. FBIS-EAS-90-243, Dec. 18, 1990: 33-34.

Agence France Presse. 1991. "New Political Party Announces Formation." Agence France Presse (Hong Kong). *Foreign Broadcast Information Service Daily Report,* No. FBIS-EAS-91-214, Nov. 5, 1991: 23.

"Akashi: 'More' Vietnamese Troops in Cambodia." 1993. Agence France Presse (Hong Kong). *Foreign Broadcast Information Service Daily Report,* No. FBIS-EAS-93-043, Mar. 8, 1992: 46.

"Akashi Rules Vietnamese Can Vote in Elections." 1992. Agence France Presse (Hong Kong). *Foreign Broadcast Information Service Daily Report,* No. FBIS-EAS-92-152, Aug. 6, 1992: 26.

Annabi, Hédi. 1992. Speech to the U.S. NGO Forum on Viet Nam, Cambodia and Laos, Stony Brook, New York, June 13, 1992.

Antara. 1992. "Cambodia's Rannariddh Arrives." Antara (Jakarta). *Foreign Broadcast Information Service Daily Report,* No. FBIS-EAS-92-092, May 12, 1992: 1.

Awanohara, Susumu. 1991. "Rouge, White and Blue." *Far Eastern Economic Review,* Nov. 21, 1991: 55-56.

Ban Muang. 1980. "Columnist Reports Conditions, Suggests PRK Will Be Recognized." Ban Muang (in Thai). *Joint Publications Research Service South and East Asia Report,* No. 903, July 10, 1980: 11-13.

Bangkok Post. 1992. "Problems of Daily Life, Peace Accord Viewed." *Bangkok Post*(Bangkok). *Foreign Broadcast Information Service Daily Report,* No. FBIS-EAS-92-037, Feb. 25, 1992: 55-56.

Bangkok Radio Thailand. 1992. "56,568 Cambodian Refugees Repatriated Since March." Bangkok (in Thai). *Foreign Broadcast Information Service Daily Report,* No. FBIS-EAS-92-146, July 29, 1992: 35.

Barron, John and Anthony Paul. 1977. *Murder of a Gentle Land.* New York: Thomas Y. Crowell Company.

"Battlefields and Ballot Boxes." 1993. *The Economist.* Vol. 326, No. 7797, Feb. 6, 1993: 36.

Becker, Elizabeth. 1983a. "Cambodia Blames Ousted Leader Not Party." *The Washington Post,* Mar. 1, 1983: A1, A12.

Becker, Elizabeth. 1983b. "Recovery After Pol Pot Relapses to Poverty." *The Washington Post,* Feb. 28, 1983: A1, A16.

Bonacci, Mark A. 1990. *The Legacy of Colonialism: Health Care in Southeast Asia.* Washington: Asia Resource Center.

Boua, Chanthou, 1982. "Women in Today's Cambodia," *New Left Review* 131:45-61.

Branigin, William. 1991. "Surging Mekong Adds Misery." *The Washington Post,* Sept. 22, 1991: A36.

Branigin, William. 1992a. "Key Phases of U.N. Peace Operation in Cambodia Seen Breaking Down." *The Washington Post,* Oct. 4, 1992: A33, A34.

Branigin, William. 1992b. "UN Starts Cambodian Repatriation." *The Washington Post,* Mar. 31, 1992: A1, A14.

Branigin, William. 1992c. "U.N. Influx Livens Phnom Penh Nights." *Washington Post,* June 22, 1992: A11, A14.

Briefing. 1991. "Phnom Penh Frees 442 Political Prisoners." *Far Eastern Economic Review,* Nov. 14, 1991: 14.

Briefing. 1992. "More Money for Cambodian Refugees." *Far Eastern Economic Review,* Apr. 2, 1992: 14.

Britannica. 1991. *1991 Britannica Book of the Year.* Chicago: Encyclopedia Britannica.

Brown, Frederick Z. 1992. "Cambodia in 1991." *Asian Survey,* Vol. 32, No. 1, Jan. 1992: 88-96.

Brown, Frederick Z. 1993. "Cambodia in 1992." *Asian Survey,* Vol. 33, No. 1, Jan. 1993: 83-90.

Cambodia Chronology. 1991. "Cambodia Chronology." *Indochina Chronology,* Vol. 10, No. 2, Apr.-June, 1991: 10-12.

Cambodian Department of Statistics. 1992. Data provided to the Asian Development Bank, Manila, Philippines.

"Cambodian Peace Prompts Banditry, 'Quick Profits'." 1991. *The Nation* (Bangkok). *Foreign Broadcast Information Service Daily Report,* No. FBIS-EAS-91-184, Sept. 11, 1991: 46-47.

Campbell, Catherine. 1982. "Anti-V'nese Khmer Groups Sign Pact, Concrete Results Uncertain." *The Asia Record,* July 1982: 1, 6.

Canesso, Claudia. 1989. *Cambodia.* New York: Chelsea.

Carney, Tim, 1989. "The Organization of Power." In: Karl Jackson, ed., *Cambodia 1975-1978.* Princeton, NJ: Princeton University Press.

Castles, Ian. ed. 1990. *Yearbook Australia 1990.* Canberra: Australian Bureau of Statistics.

Census of Cambodia. 1966. National Institute of Statistics and Economic Research. *Resultats Finals Du Recensement General De La Population 1962 [Final Results of the General Census of the Population 1962].* Phnom Penh.

Census of Cambodia. 1970. National Institute of Statistics and Economic Research. *Additif Aux Resultats Du Recensement General De La Population 1962 [Supplement to the Results of the General Census of the Population 1962].* Phnom Penh.

"Central Bank Wants to Tie Riel Rate to Thai Baht." 1992. *Bangkok Post* (Bangkok), June 29, 1992: 13, 22.

Cham Prasidh. 1992a. Speech to the U.S. NGO Forum on Viet Nam, Cambodia and Laos, Stony Brook, New York, June 13, 1992.

Cham Prasidh. 1992b. Speech to the U.S. NGO Forum on Viet Nam, Cambodia and Laos, Stony Brook, New York, June 14, 1992.

Chanda, Nayan. 1981. "The Survivors' Party." *Far Eastern Economic Review*, June 22, 1981: 22.

Chanda, Nayan. 1992a. "Ghost At the Feast." *Far Eastern Economic Review*, July 2, 1992: 8-9.

Chanda, Nayan. 1992b. "Hun Sen Warns That a Failure to Implement Cambodia Peace Plan May Benefit Khmer Rouge." *The Asian Wall Street Journal Weekly*, Apr. 6, 1992: 3, 24.

Chandler, David P. 1983. *A History of Cambodia.* Boulder: Westview.

Chandler, David P. 1991. *The Tragedy of Cambodian History: Politics, War and Revolution Since 1945.* New Haven: Yale University Press.

Chandler, David P. and Ben Kiernan, eds. 1983. *Revolution and Its Aftermath in Kampuchea: Eight Essays.* New Haven: Yale University Southeast Asia Studies.

Chipello, Christopher J. 1992. "Cambodia Gets Pledge of Aid for Rebuilding." *The Wall Street Journal,* June 23, 1992: A17.

Chongkitthawon, Kawi. 1989. "'Khmerization' of Education Reportedly Planned." *The Nation* (Bangkok). *Foreign Broadcast Information Service Daily Report,* No. FBIS-EAS-89-229, Nov. 30, 1989: 38-39.

Chongkitthawon, Kawi. 1991. "Postwar Political Developments Previewed." *The Nation* (Bangkok). *Foreign Broadcast Information Service Daily Report,* No. FBIS-EAS-91-215, Nov. 6, 1991: 33.

CIA. 1980. Central Intelligence Agency. *Kampuchea: A Demographic Catastrophe.* Washington, D.C.

Conboy, Kenneth. 1991. *U.S. and Asia: Statistical Handbook.* Washington, D.C.: The Heritage Foundation.

Coyaume, T.Y. Abdul. 1992. "Health Situation in Cambodia." Presented to the Sectoral Workshop on Health, Prosthetics and Family Planning, U.S.

NGO Forum on Viet Nam, Cambodia and Laos, Stony Brook, New York, June 13, 1992.

Criddle, Joan, & Teeda Butt Mam, 1987. *To Destroy You Is No Loss*. New York, NY: Atlantic Monthly Press.

Davies, Robin. 1992. "Economist Explains Riel Fluctuations." *Bangkok Post* (Bangkok). *Joint Publications Research Service*, No. JPRS-SEA-92-006, Apr. 8, 1992: 4-5.

de Nerciat, Charles-Antoine. 1992. "Refugee Repatriation Process Reviewed, Detailed." *Foreign Broadcast Information Service Daily Report*, No. FBIS-EAS-92-116, June 16, 1992: 28-29.

Ea, Meng-Try. 1981. "Kampuchea: A Country Adrift." *Population and Development Review*, Vol. 7, No. 2, June 1981: 209-228.

Ea, Meng-Try. 1987. "Recent Population Trends in Kampuchea." In David A. Ablin and Marlowe Hood, eds. *The Cambodian Agony*. Armonk: M.E. Sharpe: 3-15.

East-West Center. 1992. "Cambodia Primed for Oil Discoveries." *East-West Center Views*, May-June 1992: 3.

Ebihara, May. 1968. *A Khmer Village in Cambodia*. Ph.D. dissertation, Columbia University. Ann Arbor, MI: University Microfilms.

Ebihara, May. 1987. "Revolution and Reformulation in Kampuchean Village Culture." In: D. Ablin & M. Hood, eds., *The Cambodian Agony*. Armonk, NY: M.E. Sharpe.

Ebihara, May. 1990. "Return to a Khmer Village." *Cultural Survival Quarterly* 14:3:67-70.

Ebihara, May. 1993. " 'Beyond Suffering:' The Recent History of a Cambodian Village," in Borje Ljunggren, ed., *The Challenge of Reform in Indochina*, Harvard Studies in International Development, Harvard Institute for International Development.

The Economist. 1991. "Town and Country." *The Economist*, Nov. 23, 1991: 39.

Economist Intelligence Unit. 1991. *Indochina: Vietnam, Laos, Cambodia Country Profile 1991-92*. London: Business International, Ltd.

Etcheson, Craig. 1984. *The Rise and Demise of Democratic Kampuchea.* Boulder: Westview.

FAO. 1991. Food and Agriculture Organization. *FAO Yearbook 1990.* Rome.

Favret, Remi. 1992. "Cambodia: Norodom Sihanouk's Doubts." *Le Figaro* (Paris). "Sihanouk: 'No Illusions' on Peace Accord Problems," *Foreign Broadcast Information Service Daily Report,* No. FBIS-EAS-92-161, Aug. 19, 1992: 21-22.

FBIS. 1976. Foreign Broadcast Information Service. *Asia and Pacific Daily Report,* Vol. IV, No. 63.

FBIS. 1990. de Nerciat, Charles-Antoine. "Officials Note Increased Relocation of Refugees." Agence France Presse (Hong Kong). *Foreign Broadcast Information Service Daily Report,* No. FBIS-EAS-90-151, Aug. 6, 1990: 44.

FBIS. 1991a. "Khmer Rouge to Forcibly Repatriate 'Thousands'." Agence France Presse (Hong Kong). *Foreign Broadcast Information Service Daily Report,* No. FBIS-EAS-91-196, Oct. 9, 1991: 25-26.

FBIS. 1991b. "Refugees to Move to Khmer Rouge Areas." *The Nation* (Bangkok). *Foreign Broadcast Information Service Daily Report,* No. FBIS-EAS-91-208, Oct. 28, 1991: 42-43.

FBIS. 1992a. "All Cambodian Refugees To Be Repatriated by '93." Radio Thailand Network (Bangkok) in Thai. *Foreign Broadcast Information Service Daily Report,* No. FBIS-EAS-92-052, Mar. 17, 1992, p.49.

FBIS. 1992b. "Date for Refugee Repatriation May Be Imposed." Agence France Presse (Hong Kong). *Foreign Broadcast Information Service Daily Report,* No. FBIS-EAS-92-033, Feb. 19, 1992: 51.

FBIS. 1992c. de Nerciat, Charles-Antoine. "Khmer Rouge Repatriation Practices Discussed." Agence France Presse (Hong Kong). *Foreign Broadcast Information Service Daily Report,* No. FBIS-EAS-92-045, Mar. 6, 1992: 21-22.

FBIS. 1992d. "Foreign Officials on Refugee Repatriation Plan." *The Nation* (Bangkok). *Foreign Broadcast Information Service Daily Report,* No. FBIS-EAS-92-035, Feb. 21, 1992: 34-35.

FBIS. 1992e. "Government Seeks UN Assurance on Refugees." *Bangkok Post* (Bangkok). *Foreign Broadcast Information Service Daily Report*, No. FBIS-EAS-92-050, Mar. 13, 1992. pp. 52-53.

FBIS. 1992f. "KR Guerillas Detain Refugee Camp Leaders." Agence France Presse (Hong Kong). *Foreign Broadcast Information Service Daily Report*, No. FBIS-EAS-92-058, Mar. 25, 1992: 25-26.

FBIS. 1992g. "Refugee Repatriation Centers 'Almost Completed'." SPK (Phnom Penh). *Foreign Broadcast Information Service Daily Report*, No. FBIS-EAS-92-057, Mar. 24, 1992: 23-24.

FBIS. 1992h. "Thai, Indonesian Ministers on Cambodian Refugees." Voice of Free Asia, in Thai (Bangkok). *Foreign Broadcast Information Service Daily Report*, No. FBIS-EAS-92-046, Mar. 9, 1992: 46.

FBIS. 1992i. "UN Envoy on Difficulties of Mine-Clearance." SPK (Phnom Penh). *Foreign Broadcast Information Service Daily Report*, No. FBIS-EAS-91-249, Dec. 27, 1991: 50-51.

FBIS. 1992j. "UN Peacekeeping Operation Leaders Arrive." Agence France Presse (Hong Kong). *Foreign Broadcast Information Service Daily Report*, No. FBIS-EAS-92-051, Mar. 16, 1992: 42-43.

Fitzsimmons, Thomas, ed. 1957. *Cambodia*. New Haven: Hraf.

"Foreign Minister Asks World Help for Food Shortages." 1992. Agence France Presse (Hong Kong). May 23, 1992.

"Foreign Minister on KR Stance in UN Troops." 1992. Agence France Presse (Hong Kong). *Foreign Broadcast Information Service Daily Report*, No. FBIS-EAS-92-067, Apr. 7, 1992: 24-25.

Frieson, Kate, 1990. "The Pol Pot Legacy in Village Life." *Cultural Survival Quarterly* 14:3:71-73.

Grazer, Walter and Shep Lowman. 1992. "The Cambodian Repatriation: A Special Trip Report with Recommendations January 12-20, 1992." United States Catholic Conference, Migration and Refugee Services. April 1992.

Hannum, Hurst. 1989. "International Law and Cambodian Genocide: The Sounds of Silence." *Human Rights Quarterly*, No. 11: 82-138.

Hanoi Voice of Vietnam. 1992. "Cambodia Voter Registration, Khmer Rouge Viewed." *Foreign Broadcast Information Service Daily Report*, No. FBIS-EAS-92-199, Oct. 14, 1992: 41.

Hawk, David, 1989. "The Photographic Record." In: Karl Jackson, ed., *Cambodia 1975-1978*. Princeton, NJ: Princeton University Press.

Heder, Stephen, 1980. *Kampuchean Occupation and Resistance*. Bangkok: Institute of Asian Studies, Chulalongkorn University, Asian Studies Monograph No. 27.

Hiebert, Murray. 1986. "Cambodia: Perspectives on the Impasse." *Indochina Issues*, No. 64, Feb.-Mar. 1986.

Hiebert, Murray. 1989. "War Against Want." *Far Eastern Economic Review*, July 13, 1989: 72-74.

Hiebert, Murray. 1990a. "Hammerblow for Hanoi." *Far Eastern Economic Review*, July 5, 1990: 44-45.

Hiebert, Murray. 1990b. "Khmers' Other Battle." *Far Eastern Economic Review*, Nov. 8, 1990: 60-62.

Hiebert, Murray. 1991a. "A Basket Case." *Far Eastern Economic Review*, Nov. 7, 1991: 30-32.

Hiebert, Murray. 1991b. "Exit Heng Samrin." *Far Eastern Economic Review*, Oct. 31, 1991: 11-13.

Hiebert, Murray. 1992. "Baht Imperialism." *Far Eastern Economic Review*, June 25, 1992: 46-47.

Holck, Susan E. and Willard Cates, Jr. 1982. "Fertility and Population Dynamics in Two Kampuchean Refugee Camps." *Studies in Family Planning*, Vol. 13, No. 4, Apr. 1982: 118-124.

Hong Kong AFP. 1989. "80,000 Civilians Reported in Cambodia." Agence France Presse (Hong Kong). *Foreign Broadcast Information Service Daily Report*, No. FBIS-EAS-89-160, Aug. 21, 1989: 61.

Hong Kong AFP. 1991. "Chea Sim Explains Party Changes." Agence France Presse (Hong Kong). *Foreign Broadcast Information Service Daily Report*, No. FBIS-EAS-91-210, Oct. 30, 1991: 37.

Hong Kong AFP. 1992a. "Factions Refuse to be First to Mark Minefields." *Foreign Broadcast Information Service Daily Report*, No. FBIS-EAS-92-082, Apr. 28, 1992: 34.

Hong Kong AFP. 1992b. "UNTAC Deputy Says No SRV Troops Discovered." *Foreign Broadcast Information Service Daily Report*, No. FBIS-EAS-92-092, May 12, 1992: 26.

Hong Kong AFP. 1993. "SRV Says Soldiers Left Behind Are Cambodians." *Foreign Broadcast Information Service Daily Report*, No. FBIS-EAS-93-039, Mar. 2, 1993: 37.

Hou Taing Eng. 1992. Data provided to the Population Reference Bureau, Washington, D.C.

House, Karen Elliott. 1991. "Peace Rekindles Fear of Khmer Rouge." *The Asian Wall Street Journal Weekly*, Vol. 13, No. 47, Nov. 25, 1991: 16.

Hugo, Graeme. 1987. "Postwar Refugee Migration in Southeast Asia: Patterns, Problems, and Policies." in *Refugees, a Third World Dilemma*. John R. Rogge, ed. Totowa, New Jersey: Rowman & Littlefield: 237-252.

Huguet, Jerrold W. 1991. "The Demographic Situation in Cambodia." *Asia-Pacific Population Journal*, Vol. 6, No. 4, Dec. 1991: 79-91.

Hun Sen. 1991. ""Hun Sen Addresses Party Congress 17 Oct." Kampuchea Radio Network, in Cambodian (Phnom Penh). *Foreign Broadcast Information Service Daily Report*, No. FBIS-EAS-91-203, Oct. 21, 1991: 40-47.

Hunter, Brian, ed. 1991. *The Statesman's Yearbook 1991-1992*. London: MacMillan.

"If Only." 1991. *The Economist*, May 18, 1991: 42-44.

Indochina Digest. 1992. "Tension at Thai Border Camp." June 12, 1992: 2.

Intelligence. 1992. "Tree Muggers." *Far Eastern Economic Review*, July 2, 1992, p. 6.

Jenkins, David. 1984. "The Long Road Back." *Far Eastern Economic Review*, Nov. 29, 1984: 25-31.

Johnson, E. Paige. 1990. "International Law or International Politics? Recognition and Intervention: The Case of Cambodia." *Monterey Review,* Vol. 11, No. 3, Fall 1990: 35-44.

Khieu Kanharith. 1988. "The New Order in Post-Conflict Kampuchea." In: Donald H. McMillen, ed., *Conflict Resolution in Kampuchea*. Griffith University, Australia, August 1988: 42-49.

Khus, Thida. 1992. Speech to the U.S. NGO Forum on Viet Nam, Cambodia and Laos, Stony Brook, New York, June 15, 1992.

Kiernan, Ben, 1980. "Conflict in the Kampuchean Communist Movement," *Journal of Contemporary Asia* 10: 75-118.

Kiernan, Ben, 1985. *How Pol Pot Came to Power.* London: Verso.

Kiernan, Ben. 1986. "Kampuchea's Ethnic Chinese Under Pol Pot: A Case of Systematic Social Discrimination." *Journal of Contemporary Asia*, Vol. 16, No. 1: 18-29.

Kiernan, Ben. 1986a. *Cambodia: The Eastern Zone Massacres.* New York: Columbia University, Center for the Study of Human Rights, Documentation Series No. 1, 1986.

Kiernan, Ben. 1988. "Orphans of Genocide: The Cham Muslims of Kampuchea under Pol Pot," *Bulletin of Concerned Asian Scholars* 20:4, 1988: 2-33.

Kiernan, Ben, 1990. "Roots of Genocide: New Evidence on the U.S. Bombardment of Cambodia," *Cultural Survival Quarterly* 14:3:20-22.

Kiernan, Ben. 1990a. "The Genocide in Cambodia, 1975-1979." *Bulletin of Concerned Asian Scholars*, Vol. 22, No. 2: 35-40.

Kiernan, Ben. 1992. "The Cambodian Crisis, 1990-1992: The UN Plan, the Khmer Rouge, and the State of Cambodia." *Bulletin of Concerned Asian Scholars* Vol. 24, No. 2, Apr.-June 1992: 35-40.

Kiernan, Ben. 1992. Speech to the U.S. NGO Forum on Viet Nam, Cambodia and Laos, Stony Brook, New York, June 14, 1992.

Kiernan, Ben & Chanthou Boua, eds., 1982 *Peasants and Politics in Kampuchea, 1942-1981*. Armonk, NY: M.E. Sharpe.

Kuala Lumpur Radio Malaysia. 1992. "SRV Minister on Vietnamese Voting in Cambodia." *Foreign Broadcast Information Service Daily Report*, No. FBIS-EAS-92-097, May 19, 1992: 4.

Kunstadter, Peter, ed. 1967. *Southeast Asian Tribes, Minorities, and Nations.* (2 volumes). Princeton: Princeton University Press.

Kyodo. 1992. "UN Official: Cambodian Refugees Need Protection." Kyodo (Tokyo). *Foreign Broadcast Information Service Daily Report*, No. FBIS-EAS-92-080, Apr. 24, 1992: 7.

Ledgerwood, Judy, 1992. *Analysis of the Situation of Women in Cambodia.* Report for UNICEF (unpublished ms.).

Marston, John, 1989. "Metaphors of the Khmer Rouge." Paper presented in a panel on "Khmer Culture: Persistence and Process" at the annual meetings of the Association for Asian Studies.

May, Someth (edited by James Fenton), 1986. *Cambodian Witness: The Autobiography of Someth May.* New York, NY: Random House.

Le Monde. 1993. "Douze Millions d'Habitants?" *Le Monde* (Paris), Mar. 5, 1993: 5

Levy, Barry S. and Daniel C. Susott. 1986. "Historical Context and Brief Overview of the Relief Operation." In: *Years of Horror, Days of Hope.* Barry S. Levy and Daniel C. Susott, eds. Millwood, New York: Associated Faculty Press: xix-xxii.

Liden, Jon. 1991. "A Coward's War." *Far Eastern Economic Review*, Nov. 21, 1991: 58.

Liden, Jon and Murray Hiebert. 1992. "Cambodian Assault." *Far Eastern Economic Review*, June 4, 1992: 64.

Loebus, Fritz. 1992. Speech to the U.S. NGO Forum on Viet Nam, Cambodia and Laos, Stony Brook, New York, June 14, 1992.

Lynch, James F. 1989. *Border Khmer: A Demographic Study of the Residents of Site 2, Site B, and Site 8.* Bangkok: Nov. 1989.

Maniphan, Anurat. 1989. "Thai Correspondent Analyzes Economic Situation." *Bangkok Post* (Bangkok). *Foreign Broadcast Information Service Daily Report*, No. FBIS-EAS-89-244, Dec. 21, 1989: 33-35.

Mason, Linda and Roger Brown. 1983. *Rice, Rivalry and Politics: Managing Cambodian Relief.* Notre Dame: University of Notre Dame Press.

Mazel, Lou. 1992. Speech to the U.S. NGO Forum on Viet Nam, Cambodia and Laos, Stony Brook, New York, June 13, 1992.

Mehta, Harish. 1992. "Peace Dividend." *Singapore Business*, Apr. 1992: 16-23.

Migozzi, Jacques. 1973. *Cambodge: Faits et Problemes de Population.* Paris: CNRS.

Muscat, Robert J. and Jonathan Stromseth. 1989. *Cambodia: Post Settlement Reconstruction and Development.* New York: East Asian Institute.

Mysliwiec, Eva. 1988. *Punishing the Poor: The International Isolation of Kampuchea.* Oxford: Oxfam.

The Nation. 1991. "SRV Relations 'Strained' After Peace Accord." *The Nation (Bangkok).* *Foreign Broadcast Information Service Daily Report*, No. FBIS-EAS-91-226, Nov. 22, 1991: 33.

The Nation. 1992. "Bank Governor Discusses Business Activity." *The Nation* (Bangkok). *Foreign Broadcast Information Service Daily Report*, No. FBIS-EAS-92-072, Apr. 14, 1992. pp. 30-32.

Nations, Richard. 1979. "Chinese Fleeing Cambodia Pour Over Thai Border." *The Washington Post*, May 18, 1979: A32.

Newhall, Sarah. 1992. Speech to the U.S. NGO Forum on Viet Nam, Cambodia and Laos, Stony Brook, New York, June 13, 1992.

Ngor, Haing (with Roger Warner), 1987. *A Cambodian Odyssey.* New York, NY: Macmillan.

Nivolon, Francois. 1980. "Aid Distribution, Services Seen as Improved." *Le Figaro* (in French). *Joint Publications Research Service South and East Asia Report*, No. 901, June 26, 1980: 139-143.

Osborne, Milton. 1979. *Before Kampuchea: Preludes to Tragedy.* London: George Allen & Unwin.

Panaritis, Andrea. 1985. "Cambodia: The Rough Road to Recovery." *Indochina Issues,* No. 56, Apr. 1985.

Pheng Eng By. 1986. "Family Planning: The Perspective of a Cambodian Public-Health Nurse." In *Years of Horror, Days of Hope.* Barry S. Levy and Daniel C. Susott, eds. Millwood, New York: Associated Faculty Press: 214-215.

Phnom Penh Domestic Service. 1990. "Project to Expand Phnom Penh Housing Reported." Phnom Penh Domestic Service (in Cambodian). *Foreign Broadcast Information Service Daily Report,* No. FBIS-EAS-90-158, Aug. 15, 1990: 50-51.

Phnom Penh Domestic Service. 1991. "Interior Ministry Sets Deadline for ID Cards." Phnom Penh Domestic Service (in Cambodian). *Foreign Broadcast Information Service Daily Report,* No. FBIS-EAS-91-028, Feb. 11, 1991: 40.

Phnom Penh SPK. 1991a. "12th National Education Conference Opens." SPK (Phnom Penh). *Foreign Broadcast Information Service Daily Report,* No. FBIS-EAS-91-169, Aug. 30, 1991: 45.

Phnom Penh SPK. 1991b. "176 Students to Study in SRV in 1991-92." SPK (Phnom Penh). *Foreign Broadcast Information Service Daily Report,* No. FBIS-EAS-91-079, Apr. 24, 1991: 33-34.

Phnom Penh SPK. 1991c. "SPK Quotes AFP on UNICEF Seminar." SPK (Phnom Penh). *Foreign Broadcast Information Service Daily Report,* No. FBIS-EAS-91-132, July 10, 1991: 53.

Phnom Penh SPK. 1992. "Report Emphasizes Necessity of Foreign Aid." SPK (Phnom Penh). *Foreign Broadcast Information Service Daily Report,* No. FBIS-EAS-92-091, May 11, 1992: 33.

Phnom Penh SPK. 1993. "KR Ignore Election Registration Deadline." *Foreign Broadcast Information Service Daily Report,* No. FBIS-EAS-93-018, Jan. 29, 1993: 43.

Pike, Douglas. 1991. "U.S. Policy Toward Indochina." Presented at the International Symposium on Indochinese Economic Reconstruction and International Economic Co-operation, Institute of Developing Economies, Tokyo, Nov. 13 -14, 1991.

Pitaksuntipan, Surangkana. 1986. "Family Planning: The Perspective of a Thai Public-Health Worker." in *Years of Horror, Days of Hope*. Barry S. Levy and Daniel C. Susott, eds. Millwood, New York: Associated Faculty Press: 212-213.

Ponchaud, Francois. 1977. *Cambodge Annee Zero. [Cambodia: Year Zero]. Joint Publications Research Service*, No. JPRS L/7334, Aug. 23, 1977.

Ponchaud, Francois. 1979. "The Vietnamese Engage in Serious Acts of Plunder in Cambodia." *Le Monde* (Paris). "Refugees Report Hardship, Vietnamese Misconduct." *Joint Publications Research Service Translations on South and East Asia*, No. 828, June 19, 1979: 74-76.

Prasso, Sheri. 1991. "Banker Warns Foreign Investors About Problems." Agence France Presse (Hong Kong). *Foreign Broadcast Information Service Daily Report*, No. FBIS-EAS-91-225, Nov. 21, 1991: 31-33.

Prasso, Sheri. 1992a. "Akashi Refuses KR Demand on Phnom Penh Regime." Agence France Presse (Hong Kong). *Foreign Broadcast Information Service Daily Report*, No. FBIS-EAS-92-149, Aug. 3, 1992: 25.

Prasso, Sheri. 1992b. "Neighbors Show Little Sympathy for Murdered Viets." Agence France Presse (Hong Kong). *Foreign Broadcast Information Service Daily Report*, No. FBIS-EAS-92-145, July 28, 1992: 31-32.

Prasso, Sheri. 1993. "U.N. to Urge Honoring Aid Pledges." Agence France Presse (Hong Kong). *Foreign Broadcast Information Service Daily Report*, No. FBIS-EAS-93-035, Feb. 24, 1993: 37-38.

Pura, Raphael. 1992a. "Cambodia Economy Nears Collapse as Funds Dry Up." *Asian Wall Street Journal Weekly*, Vol. XIV, No. 46, Nov. 16, 1992: 1, 20.

Pura, Raphael. 1992b. "Former Cambodian Refugee Wants to Bring American-Style Democracy to His People." *Asian Wall Street Journal Weekly*, Vol. XIV, No. 45, Nov. 10, 1992, p. 10.

"Rannariddh Discusses Tokyo Aid Conference." 1992. Voice of the Khmer (in Cambodian). *Foreign Broadcast Information Service Daily Report*, No. FBIS-EAS-92-127, July 1, 1992: 30-34.

"The Refugees." 1991. *Indochina Chronology*, Vol. X, No. 1, Jan.-Mar. 1991: 25.

Robinson, Warren. 1989. "Population Trends and Policies in Laos (Lao People's Democratic Republic) and Cambodia (Democratic Kampuchea)." *International Population Conference, New Delhi* . Vol. 1, Liège, Belgium: International Union for the Scientific Study of Population: 143-153.

Rogge, John R. 1990. *Return To Cambodia*. Dallas: Intertect Institute, Mar. 1990.

Ross, Russell R., ed. 1990. *Cambodia: A Country Study* . Washington, D.C.: Library of Congress Federal Research Division.

Rowe, Trevor. 1992. "U.N. Security Council Approves Peace-Keepers for Cambodia," *The Washington Post*, Feb. 29, 1992: A18.

"Royal Huff," *The Economist*, Vol. 326, No. 7793, Jan. 9, 1993: 33-34.

Samleng Pracheachon Kampuchea. 1992. "Supreme National Council Holds Session 23 Jul." *Foreign Broadcast Information Service Daily Report* , No. FBIS-EAS-92-143, July 24, 1992: 30-31.

Sampson, W.J.. 1977. Letter to the *Economist,* 26 March.

Scoville, Orlin. 1987. "Rebuilding Kampuchea's Food Supply." In David A. Ablin and Marlowe Hood, eds. *The Cambodian Agony*. Armonk: M.E. Sharpe: 263-290.

Shallon, Nessim. 1992. Speech to the U.S. NGO Forum on Viet Nam, Cambodia and Laos, Stony Brook, New York, June 15, 1992.

Shawcross, William. 1980. *Sideshow: Kissinger, Nixon, and the Destruction of Cambodia*. London: Fontana.

Sherry, Andrew. 1992a. "Disarming to Begin June 13, 1992." Agence France Presse (Hong Kong). *Foreign Broadcast Information Service Daily Report,* No. FBIS-EAS-92-091, May 11, 1992, pp. 31-32.

Sherry, Andrew. 1992b. "UN Says Logging at Unsustainable Pace." Agence France Presse (Hong Kong). *Foreign Broadcast Information Service Daily Report*, No. FBIS-EAS-92-094, May 14, 1992, pp. 20-21.

Siam Rat. 1992. "Thai Firm Surveys Investment, Economic Conditions." Bangkok (in Thai). *Joint Publications Research Service Daily Report* , No. JPRS-SEA-92-009, Apr. 23, 1992: 1-3.

Siampos, George S. 1970. "The Population of Cambodia 1945-1980." *Milbank Memorial Fund Quarterly*, Vol. XLVIII, No. 3, July 1970: 317-360.

Silber, Irwin. 1986. *Kampuchea: The Revolution Rescued*. Oakland: Institute for Social and Economic Studies.

"Soldiers Released from Barracks to Plant Rice." 1992. Agence France Presse (Hong Kong). *Foreign Broadcast Information Service Daily Report*, No. FBIS-EAS-92-151, Aug. 5, 1992: 33.

Solomon, Jay. 1992. "Going Nowhere." *Far Eastern Economic Review*, Sept. 17, 1992: 56.

"Son Sann Urges Voting Rights for Overseas Khmer." 1992. Agence France Presse (Hong Kong). *Foreign Broadcast Information Service Daily Report*, No. FBIS-EAS-92-097, May 19, 1992: 31.

SPK. 1992. "Akashi Cites Khmer Rouge Breaches." SPK (in French). *Foreign Broadcast Information Service Daily Report,* No. FBIS-EAS-92-144, July 24, 1992: 36.

Stuart-Fox, Martin. 1985. *The Murderous Revolution: Life and Death in Pol Pot's Kampuchea*. Chippendale, Australia: Alternative Publishing Cooperative Ltd.

Sullivan, Frances. 1992. Speech to the U.S. NGO Forum on Viet Nam, Cambodia and Laos, Stony Brook, New York, June 15, 1992.

Sutter, Robert G. 1991. *The Cambodian Crisis: U.S. Policy Dilemmas.* Boulder: Westview.

Sutter, Valerie O'Connor. 1990. *The Indochinese Refugee Dilemma.* Baton Rouge: Louisiana State University.

Swank, Emory C. 1983. "The Land In Between: Ten Years Later." *Indochina Issues*, No. 36, April 1983.

SWB. 1991. *Summary of World Broadcasts.* "Education Conference Told of Increase in Student Numbers." SPK (Phnom Penh). *Summary of World Broadcasts*, No. FE/W0196, Sept. 11, 1991: A6.

Tasker, Rodney. 1989. "Khmer Rouge Role." *Far Eastern Economic Review*, June 29, 1989: 19-20.

Tasker, Rodney. 1990. "Forced March Home." *Far Eastern Economic Review*, Feb. 15, 1990: 27-28.

Tasker, Rodney. 1991. "The Odd Couple." *Far Eastern Economic Review*, Nov. 28, 1991: 10-11.

Thayer, Nate. 1992a. "Fighting Words." *Far Eastern Economic Review*, Aug. 20, 1992: 8-9.

Thayer, Nate. 1992b. "Plunder of the State." *Far Eastern Economic Review*, Jan. 9, 1992: 11.

Thayer, Nate. 1992c. "The War Party." *Far Eastern Economic Review*, June 25, 1992: 12.

Thayer, Nate and Nayan Chanda. 1993. "Shattered Peace." *Far Eastern Economic Review*, Feb. 11, 1993: 10-11.

Twining, Charles, 1990. "The Economy." In: Karl Jackson, ed., *Cambodia 1975-1978*. Princeton, NJ: Princeton University Press.

UNDP. 1989. United Nations Development Programme. *Report of the Kampuchea Needs Assessment Study*. August 1989.

UNDP. 1990. United Nations Development Programme. "Cambodia Infrastructure Survey Mission, 18 June-15 July 1990." In *Report of the Cambodia Infrastructure Survey Missions*. New York: September 1990.

UNDP. 1992. United Nations Development Programme. *Update*, Vol. 5, No. 9, May 4, 1992.

UNFPA. 1989. United Nations Population Fund. *Inventory of Population Projects in Developing Countries Around the World 1988/1989*. New York.

UNHCR. 1991. United Nations High Commissioner for Refugees. "Information Bulletin No. 1—On Cambodia Repatriation Plan." Geneva: UNHCR Public Information, Oct. 7, 1991.

UNHCR. 1992a. "Going Home." *Refugees*, No. 88, Jan. 1992: 6-11.

UNHCR. 1992b. "De-Mining." *Refugees*, No. 88, Jan. 1992: 12-15.

UNICEF. 1990. United Nations Children's Fund. *Cambodia: The Situation of Children and Women.* Phnom Penh: UNICEF Office of the Special Representative.

United Nations. 1981. *World Population Prospects as Assessed in 1980.* New York.

United Nations. 1990. *World Population Monitoring 1989: Special Report, The Population Situation in the Least Developed Countries.* New York.

"UNTAC Begins Civil Administrative Control." 1992. *Bangkok Post* (Bangkok). *Foreign Broadcast Information Service Daily Report*, No. FBIS-EAS-92-129, July 6, 1992: 34.

"UNTAC Chief Signs Cambodian Election Laws." 1992. SPK (Phnom Penh). *Foreign Broadcast Information Service Daily Report*, No. FBIS-EAS-92-161, Aug. 19, 1992: 20-21.

USAID. 1991. United States Agency for International Development. "Report to Congress, Cambodia, Humanitarian and Development Assistance Priorities." Washington, D.C.

U.S. Bureau of the Census. 1991. *Statistical Abstract of the United States: 1991.* (111th edition) Washington, D.C.

U.S. Department of Commerce. 1991. "Census Bureau Releases 1990 Census Counts on Specific Racial Groups." *United States Department of Commerce News*, June 12, 1991.

U.S. Department of State. 1987. "Background Notes—Cambodia." Washington, D.C.

U.S. Department of State. 1990. "Background Notes—Cambodia." Washington, D.C.

U.S. Department of State Bureau for Refugee Programs. 1991. *World Refugee Report.* Washington, D.C.

Vickery, Michael. 1984. *Cambodia: 1975-1982.* Singapore: South End Press.

Vickery, Michael. 1986. *Kampuchea: Politics, Economics and Society.* Boulder: Lynne Rienner, 1986.

Vickery, Michael. 1989. "Comments on Cham Population Figures." *Bulletin of Concerned Asian Scholars*, Vol. 22, No. 1, Jan.—Mar. 1989: 31-33.

Vickery, Michael. 1990. "Notes on the Political Economy of the PRK." *Journal of Contemporary Asia*, Vol. 20, No. 4.

Vickery, Michael, 1983. "Democratic Kampuchea: Themes and Variations." In: David Chandler and Ben Kiernan, eds., *Revolution and its Aftermath in Kampuchea: Eight Essays*. New Haven, CT: Yale University Southeast Asia Studies, Monograph Series no. 25.

Vickery, Michael. 1991a. "The Cambodian Economy: Where Has It Come From, Where Is It Going?" Presented at the International Symposium on Indochinese Economic Reconstruction and International Economic Co-operation, Institute of Developing Economies, Tokyo, Nov. 1991.

Vickery, Michael. 1991b. "Remarks on the Cambodian Economy and Political Situation." Speech to the International Symposium on Indochinese Economic Reconstruction and International Economic Co-operation, Institute of Developing Economies, Tokyo, Nov. 1991.

Vietnam 1989 Sample Census. 1990. *Vietnam Population Census—1989: Sample Results*. Hanoi: Central Census Steering Committee.

Voice of the Great National Union Front of Cambodia. 1992a. "Regime Naturalizing Vietnamese Before Elections." Voice of the Great National Union Front of Cambodia (in Cambodian). *Foreign Broadcast Information Service Daily Report*, No. FBIS-EAS-92-099, May 21, 1992: 24-25.

Voice of the Great National Union Front of Cambodia. 1992b. "Vietnamese 'Aggressors' Said Living in Phnom Penh." Voice of the Great National Union Front of Cambodia (in Cambodian). *Foreign Broadcast Information Service Daily Report*, No. FBIS-EAS-92-099, May 21, 1992: 25.

Voice of the Khmer. 1992. "Son Sann on 'Very Successful' Tokyo Meeting." Voice of the Khmer (in Cambodian). *Foreign Broadcast Information Service Daily Report*, No. FBIS-EAS-92-130, July 7, 1992: 40-44.

VNADK. 1990. Voice of the National Army of Democratic Kampuchea. "AIDS Cases in Phnom Penh, Koh Kong Cited." Voice of the National Army of Democratic Kampuchea (in Cambodian). *Foreign Broadcast Information Service Daily Report*, No. FBIS-EAS-90-134, July 12, 1990: 41.

Vokes, Richard. 1991. "Economy." *The Far East and Australasia 1991.* London: Europa: 272-275.

Volkmar-Andre, Josiane. 1986. "Medical Care Inside Kampuchea." In *Years of Horror, Days of Hope.* Barry S. Levy and Daniel C. Susott, eds. Millwood, New York: Associated Faculty Press: 273-285.

Walker, Susan. 1992. Speech to the U.S. NGO Forum on Viet Nam, Cambodia and Laos, Stony Brook, New York, June 13, 1992.

Willmott, W.E. 1981. "The Chinese in Kampuchea." *Journal of Southeast Asian Studies*, Vol. XII, No. 1, Mar. 1981: 38-45.

Yathay, Pin, 1987. *Stay Alive, My Son.* New York, Free Press.

Abbreviations

ASEAN   The Association of Southeast Asian Nations—
                 Cambodia's non-Communist Southeast Asian
                 neighbors. ASEAN member states are Thailand,
                 Malaysia, Singapore, Brunei, Indonesia and the
                 Philippines.

BLDP   Buddhist Liberal Democratic Party, see KPNLF.

FUNCINPEC   French acronym for the National United Front for an
                 Independent, Neutral, Peaceful, and Cooperative
                 Cambodia, faction loyal to Prince Norodom
                 Sihanouk—The faction, one of the four party to the
                 Paris Peace Agreement, is led by Sihanouk's son,
                 Prince Norodom Rannariddh. Throughout the 1980s,
                 FUNCINPEC was part of the Coalition Government
                 of Democratic Kampuchea, the coalition of three
                 resistance groups organized to displace the
                 Vietnamese-installed Phnom Penh regime.

KPNLF   Khmer People's National Liberation Front, since
                 May 1992 also known as the Buddhist Liberal
                 Democratic Party (BLDP)— The KPNLF, headed by
                 former Cambodian Prime Minister Son Sann, is one
                 of the four factions party to the Paris Peace
                 Agreement. The KPNLF was one component of the
                 Coalition Government of Democratic Kampuchea.

NGO   Non-governmental organization.

PDK   Party of Democratic Kampuchea, The Khmer
                 Rouge—The Khmer Rouge formed the strongest
                 military power in the Coalition Government of
                 Democratic Kampuchea, the coalition of three
                 resistance groups organized to displace the
                 Vietnamese-installed Phnom Penh regime. The
                 Khmer Rouge are signatories of the Paris Peace
                 Agreement.

PRK   People's Republic of Kampuchea—see SOC.

SNC	Supreme National Council—The SNC, made up of representatives of the Phnom Penh government and the three resistance factions, embodies Cambodian sovereignty until a new government can be established following the UN-supervised elections in May 1993.
SOC	State of Cambodia—the Vietnamese-installed government of Prime Minister Hun Sen. The SOC was formerly called the People's Republic of Kampuchea (PRK).
UNHCR	United Nations High Commissioner for Refugees—UNHCR is responsible for the repatriation of Cambodian refugees/displaced persons abroad.
UNTAC	United Nations Transitional Authority in Cambodia—UNTAC is the operational arm of the United Nations in implementing the Paris Peace Agreement.

Contributors

Hédi Annabi, a national of Tunisia, was Director of the Office of the Special Representative of the U.N. Secretary-General for Humanitarian Affairs in Southeast Asia. In 1992 he was appointed a Director in the Department of Peace-Keeping Operations of the United Nations.

Dr. Judith Banister is the Chief of the Center for International Research at the U.S. Bureau of the Census in Washington, D.C. She received her Ph.D. in Demography from Stanford University. Her research has focused on the demography of Asian countries, especially the People's Republic of China, Vietnam, North Korea, and Cambodia. She has published a book, several monographs, and numerous articles and papers on these subjects.

Chanthou Boua was born in Kompong Cham province, Cambodia. After attending Phnom Penh University, she gained degrees in economics, education and sociology from the University of New South Wales, Melbourne State College and the University of Wollongong. She is author of *Children of the Killing Fields* (University of Wollongong Centre for Multicultural Studies, 1990) and co-editor of *Peasants and Politics in Kampuchea, 1942-1981* (London and New York, 1982), and of *Pol Pot Plans the Future: Confidential Leadership Documents from Democratic Kampuchea, 1976-1977* (Yale Southeast Asia Council, 1988). She has worked on various aid programs in Cambodia.

Douc Rasy is a former dean of the Faculty of Law of the University of Phnom Penh and was a member of Cambodia's National Assembly from 1962 to 1972. He lived in exile in France during the 1970s and 1980s. He is now President of the Cambodian League for the Rights of Man and Citizen, in Phnom Penh.

May Ebihara is a professor of anthropology at the City University of New York. Author of *Svay: A Khmer Village in Cambodia* (1969), she was the only American anthropologist to work in a Khmer village in Cambodia before the Khmer Rouge takeover. She recently returned to the same village after thirty years' absence and is currently writing a history of the village from the 1950s to the 1990s.

Kate G. Frieson was program associate to the Joint Committee on Southeast Asia at the Social Science Research Council, New York, in 1991-1992. She received degrees in political science from the University of British Columbia before completing her doctoral dissertation at Monash University, Australia, *The Impact of Revolution on Cambodian Peasants, 1970-1975.*

Ms. Paige Johnson is a graduate student in Foreign Affairs at the University of Virginia. Her research interests include the domestic politics and foreign policies of the ASEAN states, focusing on Malaysia, Singapore, and Brunei. She spent the 1991-1992 academic year in Singapore on a Fulbright Scholarship.

Khieu Kanharith is Cambodia's Minister of Information. He was a student at the Faculty of Law in Phnom Penh when the Khmer Rouge took power in April 1975. He survived the next four years and in 1979 became founding editor of the weekly *Kampuchea*, the country's most influential newspaper. He was dismissed from that position by the Phnom Penh government in May 1990. He is the author of "The New Order in Post-Conflict Kampuchea" (1988) and of "The Prevention of the Return of Genocide" (1989), and other articles. In February 1992 he was appointed a senior adviser to Cambodian Prime Minister Hun Sen, and in February 1993 was reappointed editor of *Kampuchea*, and in June to the cabinet.

Ben Kiernan, who was born in Melbourne, Australia, in 1953, is Associate Professor of History at Yale University. He is author of *How Pol Pot Came to Power* (London and New York, 1985) and two other works on the Khmer Rouge, and co-author of four books on modern Cambodia, including *Revolution and its Aftermath in Kampuchea* (Yale Southeast Asia Council, 1983). He is completing a social and political history of the Pol Pot regime.

Gregory H. Stanton has taught in the Law School at Washington and Lee University and in the Department of Justice, Law and Society at The American University. In 1980-1 he worked for a relief program in Cambodia, and founded the Cambodian Genocide Project. He has written a number of reports urging action in the International Court of Justice to bring the perpetrators of the Cambodian genocide to account.

Serge Thion, of France's Centre National de la Recherche Scientifique, is a sociologist and Indochina specialist. He is author *Le pouvoir pâle* and *Verité historique ou verité politique?* and co-author of *Des courtisans aux partisans* (1971), and of *Khmers rouges!* (1981), and a forthcoming book on modern Cambodia. He is the only Western observer to have freely visited the Khmer Rouge zones before their 1975 victory.